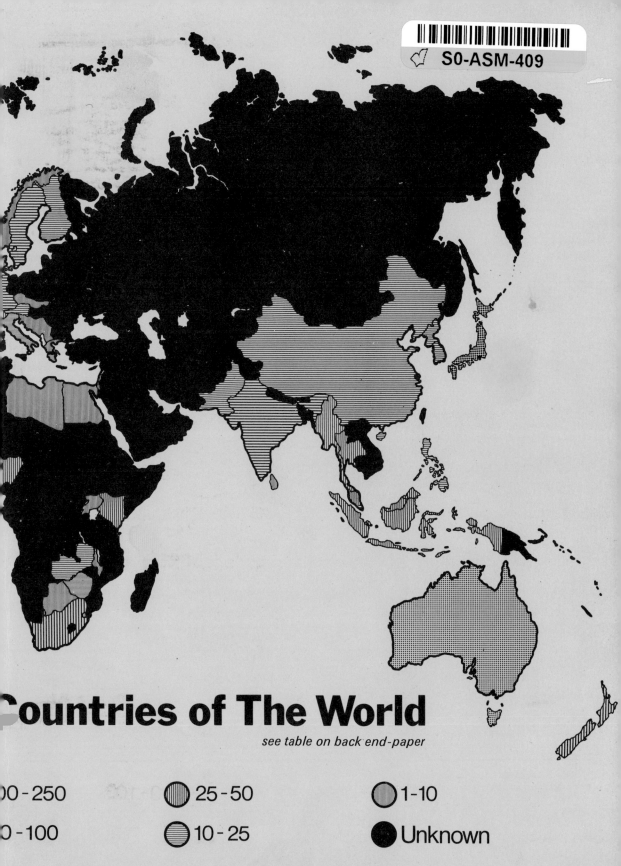

Countries of The World

see table on back end-paper

00 - 250		25 - 50		1 - 10	
0 - 100		10 - 25		Unknown	

THE GUINNESS BOOK OF

GOLF
FACTS & FEATS

DONALD STEEL

© Women Golfers' Museum

GUINNESS SUPERLATIVES LIMITED
2 Cecil Court, London Road, Enfield, Middlesex

Acknowledgements

The author and publishers wish to record their gratitude for
particular help given by:
Asia Golf Circuit (*the late Kim Hall*)
Dunlop Ltd (*John Walker*)
ETPC (*Bill Hodge*)
Golfers' Handbook (*Percy Huggins*)
Canon D Welander, Gloucester Cathedral
Japan Golf Association (*Mowa Settsu*)
LGU (*Jennie Cobb*)
LPGA of America (*Ruffin Beckwith*)
Slazenger (*Tony Lomax*)
South Herts Golf Club (*Maurice E Dorey*)
Dave Terry
US Golf Association, Golf House (*Patrick Leahy*)
USPGA (*Joe Schwendeman*)

Editor: Beatrice Frei
Design and Layout: David L Roberts
Copyright © Donald Steel
and Guinness Superlatives Ltd 1980
ISBN 0 85112 215 9

Published in Great Britain by
Guinness Superlatives Ltd, 2 Cecil Court, London Road, Enfield,
Middlesex

Set in 10 pt Plantin by Jarrold and Sons Ltd, Norwich
Printed and bound by Butler & Tanner Ltd, Frome and London

British Library Cataloguing in Publication Data

Steel, Donald
Guinness Book of Golf Facts and Feats.
1. Golf – Records
I. Title
796.352′09   GV1001

ISBN 0–85112–215–9

Contents

Introduction

When it comes to researching just how, when and where golf had its origins, it is too easy to become swallowed up in fathomless waters. For our purposes, it is safe to say that the game is at least five centuries old and that the first dramatic tales of competition concern the old challenge matches for which there were frequently high stakes.

However, championship golf is distinctly modern. The British Open, launched by the Prestwick Club, was first played in 1860 and all the early records and achievements concern British golfers. Not until after World War I did the United States assume the playing dominance so familiar today and it was still later that many of the events highlighted in this book took place.

For example, the women's professional tour in the United States, the Asia circuit, the World Cup and the World Amateur team championships have all sprung to life since World War II, a period when the game has developed out of all recognition. Even as recently as the 1950s the only lucrative circuits were in Great Britain and the United States and you had to be very good to make anything approaching a living. Now, a young tournament professional can seek to prove himself on additional circuits in the Far East, Australia, New Zealand, Europe, South Africa and South America.

One result of this expansion has been a rapid increase in the number of records, facts and feats that have to be chronicled. No other game has quite such an assortment of records and everyone who plays is intrigued by this variety.

This is because only a tiny proportion of golfers play competitively and anyone enjoying a few holes with friends is quite liable to perform a feat which the greatest players have been unable to match. It is one of the few active pastimes in which four generations, however good or bad, can take part at the same time—thanks to the handicapping system.

While a number of names in these pages may, therefore, strike few immediate chords, the real interest and the main focus of attention is upon the great players and their great deeds; those men and women whose skill has set them apart.

Allowance must be made, as in any sport, for changing times and particularly for the enormous advance in equipment. What might Willie Park or Willie Anderson have done with the benefit of a ball that flew further, or how many more putts might they have holed on greens as highly manicured as those of today? Yet it is fascinating to see how many old records survive.

Young Tom Morris remains the youngest winner of the British Open, having won in 1868 at the age of 17 years and 5 months; and there has not been anyone since to threaten his record although young golfers today can do remarkable things. Nevertheless, we are not yet accustomed to golfers being past their best at 16 like swimmers and gymnasts.

One day, Young Tom may be deposed, but it is hard to envisage another golfer succeeding his father as Open Champion as happened with the Morrises. It is rare even for father and son to take part in a modern British or American Open although Gary and Wayne Player were exceptions in 1979 at Lytham.

Of the other records which may never be broken, Bobby Jones's Impregnable Quadrilateral must head the list. I never cease to wonder at his achievement of winning the Open and Amateur championships of Britain and America in the same summer (1930); or how Byron Nelson won eleven straight tournaments on the US professional tour in 1945.

Into this highly improbable bracket we can place the 19 major victories of Jack Nicklaus (17 as a professional) although after that at St Andrews in 1978, he felt himself to be more vulnerable. All the same he will not be overtaken in a hurry; nor will Harry Vardon whose six victories in the British Open is a record.

The American Open record of victories is shared by him, Willie Anderson, Bobby Jones and Ben Hogan with four apiece and, if Nicklaus is unable to beat it before he is through, it will be some while before anyone else does.

I have mentioned the effect of modern equipment on the downward spiral of scoring but it should also be remembered that prize-money is an imperfect measurement of achievement and reference is made to it mainly because the earnings of others exert a strange fascination. To illustrate this, Nancy Lopez in three years exceeded the $359 323 which took Mickey Wright 23 seasons to accumulate (1955–78). In that time Wright won 82 tournaments, a record Lopez is unlikely to beat.

Inevitably, a large part of this book involves Britain and America, the leading golfing nations in competitive and championship terms. However, every attempt has been made to cover as large a part of the globe as possible and due regard has been paid to records from other countries. The theme is also facts and feats and here the hardest part has been to decide what to leave out.

This is a work of reference, a book to settle arguments and one that can be picked up for five minutes to induce the reaction 'fancy that'. When delving into the past, it is astonishing what unusual feats have been performed. These pages are intended to provide something for everyone—the champions, the addicts, the club players who comprise the vast and honourable majority; and those who are always promising to play a little more but never quite manage it. Perhaps this book will act as the spur.

In order to avoid repetition and also aid readability the nationalities, and dates of birth and death, where known, are included in the names index.

Le Golf. One of France's early courses, La Boulie 1904 (Illustrated London News Pic. Lib.)

Mary Queen of Scots, the first well-known lady golfer. St Andrews 1563 (The Mansell Collection)

1340–50 A stained-glass window erected in Gloucester Cathedral showing a man swinging a club at a ball. It was commissioned by Sir Thomas Broadstone to commemorate his comrades who fell at Crécy.

1353 Reference to chole, a popular cross-crountry game in Flanders. It consisted of hitting balls with clubs towards a fixed mark, eg a church door. Two parties would play; one hitting the ball across country towards the goal, the other party on every fourth stroke hitting the ball into a hazard.

1457 First of three dates when 'gouf' was banned in Scotland by an Act of Parliament. It joined football which had been banned in 1424 by James I. Similar enactments were also made by James III in 1470 and James IV in 1491.

1502 King James IV buys clubs and balls from a bow-maker in Perth.

1504 James IV played golf with the Earl of Bothwell.

1527 Sir Robert Maule (1497–1560) was the first golfer mentioned by name after King James IV and the Earl of Bothwell. Sir Robert was described in the Panmure Register as 'ane man of comlie behaviour, of hie stature, sanguine in collure both of hyd and haire, colarique of nature and subject to suddane anger. . . . He had gryt delight in haukine and hountine. . . . Lykewakes he exercisit the gowf, and ofttimes past to Barry Links, quhan the wad-sie [wager] was for drink.' Barry Links, where the Scots defeated the Danes in a great battle in 1010, is close to the modern Carnoustie.

1553 The Archbishop of St Andrews confirms the right of the community to play golf over the links of St Andrews.

1567 Mary Queen of Scots criticised for playing golf at Seton House within two weeks of her husband Darnley's death.

1589 Playing of golf forbidden in the Blackfriars Yard, Glasgow.

1592 Proclamation against the playing of golf at Leith on Sundays during the time of the 'sermonis'.

c **1600** Man injured playing golf on the links at Ayr.

c **1608** Prince of Wales played golf in the grounds of Royal Manor at Greenwich.

c **1620** First mention of the feathery ball.

Before the introduction of the feathery ball, it is generally assumed that balls used for golf were of turned boxwood, similar to those used in the kindred games of chole and pall mall.

A monopoly of sale was granted to James Melvill, the price for each golf ball being fixed at fourpence.

1621 Golf played in King's Park, Stirling.

1629 The Marquis of Montrose was a golfer, as his father the Earl had been before him. Evidence of this is shown in his golfing expenses from visits to St Andrews and Leith as well as for his home course, Montrose. He may also have had something to do with the introduction of caddies. In the Marquis's accounts for 1628, there is record of the payment of four shillings 'to the boy who carried my clubs'.

1630 Dornoch described in glowing terms by Sir Robert Gordon, 'doe surpass the fields of Montrose or St Andrews'.

1641 News of the Irish rebellion conveyed to King Charles while he was playing golf at Leith.

Feathery balls (By courtesy of the JGA Golf Museum)

1642 A golf-ball-maker licensed by the Council of Aberdeen.

1658 First mention of golf in London, at 'Up-Fields' (Vincent Square), Westminster.

1682 First International match. The Duke of York and a shoemaker defeating two English noblemen at Leith.

1721 Golf on Glasgow Green.

1724 Big crowds for a match at Leith.

The match was between Alexander Elphinstone, a younger son of Lord Balmerino, and Captain John Porteous of the Edinburgh City Guard. The stake was 20 guineas and, among the large crowd, were the Duke of Hamilton and the Earl of Morton.

1744 First meeting of the Honourable Company of Edinburgh Golfers; they competed for a silver club presented by the City of Edinburgh. Widely acclaimed as the first golf club in the world. John Rattray, a surgeon, was the first winner of the silver club.

First rules of the game (13) were drawn up.

1754 Date of the founding of the St Andrews Club, later the Royal and Ancient. Twenty-two noblemen and others of Fife held an open competition for the prize of a silver club. The first winner was Bailie William Landale, a merchant of St Andrews.

The Leith code of rules written in 1744 were adopted generally.

1759 First mention of strokeplay. Previously all golf consisted of matches.

1764 A round at St Andrews was reduced to 18 holes. Originally it had been 22.

1766 Silver driver donated for competition at Blackheath.

1773 Edinburgh Burgess Golfing Society formed.

1779 Golf played in New York by Scottish officers during the American Revolutionary War.

1780 Formation of (Royal) Aberdeen Golf Club.

1786 Crail Golfing Society formed. South Carolina Golf Association formed at Charleston, USA but no continuity.

1787 The Bruntsfield Links golfers formed themselves into a club.

1797 Burntisland Golf Club formed.

1810 First mention of a competition for ladies. It was held for the fishwives of Musselburgh.

1818 Manchester golfers—Old Manchester Club—began playing on Kersal Moor.

1824 Perth Golfing Society formed.

1829 Calcutta Golf Club, India, founded, the first in the world outside Britain. Later became Royal Calcutta.

1832 North Berwick Golf Club founded.

1833 Perth Golfing Society became Royal Perth; it was created by William IV and was the first Royal club anywhere.

1834 William IV grants the Royal and Ancient golf club of St Andrews its name.

1836 The Honourable Company of Edinburgh Golfers move from Leith to Musselburgh.

1842 Bombay Golfing Society, India, formed, later Royal Bombay.

1848 Introduction of the gutta-percha ball, better known as the 'gutty'.

1851 Prestwick Golf Club founded.

Unofficial golf played in Sydney, Australia.

1856 Royal Curragh Golf Club founded in Kildare.

Pau Golf Club, France, formed; the first on the continent of Europe.

1857 First book on golf instruction published, *The Golfer's manual*, by 'A Keen Hand' (H B Farnie).

1859 Death of the first great professional golfer, Allan Robertson (b 1815).

1860 The beginning of championship golf. The first Open at Prestwick; the winner: Willie Park, Sr. It was contested entirely by professionals, but in 1861 it was thrown open 'to all the world'.

1864 The (Royal) North Devon Club founded at Westward Ho!, the first seaside links in England.

1865 The London Scottish Golf Club founded at Wimbledon.

1867 First ladies' golf club founded at St Andrews.

1869 Birth of the (Royal) Liverpool Golf Club at Hoylake and the Alnmouth Golf Club, Northumberland.

1870 Formation of the (Royal) Adelaide Golf Club, the first in Australia.

1871 First organised golf in New Zealand.

Gutta Percha balls (By courtesy of the JGA Golf Museum)

Finish of the first tournament held at St Andrews (c 1840). Mr R Chambers (winner) putting (The Fotomas Index)

Dunedin Golf Club (later called the Otago) formed, followed a year later by the Christchurch Golf Club. However, both clubs lapsed and a new era did not dawn until 1891.

1872 Following Young Tom Morris winning the Open championship belt outright, the Prestwick and St Andrews clubs, together with the Honourable Company of Edinburgh Golfers, combined to provide a new Open championship trophy—a silver claret jug. It was won by Young Tom Morris, his fourth championship victory in succession.

1873 (Royal) Montreal Golf Club founded, the first club in Canada and the continent of North America.

1875 Oxford and Cambridge University Golf Clubs formed.

1878 Birth of the University Match (Oxford and Cambridge); the oldest club match in the world.

1880 The Tennant Cup founded by the Glasgow Club. It is the oldest surviving Open competition for amateurs.

1881 Royal Belfast Golf Club formed.

1884 Formation of the Oakhurst Golf Club, White Sulphur Springs, Virginia; but it did not last.

1885 Founding of South Africa's first club, the Royal Cape. The first recorded golf had been on a 6-hole course near the military camp at Wynberg.

The British Amateur championship founded at Hoylake, Cheshire. It is the oldest amateur championship in the world. First played on 20–23 April.

1888 Formation of the St Andrews Golf Club at Yonkers, New York; the real beginnings of golf in the United States.

Belgium's first course, Royal Antwerp; Malaysia's first course, Perak at Taiping.

1889 Hong Kong Golf Club founded, now Royal Hong Kong.

1890 Royal Bangkok Golf Club, Thailand, founded.

1891 Formation of Shinnecock Hills Golf Club on Long Island, New York; named after a tribe of Indians who once inhabited the far end of Long Island; its clubhouse is the oldest in the United States.

Ladies putting at St Andrews *c* 1867 (Illustrated London News Pic. Lib.)

Haskell balls (By courtesy of the JGA Golf Museum)

Las Palmas Golf Club, Canary Islands, founded.

Gothenburg Golf Club, Sweden, founded.

1892 First Indian Amateur championship.

Lomas Golf Club, Argentina, founded.

1893 Formation of the Ladies' Golf Union in Britain; also, the start of the British Ladies' championship.

Start of the New Zealand Amateur championship.

1894 The British Open taken to England for the first time and won by J H Taylor. He was the first English winner.

The United States Golf Association founded.

First Australian Men's Amateur and Ladies' championships. First Malaysian Amateur.

1895 First United States Open and Amateur championships played at Newport Golf Club, Rhode Island.

Canadian Amateur championship started.

Bulawayo Golf Club, Rhodesia, founded.

First two courses in Germany—Bad Homburg and Baden-Baden.

Argentinian Amateur championship started.

1897 Nine-hole course opened at Puebla, Mexico.

1898 Copenhagen Golf Club, Denmark, founded.

1901 First course in Japan, 9 holes on the slopes of Mount Rokko, near Kobe.

Invention of the Haskell (USA) rubber-cored ball.

British Professional Golfers' Association formed—first in the world.

First course in Austria at Wien-Krieau.

1902 First amateur international match between England and Scotland.

1903 The Oxford and Cambridge Golfing

Society toured the United States, the first overseas tour ever undertaken.

1904 First French Amateur championship at La Boulie.

First course in Czechoslovakia at Karlovy Vary.

First Australian and Canadian Open championships.

1905 First international golf match between Britain and the United States. The British ladies defeated the American ladies 6–1 at Cromer, England.

1906 First French Open championship started at La Boulie.

1907 Swiss Men's and Ladies' Open amateur championships first played at Interlaken.

First New Zealand Open championship.

1909 Austrian Amateur championship started.

1913 Francis Ouimet (1893–1967), a virtually unknown amateur, defeated the British professionals Harry Vardon and Ted Ray in a play-off for the US Open at the Country Club, Brookline, Boston. It marked the beginning of

Below: First course in Japan, 1901. Nine holes at Mount Rokko, near Kobe (Illustrated London News Pic. Lib.)

First international match, Hoylake 1902. England v Scotland—England 25, Scotland 32 holes (By courtesy of Royal Liverpool Golf Club)

England
Standing, l to r: B Darwin, J A T Bramston, H C Ellis, Hon O Scott, S H Fry, G F Smith *Sitting, l to r:* H G Hutchinson, John Ball, Harold Hilton, C Hutchings

Scotland
Standing, l to r: J Robb, F Mackenzie, J R Gairdner, C E Dick, J Graham Jr, E Blackwell *Sitting, l to r:* R Maxwell, L Balfour Melville, S Mure Fergusson, J E Laidley

American dominance.

1917 Golf started in Bogotá, Colombia.

1918 United States Professional Golfers' Association formed. USPGA championship started.

1919 Management of the British Open and Amateur championships taken over by the Royal and Ancient Golf Club.

Taiwan Golf and Country Club opened.

1921 The Royal and Ancient and the USPGA introduced the first limitation on the size and weight of the ball, and agreed that 'on and after May 1st, 1921, the weight of the ball shall not be greater than 1·62 ounces (45·88 g) and the size

not less than 1·62 inches (41·15 mm)'.

First amateur international between Britain and the United States at Hoylake. The US won 9–3.

1922 The Prince of Wales, later King Edward VIII, Captain of the Royal and Ancient Golf Club.

Walker Cup matches started.

1925 Steel shafted clubs legalised in the United States.

1926 First, semi-official, professional international match played at Wentworth between the United States and Britain. Britain won $13\frac{1}{2}$–$1\frac{1}{2}$.

1927 Ryder Cup matches started.

1930 Grand Slam year for Bobby Jones. He won the British and American Open and Amateur championships.

Steel-shafted clubs legalised in Britain although Bobby Jones remained loyal to hickory throughout his career. He retired after the Grand Slam.

The Duke of York, later King George VI, became Captain of the Royal and Ancient Golf Club.

1932 Curtis Cup matches started at Wentworth. The United States ladies defeated the British $5\frac{1}{2}$–$3\frac{1}{2}$.

1934 Start of the US Masters at Augusta, Georgia.

1937 European Golf Association founded.

1951 Francis Ouimet (1893–1967) became the first American Captain of the Royal and Ancient.

Left: The Prince of Wales and his caddie, Andrew Kirkaldy, before the Prince drove into office as Captain of the Royal and Ancient Golf Club 1922 (Illustrated London News Pic. Lib.)

Below: The caddies who waited to retrieve his ball were said to have stood disloyally close to the tee, but the Prince got his shot away with some nifty footwork (Illustrated London News Pic. Lib.)

The first British Ryder Cup team setting sail for America, 1927 (Illustrated London News Pic. Lib.)

Unified code of rules hammered out by the R and A and the USGA. Took effect in 1952 although one or two differences existed.
1952 Stymie abolished.
Americas Cup matches started for the amateurs of the United States, Canada and Mexico.
1953 Canada Cup, later the World Cup, started.
1958 First world amateur team championship for the Eisenhower trophy took place at St Andrews.
Bobby Jones received the Freedom of St Andrews on 9 October.
1959 Far East—now Asia circuit—professional tour started in Hong Kong by Eric Cremin, the Australian professional, and Kim Hall.

1963 Asia Golf Confederation founded.

1964 Women's world amateur team championship for Espirito Santo Trophy started in Paris.

1968 A women's team from continental Europe defeated a United States team $10\frac{1}{2}$–$7\frac{1}{2}$ in Paris.

1971 First golf shot on the Moon (February). Captain Alan Shepard, Commander of the Apollo 14 spacecraft, hit two balls with an iron-headed club which he presented to the USGA Museum in 1974.

The Royal and Ancient Golf Club sent Shepard a telegram of congratulation and a reminder of the Rules of Golf section on etiquette, '. . . before leaving a bunker, a player should carefully fill up all holes made by him therein.'

1979 Spanish golfer, Severiano Ballesteros wins the British Open.

Left: Francis Ouimet drives in as the first American Captain of the Royal and Ancient Golf Club, 1951 (Illustrated London News Pic. Lib.)

Below: A proud moment for St Andrews and Bobby Jones. Jones receives the Freedom of St Andrews, 1958 (Action Photos)

The Supreme Champions

Bobby Jones's assertion that 'there are tournament winners and major tournament winners' was a neat way of stressing the difference between the good and the great.

He, for his part, was the supreme champion, and this section is concerned solely with those men whose achievements have enriched the history of competitive golf: the legends like Jones, Hogan and Nicklaus.

It has become customary to measure success by the number of victories in the major championships, but such a measurement is not entirely fair. Before the start of the US Masters in 1934 and the USPGA championship in 1916, the only major championships were the British and American Opens; and, until the start of the jet age, it was very much the exception for anyone to play in both in the same year.

As a result, Harry Vardon, say, had far fewer chances than Jack Nicklaus who has taken part in all four major championships since first appearing as a professional in 1962. Inspired and influenced by Jones, however, he has always set his standards by the major championships and, by this insistence, has guaranteed their pre-eminence.

They remain the most cherished titles in the world of golf largely because they act as some means of comparison between the generations. In modern times, they have also become a passport to fortune, but the stunning thought today is that Jones was an amateur. His total of championship victories is, therefore, based on the Open and Amateur championships of Britain and America.

Any parallel between him and Hogan or Sarazen or Snead cannot be exact. If one includes Jones's Amateur championship successes, one has to include the two by Nicklaus and one by Arnold Palmer but, while it is impossible to argue with figures, the accompanying charts and tables illustrate what it is, by any reckoning, that sets a few golfers apart from the others.

INDIVIDUAL VICTORIES IN THE MAJOR CHAMPIONSHIPS

(These include US and British Opens, US Masters, USPGA and US and British Amateurs.)

19—JACK WILLIAM NICKLAUS
US Open, 62-67-72-80
British Open, 66-70-78
US Masters, 63-65-66-72-75
USPGA, 63-71-73-75-80
US Amateur, 59-61

13—ROBERT TYRE (BOB—USA, BOBBY—GB) JONES, Jr
US Open, 23-26-29-30
British Open, 26-27-30
US Amateur, 24-25-27-28-30
British Amateur, 1930

11—WALTER CHARLES HAGEN
US Open, 14-19
British Open, 22-24-28-29
US Masters, None
USPGA, 21-24-25-26-27

9—BENJAMIN WILLIAM (BEN) HOGAN
US Open, 48-50-51-53
British Open, 1953
US Masters, 51-53
USPGA, 46-48

9—GARY PLAYER
US Open, 1965
British Open, 59-68-74
US Masters, 61-74-78
USPGA, 62-72

8—ARNOLD DANIEL PALMER
US Open, 1960
British Open, 61-62
US Masters, 58-60-62-64
USPGA, None
US Amateur, 1954

7—EUGENE (GENE) SARAZEN
US Open, 22-32
British Open, 1932
US Masters, 1935
USPGA, 22-23-33

7—SAMUEL JACKSON SNEAD
British Open, 1946
US Masters, 49-52-54
USPGA, 42-49-51

MAJOR TITLE WINNERS

US Open, British Open, US Masters, USPGA, US Amateur
In same year None
In different years Jack Nicklaus

US Open, British Open, US Masters, US Amateur
In same year None
In different years Arnold Palmer, Jack Nicklaus

British Open, US Open, US Masters, USPGA
In same year None
In different years Gene Sarazen, Ben Hogan, Gary Player and Jack Nicklaus

British Open, US Open, British Amateur, US Amateur
In same year R T Jones, Jr (1930)
In different years None

British Open, US Open, US Masters
In same year Ben Hogan (1953)
In different years Gene Sarazen, Arnold Palmer, Gary Player and Jack Nicklaus

British Open, US Open, USPGA
In same year None
In different years Walter Hagen, Jim Barnes, Gene Sarazen, Tommy Armour, Ben Hogan, Gary Player, Jack Nicklaus and Lee Trevino.

British Open, USPGA, US Masters
In same year None
In different years Gene Sarazen, Ben Hogan, Sam Snead, Gary Player and Jack Nicklaus

US Open, USPGA, US Masters
In same year None
In different years Gene Sarazen, Byron Nelson, Ben Hogan, Gary Player and Jack Nicklaus

British Open, US Open, US Amateur
In same year R T Jones, Jr (1930)
In different years R T Jones, Jr, Jack Nicklaus, Arnold Palmer

British Open, British Amateur, US Amateur
In same year R T Jones, Jr (1930)
In different years Harold Hilton

British Open, US Open, British Amateur
In same year R T Jones, Jr (1930)
In different years None

US Open, US Amateur, British Amateur
In same year R T Jones, Jr (1930)
In different years W Lawson Little

British Open, US Open
In same year R T Jones, Jr (1926 and 1930), Gene Sarazen (1932), Ben Hogan (1953) and Lee Trevino (1971)
In different years Ted Ray, Harry Vardon, Walter Hagen, Jim Barnes, R T Jones, Jr, Tommy Armour, Arnold Palmer, Gary Player, Jack Nicklaus, Tony Jacklin, Lee Trevino and Johnny Miller

British Amateur, US Amateur
In same year Harold Hilton (1911), R T Jones, Jr (1930), W Lawson Little (1934 and 1935), Bob Dickson (1967)
In different years Walter Travis, Jess Sweetser, Willie Turnesa, Dick Chapman, Harvie Ward, Deane Beman, Steve Melnyk and Marvin Giles III

US Open, US Amateur, US Masters
In same year None
In different years Arnold Palmer, Jack Nicklaus

US Open, US Amateur
In same year Charles Evans, Jr (1916), R T Jones, Jr (1930)
In different years Francis Ouimet, Jerome D Travers, R T Jones, Jr, John Goodman, Lawson Little, Arnold Palmer, Gene Littler, Jack Nicklaus and Jerry Pate

British Open, British Amateur
In same year R T Jones, Jr (1930)
In different years John Ball, Harold Hilton

US Open, USPGA
In same year Gene Sarazen (1922), Ben Hogan (1948), Jack Nicklaus (1980)
In different years Walter Hagen, Jim Barnes, Gene Sarazen, Tommy Armour, Olin Dutra, Byron Nelson, Ben Hogan, Gary Player, Jack Nicklaus, Julius Boros and Lee Trevino

British Open, USPGA
In same year Walter Hagen (1924)
In different years Jim Barnes, Jock Hutchison, Gene Sarazen, Walter Hagen, Tommy Armour, Densmore Shute, Sam Snead, Ben Hogan, Gary Player, Jack Nicklaus and Lee Trevino

US Open, US Masters
In same year Craig Wood (1941), Ben Hogan (1951 and 1953), Arnold Palmer (1960), Jack Nicklaus (1972)
In different years Gene Sarazen, Byron Nelson, Ralph Guldahl, Cary Middlecoff, Gary Player, Jack Nicklaus, Billy Casper

British Open, US Masters
In same year Ben Hogan (1953), Arnold Palmer (1962), Jack Nicklaus (1966) and Gary Player (1974)
In different years Gene Sarazen, Sam Snead, Arnold Palmer, Gary Player, Jack Nicklaus, Tom Watson and Severiano Ballesteros

USPGA, US Masters
In same year Sam Snead (1949), Jack Burke (1956), Jack Nicklaus (1963 and 1975)
In different years Gene Sarazen, Byron Nelson, Henry Picard, Sam Snead, Ben Hogan, Doug Ford, Gary Player, Jack Nicklaus, Raymond Floyd

YOUNG TOM MORRIS

b St Andrews, Fife, 20.4.1851;
d St Andrews, 25.12.1875

Golf's first great champion, Young Tom Morris. The championship belt, presented by the Earl of Eglinton, was made of red morocco leather and silver plates (BBC Hulton Pic. Lib.)

Sooner or later most of the early championship records have been broken, but three which Young Tom Morris established are never likely to succumb. Making allowances for 1871 when there was no Open, owing to the fact that he had won the championship belt outright, he scored four successive victories; and, when he won his first title in 1868, he succeeded his father, Old Tom, as champion. In 1869, they finished first and second.

Young Tom was the man who put championship golf on the map and though he had only a handful of challengers, there is no telling how many other records he would have set if he had not died at the tragically early age of 24.

His death came on Christmas Day 1875, only three months after that of his wife and newly born son. The tale, contradicted in the local St Andrews paper, was that he died of a broken heart. His memory is perpetuated by a plaque in St Andrews Cathedral which bears the inscription, 'Deeply regretted by numerous friends and all golfers, he thrice in succession won the championship belt and held it without rivalry and yet without envy, his many amiable qualities being no less acknowledged than his golfing achievements.'

Just how keen the rivalry was between father and son, is not recorded, but Old Tom once remarked in later years, 'I could cope wi' Allan [Robertson] mysel' but never wi' Tommy'; and nor could anyone else. At the age of 13, Young Tom won an exhibition match at Perth for a prize of £15; three years later, he won a professional tournament at Carnoustie, defeating Willie Park and Bob Andrew in a play-off, and in 1868 became the youngest Open champion.

Scores have inevitably improved over the years and it is no fairer to compare them than it is to measure success by the ever-increasing prize-money, but one achievement of Young Tom's is an undoubted measure of his ability.

In winning the 1870 Open by 12 strokes, only 1 stroke less than Old Tom's record-winning margin in 1862, he covered three rounds of Prestwick's 12-hole course in 149 strokes. It was a score never equalled even by Vardon, Taylor or Braid so long as the gutty ball was in use. Tom's last round of 49, 1 under fours, included a 3 at the 1st hole which measured considerably over 500 yd (450 m) and gained him custody of the championship belt which was later presented to the Royal and Ancient Golf Club.

There was thus a gap of a year while the championship trophy, still played for today, was presented; in 1872, he won that, too. He beat Davie Strath by 3 strokes and once thereafter beat the better ball of Strath and Jamie Anderson. On another occasion, he backed himself to beat 83 round the Old course for a whole week, winning every time and then lowering his target to 81 and 80.

He had some detractors; for instance it was said that his swing lacked classic grace, but the power of his broad shoulders gave him the ability to squeeze the ball out of the bad lies that abounded in those days.

THE GREAT TRIUMVIRATE

JAMES BRAID
b Earlsferry, Fife, 6.2.1870;
d London, 27.11.1950

JOHN HENRY TAYLOR
b Northam, North Devon, 19.3.1871;
d Northam, North Devon, 10.2.1963

HARRY VARDON
b Grouville, Jersey, 9.5.1870;
d Totteridge, London, 20.3.1937

From 1894 until the outbreak of World War I in 1914 there were only five years in which the British Open championship was not won by one of the Great Triumvirate.

In that time, Harry Vardon won six times and J H Taylor and James Braid five times each. Three times they occupied the first three places and never once did one of them fail to finish in the first three. No major championship has ever been so dominated by three players over such a long period and they were the first to make the public conscious of golfing records.

Only Peter Thomson can rival them in terms of Open victories, but not even his tussle with Bobby Locke in the 1950s matched what was perhaps the most romantic period in golf.

Born within a year of one another the Triumvirate did more than anyone to establish professional golf as an honourable trade.

Without their example, the recognition of professionals at clubs may have taken even longer than it did. Taylor, in particular, was a natural speaker and a natural leader who was largely responsible for the founding of the PGA and the development of artisan golf; but it was

their contribution to the playing side of the game that undoubtedly left the biggest mark.

Although John Ball and Harold Hilton had both won the Open championship as amateurs, J H Taylor's first victory in 1894 halted the supremacy of the Scots professionals. It took place, too, at Sandwich, the first time the Open ventured into England and highlighted Taylor's almost revolutionary new style of hitting boldly up to the pin.

His swing and follow-through were a little curtailed and his stance rigidly flat-footed, but there was an abundance of defiance and determination about his golf that made him such a redoubtable bad-weather player.

When Taylor pulled down his cap, stuck out his chin and embedded his large boots in the ground, he could hit straight through the wind, especially with his trusty mashie. His last and best victory came in just such conditions at Hoylake in 1913. He won by 8 strokes, showing a control on the last day that nobody could match. He was the only player to break 80 in the third and fourth rounds and confirmed his oft-quoted saying that the best way to win is to win easily. Though a highly strung and emotional man, he was a stern competitor who, at the age of 53, had the lowest score in the 1924 Open, taking into account the qualifying rounds as well.

That was as creditable a performance as any in a career that blossomed after his first success in the Open in 1894. He defended his title with another victory at St Andrews in 1895, but lost it to Vardon the following year at Muirfield in a play-off—the first play-off since the championship was decided over four rounds.

Vardon had started the final day 6 strokes behind Taylor, but his ultimate victory was confirmation of his genius. In a career which saw him win his last Open 18 years after his first, he won a record six times. About the turn of the century when he went up and down the country, winning tournaments and breaking records, he raised the standards of those around him and had a great influence on methods of playing.

Until then, nobody had paid much attention to style, but suddenly people became aware that Vardon's upright swing was the essence of rhythm and grace. It was soon hailed as a perfect model for others to copy. Although he hit the ball a long way, he favoured light clubs and never carried more than ten.

Three of Vardon's six Opens were won after the advent of the rubber-cored ball, but it was with the gutty, before his serious illness in 1903,

In honour of the Great Triumvirate (By courtesy of the South Herts Golf Club/Photo: Chris Greenhill, AIIP)

that he reigned supreme. Most of his success was attained in Britain, but he was also a pioneer of travel in days when it was long and laborious.

In 1900, he and Taylor finished first and second in the US Open at Chicago, the first time that either Open had been won by a traveller from overseas. Thirteen years later, he returned to Brookline for one of the most famous of all championships. It was the one in which he and Ted Ray lost a play-off to Francis Ouimet, an unknown local lad, who thus started the decline of British dominance.

Vardon's first tour of America took a lot out of him and it is said that he was never as brilliant again, although he was 44 years old when he won his last Open at Prestwick in 1914. After winning in 1903 with a total of 300, one of his proudest achievements, he contracted tuberculosis and had to go to a sanatorium for treatment but, by then, the third of the Triumvirate, James Braid, was in full swing.

The son of an Elie ploughman, he was a late starter compared to his great contemporaries. By the time he won his first Open in 1901, Taylor and Vardon had each won three times but, in a sudden golden era, Braid was the first of the three to win the championship five times.

In the space of ten years, he won at St Andrews and Muirfield twice and at Prestwick once. He never succeeded in England where he spent most of his life (first of all at the Army and Navy Stores in London, then at Romford and finally at Walton Heath) but, like Taylor and Vardon, he was seldom far away when not actually winning.

Until Jack Nicklaus finished second in 1979 for the seventh time, Taylor shared the title of champion runner-up with six, but Braid and Vardon were runners-up four times, Vardon once three years in succession.

Braid, who was said by Horace Hutchinson to drive with divine fury, was the winner of the first *News of the World* matchplay championship in 1903 and won money regularly in challenge and exhibition matches. In the 1904 Open at Sandwich, he played the last two rounds in a total of 140 strokes and was the first man to return a score under 70 in the championship. It came in his third round, Jack White, the winner, equalling it later in the day and Taylor, who finished third, beating it with 68.

Of the three, Braid's game was more liable to error, but his powers of recovery were immense, particularly in the now-familiar explosion shot from sand. It is just one more example of the way in which he, Taylor and Vardon set fashions over perhaps the most important 20 years in the whole history of championship golf.

	Harry Vardon	J H Taylor	James Braid
1894	=5	1	
1895		1	
1896	1	2 (lost play-off)	6
1897	6	=10	2
1898	1	4	11
1899	1	4	5
1900	2	1	3
1901	2	3	1
1902	=2	=6	=2
1903	1	=9	5
1904	5	=2	=2
1905	=9	=2	1
1906	3	2	1
1907	=7	2	=5
1908	=5	=7	1
1909	26	1	2
1910	=16	=14	1
1911	1	=5	=5
1912	2	=11	3
1913	=3	1	=18
1914	1	2	=10
1920	=14	12	=21
1921	=23	=26	=16
1922	=8	6	
1924		5	

In addition, Vardon won the US Open in 1900 and was runner-up in 1913. He was also equal second when Ted Ray won in 1920. Taylor was second to Vardon in 1900.

JACK WILLIAM NICKLAUS

b Columbus, Ohio, 21.1.1940

To the question how good is Jack Nicklaus, the answer can only be: look at the record. The number of times his name appears in these pages is some guide, but statistics only scratch the surface. They deserve closer scrutiny.

From the time that he defeated Arnold Palmer in a play-off in his first US Open as a professional in 1962, he has started favourite in almost every tournament or championship in which he has taken part. Inevitably, he has had his bad days and his bad weeks, but what is bad for him is good for most others.

Jack Nicklaus sharing the moment of victory with Jimmy Dickinson. St Andrews 1978 (Peter Dazeley)

Fellow competitors still look over their shoulders even when Nicklaus is 7 or 8 strokes behind. He is always capable of a round that is beyond everyone else, and several have brought him victory in the major championships on which he concentrates his efforts.

To date, he has won 19—or 17 if one discounts his two US Amateur championships. These comprise four US Opens, three British Opens, five Masters and five USPGAs, but not the least impressive part of this roll of honour is the number of times that he has finished in the first ten. His consistency is phenomenal.

From 1962 to 1979 Nicklaus played 72 major championships. In only 17 of these did he finish outside the first ten; in only four did he fail to make the cut (the 1963 US Open, the 1967 Masters and the 1968 and 1978 USPGAs) and in no fewer than 39 was he in the first three.

In the 14 British Opens from 1966, he never finished worse than sixth. He has played 23 rounds under 70 (nine more than anybody else) and he has been runner-up a record seven times. In addition, he has the highest number of rounds under 70 in the US Open, the record number of victories in the Masters and the highest number (13) of top five finishes.

Jack Nicklaus has been breaking records, in fact, ever since the Eisenhower Trophy in 1960 at Merion when he first dropped a hint of what was in store. Even making due allowance for the fact that the pins were positioned without the customary severity of an Open, 269 was an absurdly low score for a young amateur. The previous year, he had made his debut in the Walker Cup at Muirfield and went home to win the US Amateur, a title he captured again in 1961 at Pebble Beach. Coincidentally, he won the US Open at Pebble Beach eleven years later—the only person to win the US Amateur and US Open on the same course. In 1960, he also set the lowest US Open aggregate by an amateur (282).

Within a few months of turning professional, he won the US Open at Oakmont although his first appearance in the British Open, which Arnold Palmer won the same summer, was easily his worst (equal 34th). However, it is the only occasion in which Palmer has finished above Nicklaus in the British Open; and there have not been very many others elsewhere in major championships.

In retrospect, it seems inevitable that Nicklaus became a great golfer. In the Foreword to Nicklaus's book, *The Greatest Game of All*, Bobby Jones recalled that as early as the age of 15 when Nicklaus first appeared in the US Amateur, 'it was not difficult to see that a new talent of the first magnitude had arrived'.

With the adoption of Jones as his hero, Nicklaus set out on his path to the top, encouraged by his father, Charlie Nicklaus, a keen golfer and qualified pharmacist; and taught from the beginning by Jack Grout to whom he still turns when he has a technical problem.

During his developmental years, Nicklaus attended high school and college but by 1961 he was known as 'the amateur the pros fear' and, in view of the opportunities which professional golf had to offer, it was inevitable that he should take the decision to join its ranks.

It was inevitable, too, that Palmer's reign as the world's leading golfer should have been ended by Nicklaus. Not that this was universally welcome in America where Palmer's popularity knew no limits. Many resented the fact that Nicklaus, little more than a young college boy, could play so well. They did not think it right that he should topple their great hero so soon. So life was not always easy for Nicklaus as a result.

Luckily, however, he had a warm regard for Palmer and understood the situation perfectly. Equally, the hysteria of his followers which Palmer experienced must have been an embarrassment to him at times, but Nicklaus quickly made himself a model champion; a champion with less of the identifiable emotion that Palmer displayed, but one whose golf was indisputably supreme.

There had been many signs of his rising genius notably in the 1960 Open when he finished second to Palmer, two strokes behind. It was the highest finish by an amateur since Johnny Goodman won in 1933 but there was still an element of suddenness about the way he became champion two years later within such a short time of turning professional.

It was the best first tournament any professional could have won, but Nicklaus enjoyed phenomenal success wherever he went. The first of the eight years (a record) that he has finished as leading money-winner in the United States was 1964, and he has won tournaments regularly ever since despite rationing his appearances and concentrating on the major championships. To date, he has won 66 tournaments which puts him in second place in the United States behind Sam Snead on 84.

A year after winning the US Open, he won the Masters and the PGA championship. He won the Masters again in 1965, breaking all records with a total of 271, 9 strokes ahead of

Palmer and Player; and he became the only person to successfully defend his title the following April.

This came only after a play-off with Tommy Jacobs and Gay Brewer, but it was the start of a summer which saw his first success in the British Open at Muirfield, the course for which he already had great affection and after which he called his own course Muirfield Village several years later.

After an inauspicious beginning in the 1962 British Open, when he made the cut only by a single stroke, he had a chance in 1963 and followed Tony Lema home at St Andrews in 1964. On the last day, Nicklaus had the lowest aggregate (134) of any last day but with the fairways narrow and the rough deep at Muirfield, he squeezed home with 1 stroke in hand.

Nicklaus had gone on record as saying that he was not a good 'fast course' player, but he was prepared to accept the course's essential demand for accuracy rather than length, taking an iron from many of the tees.

He squandered a big lead on the last 9 holes of the third round and dropped strokes at the 11th, 13th and 14th in the last round, but he managed the four 4s he needed to win, one of them a birdie.

His triumph completed victory in the four major championships, enabling him to join Gene Sarazen, Ben Hogan and Gary Player, but by 1971 he became the first person to win them all a second time and now he has won them all three times. He passed Bobby Jones's total of 13 major championships and, on the professional tour front, joined the million dollar 'Club' in 1970. Since then he has become the founder member of the two and three million dollar 'Club', and sole member of the latter.

Yet the impressive part of this recital of superlatives are some of the individual records he holds. In the Masters, he is the most frequent winner, the youngest winner, the winner by the biggest margin and has the lowest number of top five finishes.

In the US Open, Nicklaus set a new record for the lowest aggregate with 272 in 1980 and has the highest number of rounds (19) under 70. This is a record he holds, too, in the British Open (23), as well as a share of the lowest third and fourth rounds—both 65s. He has the lowest last round in the USPGA (64) and has the biggest span between his first and last victories in this (1963–75) and the US Open (1962–80).

He has six victories to his name in the Australian Open and has been a member of six winning World Cup teams, but he has accom-plished this huge catalogue of success without allowing it to dictate his whole life and without spoiling him as a person.

He has always given straight answers and the golf writers of the world have respected him for it but, early on, he could be a little abrasive. However, as the college boy image faded, he transformed his appearance and his weight and endeared himself to many by his good grace and generosity of mind.

Defeat can be harder to bear when somebody is as used to winning as he is but he accepts it calmly and philosophically and, at such moments, will continue interviews at length when some others grudge as much as a couple of minutes.

It is on these occasions that one is struck by his control, care, thoughtfulness and patience. But these are, after all, the same qualities that characterise his golf—the qualities that combine to make him unquestionably the best contemporary golfer and arguably the best that ever lived.

	British Open	US Open	US Masters	USPGA
1958	DNP	=41*		DNP
1959	DNP		F/Q*	DNP
1960	DNP	2*	=13*	DNP
1961	DNP	=4*	=7*	DNP
1962	=34	1	=15	=3
1963	3	F/Q	1	1
1964	2	=23	=2	=2
1965	=12	=32	1	=2
1966	1	3	1	=22
1967	2	1	F/Q	=3
1968	=2	2	=5	F/Q
1969	=6	=25	=24	=11
1970	1	=51	8	=6
1971	=5	2	=2	1
1972	2	1	1	=13
1973	4	=4	=3	1
1974	3	=10	=4	2
1975	=3	=7	1	1
1976	=2	=11	=3	=4
1977	2	=10	2	3
1978	1	=6	7	F/Q
1979	=2	=9	4	=65
1980	=4	1	=33	1

United States Amateur champion 1959 and 1961.
DNP Did not play.
F/Q Failed to qualify for final 36 holes.
= Finished tied.
* As Amateur.

CAREER SUMMARY
(Professional Years: From 1962 to 1980 inclusive)

Official tour victories: 66
Second place or ties: 44

Third place or ties: 31
Total victories round the world: 84
Tops in career tour averages: 70·4 strokes per round
Tops in lowest scoring average: 8 times, 1976-75-74-73-72-71-65-64; runner-up 6 times
Top money-winner: 8 times, 1976-75-73-72-71-67-65-64; runner-up 4 times
Tops in career official tour earnings: $3 408 827
Most major championship titles: 19 (Masters 5; PGA Championship 5; United States Open 5; British Open 3; US Amateur 2)
PGA Player of the Year Award: 5 times, 1976-75-73-72-67
Play-off tour record: won 12, lost 8
Lowest tournament records: all 62s
Ohio Kings Island Open, 7 October 1973, third round
Sahara Invitational, 28 October 1967, third round
Australian Dunlop International, 5 November 1971, second round
(shot 59 in exhibition with three professionals 12 March 1973, at Palm Beach, Florida)

International and other victories
British Open (3): 1978-70-66 (runner-up 7 times)
Australian Open (6): 1978-76-75-71-68-64
World Series of Golf (5): 1976-70-67-63-62 (runner-up 6 times)
Ryder Cup: member of US teams that defeated Britain in 1977-75-73-71 and tied Britain 1969
World Matchplay Championship: 1970
World Cup: winner of individual championship a record three times (1971-64-63) and 6 times a partner on US winning teams

ROBERT TYRE JONES, JR

b Atlanta, Georgia 17.3.1902;
d Atlanta, 18.12.1971

The Impregnable Quadrilateral, so much nicer a term than the Grand Slam, is the most perfect achievement in golf. In the summer of 1930, Bobby Jones won the Open and Amateur championships of Britain and America.

Nowadays, it is unthinkable for an amateur to win either Open and this is, therefore, a record that will almost certainly never be broken. It is the ultimate achievement and, though only 28 at the time, Jones understandably retired. For the previous eight years his consistency in the two

Opens remains unsurpassed even by modern giants like Hogan and Nicklaus.

In his last nine US Opens, he was first four times and second four times. From 1923 to 1930, he was either US Open or Amateur champion although strangely he never won both in the same year until 1930. He won three of the four British Opens in which he took part and, after 1923, Walter Hagen, one of the leading golfers of the 1920s, only once finished above him in either championship.

In addition to winning the US Amateur a record five times, Jones was a finalist and semi-finalist twice and eventually succeeded in winning the British Amateur, a championship with its 18-hole matches which Jones always considered was the hardest of all to win.

In 36-hole matches, however, it was a different story. His successes in the Walker Cup and US Amateur were devastating. From 1923 to 1930, he lost only once over 36 holes—to George von Elm in the Amateur final of 1926.

At various other times, he defeated Chick Evans 7 and 6; von Elm 9 and 8; Roger Wethered 9 and 8, and 7 and 6; Cyril Tolley 12 and 11; Francis Ouimet 11 and 9; John Beck 14 and 13; and T P Perkins 13 and 12, and 10 and 9—both within 14 days.

No wonder Bernard Darwin wrote, 'Like the man in the song, many of Mr Jones's opponents are tired of living but feared of dying. However, their fears are rarely unduly protracted since they usually die very soon after lunch.'

In all, Jones won 13 major titles, a figure only beaten by Jack Nicklaus who, though not born until ten years after Jones retired, regarded Jones as his hero; but comparisons are worthless. Jones belonged to a leisured age when travel to Britain was a considerable undertaking. He played, too, with hickory-shafted clubs throughout his career but he had the style and technique to have played with a stair rod. He was as much loved in Britain as in America and did more than any overseas golfer to promote the importance of the British Open in the eyes of the world.

Although immensely considerate to others and later a model of behaviour, he often allowed youthful impetuosity to get the better of him if he failed to match his own high standards. It resulted in his tearing up his card in the third round of the 1921 Open at St Andrews and may have stemmed from the sort of frustration that the Old course can invoke.

However, he made handsome amends, building up a genuine love of the Old course, extolling its virtues and when receiving the

Freedom of the Burgh of St Andrews on 9 October 1958, paying it a unique compliment. He said he would choose St Andrews if he were allowed only one course in the world on which to play and added, 'I could take out of my life everything except my experiences at St Andrews and still have a rich, full life.'

Jones was only nine when he won the junior championship of his Club, East Lake, Atlanta, and was 14 when he won the Georgia State Amateur championship for the first time. A year later, he won the Southern Amateur and in 1919 was runner-up in the Canadian Open and US Amateur.

If Jones's father had not moved house from the city to the suburb of East Lake when the young Bobby was only five, he might not have taken to golf at all. His father cared little for sport but the fascination of looking through the gates of the East Lake club had its effect. Jones clearly liked what he saw.

After being officially taken to the club by his mother, he was given the chance to try his hand and the game came easily to him. He needed few lessons but, like so many great players, he was a born imitator, basing his style on the professional at East Lake, Stewart Maiden, an emigrant Scot and friend to whom Jones always paid tribute. Without consciously trying, Jones was a supreme stylist with a smooth, drowsy, rhythmic swing. His boyish good looks and

The ultimate in achievement. Bobby Jones with his four championship trophies, 1930 (US Golf Association)

sturdy, athletic build combined to give him a magnetic personality although it would be quite wrong to suggest that he did not suffer over his golf in the manner of humbler folk.

His great and trusted friend, O B Keeler, often wrote how Bobby could scarcely eat anything until a day's play was over; how, on occasions, he felt he could not even button his shirt collar for fear of the direst consequences; how he could lose a stone in weight during a championship and how he was capable of breaking down to the point of tears, not from any distress but from pure emotional overstrain.

Bernard Darwin recalled vividly, too, the close of the 1930 Open at Hoylake, the second leg of the Impregnable Quadrilateral. 'I was writing in the room where Bobby was waiting to see if he had won. He was utterly exhausted and had to hold his glass in two hands lest the good liquor be spilt. All he would say was that he would never, never do it again.'

Later that year he remained true to his word, but back in the days of his youth his career had not yet reached full flower.

Jones played in his first US Open at the age of 18, finishing in a tie for eighth place. As so often happens with young players, too much was probably expected of him too soon and for seven years from the age of 15 he played in ten major championships without success. The 1921 British Open was one example and the British Amateur the same year another.

Then, in 1923, the Bobby Jones era really

Bobby Jones at St Andrews 1927 (BBC Hulton Pic. Lib.)

opened with victory in the US Open at Inwood, New York, after a play-off with Bobby Cruick- shank. In the last round, Cruickshank had finished with a birdie, but in the play-off Jones won with 76 to 78, the 2-stroke difference coming at the 18th hole.

Jones was second for the next two years but won the US Amateur in those years and in 1926 returned to Britain, the first time since his unfortunate baptism at St Andrews. After beating Cyril Tolley 12 and 11 in the Walker Cup and losing in the fifth round of the Amateur, he decided to stay on for the Open and had to qualify.

The fact that he qualified safely is only half the story. In so doing, he scored his famous 66 on the Old course at Sunningdale which was described as being as near flawless as any round of golf could be. He was only bunkered once, holed one long putt and hit every green in the right number except one, ten of them with a 2 iron or wood.

It was an encouraging overture to the Open at Lytham where, despite taking 39 putts in his final round, he held off Al Watrous to win. That he did so owed everything to his famous recovery at the 17th when he found the green from the sandy wilderness on the left and Watrous, confident perhaps of clinching things at that hole, took 3 putts. Jones wore the mantle of champion naturally and easily, but at lunchtime on the final day he returned to his hotel, was not recognised by the gatekeeper on his return and had to pay to get back in. He was never one to make a scene.

The following year at St Andrews he opened with a 68, led all the way and won by 6 strokes, but his third victory in three appearances at Hoylake in 1930 was rather more a triumph of character. He was asked afterwards whether he had ever played worse so successfully; to which he answered no. In the third round, he lost 8 strokes to par in the first 3 holes and in the last round took 7 at the 8th. However, the great breakthrough had been the first leg of the Impregnable Quadrilateral, the British Ama- teur at St Andrews—the championship that had hitherto eluded him. No wonder, having secured his ambition, he said, 'There has been nothing in golf I wanted so much.'

Not that it was wholly straightforward. In a marvellous match in the fourth round, Cyril Tolley took him to the 19th watched by an estimated 12000 spectators, and in the semi- final George Voigt was 2 up and 5 to play. 'I did not think Voigt was the kind of player who would toss away this sort of lead, and I was quite certain that I was not capable of the golf needed to wrest it away from him. All I could do was what I did, namely, resolve to swallow the medicine, whatever it might be, and to keep on trying as best I could.' Well, Voigt drove out of bounds at the 14th, made enough errors for Jones to take advantage and Jones swept to victory in the final by 7 and 6 against Roger Wethered.

Back in the United States the Open, played in fierce heat, was next at Interlachen CC, Minneapolis where Jones played his famous lily pad stroke. It happened in the second round and, according to Keeler, skidded on the surface of the lake at the 9th hole and covered the remaining 20 yd (18·3 m) to the far side and safety. In the end, he had 2 strokes to spare despite a final round of 75.

That was the third trick of the Slam; the remaining act taking place at Merion where Keeler described him as 'incomparably brilliant and incredibly sloppy by turns'. The results, however, make that hard to understand. He led the qualifying rounds and then won five matches, his smallest margin being 5 and 4. In the final, he beat E V Homans by 8 and 7, as convincing a way to complete golf's greatest feat as any that could be devised.

In between 1926 and 1930, he won the US Amateur in 1927 and 1928 and the Open of 1929. In the 1928 Open, he lost a play-off to Johnny Farrell and in 1927 unaccountably tied for eleventh. Otherwise, his consistency was phenomenal. Apart from 1927, he was nothing but second or first in his last nine US Opens.

Having taken the decision to retire in 1930, Jones was able to devote more time to his law practice in Atlanta. As well as being a superb golfer, he was undoubtedly the most highly educated man ever to have played the game successfully. He held degrees in engineering, literature and law, graduating at the Atlanta School of Technology and subsequently at Harvard.

After his death, a Bobby Jones Trust was set up offering scholarships to students in America and Britain. Jones's influence on golf remained—and a goodly and active influence it was.

Augusta National golf course was built under his guidance and the Masters tournament (first played in 1934) was his inspiration and later his memorial.

Jones was always in attendance with his wise counsel and kindly praise such as when Jack Nicklaus had his great year in 1965. 'He plays a game with which I am not familiar.'

There was nothing of the Muhammad Ali about Jones. His modesty and quietness were remarkable for a man of such talent, but those who saw and knew him in later life when a cruel affliction confined him to a wheelchair, will testify that his forbearance at such misfortune was his greatest triumph of all.

The best epitaph was that of Herbert Warren Wind, the great American writer. 'As a young man he was able to stand up to just about the best that life can offer, which is not easy, and later he stood up, with equal grace, to just about the worst.'

IMPREGNABLE QUADRILATERAL OR GRAND SLAM

This was the achievement of Bobby Jones in 1930 when, in the same summer, he won the Open and Amateur championships of Britain and the United States.

The sequence of victories was: British Amateur, British Open, US Open and US Amateur.

Details as follows:

British Amateur Championship at St Andrews

Round	Date	Opponent	Score
2	Monday, 26 May	S Roper (Wollaton Park)	3 and 2
3	Tuesday, 27 May	C Shankland (St George's Hill)	3 and 2
4	Wednesday, 28 May	Cyril J H Tolley (Royal & Ancient)	19th hole
5	Thursday, 29 May	G O Watt (Broughty)	7 and 6
6	Thursday, 29 May	H R Johnston (USA)	1 hole
7	Friday, 30 May	E W Fiddian (Stourbridge)	4 and 3
Semi-final	Friday, 30 May	G J Voigt (USA)	1 hole
Final	Saturday, 31 May	R H Wethered (Worplesdon)	7 and 6

British Open (Hoylake) 18, 19, 20 June

Name	Score	Total
R T Jones, USA	70 72 74 75	291
L Diegel, Agua Caliente, Mexico	74 73 71 75	293
Macdonald Smith, USA	70 77 75 71	293
F Robson, Cooden Beach	71 72 78 75	296
Horton Smith, Cragston, USA	72 73 78 73	296
A Compston, Coombe Hill	74 73 68 82	297
J Barnes, Pelham Manor, USA	71 77 72 77	297

US Open at Interlachen GC, Minneapolis 10, 11, 12 July

Name	Score	Total
R T Jones	71 73 68 75	287
Macdonald Smith	70 75 74 70	289
Horton Smith	72 70 76 74	292
Harry Cooper	72 72 73 76	293
John Golden	74 73 71 76	294
Tommy Armour	70 76 75 76	297

US Amateur Championship (Merion Cricket Club) 22–27 September

Having been medallist in the qualifying rounds with a score of 142, 1 stroke better than George von Elm (Rancho), Jones won the matchplay section as follows:

Round	Date	Holes	Opponent	Score
1	24 September	18	C Ross Somerville (Canada)	5 and 4
2	24 September	18	F G Hoblitzel (Canada)	5 and 4
3	25 September	36	Fay Coleman (California)	6 and 5
Semi-final	26 September	36	Jess W Sweetser (Siwanoy)	9 and 8
Final	27 September	36	Eugene V Homans (Englewood)	8 and 7

	US Open	British Open	US Amateur	British Amateur
1916	DNP	DNP	third round	DNP
1919	DNP	DNP	finalist	DNP
1920	=8	DNP	semi-final	DNP
1921	=5	Picked up in third round	third round	fourth round
1922	=2	DNP	semi-final	DNP
1923	1	DNP	second round	DNP
1924	2	DNP	winner	DNP
1925	2 (lost play-off)	DNP	winner	DNP
1926	1	1	finalist	sixth round
1927	=11	1	winner	DNP
1928	2 (lost play-off)	DNP	winner	DNP
1929	1	DNP	first round	DNP
1930	1	1	winner	winner

DNP Did not play.
= Finished tied.

WALTER CHARLES HAGEN

b Rochester, New York, 21.12.1892;
d Traverse City, Michigan, 5.10.1969

Walter Hagen was a joy to the headline writers and, more than anyone else, made golf front-page news. He did so as much by a flamboyant personality and fine disregard for convention as he did by a dashing approach to his game which was an ample reflection of the man himself.

His style of life set new standards for the professional golfer and he became the pioneer for many of the privileges which subsequent generations quickly took for granted. Nobody appreciated this more than his great contemporary, Gene Sarazen, who was never slow to acknowledge the debt to Hagen although

A study in elegance—Walter Hagen (BBC Hulton Pic. Lib.)

Hagen himself was ever mindful of the opportunity to do good.

In 1920, when the Inverness Club in Toledo, Ohio became the first to open its doors to professionals at a US Open championship, Hagen was the first to raise a collection among his fellow players for a grandfather clock to be presented to the club. However, he could be just as quick to voice a protest.

In 1923, after finishing runner-up to Arthur Havers in the British Open, he declined to enter the clubhouse for the presentation ceremony because none of the professionals had been allowed to enter it during the week. Instead, while thanking officials for their courtesy, he invited spectators to the pub where he was staying.

For someone who entered golf earning 10 cents an hour as a caddie, he certainly did not acquire a taste for high living from his boyhood. His parents, of thrifty German stock, had to work hard to raise a family of five of which he was the only boy. His father made $18 a week as a blacksmith in the car shops of East Rochester and so the odd dollar from caddying came in very useful; but the urge to play could not be suppressed. He signed on as assistant at the Country Club of Rochester and quickly became a successful player—a player embarking on one of the most glamorous careers in the whole of professional sport.

Everyone knew Walter Hagen; everyone flocked to see him play. They admired his dashing style on the course and they were amused by the sometimes outrageous things that occupied him off it. But not all the countless stories of Hagen are true; nor was the image portrayed of him always accurate.

He drank only about half the drinks he accepted but he certainly never kept strict hours.

When told once that his opponent of the following day had been in bed for some time, he made the famous reply, 'Yeah, but he ain't sleeping.' The incident occurred in an Edinburgh night-club before the last day of the 1929 British Open at Muirfield where Hagen won. The opponent most feared to catch him, Leo Diegel, finished third.

There were other equally famous remarks, but all tended to emphasise the free and easy nature of a player who realised that golf was not necessarily a tight-lipped, solemn game; and that everyone has to cultivate his own way of relaxing. He could turn up on the first tee at the last minute, break his concentration between shots by chatting nonchalantly to spectators and still give of his best.

He was the first golfing showman and perhaps the first to indulge in any form of gamesmanship. Even in defeat, he seldom did anything by halves. In 1928, he lost a challenge match over 72 holes by 18 and 17 to Archie Compston, but a few days later, he won the Open championship at Sandwich.

He also gained the reputation of being a marvellous putter, but that sort of compliment is frequently used to hide a lack of other golfing virtues. In Hagen's case, that was not so. Before the days of the Masters, he won two US Opens, four British Opens and five USPGA championships, four of them in succession. One could not win all those simply with a putter.

What is more, his career covered a wide span. He first won the US Open in 1914 and finished third 21 years later. However, the 1920s were his best years. He was the first American-born winner of the British Open (1922) and the first American to win both the American and British titles.

His second British title was gained at Hoylake and he won for a third time at Sandwich in 1928. Although he only once finished in front of Bobby Jones in Jones's last eight US Opens, his second victory had come in 1919, but his most notable supremacy was in the USPGA championship. By winning from 1924 to 1927, he scored 22 straight matches against America's best professionals.

This proved how he made his mark at both strokeplay and matchplay. He played in all the Ryder Cup matches until 1937 and, with Jones and Sarazen, helped to foster close ties between British and American golf. In addition, he won the French, Canadian and Belgian Opens but it was his fourth victory in the British Open at Muirfield that gave him as much pleasure as any.

He won by 6 strokes from a strong field including the American Ryder Cup team, never took more than 5 at any hole and received the trophy in 1929 from the Prince of Wales who had watched him play his final round. It probably never occurred to Hagen that he should have received it from anyone else.

An admiring gallery watching Ben Hogan. World Cup, 1956 (Action Photos)

	US Open	British Open	Masters	USPGA
1913	=4			
1914	1			
1915	=10			
1916	7			
1919	1			DNP
1920	11	53		DNP
1921	=2	=6		1
1922	5	1		DNP
1923	=18	2		finalist
1924	=4	1		1
1925	=5			1
1926	7	=3		1
1927	6			1
1928	=4	1		quarter-final
1929	=19	1		quarter-final
1930	=17			DNP
1931	=7			DNP
1932	10			first round
1933	4	=22		DNP
1934	=58		=13	first round
1935	3		=15	DNP
1936	=33		=11	DNP
1937		=26		
1938				
1939			=33	

DNP Did not play.
F/Q Failed to qualify.
=   Finished tied.

BENJAMIN (BEN) WILLIAM HOGAN

b Dublin, Texas, 13.8.1912

Many golfers, like most actors, tend to linger for one more curtain call; but Ben Hogan was no sentimentalist. When he felt that he could no longer compete and win, he left the stage to others.

When the time comes, Jack Nicklaus will do the same, just as Bobby Jones did for slightly different reasons. Having conquered all worlds in 1930 at the age of 28, there were no more peaks for Jones to climb. The years of competition left their mark, too, although in Hogan's case, he survived a terrible car crash when his golf was in full bloom and was still able to play the lowest round in the Masters at 54.

He would never appear in public unless he could summon his best and certainly not for old times' sake. He was probably the finest shot-maker the game has ever known and preferred to be remembered as such. Gene Sarazen, whose knowledge of golfers is second to none, is emphatic about his rating of Hogan: 'nobody covered the flag like he did'.

His control from tee to green was legendary. More than any other player, he thought not of hitting the fairway, but which part of the fairway and where he should be to make the next shot simpler. This was the strategy, in fact, of an expert snooker player who is planning several shots ahead. He could shape the ball at will, fading it, drawing it, hitting it high or low. 'You felt', someone once said of Hogan, 'the ball had no option.'

Large crowds were no doubt a motivating force to him, but in an age when public image and cheap publicity is the concern of many professionals, Hogan spurned adulation. He could see nothing remarkable in a round of 68 or 69 and was a man of few words. For some years, it was frequently related that all he might say to his playing partners, during the course of a round was 'You're away.' With Hogan, his golf did the talking.

He won the US Open four times, the Masters and PGA championship twice each and the British Open on his only appearance. In 14 consecutive Open championships up to 1960, and the same number of Masters, he was never outside the first ten, and 18 times was in the first four. Only Nicklaus can match that sort of consistency and then not in the US Open. But golf to Hogan was an intensely serious business and he practised with fantastic single-mindedness that later had a big influence on Gary Player.

Considering his tough boyhood and his introduction to golf through caddying, Hogan's fierce application was no surprise to his friends. Nor, indeed, was his reaction to playing again after the car accident, on the foggy morning of 2 February in 1949 in Texas, which left him with multiple injuries and a month in hospital. Many believe it was the same strong will that guided his golf, so keeping him alive. Though hobbling badly, he made the trip to England later that year to captain the Ryder Cup team at Ganton, and in January 1950 filed an entry for the Los Angeles Open to see how he would stand up to it.

He stood up to it so well that he tied for first place with Sam Snead and, a month later, tied with Lloyd Mangrum and George Fazio for the US Open at Merion; and, despite wondering whether he would get round he won the play-off.

Hogan's debut in the US Open was in 1936 when he failed to make the cut for the last 36 holes, and his first victory came in 1948 at the Riviera CC, Los Angeles. In between, his best finish was tied third in 1941, but his aggregate in 1948 (276) set a new record for the championship. It contained three rounds under 70, another record at that time.

His accident meant that he played none of the major championships in 1949, but he successfully defended his title in 1951 and, after finishing third in 1952, won again in his great year of 1953.

His victory in 1951, at Oakland Hills is remembered for his remark, 'I vowed I would bring this monster to its knees.' Probably because of the threat he posed to low scoring, the USGA began to doctor their Open courses but, though Hogan felt they had gone too far at Oakland Hills, he was determined to show there was a way to play it.

By now, his dedication was a by-word and from then on it was a regular sight for other professionals to congregate on the practice ground to watch him. His sessions were an education in themselves, but 1953 was a perfect example of how he transferred much of that mechanical precision to the course itself.

Hogan won the Masters for a second time with what he considers perhaps the best golf of his career. His total of 274 (70, 69, 66, 69) was a record which stood for twelve years, and he followed it by adding a fourth victory in the US Open, equalling the record of Bobby Jones and Willie Anderson.

By finishing at Oakmont with a par and two birdies, he won by 6 strokes from Sam Snead with the biggest margin since 1938. He led throughout—the first to do so for 42 years.

After his accident, Hogan was not keen on travelling, but he was persuaded to make the journey to Carnoustie for the British Open and never regretted it.

He was surprised to see how much people in Britain wanted him to win and even more surprised at the enormous size of the crowds. He would have been less happy with the informal nature of the stewarding; it was some years before it became the controlled art it is today.

As usual, Hogan's preparations were thorough. He arrived two weeks early to acquaint himself with the course and the small ball which he had never played; and though he was not entirely happy with his putting, he had each round lower than the one before (73, 71, 70, 68), and eventually won with one of the finest last rounds ever played.

His victory gave him the unique distinction of winning the Masters and both Opens in the same summer and meant that he had emulated Gene Sarazen in winning the four major championships. Hogan rarely played in the PGA championship, decided by matchplay until 1958, and did not take part in it in 1953 because it clashed with the British Open—a tragedy.

The year 1953 would have been a good time for him to have retired, but golf was his life; ambition still burned within him and, most important of all, he felt he had not yet attained perfection. He would have liked to have won the US Open for a fifth time, but was thwarted more than once.

His most astonishing failure was in losing a play-off with the little-known Jack Fleck at the Olympic Club, San Francisco, in 1955. It was also the scene of Arnold Palmer's bewildering failure in 1966, although that is no consolation to either.

In 1956, Hogan needed two 4s to tie Cary Middlecoff, but missed from no more than a yard on the 71st green; and he had a chance again in 1960 at the age of 48. He was not helped by the fact that putting, particularly the holing out, had become a terrible affliction to him. He was not the first, or the last, to confront these agonies and, while he overcame them for a period thanks to his superlative long game, they got the better even of Hogan.

There were other aches and pains; and a shoulder injury that required surgery, but he gave Augusta one last treat in 1967, going out in 30 on the Saturday and looking for a moment as though he might just turn back the years.

Altogether, Hogan won 62 tournaments on the US tour, one more than Palmer. He won all his three Ryder Cup games (two foursomes and one single) and won a famous victory for the United States in the Canada Cup at Wentworth with Sam Snead as his partner.

It made up in some measure for the fact that he never played a second time in the British Open, and he certainly put on a memorable show, his aggregate of 277 being the lowest.

He hit a variety of strokes all round the pin and might once have been out in 29, but he has done that sort of thing all his life. In the 1960 US Open, in fact, he hit 34 consecutive greens

in the right number on the final day only to go in the water on the last two holes. If golf were decided without the need to putt, Hogan would hardly ever have been beaten, but let us forget his putting and remember him as the man who has come nearer than anyone to reaching perfection in the part of the game that ordinary mortals find next to impossible.

	US Open	British Open	Masters	USPGA
1936	F/Q	DNP		
1937		DNP		
1938		DNP	=25	
1939		DNP	9	third round
1940	=5	DNP	=10	fourth round
1941	=3	DNP	4	fourth round
1942			2 (lost play-off)	third round
1946	=4	DNP	2	1
1947	=6	DNP	=4	first round
1948	1	DNP	=6	1
1949	DNP	DNP	DNP	DNP
1950	1	DNP	=4	DNP
1951	1	DNP	1	DNP
1952	3	DNP	=7	DNP
1953	1	1	1	DNP
1954	=6	DNP	2 (lost play-off)	DNP
1955	2 (lost play-off)	DNP	2	DNP
1956	=2	DNP	=8	DNP
1957	DNP	DNP	F/Q	DNP
1958	=10	DNP	=14	DNP
1959	=8	DNP	=30	DNP
1960	=9	DNP	=6	F/Q
1961	=14	DNP	=32	DNP
1962		DNP	35	DNP
1963		DNP	DNP	DNP
1964		DNP	=9	=9
1965		DNP	=21	=15
1966	12	DNP	=13	DNP
1967		DNP	=10	DNP

DNP Did not play.
F/Q Failed to qualify.
=   Finished tied.

GARY PLAYER

b Johannesburg, Transvaal, 1.11.1935

Gary Player was the first overseas professional to make a prolonged assault on the US tour and to become an outstanding champion. He was the first overseas winner of the Masters; the first US Open champion from overseas since 1920;

Gary Player on his first visit to Britain with two other South Africans, Trevor Wilkes (middle) and Bobby Locke (Action Photos)

he is the only non-American to have won the world's four major championships and one of only two born outside the United States to have won more than a million dollars on the professional circuit.

He has won the British Open in three different decades and is one of the best known and best respected of all golfers. But not the least remarkable aspect of a remarkable story is that, when he first played in Britain, there were many who thought he did not have a chance. Player soon built up the knack of surprising everyone and has gone on surprising them.

Nobody without the necessary devotion and dedication would have contemplated the idea of going to Britain in 1955 in the first place. His small physique ('Jack Nicklaus was my size when he was twelve', Player often used to joke in later years) and a number of technical faults,

were hardly the ideal credentials for the sort of life that shows no mercy. Player possessed a lion-sized will to learn, an insatiable capacity for practice, a rare zest for physical fitness and a limitless ambition.

Six years before he set out for England, he had not even taken up the game. Player's father, a mine captain, persuaded Gary to play with him one day. He soon became hooked and later took up his post as Assistant Professional to Jock Verwey whose daughter, Vivienne, he later married.

Player, whose mother died when he was eight, always enjoyed an outdoor life, like so many of his countrymen, and was in little doubt that, once he had decided to become a tournament golfer, he had to travel to England—the 'Mother country', as he described it in one of his books.

It was a big decision, but within a year or so of arriving in England and within four years of turning professional, he won the Dunlop tournament at Sunningdale in 1956 and soon set forth for his first taste of golf in America. If there were critics of his swing there, they were quietened, if not silenced, when he finished second to Tommy Bolt in the 1958 US Open at Southern Hills, Tulsa; but his first major championship success was back in Britain when he won the 1959 Open championship at Muirfield.

It was not a strong field by today's standards but Player, 8 strokes behind the leader at the start of the final day, had a steady downward progression of rounds (75, 71, 70, 68) and won by 2 strokes despite taking 6 at the 72nd hole.

It was the victory he was seeking and one which made him believe more strongly than ever that he could succeed in America. Although he had been a regular competitor in the British Open, he did not do as well again for some time but in two years he was Masters champion and soon to be compared with Arnold Palmer and Jack Nicklaus—the Big Three, as the American Press christened them.

Player's first victory at Augusta in 1961 could hardly have been more dramatic. On the final hole, he got down in 2 from the same bunker from which Palmer later took 4 more. Player won by a stroke from Palmer with 280, at a time when Palmer was at the very height of his powers. This was part of Player's graduation towards the Big Three although, in the public imagination at least, Player was the under-dog. That he was able to equal and sometimes dominate Palmer and Nicklaus underlined his ruthless self-discipline.

That same April, Nicklaus played in the Masters as an amateur but, far from his entrance on to the professional scene damping Player's hopes, it seemed to push him to new limits. In 1962, he won the USPGA championship in spite of recounting in *Grand Slam Golf*, how he was on the verge beforehand of 'quitting this ridiculous life'.

He had failed to qualify for the British Open at Troon where the ground was very hard and dry, but the sight of Aronimink and its softer, greener fairways inspired him to a 1-stroke victory and the third leg of the major championships. The US Open was the missing link and he had to wait until 1965 before making up an exalted trio with Gene Sarazen and Ben Hogan.

Player was thoroughly at home in America and it is some measure of his achievement that he completed his sequence of major championship victories in the space of six years. The pace of life was hot and it became hotter as Player's commitments grew with his success, but he never lost the urge to continue as a champion or the dedication needed to preserve his aim.

His record in the major championships lacks the consistency of Nicklaus, but he was forever popping up with a victory and, even today, can never be disregarded. After his US Open victory, he went until his second British Open in 1968 without another major success and he waited a further four years for his next, the 1972 USPGA.

However, he got something of a second wind, winning the Masters and the British Open in 1974 and then a third Masters in 1978. The US Open remains the only major title he has failed to win more than once.

One of his best performances was the 1974 British Open at Lytham when he was never behind in a championship which was the first to be played with the big ball. As it happened, conditions were windy almost throughout, but Player broke 70 twice—the only person to do so. He won by 4 strokes although he nearly lost his ball with his second shot at the 71st hole and ended up at the 72nd playing his third shot left-handed with a putter. The clubhouse wall prevented him from playing right-handed.

In the next three years, he played all four major championships without once finishing in the first ten, but the 1978 Masters was yet another example of his resilience, his continued fitness and enduring ability. As in 1961, it needed some faltering by his principal rivals, whom he was able to watch after he had completed his final round, in order for Player to succeed.

At the age of 42, Player entered the last round 7 strokes behind the leader, Hubert Green, and around the final turn the Augusta crowd had not yet looked upon him as a possible winner; but he came home in 30, had 7 birdies in the last 10 holes and equalled Augusta's course record with 64. After that, he sat and waited as the chances of Tom Watson, Green and Rod Funseth came and went.

Nevertheless, the major events form only part of the Player story. Nobody has travelled further as a professional golfer in pursuit of success. There are a record seven victories in the Australian Open to consider as well as a record twelve in his own South African Open. In addition, he played some of his best golf in capturing the World Cup of 1965 for his country in partnership with Harold Henning and, within a week, he had won yet another victory with a fictional ring about it. This occurred in the world matchplay championship at Wentworth when he was 7 down to Tony Lema on the second tee of the afternoon round and beat him at the 37th. This is a championship in which Player invariably excels and the following year he was far too good for Jack Nicklaus in a final which Player won 6 and 4.

For someone who has led such a hectic life for 25 years, Player remains a marvel. His figure is still trim and his enthusiasm undiminished but he has always loved spending time with his family and his busy programme is increasingly organised in order that he can do just that.

In his farm near Johannesburg with his string of horses, he has the perfect escape from a life, the better part of which has been spent in aeroplanes and hotel rooms.

When the time comes for him to quit the tour, he is well qualified to take on the full-time role of farmer; but he has repeatedly told Press interviewers that he believes he can play better; so maybe he has a fourth British Open in a fourth decade up his sleeve. He has amazed people throughout his career and proved many wrong. Why should he stop now?

	US Open	British Open	Masters	USPGA
1955		F/Q		
1956		4		
1957		24	=24	
1958	2	7	F/Q	
1959	=15	1	=8	
1960	=19	7	=6	
1961	=9	retired	1	=29
1962	=6	F/Q	2	1
1963	=8	=7	=5	=8
1964	=23	=8	=5	=13
1965	1	retired	=2	=33
1966	=15	=4	=28	=3
1967	=12	=3	=6	2
1968	=16	1	=7	=12
1969	=48	=23	=33	2
1970	=44	F/Q	3	=12
1971		=7	=6	=4
1972	=15	6	=10	1
1973	12	=14	DNP	=51
1974	=8	1	1	7
1975	=43	=32	=30	=33
1976	=23	=28	=28	=13
1977	=10	=22	=19	=31
1978	=6	=34	1	=26
1979	=2	=19	=17	=23

DNP Did not play.
F/Q Failed to qualify.
=   Finished tied.

ARNOLD DANIEL PALMER

b Latrobe, Pennsylvania, 10.9.1929

On the last afternoon of the 1960 US Open at Cherry Hills, Arnold Palmer drove the 1st green, went out in 30, made up 7 strokes on the 54-hole leader, Mike Souchak, and won the championship.

Six years later, at the Olympic Club in San Francisco, he was 7 strokes ahead of Billy Casper with 9 holes to play on the Lake course. He finished in a tie and lost the play-off next day after leading at the turn.

These two contrasting episodes mark the best comebacks by a champion after 54 and 63 holes; but more cogently, they represent the extremes of Palmer's career which set in motion a new golden era of development in the game and sustained it amid the most passionate acclaim ever afforded any golfer.

For a time, both before and after his great days, Palmer was the best-known and best-loved figure in the golfing world; one who never betrayed, by word or deed, himself, his followers or the standards expected of him.

Palmer did more than win tournaments; he made golf exciting for millions who previously had paid little heed to it.

As the professionals of the 1920s owed an enormous debt to Walter Hagen, so their successors in the 1960s owed the same debt to Palmer. Whether he was the cause or beneficiary of this golden era it is hard to say, but despite being a fairly regular competitor at the age of 50, his major championship victories were confined to all too short a period.

To be precise, they were confined to the years between his first Masters victory in 1958 and his last in 1964, although he won the US Amateur in 1954, the first indication nationally that a rare talent was unfolding. This talent was based on a huge pair of hands and a good grip which his father, a worker in the Pennsylvania steelmills before becoming a professional, maintained were vital.

He inherited much of his father's strength, humour and respect for the game's traditions but nobody could have predicted the tumultuous years ahead. From the moment in 1958 that he won at Augusta with birdies on the last 2 holes when nothing else would have done, he was front-page news.

Having won the Masters and US Open in

Hard to say who is the more delighted, Winnie or Arnie Palmer. Birkdale 1961 (Action Photos)

1960, he went to St Andrews in the same summer to try and emulate Ben Hogan by winning the British Open at his first attempt. In Hogan's case, it was his only attempt.

For his part, Palmer started a great revival in the popularity of the British Open among overseas players and, although he was foiled in the Centenary Open by Kel Nagle, he finished as runner-up and won in 1961 and 1962. His finishes in his first three British Opens were, in fact, second, first, first—a record unmatched even by Young Tom Morris.

He concealed his disappointment admirably at not equalling Hogan's feat of winning three

major championships of the world in the same year and returned to Birkdale in 1961 to win the British by a single stroke in a championship dogged for a day or two by stormy weather.

His playing of the first 6 holes of his second round in 3 under par is still regarded by him as perhaps the best golf of his life, but in 1962 at Troon he showed he could cope equally well with a fast-running seaside links. It was a year in which Gary Player failed to qualify and Nicklaus succeeded with only a stroke to spare.

These were not conditions which Palmer exactly relished, but he played the back 9 commandingly each day and beat Kel Nagle by

6 strokes and the rest of the field by 13. His total of 276 set a new record aggregate.

This was some consolation for Palmer who, a month previously, had lost the US Open in a play-off with Jack Nicklaus. In April, he had won a third Masters after a play-off with Player and Dow Finsterwald, but his defeat by Nicklaus was the first sign of the rising threat to his supremacy. Not that it blunted the devotion of Palmer's followers. His inclination to give and attempt everything with every shot was what they wanted to see—plus a remarkable flair for recovery play.

His bold putting, glove tucked into his hip pocket, could be deadly and undoubtedly helped him become leading money-winner in 1958–60–62–63. In 1963, he was the first player to top the $100 000 mark in a season and in the 1968 PGA championship, in which he was second, he became the first player to pass the million dollar mark.

In the same way, however, that Sam Snead never won the US Open, the PGA title has always eluded Palmer; nevertheless he has three times been second, the last time in 1970. In all, he has won 61 tour events, one less than Hogan, and remained a real force until 1971 when he was third in the money list.

He won the Bob Hope Classic in 1973, a year in which he was 27th in the money list, but his last victory in a major championship was the 1964 Masters.

Happily, it was one of his most convincing. The Masters saw many of his best days; and rounds that year of 69, 68, 69, 70 gave him victory by 6 strokes over Nicklaus and Dave Marr. He was still then at the height of his powers, setting standards perceptibly higher than had existed before and forcing others to follow.

In addition, his good humour, friendliness and magnetic appeal made him an extremely marketable figure for whom Mark McCormack, a member of the same golf team at Wake Forest University, built up a vast financial empire which made people aware of how famous golfers had become. However, Palmer never lost the urge to go on doing what he liked best—playing golf.

Despite trouble with a hip injury and the need to wear glasses for a time, he continued to draw crowds even when his chances of victory waned. He won the Spanish Open and the British PGA championship in 1975 in windy conditions at Sandwich which revived memories of Birkdale in 1961.

In the modern golfing world, there is a natural search for players to idolise and respect not only as masters of their craft but as the personification of what heroes should be. Nobody has fitted that bill better than Palmer.

	US Open	British Open	Masters	USPGA
1958	=23	DNP	1	
1959	=5	DNP	3	=14
1960	1	2	1	7
1961	=14	1	=2	=5
1962	2	1	1	=17
1963	=2	=26	=9	=40
1964	=5	DNP	1	=2
1965		=12	=2	=33
1966	2	=8	=4	=6
1967	2	DNP	4	=14
1968	59	=10	F/Q	=2
1969	=6	DNP	27	F/Q
1970	=54	12	36	=2
1971	=24	F/Q	=18	=18
1972	3	=7	=33	=16
1973	=4	=14	=24	F/Q
1974	=5	DNP	=11	=28
1975	=9	=16	=13	=33
1976	=50	=55	F/Q	=14
1977	=19	7	=24	=19
1978		=34	=37	F/Q
1979	=56	DNP	F/Q	F/Q

DNP Did not play.
F/Q Failed to qualify.
=   Finished tied.
In 1962, 63 and 66 he lost a play-off in US Open.

GENE SARAZEN

b Harrison, New York 27.2.1902

Of all the great winners of the major championships down the years, Gene Sarazen was undoubtedly the smallest in stature. In some ways, he came into golf by accident, but his playing career spanned more than half a century and is among the most distinguished in the history of the game.

He is remembered for many things, but four feats of his must be recorded straightaway since they founded and preserved his reputation.

In the course of winning the British and American Opens in the same summer of 1932, he played 28 holes in 100 strokes at Fresh Meadow in the latter. Bobby Jones described it as 'the finest competitive exhibition on record'.

He became the first player to win all four major championships of the world, having been American champion for the first time at the age of 20; and he has to his credit two of the most famous single strokes ever played.

In only the second US Masters in 1935, he holed his second with a 4 wood at the 15th in the final round to turn a good chase into victory; and in the 1973 British Open at Troon, he holed in one at Troon's 8th, the celebrated Postage Stamp. To add piquancy to the tale, it was the 50th anniversary of his first appearance in the championship, also at Troon, and the shot was caught by the television cameras.

Sarazen was born in Harrison, New York, the son of a carpenter and christened Eugene Saraceni; the change of name came about because he felt he might be mistaken for a violinist. His father, who had studied for the priesthood back in Italy, was never in favour of his son becoming a golfer and it is possible that Gene might never have played at all if he had not contracted pleurisy while apprenticed to his father in Connecticut.

On medical advice, he found less strenuous work and, in the course of recuperation, tried his hand at golf. In a matter of months, he landed an assistant's post and before long he was Open champion. Having qualified for the championship in 1920 and 1921, his victory came at Skokie near Chicago where he was little known and spent the championship, so the story goes, sleeping in a dormitory of fellow professionals.

He practised extremely hard that week and had a premonition that he would win. He began with a 72 and 73 which put him in third place only to fall back with a moderate third round; but a 68, the first under 70 by a champion and the lowest last round until he beat it himself ten years later, gave him victory by a single stroke over John Black and Bobby Jones.

Golf has always been a full profession and a continuous business for Sarazen and, after the Open, he was inundated with invitations to take part in exhibition matches.

He won the PGA championship the same year and challenged Walter Hagen to a special match over 72 holes for the unofficial world championship. Not in the least daunted by the prospect, he beat 'The Haig' and then beat him again the following year at the 38th hole of the final of the PGA. They became good friends, dominated American professional golf for a number of years and, between them, put the professionals on the map, although Sarazen was always generous enough to give the lion's share of the credit to Hagen.

They became keen rivals and great contemporaries who, with Jones, set the tradition of supporting the British Open. Sarazen's first attempt in 1923 foundered even before he reached first base. He went to Troon, suitably hailed as the new star in the firmament, but failed to qualify in bad weather. With a humiliation that Hagen could understand after his experience in 1920, he vowed that he would be back even if he had to swim across the Atlantic.

As Herbert Warren Wind wrote of Hagen in *The Story of American Golf*, 'he had been press-agented as the golfer who would show British golf a thing or two' at Deal in 1920. 'Walter showed them four rounds in the eighties and finished a lurid fifty-fifth.'

Nobody doubted that Sarazen would be true to his word, but he had to wait until 1932 when the British Open was held at Prince's, Sandwich, for the first and only time. Accompanied by Daniels who had caddied for Hagen, Sarazen led from start to finish on a fast-running course, firmly obeying the advice of Daniels.

In 1928 over the fence at Royal St Georges, Sarazen took 7 on the 14th and lost to Hagen, but Daniels consoled him mightily by saying, 'I am going to win this championship for you if it

Gene Sarazen (left) with Bobby Jones (right), July 1923 (BBC Hulton Pic. Lib.)

is the last thing I do before I die.' Daniels kept his promise. Sarazen was never in danger and in the end had 5 strokes in hand over Macdonald Smith.

On the last day, in 1932, Daniels had been round the course early, checking the positions of the flags, showing that the modern propensity for pacing is nothing new but, in some ways, Sarazen's victory at Prince's was overshadowed by his second victory in the US Open before he left for England that same summer.

In the previous months and years, he had not enjoyed the best of success and, for once in his life, he dabbled with technique.

He had always felt that his size had militated against him but, among other things, he experimented with the idea of a sand wedge with which he became a wizard; and, whether or not it was a big influence on his year of 1932, it gave him increased confidence.

Ironically, however, he started by playing cautiously and conservatively at Fresh Meadow in contrast to his normal approach of giving it everything he had. This seemed particularly misguided since the course encouraged players to attack from the tee and then to think about their second shots to well-bunkered greens.

With Sarazen's skill with his new bunker club, it seemed to further justify an attacking policy, but he decided otherwise and began with a 74 and a 76.

He persisted for a further 9 holes, but then was driven to return to his old ways. The results were as dramatic as could be. He played the last 28 holes in exactly 100 strokes, including a last round of 66. This was unheard of in those days and it remained the lowest last round by an American champion until Arnold Palmer returned 65 in 1960.

It was one of those almost fictional happenings that were such a feature of Sarazen's golfing life. His victory at the Masters and his hole in one at Troon are other examples, but 1932 marked the last of his victories in national championships although he came close more than once.

In his defence of the British Open at St Andrews in 1933, he finished 1 stroke away from a play-off with Densmore Shute and Craig Wood. Ironically, however, his trusty bunker club twice let him down. A lengthy argument with the Hill bunker cost him 6 at the short 11th in the second round and, in his final round, he failed to recover from Hell bunker on the 14th at his first attempt.

Sarazen also lost by 1 stroke to Olin Dutra in the US Open in 1934 at Merion, but he

	US Open	British Open	Masters	USPGA
1920	=30			DNP
1921	17			third round
1922	1			1
1923	=16	F/Q		1
1924	=17			first round
1925	=5			first round
1926	=3			second round
1927	3			third round
1928	=6	2		quarter final
1929	=3	=8		third round
1930	=28			finalist
1931	=4	=3		quarter final
1932	1	1		DNP
1933	=26	=3		1
1934	2			second round
1935	=6		1	second round
1936	=28	=5	3	first round
1937	=10		24	second round
1938	10		=13	third round
1939	=47		5	first round
1940	2		=21	fourth round
1941	7			quarter final
1942			=29	
1946			DNP	
1947	=39		26	
1948			=23	
1949			=39	
1950			=10	
1951			=12	
1952			withdrew	
1953			=34	
1954			=52	
1955			withdrew	
1956			=49	
1963			49	

DNP Did not play.
F/Q Failed to qualify.
=   Finished tied.

remained a regular competitor long after most of his contemporaries had retired. He could hold his own, too, and was instantly recognisable with his tanned, olive complexion and the knickers, or plus-fours, which became his trademark.

There have been better technicians and more elegant swingers but, rather like Gary Player some years later, Sarazen's consistent hitting, month after month and year after year, proved itself in the record books—and one cannot argue with figures.

His nostalgic appearance in the British Open of 1973 was made possible by the exemption of all past Open champions, but Sarazen again stole the headlines on the first day by holing a punched 5 iron at the 8th. The following day, he holed a bunker shot for a 2 on the same hole and thereby set an incomparable record: An aggregate of 3 strokes for 1 hole in two days at the age of 71.

Sarazen has seen all the famous players from

Vardon to Watson and has kept in touch with the game's development. He became an adviser in designing new courses and compered the popular film series, 'Shell's Wonderful World of Golf'. He has introduced telecasts from the Masters and was made an Honorary Member of the Royal and Ancient Golf Club, but he will be best remembered as a champion golfer, an honest person and a man of charm and energy who is at home in all realms of society.

Known universally as 'The Squire', he has remained a popular figure for almost 60 years who, though not without his setbacks, knew how to win. In the words of someone summing up what he felt to be Sarazen's belief of himself after his first US Open victory, 'All men are created free and equal, and I am one shot better than the rest.'

SAMUEL JACKSON (Sam) SNEAD

b Hot Springs, Virginia, 27.5.1912

Only the Gods really know why Sam Snead never won the US Open. For a player who achieved every other distinction in over 40 years of regular, high-level competition, and was widely believed to possess the best swing in the world, it is a strange anomaly.

One possible explanation is that, since his approach to the game has been entirely intuitive, his tactical awareness was not always razor sharp in the crucial moments which decide major championships.

The other point is that, having come close to winning the Open once or twice in the early stages of a career which saw him beat his age (67) in the 1979 Quad Cities Open, he became haunted by the prospect of another chance of victory slipping away. Even the best golfers and the best methods are not immune to gnawing pressures.

In his first appearance in the US Open in 1937, he lost to Ralph Guldahl by 2 strokes and two years later took 8 on the 72nd hole at the Philadelphia CC, although he was unaware at the time that a 5 would have been enough. In 1940, a last round of 81 destroyed the challenging position he held at lunchtime and in 1947 he missed from under a yard on the 18th green at St Louis to prolong a play-off with Lew Worsham. In 1949, he finished 1 stroke behind Cary Middlecoff; in 1953, he was second to Ben Hogan and sadly he never came as near again.

Classical poise and balance—Sam Snead (Action Photos)

However, in every other respect, his record is incomparable especially in its durability. He won the Masters and USPGA titles three times each, the British Open once, and has scored no fewer than 84 victories on the US tour, and 135 in all. Three times he beat Ben Hogan, his great contemporary and rival, in play-offs; he was the first man to break 60 in a major event (at Greenbrier in 1959); and in official money, has earned over $620 000—a figure that would have been immeasurably more if he had been born 30 years later.

Snead was, in fact, raised in golfing terms at the Greenbrier Hotel course at White Sulphur Springs although he once said, 'none of us peckerwoods ever expected to get inside the gate, let alone out there with a club in our hands!'. He was first a caddie and then a teaching professional, but he was astute enough, as his own golf developed, to win money from matches with members and guests.

As he wrote in his book *The Education of a Golfer*, 'My reputation for being so tight with money that I buried my winnings in tin cans in my backyard began about then, mostly due to my unwillingness to hang around clubhouse bars after tournaments and swap drink checks with the boys'; but his talents could not be checked and it was not long before he was one of the leading names on the tour.

It is an indication of the ever-growing wealth of the US tour that in the PGA's career money-winning list, he has already been passed by players of lesser ability who will certainly not be playing in the PGA championship in 40 years' time. But that is no disgrace. There will never be another Snead and nobody would dream of evaluating his success purely in monetary terms.

Nobody has brought to the game quite the same expression of power, grace and beauty. Nobody has hit more perfect shots and, even with the blemish of his failure to win the US Open, nobody could shortlist the ten best golfers of all time and omit the name of Sam Snead.

His swing, which owed little to practice or teaching, was based on a well-proportioned and extremely supple body. This made it possible for him to make an effortless, thorough and unhurried turn of hips and shoulders without detriment to control or balance. He could unleash tremendous power in his hands, but it was his sense of rhythm and timing which set him apart.

He did not devote the same effort of concentration that characterises other champions; he did not have to. But he has gone on playing long after many others have given up, despite problems with his putting which he never allowed to be a deterrent to low scoring.

By adopting a side-saddle method, he overcame the problem remarkably well, finishing in the top ten in the US Open, Masters and PGA while in his mid-fifties. He also remains the oldest winner of a tournament on the PGA circuit (the 1965 Greater Greensboro Open when he was 52 years and 10 months); and he is the only player to beat his age in an official PGA event.

He did not play a great deal outside America and was an infrequent visitor to the British Isles. He once likened staying in Britain to 'camping out'. However, he added his name to the list of Open winners at St Andrews in 1946; took part in three Ryder Cup matches and is principally remembered for his play in two World Cups, one at Wentworth in 1956 and the second at Portmarnock in Eire four years later.

At Wentworth, he partnered Ben Hogan, and at Portmarnock, Arnold Palmer who was on his way to his first British Open. On both occasions the Americans won and, on both occasions, they attracted enormous crowds.

It is no wonder that Snead drew the crowds with such a classical swing. He has done so all his life, giving pleasure to millions and, at the same time, casting waves of envy that anyone could hit the ball so easily and elegantly. If Snead's skill could be transmitted and auctioned, the bidding would be never ending.

	US Open	British Open	Masters	USPGA
1937	2	=11	18	quarter final
1938	=38	DNP	=31	2 (runner-up)
1939	5	DNP	2	DNP
1940	=16	DNP	=7	2
1941	=13	DNP	=6	semi-final
1942		DNP	=7	1
1946	=19	1	=7	second round
1947	2 (lost play-off)	DNP	=22	second round
1948	5	DNP	=16	semi-final
1949	=2	DNP	1	1
1950	=12	DNP	3	second round
1951	=10	DNP	=8	1
1952	=10	DNP	1	first round
1953	2	DNP	=16	second round
1954	=11	DNP	1	semi-final
1955	=3	DNP	3	second round
1956	=24	DNP	=4	semi-final
1957	=8	DNP	2	quarter-final
1958		DNP	=13	3
1959	=8	DNP	=22	=8
1960	=19	DNP	=11	=3
1961	=17	DNP	=15	=27
1962	=38	=6	=15	=17
1963	=42		=3	=27
1964	=34		F/Q	DNP
1965	=24		F/Q	=6
1966			=42	=6
1967			=10	DNP
1968	=9		42	=30
1969			F/Q	=62
1970			=23	=12
1971			F/Q	=34
1972			=27	=4
1973			=29	=9
1974			=20	=3
1975			withdrew	F/Q
1976			F/Q	F/Q
1977			withdrew	=54
1978			F/Q	DNP
1979			F/Q	42

DNP Did not play.
F/Q Failed to qualify.
=   Finished tied.

The Four Major Championships

BRITISH OPEN

First played 1860

The oldest Open championship in the world was started by the Prestwick Club, Ayrshire, in October 1860 and, apart from 1871 and the war years, has been contested annually. There was no championship in 1871 because Young Tom Morris had won the previous three and had made the Open championship belt his own.

In 1872, a new trophy, a silver claret jug, was presented and the championship was then organised jointly by the Prestwick Club, the Royal and Ancient and the Honourable Company of Edinburgh Golfers. Until 1892, the championship was completed over 36 holes in one day. In 1892, it became 72 holes and the list of courses increased from three to include Royal St George's Sandwich (1894) and Royal Liverpool, Hoylake (1897).

The Royal and Ancient took over full responsibility for running the Open in 1920 and have seen it develop steadily into the major competition that it is today.

In the 1920s, Bobby Jones, Walter Hagen and Gene Sarazen led the American invasion that gave it true international status and this has continued on and off ever since. Arnold Palmer revived the American interest in 1960, although Sam Snead won the championship in 1946 and Ben Hogan triumphed on his lone mission to Carnoustie in 1953.

Nowadays, the Open is watched by over 130 000 spectators during the week and is seen by many millions on television all over the world. In the ten years from 1970 to 1980, the total prize-money has risen from £40000 to £200000.

It is traditional for the Open to be staged on a seaside links. As a result, the rota has always been limited. A total of only 14 courses have been used compared with over 40 for the American Open. Of the 14, three have only been used once, but modern needs dictate that more than just playing quality be taken into account. Such things as ease of crowd movement, car parking, hotel accommodation, access and the ability to house a vast tented village are vital considerations.

MILESTONES

1860 Birth of championship golf on Wednesday, 17 October at Prestwick.

Eight entries for first Open at Prestwick. Not strictly 'Open' as the field comprised all professionals. The death of Allan Robertson the previous year left the need to find a new top golfer, but it was not until 1861, after complaints from amateurs, that the championship was thrown open 'to all the world'.

One competitor took 21 for 1 hole, the highest ever recorded for a single hole.

Willie Park, Sr, was first champion with a score of 174 for three rounds of Prestwick's 12-hole course.

1862 Old Tom Morris's margin of victory: 13 strokes. This is a record which still stands.

1863 Prize-money instituted for the first time.

1865 Official score-cards introduced.

1868 Young Tom Morris succeeded his father

Old Tom Morris (Badminton Library)

as champion. At 17, he is still the youngest winner.

Young Tom also performed the first hole in one in championship golf at Prestwick's 8th hole.

1870 Young Tom Morris's third victory. In accordance with the rule, passed by the Prestwick Club in 1860, he won the championship belt outright.

Young Tom's total of 149 for three rounds of the Prestwick course was never equalled with the gutty ball.

1871 No championship while new trophy was found.

1872 The first championship for the silver trophy (a claret jug) that has been so envied by golfers. The permanent trophy was presented by the Prestwick Club, the Royal and Ancient and the Honourable Company of Edinburgh Golfers.

These three joined forces to manage the championship which was then played in rotation over the links of Prestwick, St Andrews and Musselburgh.

Young Tom won his fourth title in succession, an achievement never equalled.

1873 Record entry of 26 for St Andrews' first Open, the first, indeed, away from Prestwick.

1876 Total prize-money £20. First prize of £10 going to Bob Martin, but he tied for the title with David Strath and there was doubt over the procedure to be adopted as well as a call for Strath's disqualification over a technicality. A decision was delayed, Strath refused to play-off and Martin was awarded the title.

1878 John Ball finished fifth at the age of 14.

1879 Jamie Anderson makes it three wins in a row at the age of 37. He was runner-up in 1873.

1880 Bob Ferguson deposed Jamie Anderson and began his run of three victories in a row. Ferguson, a former caddie at Musselburgh, accepted the post of greenkeeper when he withdrew from the competition scene.

1883 Play-off needed to deny Ferguson his fourth title in a row. In the first play-off which was actually held, Willie Fernie got home at the last hole. With the two golfers level, Fernie drove the green and holed a long 'steal' for a 2.

In the last round at Musselburgh, Ferguson finished with three 3s to tie and Fernie's total of 159 included a 10. This is the only time that a winner of a major championship has completed a hole in double figures.

1884 Until then, the winners had come from Prestwick, St Andrews or Musselburgh. The new champion, Jack Simpson, was a Carnoustie man.

1885 Bob Martin's second win at St Andrews. He, James Braid, J H Taylor and Jack Nicklaus are the only players to have won twice at St Andrews.

Record entry of 51.

Left: The first model for style, Harry Vardon. (By courtesy of the South Herts Golf Club/Photo: Chris Greenhill, AIIP)

Below: The Vardon Grip (By kind permission of the Jersey Post Office)

1886 and 1888 Open won by 'artisan' golfers. David Brown, a slater by trade, in 1886 and by Jack Burns, a plasterer, in 1888.

1890 End of Scottish monopoly. First English winner and first amateur winner, John Ball.

1891 Prize-money total £28.50. First prize £10. Record entry of 82.

1892 Second amateur winner, Harold Horsfall Hilton (1869–1942).

First championship held at Muirfield which replaced Musselburgh as the home of the Honourable Company of Edinburgh Golfers.

Championship extended to 72 holes and two days, 36 holes each day.

Entry money imposed. Prize-money increased to £110.

1894 First championship to be held in England (Sandwich).

First victory by an English professional, J H Taylor.

First of 16 victories by the Triumvirate of Taylor, Harry Vardon and James Braid. Dawn of a new era.

1896 First victory by Harry Vardon.

1897 First Open at Hoylake. Won for a second time by Harold Hilton, a local member.

Hilton, an amateur, received plate valued at £40, James Braid taking the second prize of £20. It is of note that 70 years later, the Royal and Ancient's limit on the value of any prize for an amateur was £50.

1898 First Open to be won with four rounds under 80. Harry Vardon was the winner. Qualifying limit imposed after two rounds.

1899 Talk of a strike if the prize-money was not increased. Vardon, Park, Taylor and Braid against the idea, but during the championship the first prize was raised to £50.

1901 James Braid's first victory.

1902 Victory for Sandy Herd, the first with the new, revolutionary Haskell ball.

Herd was noted as the first club waggler at address.

1904 First winning total under 300 and the first individual round under 70. Jack White won a notable championship at Sandwich with a score of 141 for the last two rounds, hoisting an aggregate of 296. His 141 was not beaten until 1935, but Braid and Taylor, tied on 297, also beat 300. Braid's aggregate for the final two rounds was one less than White's and his third round of 69 was the first to break 70 since the Open began. However, in a championship of low scores, Taylor had a last round of 68, a score which was not bettered for 30 years.

Until Braid's 69, James Sherlock's second-round 71 was an individual record.

(Action Photos)

Sandy Herd (Badminton Library)

1906 The Triumvirate of Braid, Taylor and Vardon finished first, second and third.

1907 Qualifying rounds first introduced. First overseas victor: Arnaud Massy (1877–1958) of France.

1908 James Braid lowered Jack White's record aggregate by 5 strokes to 291. His 142 for the first two rounds was also a record.

1910 First round at St Andrews abandoned at 1.30 pm because of a thunderstorm.

Prize-money increased to £125. Golden Jubilee of championship. Braid's fifth victory.

1914 The year of Harry Vardon's record sixth victory.

Two qualifying rounds introduced, lowest 80 and ties going forward to the championship proper. First newsreel film made of Open.

1919 Management taken over by the Royal and Ancient Golf Club, but no championship until 1920.

1920 George Duncan, 13 strokes behind Abe Mitchell after 36 holes, won by 2 strokes from Sandy Herd. He made up the 13 strokes in the third round with a 71 to 84 at Deal. Duncan added a 72 in the afternoon while Mitchell finished fourth.

Duncan's score of 143 for the final 36 holes was the best since Jack White's 141 in 1904 and was not beaten until 1935.

Total prize-money £225. First prize reached £100.

1921 The first time the Open trophy was taken to America. It was won at St Andrews by Jock Hutchison, a St Andrean based in America. In a play-off, he defeated Roger Wethered by 9 strokes.

In the first round, Hutchison holed in one at the 8th and was within an inch or two of another one at the 9th. However, successive holes in a total of 3 strokes is a major championship record.

In the third round, Wethered, attempting to become the third amateur to win, was penalised one stroke for inadvertently stepping on his ball. Wethered, who began with a 78, had the lowest last day score of 143, including the penalty stroke. Three times, however, he took 5 at the 18th including the 72nd hole.

Bobby Jones tore up his card at the 11th in the third round.

1922 Walter Hagen's first victory—the first by an American-born player. Starting the final round, 2 strokes behind the defending champion, Jock Hutchison, Hagen returned a 72, but tremendous golf by George Duncan nearly caught him. He came to the final hole, needing a 4 for a 68, but his second to the 18th at Sandwich missed the green, his pitch was short and he took 2 putts.

1923 Victory for Arthur Havers, the last by a British golfer, as it turned out, for eleven years.

First appearance of Gene Sarazen, the US champion, but he failed to qualify, being caught in a terrible storm.

1924 Hagen's second victory.

J H Taylor finished fifth at the age of 53. He had the lowest score for the six rounds including the qualifying rounds.

Record entry of 277.

1925 Prestwick's last Open. Victory for Jim Barnes, but tragedy for Macdonald Smith.

Macdonald Smith, facing his best chance to win an Open at last, and needing a 78 to do so, finished in 82.

1926 Having returned a 66 in one of his qualifying rounds at Sunningdale, by general consent as near flawless a round as had been played, Bobby Jones won the first of his three Opens at Royal Lytham, making its debut as an Open course.

After two rounds of 72, Jones was 2 ahead of Al Watrous, but in the third round, Watrous (Jones's partner) had a 69 to Jones's 73. Jones, 2 behind with 5 holes left, was level with Watrous on the 17th tee, but he hooked into sandy ground off the tee. Watrous, on the green in 2, was well placed, but Jones played one of the famous strokes of history. His shot of 170 yd (155 m) with a mashie iron finished inside Watrous's ball. Watrous took 3 putts to Jones's 2 and a par 4 at the 18th by Jones saw him home. Gate money introduced.

1927 Jones again: having opened with a 68, his only round under 70 in any Open (qualifying rounds apart), his total of 285 set a new Open record. He led from the start.

Last appearance of John Ball, aged 65. He first played in 1878.

All entrants played two qualifying rounds on the Monday and Tuesday, one on the championship course and one on an adjacent course. The leading 100 and ties qualified for the championship. One round was played on Wednesday and one on Thursday after which those 15 or more strokes off the lead were eliminated. The remainder played two rounds on Friday. Championship, therefore, extended to three days.

1928 and 1929 A double for Walter Hagen.

1930 Part two of the Grand Slam for Bobby Jones was at Hoylake, a sound victory in which he led for three rounds and edged out Leo Diegel and Macdonald Smith with a final 75. A Tingey, Jr, hit three shots out of bounds at

Walter Hagen winning the British Open, Muirfield 1929 (BBC Hulton Pic. Lib.)

the 1st hole. They were his shots to the green. The hole cost him 11.

1931 The first ever British Open held at Carnoustie. Watched by the Duke of Windsor (then Prince of Wales) the Argentine player, Jose Jurado, had a chance to win. He needed a 75 in the fourth round, but took 77. A final 71 for Tommy Armour, born in Edinburgh, saw him home.

1932 Prince's only championship produced Gene Sarazen's only win. It was popular, deserved and impressive. He led from start to finish on ground that was fast and full running. It was a low-scoring championship and his total of 283 was the best recorded up until then. It was not beaten for 18 years.

Rules altered to allow 60 and ties on final day.

1933 After Britain had won the Ryder Cup, the Americans replied by having five in the first six at St Andrews. Sarazen looked as though he would defend his title successfully, but in the second round he took 6 at the short 11th to finish in 73 and on the last day tried, and failed, to carry Hell bunker when quite unnecessary. He was part of a triple tie for third place, one stroke behind Densmore Shute and Craig Wood. It was the first all-American play-off. Shute's rounds in the championship were 73, 73, 73, 73. Only champion with every round the same.

At the first hole of the play-off which Shute won, Craig Wood played his second shot of the day out of the Swilcan Burn, but the stroke for

which he is undoubtedly best remembered was a drive at the par-5 5th (530 yd (484 m)). It finished in one of the bunkers in the face of the hill about 100 yd (91 m) from the hole.

1934 Henry Cotton brought a new dawn for British golf. It was the first British victory for eleven years and Cotton celebrated in style. His second-round 65 remained the lowest round (or equal lowest) until 1977. His total of 132 for the first 36 holes has never been beaten and he led from start to finish.

Cotton led by 9 strokes at half-way and by 10 with one round to play. His fourth round was full of anxiety and his 79 spoiled a brilliant sequence, but he still had 5 strokes to spare over the South African, Sid Brews (the first Commonwealth golfer to do so well); and he equalled the record aggregate.

The entry was over 300 for the first time.

1935 A virtual unknown, Sam Parks, won the US Open in 1935, and though Alf Perry was a golfer of proven worth, he was, nevertheless, a surprise winner at Muirfield.

One Scottish professional started 7, 10, 5, 10 and took 65 to reach the turn. He had another 10 at the 11th and retired at the 12th.

1936 Reward for Alf Padgham after finishing second and third the previous two years. Before his final round, Padgham discovered that his clubs were locked in a local clubmaker's shop with his caddie nowhere to be seen. Padgham eventually smashed a window, rescued his clubs and hired a new caddie.

Henry Cotton, 1934. The only British golfer since World War I to win the Open championship more than once. Cotton won three times—1934, 1937, 1948 (BBC Hulton Pic. Lib.)

COTTON SMASHES ALL RECORDS

Making Sure of Golf 'Open' for Britain

ROUND OF 65 ASTOUNDS THE AMERICANS

Henry Cotton (bareheaded) at Sandwich yesterday with ex-champions, J. H. Taylor (wearing glasses), James Braid and Ted Ray (smoking).

(*Daily Mirror*, 29 June 1934/Photo:Syndication International/John Frost, Historical Newspaper Service)

BY THE MOST BRILLIANT ROUND EVER PLAYED IN CHAMPIONSHIP GOLF, HENRY COTTON, THE TWENTY-SEVEN-YEAR-OLD ENGLISH PROFESSIONAL, YESTERDAY MADE ALMOST CERTAIN OF WINNING THE OPEN CHAMPIONSHIP CUP—FOR TEN SUCCESSIVE YEARS CARRIED OFF BY AMERICA—FOR BRITAIN.

COTTON'S amazing round of 65 at Sandwich staggered all his rivals—none more so than the Americans. For it broke every known record. It—

Brought his aggregate to 132 tor 36 holes, the best ever known, and seven strokes under Gene Sarazen's existing record of 139 for two successive rounds;

Removed from the record-book Walter Hagen's historic 67 made in his second round at Muirfield in May, 1929, hitherto the lowest single round in the event except Cotton's own 67 on Wednesday;

Broke the Royal St. George's course record of 66 which Cotton himself created on Monday; and, finally

Gave him a lead over the field of nine strokes, the largest ever established at this stage.

There was only one thing he did not do—he did not achieve the ambition of all great players and do twenty-seven consecutive holes in less than 100, as Bobby Jones once did. Cotton took exactly 100.

"What's This—A Tom Thumb Course?"

The one big question everyone was asking last night was: Can Cotton keep it up to-day?

The answer is: He played with such masterly ease and composure yesterday and dealt so confidently with difficulties that a break in his wonderful consistency need hardly be contemplated.

This is what the American "tigers" said:—

DENNY SHUTE (the holder): That gives no one else any chance. It is surely the best round ever. I never thought 65 would be possible on any of your championship courses. Anyway, I am glad to see a Briton do it at last.

GENE SARAZEN: What's this? A Tom Thumb course? I sure is the most wonderful round in golf. If I go out now and do a '70 I will still be thirteen strokes behind. The American boys who did not make the trip to England must count themselves lucky, and when they hear of Cotton's score they will say to themselves, "We are the wise guys to be out of that."

Alfred Padgham (Sundridge Park, Kent) is Cotton's nearest rival with an aggregate of 141.

Four British Open champions: Alf Padgham (1936), Alf Perry (1935), George Duncan (1920) and Arthur Havers (1923). They are pictured at a Seniors championship with Mr Ronald Teacher. (Action Photos)

1937 Henry Cotton's triumph, often regarded as his greatest, over the American Ryder Cup team at Carnoustie.

Number of qualifiers increased to 140 and ties.

1938 Reg Whitcombe survived gales on the final day. Flags rent to tatters, exhibition tents blown down and Alf Padgham drove the 11th (380 yd (347 m)). The Whitcombes were regular competitors but Reg's triumph, at the age of 40, was one which escaped his brothers, Ernest and Charles.

One player took 14 at the 12th, the third highest ever recorded in the Open for a single hole.

Qualifiers reduced to 130 and the last day to a maximum of 40 players.

1939 Victory for Dick Burton, the last British golfer to win the Open at St Andrews. A third round of 77 lost him the lead but, needing a 72 to win, Burton holed for a 3 on the 18th to have 2 strokes to spare. Johnny Bulla, who finished two hours before Burton, was second.

1946 Sam Snead's only victory in either the US or British Opens. It was his second of only three appearances in the British Open. Johnny Bulla, another American, was second—as he was in 1939, also at St Andrews.

Total prize-money £1000.

German prisoners of war were employed to do some rough clearance before the championship.

1947 Fred Daly's victory at Hoylake included a third round of 78. Since then, no winner has had a round higher than 75.

1948 Play watched by King George VI. Third victory for Henry Cotton. No other Briton has won three victories in the last 60 years. Indeed, no other British player has won more than one.

1949 The beginning of the Locke/Thomson

German prisoners of war clearing the Old course at St Andrews prior to the 1946 Open championship. They are watched by the Head Greenkeeper's dog (Illustrated London News Pic. Lib.)

era. They won eight times in ten years. In 1949 at Sandwich, Locke defeated Harry Bradshaw in a play-off. It was a championship remembered for a drive of Bradshaw's finishing in a broken bottle at the 5th hole in the second round. It led to a change in the Rules of Golf but, at the time, he had to play the ball and bottle.

First prize £300.

1950 Locke lowered the record aggregate to 279 at Troon.

1951 Portrush's only Open and the last British victory for 18 years. Max Faulkner was champion.

Total prize-money £1700.

1952 Locke's third victory in four years, but Peter Thomson finished runner-up in his second Open.

1953 Ben Hogan's year. US Open and Masters champion, he added a third leg of the modern quadrilateral, the only player to perform the feat in the same year. His scores were 73, 71, 70, 68; the only other champions to have each round lower than the previous one are Jack

White (1904), James Braid (1906) and Gary Player (1959).

First prize £515.

1954 Peter Thomson's first victory; also the first by an Australian and the first Open to be held at Birkdale.

Dai Rees, who came close on a number of occasions, finished joint second.

1955 £1000 first prize for the first time. First live coverage by BBC Television on 7 July.

Thomson's second victory; championship held at St Andrews.

1956 Thomson's third victory in three years, the only player to accomplish the feat in modern times. At Hoylake, he won by 3 strokes. Flory van Donck (Belgium), Roberto de Vicenzo (Argentina) and Gary Player (South Africa) were second, third and fourth.

1957 Championship transferred at late notice from Muirfield to St Andrews owing to petrol shortage during the Suez crisis. Locke won for the fourth time, but survived a technicality over the Rules. On the 72nd green, he marked his ball a putter's head length from the spot, but

Above: As big a smile for Bobby Locke's fourth Open title as for his first. St Andrews 1957 (Action Photos)

Right: Five times British Open champion—Peter Thomson (Action Photos)

Below: Success of a mission. Ben Hogan with the Open championship trophy, Carnoustie 1953 (Action Photos)

Gary Player's wife, Vivienne, tries to console him after he had taken 6 at the 72nd hole of the 1959 British Open at Muirfield (Action Photos)

replaced it on the marker's spot, not a putter's head length away. He holed the short putt for a 3-stroke victory over Thomson. The likelihood is, therefore, that he could have stood a 2-stroke penalty.

Characteristic power and defiance—Arnold Palmer (Action Photos)

1958 Thomson's fourth victory in five years. Only Young Tom Morris can match this feat.

1959 Victory for Gary Player at Muirfield despite the highest first round by a champion for 30 years—a 75; and an agonising wait after a 6 on the 72nd hole looked as though it might lose him the championship.

Player's 6 was the highest score by a champion at the last hole for many years.

Flory van Donck of Belgium finished second. Apart from Arnaud Massy who finished first in 1907 and second in 1911, van Donck's performance was the best by a continental professional until Ballesteros tied second in 1976.

Total prize-money £5000.

1960 Centenary Open. Arnold Palmer's first appearance. He finished runner-up to Kel Nagle, the second Australian winner.

A violent storm washed out play on Friday afternoon. Final round played on Saturday.

Prize-money £7000. First prize £1250.

1961 Another Saturday finish owing to another storm washing out a day's play.

Arnold Palmer's supremacy confirmed by his victory. His play in the gale in the second round was considered among his finest. A plaque later erected on the old 15th hole to commemorate one particularly fine second shot.

Prize-money £8500. First prize £1400.

Qualifiers reduced to a maximum of 120 and the 36-hole cut altered to allow a maximum of 50 for the final 36 holes.

1962 Palmer powered his way to a second victory on a course running freely. Set record aggregate of 276. Six-stroke victory, the biggest since Walter Hagen in 1929.

Jack Nicklaus's first appearance. He took 10 at the 11th. Made cut on margin. His first round was 80. Since then his worst round has been 77 in 1965.

Attendance 37 098 with many more thought to have got in along the seashore without paying. Crowd scenes led to much stricter crowd control.

1963 First victory in any major championship by a left-handed player. Bob Charles beat Phil Rodgers in a play-off, the last to be decided over 36 holes.

Qualifying rounds took place for first time ahead of the championship on neighbouring courses. System of exemptions introduced for the leading players.

The 36-hole cut admitted 45 and ties to the final 36 holes.

1964 Tony Lema won with little more than a day's preparation. Five-stroke victory would have been greater but for Jack Nicklaus

He came, he saw, he conquered. . . . All within the space of five days. The world raised its glass, too, to Tony Lema. British Open, St Andrews 1964 (Action Photos)

Well worth the wait. Tony Jacklin, the first British-born Open champion for 18 years. Lytham 1969 (Action Photos)

completing the last two rounds in 134 strokes—a record at the time. It was Lema's first British Open.

1965 Peter Thomson joined James Braid and J H Taylor by winning his fifth and best victory at Birkdale. It was the last year that two rounds were played on the last day (Friday) and he is the only person to have won two Opens at Birkdale.

He was 6 strokes behind Tony Lema, the defending champion, at the end of the first round, but won by 2 strokes.

Number of qualifiers for the championship (including those exempt) increased to 130.

Total prize-money up to £10 000.

1966 The first championship scheduled to end on a Saturday and the first victory for Jack Nicklaus on a course where the fairways were narrow and the rough knee high. David Thomas, with two 69s to finish, was runner-up for the second time.

It was Tony Lema's last championship. He was killed on 24 July 1966 in an air crash.

Attendance topped 40 000.

Thirty-six hole cut admitted 55 and ties.

1967 Sentimental acclaim for the victory of Roberto de Vicenzo on what may prove to be Hoylake's last Open. Having been a loyal supporter of the Open, it was a popular and deserved triumph. Third in 1948 and 1949, second in 1950, third again in 1956 and third equal in 1960, there were those who believed that would be as close as he came, but he had

final rounds of 67 and 70 and held off the strong golf of Jack Nicklaus.

1968 Gary Player's second victory in a generally high-scoring championship. His total of 289 was the highest for 21 years. Of the leading 30 players, only Casper and Nicklaus broke 70—only once. At 7252 yd (6631 m), the course was the longest for an Open.

Prize-money reached £15 000 with a first prize of £3000.

1969 British victory drought ended by the success of Tony Jacklin at Lytham. He ended the longest run in history without a British champion—18 years.

For the first time in ten years no American finished in the first five. The nationalities of the top five, being English, New Zealand, Argentine, Australian and Irish.

First prize £4250 which is £3925 more than the previous British champion, Max Faulkner, received in 1951.

1970 Second all-American play-off; and it took place at St Andrews on a Sunday—an unprecedented step. Jack Nicklaus drove through the 18th green, chipped back and holed for a birdie to win by 1 stroke, but he might not have had the chance of a play-off. Doug Sanders who had to pre-qualify, took 3 putts on the 18th green on the fourth afternoon. Nobody else who had had to pre-qualify has come as close to winning. It was the first play-off to be decided by a birdie. Hitherto, the play-offs were more one-sided.

Total prize-money £40 000.

A gallery of Open champions. St Andrews 1970. *Back row:* Arthur Havers, Gene Sarazen, Dick Burton, Fred Daly, Roberto de Vicenzo, Arnold Palmer, Kel Nagle, Bobby Locke, Henry Cotton, Peter Thomson. *Front row:* Densmore Shute, Bob Charles, Max Faulkner, Jack Nicklaus, Tony Jacklin, Gary Player (Action Photos)

Storm on first evening ended play early. Tony Jacklin, defending champion and out in 29, had to mark his ball for the night on the 14th hole and finish next day.

His 29 was the lowest 9 holes at St Andrews as was Neil Coles's 65 for 18 holes.

1971 Lee Trevino's victory at Birkdale completed a unique treble. Within the space of about a month he captured the American, Canadian and British titles.

A final outward half of 31 left the Open at Trevino's mercy, but errors at the 10th and 14th were followed by a 7 at the 17th which might easily have been worse as his ball lodged in the dunes. Thoughts of breaking the aggregate record of 276 were gone, but his 278 gave him a stroke to spare over Lu Liang Huan of Formosa.

It was the first time that an Asian golfer had made such a mark.

It was the 100th Open for which the prize-money was raised to £47 500.

Number of qualifiers increased to 150, including exempt players. Fifty-four-hole cut increased to 60 and ties.

1972 Lee Trevino again at Muirfield and definitely his week. He holed two chips and a bunker shot, the last chip on the 35th green for a 5 after seemingly having acknowledged defeat. Tony Jacklin promptly took 3 putts and Trevino recorded a total of 278, the first at Muirfield below 280.

Four qualifying courses used. Total prize-money £50 000.

1973 Tom Weiskopf led from start to finish, uncertain to begin with but helped later by still, damp conditions in which he excelled. His 276 tied the record set by Arnold Palmer, also at Troon in 1962. Gene Sarazen holed in one at the 8th in the first round. It was 50 years since he first played in the Open.

1974 From the moment he began 69, 68, Gary Player was a hot favourite. Of the others, only John Morgan had a round under 70. His 69 tied Player after 18 holes, but Player's halfway lead was 5 strokes and his 54-hole lead was 3.

Use of the large ball made compulsory.

1975 Another close play-off between Tom Watson and Jack Newton, but three or four others had chances of victory on Saturday, notably the South African, Bobby Cole. There was consistent low scoring, the like of which Carnoustie had not seen in an Open. Newton had a third round of 65.

1976 Johnny Miller won by 6 strokes but was given a long, hard tussle by the young Spaniard, Severiano Ballesteros, almost unknown in those days. Peter Dawson holed in one at the 4th, the first by a left-hander in the Open.

Britain's hottest summer of the century led to a part of the course catching fire on the first day.

1977 A championship of records galore for Turnberry's first.

Tom Watson lowered the record aggregate by 8 strokes, Jack Nicklaus by 7.

Mark Hayes's second round of 63 was the lowest individual round in any Open.

Watson had the lowest last two rounds on record, the lowest aggregate for the first 54 holes and the lowest aggregate for the last 54 holes.

There were eleven scores of 66 or under. Those completing 72 holes had 40 rounds under 70 between them, 70 being Turnberry's par.

The first eight were all Americans.

The crowd total of 92 200 was a record for Scotland.

The top 20 all received four-figure prizes. Total prize-money £100 000.

Regional qualifying introduced, followed by standard qualifying over three courses.

1978 Jack Nicklaus's third victory, his second at St Andrews. For second year running, his last two rounds were under 70. He accomplished the same feat in 1964, also at St Andrews.

His total of 281 in 1978 was 2 lower than in 1970.

Isao Aoki finished equal 7th, the highest placing ever by a Japanese golfer.

First prize, £12 500. Record attendance of 125 271.

1979 Victory for Severiano Ballesteros, the first by a Spaniard and the first by a professional from continental Europe since Arnaud Massy in 1907.

Lytham, therefore, kept its record that no American professional has won in seven Opens; Bobby Jones, an amateur, won in 1926.

After equalling the course record of 65 in the second round, Ballesteros hit only two fairways with his driver on the last two days, but finished on 283, winner by 3 strokes.

Ben Crenshaw was equal second for the second year running; Jack Nicklaus second for a record seventh time. In his first round, Nicklaus holed in one at the 5th.

Hale Irwin, the US Open champion, was the 54-hole leader but, partnered by Ballesteros in the final round, finished sixth.

Bill Longmuir equalled the Lytham record with 65 on the first morning.

Prize-money totalled £155 000 and the attendance was 134 571—a record. The Open was estimated to cost £800 000 to stage.

DETAILED RECORDS

Most victories
6, Harry Vardon, 1896-98-99-1903-11-14
5, James Braid, 1901-05-06-08-10; J H Taylor, 1894-95-1900-09-13; Peter Thomson, 1954-55-56-58-65

Most times runner-up or joint runner-up
7, Jack Nicklaus, 1964-67-68-72-76-77-79
6, J H Taylor, 1896-1904-05-06-07-14

Oldest winner
Old Tom Morris, 46 years 99 days, 1867
Roberto de Vicenzo, 44 years 93 days, 1967
Harry Vardon, 44 years 51 days, 1914

Youngest winner
Young Tom Morris, 17 years 5 months 8 days, 1868
Willie Auchterlonie, 21 years 24 days, 1893
Severiano Ballesteros, 22 years 3 months 12 days, 1979

Youngest and oldest competitor
John Ball, 14 years, 1878
Gene Sarazen, 71 years 4 months 13 days, 1973

Biggest margin of victory
13 strokes, Old Tom Morris, 1862
12 strokes, Young Tom Morris, 1870
8 strokes, J H Taylor 1900 and 1913; James Braid, 1908
6 strokes, Bobby Jones, 1927; Walter Hagen, 1929; Arnold Palmer, 1962; Johnny Miller, 1976

Lowest winning aggregates
268 (68, 70, 65, 65). Tom Watson, Turnberry, 1977
271 (68, 70, 64, 69). Tom Watson, Muirfield, 1980
276 (71, 69, 67, 69). Arnold Palmer, Troon, 1962
276 (68, 67, 71, 70). Tom Weiskopf, Troon, 1973

Lowest aggregates by runner-up
269 (68, 70, 65, 66), Jack Nicklaus, Turnberry, 1977
275 (68, 67, 71, 69). Lee Trevino, Muirfield, 1980

Lowest aggregate by an amateur
283 (74, 70, 71, 68), Guy Wolstenholme, St Andrews, 1960

Lowest individual round
63, Mark Hayes, second round, Turnberry, 1977; Isao Aoki, third round, Muirfield, 1980
(out: 4,3,3,3,4,3,4,4,4 = 32;
in: 4,2,3,4,4,3,3,3,5 = 31)

Lowest individual round by an amateur
66, Frank Stranahan, fourth round, Troon, 1950

Lowest first round
65, Neil Coles, St Andrews, 1970; Bill Longmuir, Royal Lytham, 1979

Lowest second round
63, Mark Hayes, Turnberry, 1977

Lowest third round
63, Isao Aoki, Muirfield, 1980
64, Hubert Green and Tom Watson, Muirfield, 1980

Lowest fourth round
65, Jack Nicklaus, Troon, 1973; Tom Watson, Turnberry, 1977

Lowest first 36 holes
132 (67, 65), Henry Cotton, Sandwich, 1934

Lowest second 36 holes
130 (65, 65), Tom Watson, Turnberry, 1977

Lowest first 54 holes
202 (68, 70, 64), Tom Watson, Muirfield, 1980
203 (68, 70, 65), Jack Nicklaus and Tom Watson, Turnberry, 1977

Lowest final 54 holes
200 (70, 65, 65), Tom Watson, Turnberry, 1977

Lowest 9 holes
29, Peter Thomson and Tom Haliburton, first 9, Royal Lytham, 1958; Tony Jacklin, first 9, St Andrews, 1970; Bill Longmuir, first 9, Royal Lytham, 1979

30, Eric Brown, first 9, St Andrews, 1957; Eric Brown, second 9, Royal Lytham, 1958; Leopoldo Ruiz, first 9, Royal Lytham, 1958; Phil Rodgers, second 9, Muirfield, 1966; Jimmy Kinsella, first 9, Royal Birkdale, 1971; Harry Bannerman, first 9, Muirfield, 1972; Bert Yancey, first 9, Troon, 1973; Christy O'Connor, Jr, first 9, Royal Birkdale, 1976; Arnold Palmer, second 9, Turnberry, 1977; Jack Nicklaus, first 9, Royal Lytham, 1979; Tom Watson, second 9, Muirfield, 1980

Biggest span between first and last victories
19 years, J H Taylor, 1894–1913
18 years, Harry Vardon, 1896–1914
15 years, Gary Player, 1959–74
14 years, Henry Cotton, 1934–48

Successive victories
4, Young Tom Morris, 1868–72. No championship in 1871

3, Jamie Anderson, 1877–79; Bob Ferguson, 1880–82, Peter Thomson, 1954–56

2, Old Tom Morris, 1861–62; J H Taylor, 1894–95; Harry Vardon, 1898–99; James Braid, 1905–06; Bobby Jones, 1926–27); Walter Hagen, 1928–29; Bobby Locke, 1949–50; Arnold Palmer, 1961–62;. Lee Trevino, 1971–72

Victories by amateurs
3, Bobby Jones, 1926-27-30
2, Harold Hilton, 1892-97
1, John Ball, 1890
Roger Wethered lost a play-off in 1921

Winners of the British Amateur and British Open on the same course
John Ball, Open 1890, Amateur 1888 and 1899, Prestwick
Bobby Jones, Open 1927, Amateur 1930, St Andrews

Highest number of top five finishes
16, J H Taylor
15, Harry Vardon; James Braid and Jack Nicklaus

Highest number of rounds under 70
25, Jack Nicklaus
15, Peter Thomson
13, Gary Player
12, Bobby Locke
11, Arnold Palmer

First player to break 70
James Braid, 69, third round, Sandwich, 1904

Outright leader after every round
Willie Auchterlonie, 1893; J H Taylor, 1894 and 1900; James Braid, 1908; Ted Ray, 1912; Bobby Jones, 1927; Gene Sarazen, 1932; Henry Cotton, 1934; Tom Weiskopf, 1973

Hot sequences
1896–1904: Harry Vardon never finished lower than 6th. From 1911 (when he was 41) to 1914, his placings were 1st, 2nd, =3rd, 1st
1922–1930: Bobby Jones's placings were =2nd, 1st, 2nd, 2nd, 1st, =11th, 2nd, 1st, 1st
1966–1980: Jack Nicklaus never finished lower than 6th

Left-handed champion
Bob Charles, Royal Lytham, 1963

Bespectacled champions
None

Best placings on first three appearances
Arnold Palmer, 2nd, 1st, 1st, 1960–62

Play-offs
12, 1876 (tie but play-off never took place) 1883, 1889, 1896, 1911, 1921, 1933, 1949, 1958, 1963, 1970, 1975

By comparison, the US Open has had 26 play-offs in 29 fewer championships

Lowest round in a play-off
67, Bobby Locke, Sandwich, 1949
68, Peter Thomson, Royal Lytham, 1958; Bobby Locke, Sandwich, 1949.

Most holes in one
2, Charles H Ward, 8th, St Andrews 1946; 13th, Muirfield 1948

First overseas winner
Arnaud Massy (France), 1907

First winner from America
Jock Hutchison, 1921

First American-born winner
Walter Hagen, 1922

Record leads (since 1892)
After 18 holes:
4 strokes, James Braid, 1908; Bobby Jones, 1927; Henry Cotton, 1934
After 36 holes:
9 strokes, Henry Cotton, 1934
After 54 holes:
10 strokes, Henry Cotton, 1934
  7 strokes, Tony Lema, 1964
  6 strokes, James Braid, 1908
  5 strokes, Arnold Palmer, 1962

Champions with each round lower than previous one
Jack White, 1904, Sandwich, 80, 75, 72, 69
James Braid, 1906, Muirfield, 77, 76, 74, 73
Ben Hogan, 1953, Carnoustie, 73, 71, 70 68
Gary Player, 1959, Muirfield, 75, 71, 70, 68

Champion with four rounds the same
Densmore Shute, 1933, St Andrews, 73, 73, 73, 73 (excluding the play-off)

Biggest variation between rounds of a champion
14 strokes, Henry Cotton, 1934, second round 65 fourth round 79
11 strokes, Jack White, 1904, first round 80 fourth round 69

Best comeback by champions
After 18 holes:
Harry Vardon, 1896, 11 strokes behind the leader
After 36 holes:
George Duncan, 1920, 13 strokes behind the leader
After 54 holes:
Jim Barnes, 1925, 5 strokes behind the leader

Champions with four rounds under 70
None

Arnold Palmer, 1962 and Tom Watson, 1977 and 1980, had three rounds under 70

Of non-champions, Phil Rodgers, 1963 and Jack Nicklaus, 1977 and Lee Trevino, 1980, had three rounds under 70

Best finishing round by a champion
65, Tom Watson, Turnberry, 1977
66, Johnny Miller, Birkdale, 1976

Worst finishing round by a champion since 1920
79, Henry Cotton, Sandwich, 1934
78, Reg Whitcombe, Sandwich, 1938
77, Walter Hagen, Hoylake, 1924

Worst opening round by a champion since 1919
80, George Duncan, Deal, 1920 (he also had a second round of 80)
77, Walter Hagen, Hoylake, 1924

Best opening round by a champion
66, Peter Thomson, Royal Lytham, 1958
67, Henry Cotton, Sandwich, 1934

Biggest recovery in 18 holes by a champion
George Duncan, Deal, 1920, was 13 strokes behind the leader, Abe Mitchell, after 36 holes and level after 54

Champions with a 7 in final round
Bobby Jones, 1930; Peter Thomson, 1955

Championship with highest number of rounds under 70
Turnberry, 1977. There were 40 rounds which beat the par of 70

Championship since 1946 with the fewest rounds under 70
St Andrews, 1946; Hoylake, 1947; Portrush, 1951; Hoylake, 1956; Carnoustie, 1968. All had only two rounds under 70

Lowest total for two consecutive holes
3, Jock Hutchison, St Andrews, 1921. He had a 1 at the 8th and a 2 at the 9th in his first round

Oldest player to hole in one
Gene Sarazen, 71 years 4 months, Troon, 1973

Champions who led after three rounds (1892–1979)
A total of 41 champions out of 78:
Willie Auchterlonie, 1893; J H Taylor, 1894; Harry Vardon, 1899; J H Taylor, 1900; James Braid, 1901; Sandy Herd, 1902; Harry Vardon, 1903; James Braid, 1905; James Braid, 1908; J H Taylor, 1909; Harry Vardon, 1911; Ted Ray, 1912; J H Taylor, 1913; Arthur Havers, 1923; Bobby Jones, 1927; Walter Hagen, 1928; Walter Hagen, 1929; Gene Sarazen, 1932; Henry Cotton, 1934; Alf Perry, 1935; Reg Whitcombe, 1938; Henry Cotton, 1948; Max

Prize-money		
Year	Total	First Prize
	£	£
1920	225	75
1927	275	100
1930	400	100
1931	500	100
1946	1000	150
1949	1700	300
1953	2450	500
1954	3500	750
1955	3750	1000
1958	4850	1000
1959	5000	1000
1960	7000	1250
1961	8500	1400
1963	8500	1500
1965	10000	1750
1966	15000	2100
1968	20000	3000
1969	30000	4250
1970	40000	5250
1971	45000	5500
1972	50000	5500
1975	75000	7500
1977	100000	10000
1978	125000	12500
1979	155000	15500
1980	200000	25000

Attendance and Gate Money		
Year	Attendance	Gate Money £
1962	37098	15207
1963	24585	14173
1964	35954	14704
1965	32927	21214
1966	40182	23075
1967	29880	20180
1968	51819	31907
1969	46001	46188
1970	81593	62744
1971	70076	90052
1972	84746	98925
1973	78810	115000
1974	92796	158729
1975	85258	176012
1976	92021	243793
1977	87615	249073
1978	125271	421474
1979	134501	467898

The largest single day attendance was 32072 on the Friday of the 1979 championship.

Faulkner, 1951; Peter Thomson, 1955; Peter Thomson, 1956; Bobby Locke, 1957; Peter Thomson, 1958; Kel Nagle, 1960; Arnold Palmer, 1961; Arnold Palmer, 1962; Bob Charles, 1963; Tony Lema, 1964; Peter Thomson, 1965; Roberto de Vicenzo, 1967; Tony Jacklin, 1969; Lee Trevino, 1971; Lee Trevino, 1972; Tom Weiskopf, 1973; Gary Player, 1974; Tom Watson, 1977; Tom Watson, 1980

Longest course
Carnoustie, 1968, 7252 yd (6631 m)

Courses most often used (up to and including 1980)
Prestwick, 24 (but not since 1925); St Andrews, 22; Muirfield, 12; Hoylake, 10; Sandwich, 9; Royal Lytham, 7; Musselburgh, 6; Royal Birkdale and Carnoustie, 5; Royal Troon, 4; Deal, 2; Royal Portrush, Princes and Turnberry, 1

Lowest rounds on Open courses in an Open

Prestwick	69, Macdonald Smith, 1925
St Andrews	65, Neil Coles, 1970
Muirfield	63, Isao Aoki, 1980
Hoylake	67, Roberto de Vicenzo and Gary Player, 1967
Sandwich	65, Henry Cotton, 1934
Royal Lytham and St Annes	65, Eric Brown and Leopoldo Ruiz, 1958; Christy O'Connor, Sr, 1969; Bill Longmuir and Severiano Ballesteros, 1979
Prince's	68, Arthur Havers, 1932
Royal Birkdale	66, Peter Oosterhuis, 1971; Johnny Miller and Mark James, 1976
Carnoustie	65, Jack Newton, 1975
Royal Troon	65, Jack Nicklaus, 1973
Turnberry	63, Mark Hayes, 1977
Deal	71, George Duncan and Len Holland, 1920
Musselburgh	77, Willie Park, Jr, and Andrew Kirkaldy, 1889

RESULTS

British Open Championship Finals

1860 Prestwick

Willie Park, Musselburgh	174
Tom Morris, Sr, Prestwick	176
Andrew Strath, St Andrews	180
Bob Andrew, Perth	191
Daniel Brown	192
Charlie Hunter, Prestwick	195

1861 Prestwick

Tom Morris, Sr, Prestwick	163
Willie Park, Musselburgh	167
William Dow, Musselburgh	171
David Park, Musselburgh	172
Bob Andrew, Perth	175
Peter McEwen	178

1862 Prestwick

Tom Morris, Sr, Prestwick	163
Willie Park, Musselburgh	176
Charlie Hunter, Prestwick, St Nicholas	178
William Dow, Musselburgh	181
James Knight	186
J J Johnstone	208

1863 Prestwick

Willie Park, Musselburgh	168
Tom Morris, Sr, Prestwick	170
David Park, Musselburgh	172
Andrew Strath, St Andrews	174
Daniel Brown	176
Bob Andrew, Perth	178

1864 Prestwick

Tom Morris, Sr, Prestwick	167
Andrew Strath, St Andrews	169
Bob Andrew, Perth	175
Willie Park, Musselburgh	177

1865 Prestwick

Andrew Strath, St Andrews	162
Willie Park, Musselburgh	164
Bob Kirk, St Andrews	173
Tom Morris, Sr, Prestwick	174
William Doleman, Glasgow	178
Bob Andrew, Perth	179

1866 Prestwick

Willie Park, Musselburgh	169
David Park, Musselburgh	171
Bob Andrew, Perth	176
Tom Morris, Sr, St Andrews	178
Bob Kirk, St Andrews	180
Andrew Strath, St Andrews	182

1867 Prestwick

Tom Morris, Sr, St Andrews	170
Willie Park, Musselburgh	172
Andrew Strath, St Andrews	174

1868 Prestwick

Tom Morris, Jr, St Andrews	157
Bob Andrew, Perth	159
Willie Park, Musselburgh	162
Bob Kirk, St Andrews	171
J Allen	172
Charlie Hunter, Prestwick	172

1869 Prestwick

Tom Morris, Jr, St Andrews	154
Tom Morris, Sr, St Andrews	157
S Mure Ferguson, Prestwick	165
Tom Dunn	167
Bob Kirk, St Andrews	168
David Strath, St Andrews	169

1870 Prestwick

Tom Morris, Jr, St Andrews	149
Bob Kirk, St Andrews	161
David Strath, St Andrews	161
Tom Morris, Sr, St Andrews	162
William Doleman, Glasgow	169
Jamie Anderson, St Andrews	174

1871 No championship

1872 Prestwick

Tom Morris, Jr, St Andrews	166
David Strath, St Andrews	169
William Doleman, Musselburgh	177
David Park, Musselburgh	179
Tom Morris, Sr, St Andrews	179
Charlie Hunter, Prestwick	189

1873 St Andrews

Tom Kidd, St Andrews	179
Jamie Anderson, St Andrews	180

1874 Musselburgh

Mungo Park, Musselburgh	159
Tom Morris, Jr, St Andrews	161
George Paxton, Musselburgh	162

1875 Prestwick

Willie Park, Musselburgh	166
Bob Martin, St Andrews	168
Mungo Park, Musselburgh	171
Bob Ferguson, Musselburgh	172
James Rennie	177
David Strath, St Andrews	178

1876 St Andrews

Bob Martin, St Andrews	176
David Strath, St Andrews	176

(Martin was awarded the title when Strath refused to play-off)

Willie Park, Musselburgh	183
J O F Morris, Sr, St Andrews	185
William Thomson, Elie	185
Mungo Park, Musselburgh	185

1877 Musselburgh

Jamie Anderson, St Andrews	160
Bob Pringle, Musselburgh	162
Bob Ferguson, Musselburgh	164
William Cosgrove, Musselburgh	164

1878 Prestwick

James Anderson, St Andrews	157
Bob Kirk, St Andrews	159
J O F Morris, Sr, St Andrews	161
John Ball, Royal Liverpool	165
Bob Martin, St Andrews	165
Willie Park, Musselburgh	166

1879 St Andrews

Jamie Anderson, St Andrews	170
Andrew Kirkaldy, St Andrews	170

(Anderson won play-off)

1880 Musselburgh

Bob Ferguson, Musselburgh	162
Peter Paxton, Musselburgh	167
Ned Cosgrove, Musselburgh	168

1881 Prestwick

Bob Ferguson, Musselburgh	170
Jamie Anderson, St Andrews	173
Ned Cosgrove, Musselburgh	177
Bob Martin, St Andrews	178
Tom Morris, Sr, St Andrews	181
Willie Campbell, Prestwick	181
Willie Park, Jr, Musselburgh	181

1882 St Andrews

Bob Ferguson, Musselburgh	171
Willie Fernie, Dumfries	174

1883 Musselburgh

Willie Fernie, Dumfries (won play-off)	159
Bob Ferguson, Musselburgh	159
F Boothby	163

1884 Prestwick

Jack Simpson, Carnoustie	160
Willie Fernie, Troon	164
Douglas Rolland	164
Willie Park, Jr, Musselburgh	169
Willie Campbell, Prestwick	169
Ben Sayers, North Berwick	171
Tom Dunn	171
George Fernie	171

1885 St Andrews

Bob Martin, St Andrews	171
Archie Simpson, Carnoustie	172
David Ayton, St Andrews	172

1886 Musselburgh

David Brown, Musselburgh	157
Willie Campbell, Musselburgh	159
Ben Campbell, Musselburgh	160

1887 Prestwick

Willie Park, Jr, Musselburgh	161
Bob Martin, St Andrews	162
Willie Campbell, Prestwick	164
Johnny E Laidlay, Honourable Company	166
Ben Sayers, North Berwick	168
Archie Simpson	168

1888 St Andrews

Jack Burns, Warwick	86	85	171
David Anderson, Jr, St Andrews	87	85	172
Ben Sayers, North Berwick	85	87	172
Willie Campbell, Prestwick	84	90	174
Leslie Balfour, Edinburgh	86	89	175
Andrew Kirkaldy, St Andrews	87	89	176
Davie Grant, North Berwick	88	88	176

1889 Musselburgh

Willie Park, Jr, Musselburgh	78	77	155
Andrew Kirkaldy, St Andrews	77	78	155

(Park won play-off 158 to 163)

Ben Sayers, North Berwick	79	80	159
Johnny E. Laidlay, Honourable Company	81	81	162
David Brown, Musselburgh	82	80	162
Willie Fernie, Troon	84	80	164

1890 Prestwick

John Ball, Royal Liverpool	82	82	164
Willie Fernie, Troon	85	82	167
A Simpson, Carnoustie	85	82	167
Willie Park, Jr, Musselburgh	90	80	170
Andrew Kirkaldy, St Andrews	81	89	170
Horace Hutchinson, Royal North Devon	87	85	172

1891 St Andrews

Hugh Kirkaldy, St Andrews	83	83	166
Willie Fernie, Troon	84	84	168
Andrew Kirkaldy, St Andrews	84	84	168
S Mure Fergusson, Royal and Ancient	86	84	170
W D More, Chester	84	87	171
Willie Park, Jr, Musselburgh	88	85	173

(From 1892 the competition was extended to 72 holes)

1892 Muirfield

Harold Hilton, Royal Liverpool	78	81	72	74	305
John Ball, Jr, Royal Liverpool	75	80	74	79	308
James Kirkaldy, St Andrews	77	83	73	75	308
Sandy Herd, Huddersfield	77	78	77	76	308
J Kay, Seaton Carew	82	78	74	78	312
Ben Sayers, North Berwick	80	76	81	75	312

1893 Prestwick

Willie Auchterlonie, St Andrews	78	81	81	82	322
Johnny E Laidlay, Honourable Company					
	80	83	80	81	324
Sandy Herd, Huddersfield	82	81	78	84	325
Hugh Kirkaldy, St Andrews	83	79	82	82	326
Andrew Kirkaldy, St Andrews	85	82	82	77	326
J Kay, Seaton Carew	81	81	80	85	327
R Simpson, Carnoustie	81	81	80	85	327

1894 Sandwich

J H Taylor, Winchester	84	80	81	81	326
Douglas Rolland, Limpsfield	86	79	84	82	331
Andrew Kirkaldy, St Andrews	86	79	83	84	332
A Toogood, Eltham	84	85	82	82	333
Willie Fernie, Troon	84	84	86	80	334
Harry Vardon, Bury St Edmunds	86	86	82	80	334
Ben Sayers, North Berwick	85	81	84	84	334

1895 St Andrews

J H Taylor, Winchester	86	78	80	78	322
Sandy Herd, Huddersfield	82	77	82	85	326
Andrew Kirkaldy, St Andrews	81	83	84	84	332
G Pulford, Royal Liverpool	84	81	83	87	335
Archie Simpson, Aberdeen	88	85	78	85	336
Willie Fernie, Troon	86	79	86	86	337
David Brown, Malvern	81	89	83	84	337
David Anderson, Panmure	86	83	84	84	337

1896 Muirfield

Harry Vardon, Ganton	83	78	78	77	316
J H Taylor, Winchester	77	78	81	80	316
(Vardon won play-off 157 to 161)					
Freddie G Tait, Black Watch	83	75	84	77	319
Willie Fernie, Troon	78	79	82	80	319
Sandy Herd, Huddersfield	72	84	79	85	320
James Braid, Romford	83	81	79	80	323

1897 Hoylake

Harold H Hilton, Royal Liverpool	80	75	84	75	314
James Braid, Romford	80	74	82	79	315
Freddie G Tait, Black Watch	79	79	80	79	317
G Pulford, Royal Liverpool	80	79	79	79	317
Sandy Herd, Huddersfield	78	81	79	80	318
Harry Vardon, Ganton	84	80	80	76	320

1898 Prestwick

Harry Vardon, Ganton	79	75	77	76	307
Willie Park, Musselburgh	76	75	78	79	308
Harold H Hilton, Royal Liverpool	76	81	77	75	309
J H Taylor, Winchester	78	78	77	79	312
Freddie G Tait, Black Watch	81	77	75	72	315
D Kinnell, Leven	80	77	79	80	316

1899 Sandwich

Harry Vardon, Ganton	76	76	81	77	310
Jack White, Seaford	79	79	82	75	315
Andrew Kirkaldy, St Andrews	81	79	82	77	319
J H Taylor, Mid-Surrey	77	76	83	84	320
James Braid, Romford	78	78	83	84	322
Willie Fernie, Troon	79	83	82	78	322

1900 St Andrews

J H Taylor, Mid-Surrey	79	77	78	75	309
Harry Vardon, Ganton	79	81	80	78	317
James Braid, Romford	82	81	80	79	322
Jack White, Seaford	80	81	82	80	323
Willie Auchterlonie, St Andrews	81	85	80	80	326
Willie Park, Jr, Musselburgh	80	83	81	84	328

1901 Muirfield

James Braid, Romford	79	76	74	80	309
Harry Vardon, Ganton	77	78	79	78	312
J H Taylor, Royal Mid-Surrey	79	83	74	77	313
Harold H Hilton, Royal Liverpool	89	80	75	76	320
Sandy Herd, Huddersfield	87	81	81	76	325
Jack White, Seaford	82	82	80	82	326

1902 Hoylake

Sandy Herd, Huddersfield	77	76	73	81	307
Harry Vardon, South Herts	72	77	80	79	308
James Braid, Walton Heath	78	76	80	74	308
R Maxwell, Honourable Company	79	77	79	74	309
Tom Vardon, Ilkley	80	76	78	79	313
J H Taylor, Mid-Surrey	81	76	77	80	314
D Kinnell, Leven	78	80	79	77	314
Harold Hilton, Royal Liverpool	79	76	81	78	314

1903 Prestwick

Harry Vardon, South Herts	73	77	72	78	300
Tom Vardon, Ilkley	76	81	75	74	306
Jack White, Sunningdale	77	78	74	79	308
Sandy Herd, Huddersfield	73	83	76	77	309
James Braid, Walton Heath	77	79	79	75	310
R Thompson	83	78	77	76	314
A H Scott	77	77	83	77	314

1904 Sandwich

Jack White, Sunningdale	80	75	72	69	296
James Braid, Walton Heath	77	80	69	71	297
J H Taylor, Mid-Surrey	77	78	74	68	297
Tom Vardon, Ilkley	77	77	75	72	301
Harry Vardon, South Herts	76	73	79	74	302
James Sherlock, Stoke Poges	83	71	78	77	309

1905 St Andrews

James Braid, Walton Heath	81	78	78	81	318
J H Taylor, Mid-Surrey	80	85	78	80	323
R Jones, Wimbledon	81	77	87	78	323
J Kinnell, Purley Downs	82	79	82	81	324
Arnaud Massy, La Boulie	81	80	82	82	325
E Gray, Littlehampton	82	81	84	78	325

1906 Muirfield

James Braid, Walton Heath	77	76	74	73	300
J H Taylor, Mid-Surrey	77	72	75	80	304
Harry Vardon, South Herts	77	73	77	78	305
J Graham, Jr, Royal Liverpool	71	79	78	78	306
R Jones, Wimbledon Park	74	78	73	83	308
Arnaud Massy, La Boulie	76	80	76	78	310

1907 Hoylake

Arnaud Massy, La Boulie	76	81	78	77	312
J H Taylor, Mid-Surrey	79	79	76	80	314
Tom Vardon, Sandwich	81	81	80	75	317
G Pulford, Royal Liverpool	81	78	80	78	317
Ted Ray, Ganton	83	80	79	76	318
James Braid, Walton Heath	82	85	75	76	318

1908 Prestwick

James Braid, Walton Heath	70	72	77	72	291
Tom Ball, West Lancashire	76	73	76	74	299
Ted Ray, Ganton	79	71	75	76	301
Sandy Herd, Huddersfield	74	74	79	75	302
Harry Vardon, South Herts	79	78	74	75	306
D Kinnell, Prestwick St Nicholas	75	73	80	78	306

1909 Deal

J H Taylor, Mid-Surrey	74	73	74	74	295
James Braid, Walton Heath	79	73	73	74	299
Tom Ball, West Lancashire	74	75	76	76	301
C Johns, Southdown	72	76	79	75	302
T G Renouf, Manchester	76	78	76	73	303
Ted Ray, Ganton	77	76	76	75	304

1910 St Andrews

James Braid, Walton Heath	76	73	74	76	299

Sandy Herd, Huddersfield	78	74	75	76	303
George Duncan, Hanger Hill	73	77	71	83	304
Laurie Ayton,. Bishops Stortford	78	76	75	77	306
Ted Ray, Ganton	76	77	74	81	308
W Smith, Mexico	77	71	80	80	308
J Robson, West Surrey	75	80	77	76	308

1911 Sandwich

Harry Vardon, South Herts	74	74	75	80	303
Arnaud Massy, St Jean de Lux	75	78	74	76	303

(Play-off; Massy conceded at the 35th hole)

Harold Hilton, Royal Liverpool	76	74	78	76	304
Sandy Herd, Coombe Hill	77	73	76	78	304
Ted Ray, Ganton	76	72	79	78	305
James Braid, Walton Heath	78	75	74	78	305
J H Taylor, Mid-Surrey	72	76	78	79	305

1912 Muirfield

Ted Ray, Oxhey	71	73	76	75	295
Harry Vardon, South Herts	75	72	81	71	299
James Braid, Walton Heath	77	71	77	78	303
George Duncan, Hanger Hill	72	77	78	78	305
Laurie Ayton, Bishops Stortford	74	80	75	79	308
Sandy Herd, Coombe Hill	76	81	76	76	309

1913 Hoylake

J H Taylor, Mid-Surrey	73	75	77	79	304
Ted Ray, Oxhey	73	74	81	84	312
Harry Vardon, South Herts	79	75	79	80	313
M Moran, Dollymount	76	74	89	74	313
Johnny J McDermott, USA	75	80	77	83	315
T G Renouf, Manchester	75	78	84	78	315

1914 Prestwick

Harry Vardon, South Herts	73	77	78	78	306
J H Taylor, Mid-Surrey	74	78	74	83	309
H B Simpson, St Annes Old	77	80	78	75	310
Abe Mitchell, Sonning	76	78	79	79	312
Tom Williamson, Notts	75	79	79	79	312
R G Wilson, Croham Hurst	76	77	80	80	313

1920 Deal

George Duncan, Hanger Hill	80	80	71	72	303
Sandy Herd, Coombe Hill	72	81	77	75	305
Ted Ray, Oxhey	72	83	78	73	306
Abe Mitchell, North Foreland	74	73	84	76	307
Len Holland, Northampton	80	78	71	79	308
Jim Barnes, USA	79	74	77	79	309

1921 St Andrews .

Jock Hutchison, USA	72	75	79	70	296
Roger H Wethered, R and A	78	75	72	71	296

(Hutchison won play-off 150 to 159)

T Kerrigan, USA	74	80	72	72	298
Arthur G Havers, West Lancs	76	74	77	72	299
George Duncan, Hanger Hill	74	75	78	74	301

1922 Sandwich

Walter Hagen, USA	76	73	79	72	300
George Duncan, Hanger Hill	76	75	81	69	301
Jim Barnes, USA	75	76	77	73	301
Jock Hutchison, USA	79	74	73	76	302
Charles A Whitcombe, Dorchester	77	79	72	75	303
J H Taylor, Mid-Surrey	73	78	76	77	304

1923 Troon

Arthur G. Havers, Coombe Hill	73	73	73	76	295
Walter Hagen, USA	76	71	74	75	296
Macdonald Smith, USA	80	73	69	75	297
Joe Kirkwood, Australia	72	79	69	78	298
Tom R Fernie, Turnberry	73	78	74	75	300
George Duncan, Hanger Hill	79	75	74	74	302
Charles A Whitcombe, Landsdowne	70	76	74	82	302

1924 Hoylake

Walter Hagen, USA	77	73	74	77	301
Ernest R Whitcombe, Came Down	77	70	77	78	302
Macdonald Smith, USA	76	74	77	77	304
F Ball, Langley Park	78	75	74	77	304
J H Taylor, Mid-Surrey	75	74	79	79	307
George Duncan, Hanger Hill	74	79	74	81	308
Aubrey Boomer, St Cloud, Paris	75	78	76	79	308

1925 Prestwick

Jim Barnes, USA	70	77	79	74	300
Archie Compston, North Manchester	76	75	75	75	301
Ted Ray, Oxhey	77	76	75	73	301
Macdonald Smith, USA	76	69	76	82	303
Abe Mitchell, Unattached	77	76	75	77	305

1926 Royal Lytham

*Bobby T Jones, Jr, USA	72	72	73	74	291
Al Watrous, USA	71	75	69	78	293
Walter Hagen, USA	68	77	74	76	295
George von Elm, USA	75	72	76	72	295
Abe Mitchell, Unattached	78	78	72	71	299
T Barber, Cavendish	77	73	78	71	299

1927 St Andrews

*Bobby T Jones, Jr, USA	68	72	73	72	285
Aubrey Boomer, St Cloud	76	70	73	72	291
Fred Robson, Cooden Beach	76	72	69	74	291
Joe Kirkwood, Australia	72	72	75	74	293
Ernest R Whitcombe, Bournemouth	74	73	73	73	293
Charles A Whitcombe, Crews Hill	74	76	71	75	296

1928 Sandwich

Walter Hagen, USA	75	73	72	72	292
Gene Sarazen, USA	72	76	73	73	294
Archie Compston, Unattached	75	74	73	73	295
Percy Alliss, Berlin	75	76	75	72	298
Fred Robson, Cooden Beach	79	73	73	73	298
Jose Jurado, Argentina	74	71	76	80	301
Aubrey Boomer, St Cloud	79	73	77	72	301
Jim Barnes, USA	81	73	76	71	301

1929 Muirfield

Walter Hagen, USA	75	67	75	75	292
John Farrell, USA	72	75	76	75	298
Leo Diegel, USA	71	69	82	77	299
Abe Mitchell, St Albans	72	72	78	78	300
Percy Alliss, Berlin	69	76	76	79	300
Bobby Cruickshank, USA	73	74	78	76	301

1930 Hoylake

*Bobby Jones, Jr, USA	70	72	74	75	291
Leo Diegel, USA	74	73	71	75	293
Macdonald Smith, USA	70	77	75	71	293
Fred Robson, Cooden Beach	71	72	78	75	296
Horton Smith, USA	72	73	78	73	296
Archie Compston, Coombe Hill	74	73	68	82	297
Jim Barnes, USA	71	77	72	77	297

1931 Carnoustie

Tommy D Armour, USA	73	75	77	71	296
Jose Jurado, Argentina	76	71	73	77	297
Percy Alliss, Berlin	74	78	73	73	298
Gene Sarazen, USA	74	76	75	73	298
Macdonald Smith, USA	75	77	71	76	299
John Farrell, USA	72	77	75	75	299

1932 Prince's

Gene Sarazen, USA	70	69	70	74	283
Macdonald Smith, USA	71	76	71	70	288
Arthur G Havers, Sandy Lodge	74	71	68	76	289
Charles A Whitcombe, Crews Hill	71	73	73	75	292

Percy Alliss, Beaconsfield	71	71	78	72	292
Alf H Padgham, Royal Ashdown Forest	76	72	74	70	292

1933 St Andrews

Densmore Shute, USA	73	73	73	73	292
Craig Wood, USA	77	72	68	75	292
Sid Easterbrook, Knowle	73	72	71	77	293
Gene Sarazen, USA	72	73	73	75	293
Leo Diegel, USA	75	70	71	77	293
Olin Dutra, USA	76	76	70	72	294

1934 Sandwich

Henry Cotton, Waterloo (Brussels)	67	65	72	79	283
Sid F Brews, Durban (South Africa)	76	71	70	71	288
Alf H Padgham, Sundridge Park	71	70	75	74	290
Macdonald Smith, USA	77	71	72	72	292
Joe Kirkwood, USA	74	69	71	78	292
Marcel Dallemagne, St Germain (France)	71	73	71	77	292

1935 Muirfield

Alf Perry, Leatherhead	69	75	67	72	283
Alf Padgham, Sundridge Park	70	72	74	71	287
Charles Whitcombe, Crews Hill	71	68	73	76	288
Bert Gadd, Brand Hall	72	75	71	71	289
Lawson L Little, Presidio (USA)	75	71	74	69	289
Henry Picard, Hershey (USA)	72	73	72	75	292

1936 Hoylake

Alf H Padgham, Sundridge Park	73	72	71	71	287
Jimmy Adams, Romford	71	73	71	73	288
Henry Cotton, Waterloo (Belgium)	73	72	70	74	289
Marcel Dallemagne, St Germain (France)	73	72	75	69	289
Percy Alliss, Leeds Municipal	74	72	74	71	291
T Green, Burnham Beeches	74	72	70	75	291
Gene Sarazen, USA	73	75	70	73	291

1937 Carnoustie

Henry Cotton, Ashridge	74	72	73	71	290
Reg A Whitcombe, Parkstone	72	70	74	76	292
Charles Lacey, USA	76	75	70	72	293
Charles A Whitcombe, Crews Hill	73	71	74	76	294
Bryon Nelson, USA	75	76	71	74	296
Ed Dudley, USA	70	74	78	75	297

1938 Sandwich

Reg A Whitcombe, Parkstone	71	71	75	78	295
Jimmy Adams Royal, Liverpool	70	71	78	78	297
Henry Cotton, Ashridge	74	73	77	74	298
Alf H Padgham, Sundridge Park	74	72	75	82	303
Jack J Busson, Pannal	71	69	83	80	303
Dick Burton, Sale	71	69	78	85	303
Allan Dailey, Wanstead	73	72	80	78	303

1939 St Andrews

Dick Burton, Sale	70	72	77	71	290
Johnny Bulla, Chicago	77	71	71	73	292
Johnny Fallon, Huddersfield	71	73	71	79	294
Bill Shankland, Templenewsam	72	73	72	77	294
Alf Perry, Leatherhead	71	74	73	76	294
Reg A Whitcombe, Parkstone	71	75	74	74	294
Sam L King, Knole Park	74	72	75	73	294

1946 St Andrews

Sam Snead, USA	71	70	74	75	290
Bobby Locke, South Africa	69	74	75	76	294
Johnny Bulla, USA	71	72	72	79	294
Charlie H Ward, Little Aston	73	73	73	76	295
Henry Cotton, Royal Mid-Surrey	70	70	76	79	295
Dai J Rees, Hindhead	75	67	73	80	295
Norman von Nida, Australia	70	76	74	75	295

1947 Hoylake

Fred Daly, Balmoral (Belfast)	73	70	78	72	293
Reg W Horne, Hendon	77	74	72	71	294
Frank R Stranahan, USA	71	79	72	72	294
Bill Shankland, Templenewsam	76	74	75	70	295
Dick Burton, Coombe Hill	77	71	77	71	296
Charlie Ward, Little Aston	76	73	76	72	297
Sam L King, Wildernesse	75	72	77	73	297
Arthur Lees, Dore and Totley	75	74	72	76	297
Johnny Bulla, USA	80	72	74	71	297
Henry Cotton, Royal Mid-Surrey	69	78	74	76	297
Norman von Nida, Australia	74	76	71	76	297

1948 Muirfield

Henry Cotton, Royal Mid-Surrey	71	66	75	72	284
Fred Daly, Balmoral	72	71	73	73	289
Norman G von Nida, Australia	71	72	76	71	290
Roberto de Vicenzo, Argentina	70	73	72	75	290
Jack Hargreaves, Sutton Coldfield	76	68	73	73	290
Charlie Ward, Little Aston	69	72	75	74	290

1949 Sandwich

Bobby Locke, South Africa	69	76	68	70	283
Harry Bradshaw, Kilcroney (Eire)	68	77	68	70	283
(Locke won play-off 135 to 147)					
Roberto de Vicenzo, Argentina	68	75	73	69	285
Sam King, Knole Park	71	69	74	72	286
Charlie Ward, Little Aston	73	71	70	72	286
Arthur Lees, Dore and Totley	74	70	72	71	287
Max Faulkner, Royal Mid-Surrey	71	71	71	74	287

1950 Troon

Bobby Locke, South Africa	69	72	70	68	279
Roberto de Vicenzo, Argentina	72	71	68	70	281
Fred Daly, Balmoral, Belfast	75	72	69	66	282
Dai J Rees, South Herts	71	68	72	71	282
E Moore, South Africa	74	68	73	68	283
Max Faulkner, Royal Mid-Surrey	72	70	70	71	283

1951 Royal Portrush

Max Faulkner, Unattached	71	70	70	74	285
Tony Cerda, Argentina	74	72	71	70	287
Charlie Ward, Little Aston	75	73	74	68	290
Fred Daly, Balmoral	74	70	75	73	292
Jimmy Adams, Wentworth	68	77	75	72	292
Bobby Locke, South Africa	71	74	74	74	293
Bill Shankland, Templenewsam	73	76	72	72	293
Norman Sutton, Leigh	73	70	74	76	293
Harry Weetman, Croham Hurst	73	71	75	74	293
Peter W Thomson, Australia	70	75	73	75	293

1952 Royal Lytham

Bobby Locke, South Africa	69	71	74	73	287
Peter W Thomson, Australia	68	73	77	70	288
Fred Daly, Balmoral	67	69	77	76	289
Henry Cotton, Royal Mid-Surrey	75	74	74	71	294
Tony Cerda, Argentina	73	73	76	73	295
Sam L King, Knole Park	71	74	74	76	295

1953 Carnoustie

Ben Hogan, USA	73	71	70	68	282
*Frank R Stranahan, USA	70	74	73	69	286
Dai J Rees, South Herts	72	70	73	71	286
Peter W Thompson, Australia	72	72	71	71	286
Tony Cerda, Argentina	75	71	69	71	286
Roberto de Vicenzo, Argentina	72	71	71	73	287

1954 Royal Birkdale

Peter W Thomson, Australia	72	71	69	71	283
Sid S Scott, Carlisle City	76	67	69	72	284
Dai J Rees, South Herts	72	71	69	72	284
Bobby Locke, South Africa	74	71	69	70	284

Jimmy Adams, Royal Mid-Surrey	73	75	69	69	286
Tony Cerda, Argentina	71	71	73	71	286
J Turnesa, USA	72	72	71	71	286

1955 St Andrews

Peter W Thomson, Australia	71	68	70	72	281
Johnny Fallon, Huddersfield	73	67	73	70	283
Frank Jowle, Edgbaston	70	71	69	74	284
Bobby Locke, South Africa	74	69	70	72	285
Tony Cerda, Argentina	73	71	71	71	286
Ken Bousfield, Coombe Hill	71	75	70	70	286
Harry Weetman, Croham Hurst	71	71	70	74	286
Bernard J Hunt, Hartsbourne	70	71	74	71	286
Flory van Donck, Belgium	71	72	71	72	286

1956 Hoylake

Peter W Thomson, Australia	70	70	72	74	286
Flory van Donck, Belgium	71	74	70	74	289
Roberto de Vicenzo, Mexico	71	70	79	70	290
Gary Player, South Africa	71	76	73	71	291
John Panton, Glenbervie	74	76	72	70	292
Henry Cotton, Temple	72	76	71	74	293
E Bertolino, Argentina	69	72	76	76	293

1957 St Andrews

Bobby Locke, South Africa	69	72	68	70	279
Peter W Thomson, Australia	73	69	70	70	282
Eric C Brown, Buchanan Castle	67	72	73	71	283
Angel Miguel, Spain	72	72	69	72	285
David C Thomas, Sudbury	72	74	70	70	286
Tom B Haliburton, Wentworth	72	73	68	73	286
*Dick W Smith, Prestwick	71	72	72	71	286
Flory van Donck, Belgium	72	68	74	72	286

1958 Royal Lytham

Peter W Thomson, Australia	66	72	67	73	278
David C Thomas, Sudbury	70	68	69	71	278
(Thomson won play-off 139 to 143)					
Eric C Brown, Buchanan Castle	73	70	65	71	279
Christy O'Connor, Killarney	67	68	73	71	279
Flory van Donck, Belgium	70	70	67	74	281
Leopoldo Ruiz, Argentina	71	65	72	73	281

1959 Muirfield

Gary Player, South Africa	75	71	70	68	284
Flory van Donck, Belgium	70	70	73	73	286
Fred Bullock, Prestwick St Ninians	68	70	74	74	286
Sid S Scott, Roehampton	73	70	73	71	287
Christy O'Connor, Royal Dublin	73	74	72	69	288
*Reid R Jack, Dullatur	71	75	68	74	288
Sam L King, Knole Park	70	74	68	76	288
John Panton, Glenbervie	72	72	71	73	288

1960 St Andrews

Kel D G Nagle, Australia	69	67	71	71	278
Arnold Palmer, USA	70	71	70	68	279
Bernard J Hunt, Hartsbourne	72	73	71	66	282
Harold R Henning, South Africa	72	72	69	69	282
Roberto de Vicenzo, Argentina	67	67	75	73	282
*Guy B Wolstenholme, Sunningdale	74	70	71	68	283

1961 Royal Birkdale

Arnold Palmer, USA	70	73	69	72	284
Dai J Rees, South Herts	68	74	71	72	285
Christy O'Connor, Royal Dublin	71	77	67	73	288
Neil C Coles, Coombe Hill	70	77	69	72	288
Eric C Brown, Unattached	73	76	70	70	289
Kel D G Nagle, Australia	68	75	75	71	289

1962 Troon

Arnold Palmer, USA	71	69	67	69	276
Kel D G Nagle, Australia	71	71	70	70	282
Brian Huggett, Romford	75	71	74	69	289

Phil Rodgers, USA	75	70	72	72	289
Bob Charles, NZ	75	70	70	75	290
Sam Snead, USA	76	73	72	71	292
Peter W Thomson, Australia	70	77	75	70	292

1963 Royal Lytham

Bob Charles, NZ	68	72	66	71	277
Phil Rodgers, USA	67	68	73	69	277
(Charles won play-off 140 to 148)					
Jack Nicklaus, USA	71	67	70	70	278
Kel D G Nagle, Australia	69	70	73	71	283
Peter W Thomson, Australia	67	69	71	78	285
Christy O'Connor, Royal Dublin	74	68	76	68	286

1964 St Andrews

Tony Lema, USA	73	68	68	70	279
Jack Nicklaus, USA	76	74	66	68	284
Roberto de Vicenzo, Argentina	76	72	70	67	285
Bernard J Hunt, Hartsbourne	73	74	70	70	287
Bruce Devlin, Australia	72	72	73	73	290
Christy O'Connor, Royal Dublin	71	73	74	73	291
Harry Weetman, Selsdon Park	72	71	75	73	291

1965 Royal Birkdale

Peter W Thomson, Australia	74	68	72	71	285
Christy O'Connor, Royal Dublin	69	73	74	71	287
Brian Huggett, Romford	73	68	76	70	287
Roberto de Vicenzo, Argentina	74	69	73	72	288
Kel D G Nagle, Australia	74	70	73	72	289
Tony Lema, USA	68	72	75	74	289
Bernard J Hunt, Hartsbourne	74	74	70	71	289

1966 Muirfield

Jack Nicklaus, USA	70	67	75	70	282
David C Thomas, Dunham Forest	72	73	69	69	283
Doug Sanders, USA	71	70	72	70	283
Gary Player, South Africa	72	74	71	69	286
Bruce Devlin, Australia	73	69	74	70	286
Kel D G Nagle, Australia	72	68	76	70	286
Phil Rodgers, USA	74	66	70	76	286

1967 Hoylake

Roberto de Vicenzo, Argentina	70	71	67	70	278
Jack Nicklaus, USA	71	69	71	69	280
Clive A Clark, Sunningdale	70	73	69	72	284
Gary Player, South Africa	72	71	67	74	284
Tony Jacklin, Potters Bar	73	69	73	70	285
Sebastian Miguel, Spain	72	74	68	72	286
Harold Henning, South Africa	74	70	71	71	286

1968 Carnoustie

Gary Player, South Africa	74	71	71	73	289
Jack Nicklaus, USA	76	69	73	73	291
Bob J Charles, NZ	72	72	71	76	291
Billy Casper, USA	72	68	74	78	292
Maurice Bembridge, Little Aston	71	75	73	74	293
Brian Barnes, Burnham & Berrow	70	74	80	71	295
Neil C Coles, Coombe Hill	75	76	71	73	295
Gay Brewer, USA	74	73	72	76	295

1969 Royal Lytham

Tony Jacklin, Potters Bar	68	70	70	72	280
Bob J Charles, NZ	66	69	75	72	282
Peter W Thomson, Australia	71	70	70	72	283
Roberto de Vicenzo, Argentina	72	73	66	72	283
Christy O'Connor, Royal Dublin	71	65	74	74	284
Jack Nicklaus, USA	75	70	68	72	285
Denis M Love, Jr, USA	70	73	71	71	285

1970 St Andrews

Jack Nicklaus, USA	68	69	73	73	283
Doug Sanders, USA	68	71	71	73	283
(Nicklaus won play-off 72 to 73)					

Harold Henning, South Africa | 67 72 73 73 285
Lee Trevino, USA | 68 68 72 77 285
Tony Jacklin, Potters Bar | 67 70 73 76 286
Neil C Coles, Coombe Hill | 65 74 72 76 287
Peter A Oosterhuis, Dulwich and Sydenham
      73 69 69 76 287

1971 Royal Birkdale

Lee Trevino, USA | 69 70 69 70 278
Lu Liang Huan, Taiwan | 70 70 69 70 279
Tony Jacklin, Potters Bar | 69 70 70 71 280
Craig de Foy, Coombe Hill | 72 72 68 69 281
Jack Nicklaus, USA | 71 71 72 69 283
Charles Coody, USA | 74 71 70 68 283

1972 Muirfield

Lee Trevino, USA | 71 70 66 71 278
Jack Nicklaus, USA | 70 72 71 66 279
Tony Jacklin, Potters Bar | 69 72 67 72 280
Doug Sanders, USA | 71 71 69 70 281
Brian W Barnes, Fairway DR | 71 72 69 71 283
Gary Player, South Africa | 71 71 76 67 285

1973 Troon

Tom Weiskopf, USA | 68 67 71 70 276
Neil C Coles, Holiday Inns | 71 72 70 66 279
Johnny Miller, USA | 70 68 69 72 279
Jack Nicklaus, USA | 69 70 76 65 280
Bert Yancey, USA | 69 69 73 70 281
Peter J Butler, Golf Domes | 71 72 74 69 286

1974 Royal Lytham

Gary Player, South Africa | 69 68 75 70 282
Peter Oosterhuis, Pacific Harbour | 71 71 73 71 286
Jack Nicklaus, USA | 74 72 70 71 287
Hubert M Green, USA | 71 74 72 71 288
Danny Edwards, USA | 70 73 76 73 292
Lu Liang Huan, Taiwan | 72 72 75 73 292

1975 Carnoustie

Tom Watson, USA | 71 67 69 72 279
Jack Newton, Australia | 69 71 65 74 279
(Watson won play-off 71 to 72)
Bobby Cole, South Africa | 72 66 66 76 280

Jack Nicklaus, USA | 69 71 68 72 280
Johnny Miller, USA | 71 69 66 74 280
Graham Marsh, Australia | 72 67 71 71 281

1976 Birkdale

Johnny Miller, USA | 72 68 73 66 279
Jack Nicklaus, USA | 74 70 72 69 285
Severiano Ballesteros, Spain | 69 69 73 74 285
Raymond Floyd, USA | 76 67 73 70 286
Mark James, Burghley Park | 76 72 74 66 288
Hubert Green, USA | 72 70 78 68 288
Christy O'Connor, Jr, Shannon | 69 73 75 71 288
Tom Kite, USA | 70 74 73 71 288
Tommy A Horton, Royal Jersey | 74 69 72 73 288

1977 Turnberry

Tom Watson, USA | 68 70 65 65 268
Jack Nicklaus, USA | 68 70 65 66 269
Hubert Green, USA | 72 66 74 67 279
Lee Trevino, USA | 68 70 72 70 280
Ben Crenshaw, USA | 71 69 66 75 281
George Burns, USA | 70 70 72 69 281

1978 St Andrews

Jack Nicklaus, USA | 71 72 69 69 281
Simon Owen, New Zealand | 70 75 67 71 283
Ben Crenshaw, USA | 70 69 73 71 283
Raymond Floyd, USA | 69 75 71 68 283
Tom Kite, USA | 72 69 72 70 283
Peter Oosterhuis, GB | 72 70 69 73 284

1979 Royal Lytham

Severiano Ballesteros, Spain | 73 65 75 70 283
Jack Nicklaus, USA | 72 69 73 72 286
Ben Crenshaw, USA | 72 71 72 71 286
Mark James, Burghley Park | 76 69 69 73 287
Rodger Davis, Australia | 75 70 70 73 288
Hale Irwin, USA | 68 68 75 78 289

1980 Muirfield

Tom Watson, USA | 68 70 64 69 271
Lee Trevino, USA | 68 67 71 69 275
Ben Crenshaw, USA | 70 70 68 69 277
Jack Nicklaus, USA | 73 67 71 69 280
Carl Mason, USA, unattached | 72 69 70 69 280
*Amateur

US OPEN

First played 1895

The United States Open and the British Open championships are the two most important in the world. Although junior by 35 years and dominated in its early stages by the British professionals who settled in America, the US Open soon reached its exalted position because it is the title which American golfers covet most.

This is primarily for prestige, but increasingly because of the benefits which accrue from being champion. The championship has always been run by the United States Golf Association whose organisation has kept pace with the development of championship golf. The modern entry of about 4500 has to be whittled down to more manageable proportions and then assembled at the appointed club where arrangements are made two or three years ahead.

The preparation of the course itself has become a matter of almost scientific detail: the fairways cut to the nearest millimetre; the rough grown to deter much in the way of a recovery and the greens geared to speed and treachery.

Frequently there are complaints that these things are overdone but, unlike the British Open which has been confined to 14 courses since 1860, the US Open has been housed at 47 clubs since 1895 when it was launched on a 9-hole course at Newport, Rhode Island.

It has been suggested that the USGA develop a smaller rota of championship courses but, with such a big country, they rightly feel a responsibility to move it around and the idea has never really caught on. New courses of quality are always in the making and of the last twelve US Opens four courses were played for the first time. These included the Atlanta Athletic Club in 1976, the first time the US Open had been held in the South.

So the mixture has become many of the old, traditional favourites and several new creations. It is a mixture that is readily acceptable, but there is a feeling that some over-preparation of courses has led to one or two surprising winners in recent years.

MILESTONES

1895 First Open held at Newport, Rhode Island, on 4 October, during the same week and on the same 9-hole course as the first United States Amateur championship. The championships were arranged for September but postponed because of a clash with the America's Cup yacht races.

There were five money prizes of $150, $100, $50, $25 and $10. Ten professionals and one amateur took part, the winner being Horace Rawlins, an English professional, with a score of 173 (91,82).

1896 Second Open held at Shinnecock Hills on Long Island. Thirty-five players took part but it was again a sideshow to the US Amateur. The course measured only 4423 yd (4044 m), the shortest in US Open history. Jim Foulis, a Scottish professional, became champion with 152 (78,74). His 74 was not beaten for seven years and never with a gutty ball.

1898 The Open and Amateur championships were played separately and on different courses. The championship was also extended to 72 holes. The Open, won by Fred Herd, was held at the Myopia Hunt Club, a 9-hole course in those days.

First golfer to win four US Opens—Willie Anderson (US Golf Association)

1899 Willie Smith's winning margin was 11 strokes, one which has never been equalled. Total purse increased to $650.

1900 The title went abroad for the first time although earlier winners had all been British. Harry Vardon beat J H Taylor by 2 strokes, his total of 313 including a stroke on the final green when he stabbed carelessly at the ball on a short putt and missed altogether.

1901 First play-off. Willie Anderson, the winner, and Alex Smith tied.

1902 The new champion, Laurie Auchterlonie, became the first man to break 80 in all four rounds. This feat was said to owe a lot to the new Haskell rubber-cored ball.

New record entry of 90, prize-money totalling $970.

1903 Willie Anderson became first man to win twice. His first round of 73 was a new low, but he needed another play-off before defeating David Brown with 82 to 84.

1904 Willie Anderson won twice in succession, his third win in all, but his first without a play-off. His 72 in the last round beat his own low round record.

1905 Willie Anderson set a record of three wins in a row, one which has never been equalled. His total of four victories was not equalled for 25 years, Bobby Jones's feat being later equalled by Ben Hogan and Jack Nicklaus.

1906 Anderson's run ended by Alex Smith whose total of 295 was the lowest to date in either the US Open or the British Open. The total purse was $900 and the first prize $300.

1908 Fred McLeod, only 108 lb (48.9 kg), was the smallest winner ever. The championship marked the Myopia Hunt Club's last year as host.

1909 First round under 70. Dave Hunter had 68 in the opening round, Tom McNamara 69 in the second. George Sargent's 290 set record low aggregate.

1910 First three-way play-off, the participants being Alex Smith (the winner), Johnny McDermott and Smith's brother, Macdonald.

1911 Johnny McDermott became America's first home-bred champion.

1912 McDermott's second win. Tom McNamara had new final round record of 69 but McDermott was the first to be under par for the four rounds in total. Use of par adopted.

1913 The Open which changed the course of history. It ended British playing dominance. Story-book victory for Francis Ouimet, a 20-year-old coachman's son living across the street from the Country Club, Brookline. Ouimet defeated Harry Vardon and Ted Ray, the highly experienced English professionals, in a play-off. First victory by an amateur.

A total of 165 entries required the first qualifying round to be played. Half the field played two rounds on Tuesday and the other half two rounds on Wednesday, the low 32 and ties on each day making up the championship field on Thursday and Friday.

1914 Walter Hagen led every round and recorded his first victory at Midlothian CC. Chick Evans, needing 2 to tie on the last hole, hit the cup with his pitch and bounced out.

1915 Jerome Travers became the second amateur to win. He played the last 6 holes in 1 under par to beat Tom McNamara by one stroke.

1916 The crown taken over by another amateur, Chick Evans (1890–1979) the only time amateurs have won back to back. Evans was the third amateur winner in four years. His total of 286 meant he was the second man to beat par; it was a total which was not beaten for 20 years. Jock Hutchison's closing 68 bettered the low final round record. Evans won US Amateur three months later, the first man to win both titles the same year.

Prize-money increased to $1200 with $500 for leading professional.

1917–18 No championships.

1919 Hagen's second victory. He played the last 6 holes in 1 under 4s to tie Mike Brady and then beat him in a play-off, marked by several controversies over the Rules.

Willie Chisholm took 18 on the 185 yd (169 m) 8th hole at Brae Burn in the first round.

Total prize-money $1745 with prizes for twelve players. Play extended to three days, one round on each of the first two days and two rounds on the final day.

1920 Second victory by an Englishman and the last for 50 years. Ted Ray was the winner, Harry Vardon playing the last 7 holes in a gale at Inverness in level fives having led by five. Ray remains oldest winner at 43.

Bobby Jones's first appearance at 18. Tied eighth.

Two-day playing format restored; record entry of 265. Also first time anywhere in a major championship and the professionals were allowed to use the full clubhouse facilities.

1921 The 25th championship won by Jim Barnes. Led after every round and won by 9 strokes. Trophy presented by President of the United States, Warren G Harding.

1922 Victory for Gene Sarazen, aged 20. Finished with a birdie for a 68 and a 1-stroke victory. First winner to break 70 in last round.

Friends, rivals and great contemporaries—Gene Sarazen and Walter Hagen (BBC Hulton Pic. Lib.)

Record entry of 323, the qualifying at the scene of the championship being extended to three days.

Gate money charged for the first time.

1923 Dawn of the Bobby Jones era. Victory after a play-off with Bobby Cruickshank. On the 72nd hole, Jones had a 6 and Cruickshank a birdie.

Record entry of 360.

1924 First elements of sectional qualifying introduced. Use of the steel-shafted putter allowed for first time. Victory for American-based Englishman Cyril Walker.

1925 Bobby Jones beaten in play-off by Willie Macfarlane; or rather after two play-offs, the first having ended even. Macfarlane, a Scotsman, representing Oak Ridge, was the first US Open champion who wore spectacles. His second round of 67 was a new low.

1926 Bobby Jones became first person to win British and US Opens in the same year.

Championship again extended to three days. Record entry of 694. Prize-money increased to $2145, the first 20 professionals winning money.

1927 Tommy Armour defeated Harry Cooper in a play-off, Armour holing a 10-ft (3-m) birdie

putt on the 72nd green and Cooper taking 3 putts.

Record entry of 898.

1928 Johnny Farrell defeated Bobby Jones in the first play-off over 36 holes. It was Jones's second play-off defeat in four years.

Entry over 1000 for the first time.

1929 Bobby Jones defeated Al Espinosa in a play-off despite having two 7s in his final round and then holing a 12-ft (3·6-m) putt to tie.

Third play-off in a row.

Prize-money $5000, the leading professional prize $1000.

1930 Third leg of Bobby Jones's Grand Slam. His third-round 68 at Merion was his lowest in the Open and his total of 287 marking only the third time that par has been broken over four rounds.

Entry of 1177 and the championship the last to be played with the 1·62-in (41·14-mm) ball.

1931 Longest championship on record, a 72-hole play-off (36 holes twice) being necessary to separate Billy Burke, the winner, and George von Elm.

1932 Gene Sarazen added the US title to his British title but played the last 28 holes in 100 strokes in order to do so. On the 9th tee of the

Perfect balance of Bobby Jones

First appearance of Ben Hogan who failed to qualify for last 36 holes.

1937 Manero's record broken by Ralph Guldahl with 281. He beat Sam Snead, playing his first Open, by 2 strokes. In all, five players were under par for the four rounds.

1938 Guldahl became fourth player to win in successive years, but a new record for a single hole was also set. Ray Ainsley who became a hero overnight took 19 on the par-4 16th at Cherry Hills in the second round. Most of these were taken in a swift-moving creek bordering the green. When finally he did get it out a little girl turned to her mother and said, 'Mummy, it must be dead now because the man has quit hitting at it'. Prize-money increased to $6000.

1939 Byron Nelson's year, but only after a three-way play-off and Sam Snead had come to the 72nd hole at the Philadelphia CC needing as it transpired later a par-5 to win. He took 8 and finished fifth but he was out early and might have adopted different tactics had he not been enthusiastic to set a hot pace. In the play-off, Densmore Shute was eliminated after 18 holes, but Nelson and Craig Wood, who both had 68s, had to play a second 18 holes, Nelson winning with a 70 to Wood's 73. At the 4th hole of the

Ralph Guldahl (US Golf Association)

third round, he was 7 strokes behind the leader. His total of 286 equalled that set by Chick Evans in 1916, and his final round of 66 broke the individual record for any round as well as the lowest finishing round by a winner.

1933 Victory for Johnny Goodman, the fifth and last amateur to win.

1934 The winner, Olin Dutra, made up an 8-stroke deficit over the last two rounds, a record matched by Arnold Palmer in 1960.

1935 Victory for unknown Sam Parks. None of the 20 leaders broke 75 in the final round at Oakmont.

1936 Final round of 67 gave Tony Manero a new record total of 282.

second play-off, Nelson holed a full 1 iron for an eagle 2.

1940 Gene Sarazen made a bid to win the title 18 years after his first victory, but he lost a play-off to Lawson Little.

Six players were disqualified for starting their final round ahead of their starting time in an attempt to beat an impending storm. One of them, Ed Oliver, made an 'unofficial' total of 287, the same as Little and Sarazen.

1941 Craig Wood won with 284. He considered withdrawing before the championship with a back injury which necessitated wearing a corset.

1942–45 No championships.

1946 Another three-way tie, war hero Lloyd Mangrum defeating Byron Nelson and Vic Ghezzi in a play-off. All three tied the first play-off with 72s but, surviving a thunderstorm, Mangrum, 3 behind Ghezzi and 2 behind Nelson with 6 holes left, won with 72 to two 73s.

Prize-money increased to $8000; first prize $1500.

1947 Victory for Lew Worsham, but another of Sam Snead's near misses. Having holed an 18-ft (5·5-m) putt to earn a tie, he missed from less than a yard on the 18th green of the play-off after Worsham had interrupted him to ask for a measurement.

James B McHale, an amateur, set new low round record, a 65 in the third round.

Prize-money $10 000. First prize $2000.

1948 Ben Hogan's first victory with record score of 278.

Record entry of 1411.

1949 Victory for Cary Middlecoff. Hogan unable to compete after his terrible car accident.

1950 Ben Hogan achieved a 'miracle' victory in the 50th championship. Still walking with great

Ben Hogan on one of only two visits to Britain (Action Photos)

Cary Middlecoff (US Golf Association)

discomfort after his near-fatal accident, he tied with Lloyd Mangrum and George Fazio on 287 and won the play-off with a superb 69 to Mangrum's 73 and Fazio's 75. Trailing the play-off by one stroke with 3 holes to play, Mangrum was penalised 2 strokes for picking up his ball to blow off a fly.

Prize-money $15 000. First prize $4000. Every professional who completed 72 holes received $100.

1951 Back-to-back win for Ben Hogan at Oakland Hills. The presentation of the course and its remodelling were the subject of much controversy and only Hogan and Clayton Heafner broke the par of 70 in the last round, but Hogan's 67 is generally regarded as one of

Ed Furgol, the man who overcame a remarkable physical disability to win the 1954 US Open (Action Photos)

1955 Ben Hogan's record-breaking fifth Open foiled by Jack Fleck, a municipal course professional from Iowa. Fleck made two birdies at the last 2 holes to tie Hogan and then, almost as incredibly, beat him in a play-off. One of the classic examples of David slaying Goliath.
1957 Prize-money $30 000. First prize $7200.
1958 Entry of 2132 from which Tommy Bolt emerged as winner. Sam Snead failed to qualify for final 36 holes, the first time in 18 Opens.
1959 Billy Casper triumphed with a hot putting streak. Thunderstorms struck in the third round and the final round was postponed a day for the first time. Attendance 43 377; entry 2385. Prize-money $49 200. First prize $12 000.
1960 Arnold Palmer made record comeback to win. Trailed by 7 strokes after 54 holes. Had 6 birdies in first 7 holes of final round. His 65 was the lowest ever (at the time) in the fourth round by a winner; his 30 for the first 9 tied the record held by James McHale.

Jack Nicklaus recorded the lowest aggregate (282) ever returned by an amateur. He finished second. Ben Hogan lost in what proved to be his last good chance of a fifth victory.

Billy Casper, US Open champion 1959 and 1966 (Action Photos)

his greatest single rounds. He did the last 9 in 32 on a course of which he said, 'I vowed I'd bring this monster to its knees.'

Entry 1511.
1952 Won by Julius Boros who had been a professional for less than three years.
Entry 1688.
1953 Fourth victory for Ben Hogan, equalling the record of Willie Anderson and Bobby Jones. Led after every round, his 283 at Oakmont beating Sam Snead, runner-up for the fourth time, by 6 strokes. His four victories came in the space of only six years, a supremacy not matched by Jones. Hogan was the first to hold the lead throughout since 1921, and the margin was the widest for 15 years. However, there were only two rounds under 70, Hogan's first round and Snead's second.
Prize-money $20 400. First prize $5000.
1954 Amazing victory by Ed Furgol who shattered his left elbow, leaving his arm withered and crooked at the elbow. He scored 284, 1 stroke better than Gene Littler.

Open televised for the first time. Record entry of 1928; record crowd of 39 600 and record prize-money of $23 280 with a first prize of $6000.

Simplicity of style—Gene Littler (Frank Gardner)

Art Wall set a qualifying record with 63, 65 (128) at Twin Hills CC, Oklahoma.

Entry 2453. Prize-money $60 720. First prize $14 400.

1961 Gene Littler's victory at Oakland Hills made him the eighth player to win the US Open and US Amateur.

Ben Hogan failed to finish in first ten for first time since 1940. He did not play in 1949 and 1957. Four former champions: Boros, Middlecoff, Worsham and Furgol failed to make the 36-hole cut.

1962 Beginning of the professional reign of Jack Nicklaus. He beat Arnold Palmer at Oakmont in a play-off.

Attendance 62 300. Prize-money $73 800.

1963 Return to the Country Club, Brookline, for first time since 1913. Julius Boros won,

defeating Arnold Palmer and Jacky Cupit in a play-off. Severe playing conditions, but Boros became oldest American to win, eleven years after his first victory.

Defending champion Jack Nicklaus failed to qualify and, for the first time, no amateur survived the 36-hole cut.

1964 Dramatic emergence from a dramatic slump by the winner, Ken Venturi, who survived a position of near exhaustion to win at Congressional CC, Washington, DC. It was the last year that two rounds were played on the final day. Six strokes behind after 36 holes, Venturi turned in a first half of 30 in a third round of 66. He needed a doctor's examination before continuing, but overhauled the 54-hole leader Tommy Jacobs and, walking with difficulty, parred the last 4 holes to finish four ahead of Jacobs. Jacobs had a second round of 64 which tied the lowest recorded at that time.

Studying the line—Tony Jacklin (Action Photos)

1965 Gary Player's victory after a tie with Kel Nagle, was the first by an overseas player since 1920. He was the first champion who was neither American nor British and he gave $25 000 of his $26 000 first prize to the USGA, $5000 for cancer relief work and $20 000 to promote junior golf.

Defending champion, Ken Venturi, with ailing hands, failed to qualify for the final 36 holes.

Attendance 72 052. Prize-money $123 890.

For the first time the 72 holes were spread over four days.

1966 Another dramatic finish at Olympic CC, San Francisco. Arnold Palmer, 7 strokes ahead of Billy Casper, was caught by Casper and beaten next day in a play-off.

A relatively unknown professional Rives McBee equalled the single-round scoring record with a second-round 64.

Prize-money $147 490.

1967 New Open scoring record of 275 by Jack Nicklaus at Baltusrol. It beat Hogan's 276 in 1948.

Attendance 88 414. Entry 2649.

1968 Lee Trevino played four rounds under par and equalled Nicklaus's aggregate of 275 by winning at Oak Hills CC, Rochester. First man to be under par in all four rounds, and in the 60s.

Bert Yancey tied the record of 135 for the first 36 holes. A third-round 70 for 205 broke the 54-hole record, but he was only 1 stroke better than Trevino who had a final 69 to win by 4 strokes.

Entry 3007. Prize-money $188 800.

1969 Orville Moody, until 1967 a sergeant in the Army, became champion at the Champions Club, Houston in only his second Open.

For the second time no amateur made the 36-hole cut.

Entry 3397. Prize-money $205 300.

1970 Tony Jacklin, the only player to beat par, became the first English winner since Ted Ray in 1920. He led after every round and his winning margin of 7 strokes was the biggest since Jim Barnes won by 9 in 1921.

The championship was notable for first rounds of 79, 80 and 81 by Arnold Palmer, Gary Player and Jack Nicklaus. Nicklaus's 81 being his worst Open round by 3 strokes. The week was also notable for the criticism of the course by runner-up Dave Hill who was later fined for his remarks.

Orville Moody failed to qualify for the final two rounds, the fifth defending champion in eight years to fail.

Hazeltine was the second longest course ever to house a USGA championship.

1971 Lee Trevino's second victory earned after a play-off in which Jack Nicklaus twice left shots in bunkers.

A 21-year-old amateur, Jim Simons, needed a birdie on the 72nd hole to tie Trevino and Nicklaus, but took 6, his total of 283 being 1 off Nicklaus's record aggregate for an amateur. His third-round 65, however, tied the record for the lowest individual round by an amateur.

Got it! Lee Trevino (Action Photos)

Defending champion, Tony Jacklin, failed to make the cut, the sixth champion to fail in nine years.

It was Merion's 13th USGA event—a record.

1972 Jack Nicklaus won his third US Open, leading or tying for the lead throughout. It was Pebble Beach's first Open. Nicklaus won the 1961 US Amateur, also at Pebble Beach.

Only 48 of the 150 starters broke 80 on both the first two days and only 40 rounds beat the par of 72 by the 70 contestants who played all four rounds.

Jerry McGee holed in one at the 8th on the third day, the first hole in one in the Open since 1956. Bobby Mitchell repeated the feat at the same hole next day.

Entry 4196. Prize-money $202 400.

1973 Johnny Miller broke the record for the lowest individual round and the lowest finishing round. His 63 gave him a total of 279, the lowest in five Opens at Oakmont, and victory by 1 stroke. Miller, starting his last round an hour

ahead of the leaders, made up 4 strokes on John Schlee and then went ahead.

It was Sam Snead's third Open at Oakmont and he played through his 27th Open, breaking a record he shared with Gene Sarazen.

Entry 3580. Prize-money $219 400.

1974 On a Winged Foot course which proved very difficult Hale Irwin, the second bespectacled champion, beat Forrest Fezler by 2 strokes.

Only 23 out of 150 players scored lower than 75 on the first day.

Entry 3914. Prize-money $227 000.

1975 The 25th play-off in Open history brought victory for Lou Graham over John Mahaffey; a championship in which play in the second round was interrupted by an electrical storm.

Johnny Miller who played the lowest single round in the history of the US Open at Oakmont, 1973 (Action Photos)

Entry 4214. Attendance 97 345 plus 6246 for the play-off. Prize-money $235 700. First Prize $40 000.

1976 A championship at the Atlanta Athletic Club, the first to be held in the South, in which four players had a chance of victory on the 72nd hole. Jerry Pate, who birdied the hole by hitting a 5 iron across water to 3 ft (0·90 m), was 1 stroke in front of John Mahaffey, Al Geiberger and Tom Weiskopf on the tee. His birdie was unanswerable as Mahaffey hit his second into the water and Weiskopf and Geiberger, having driven poorly, played short.

Attendance 113 084. Entry 4436.

1977 Hubert Green became champion at Southern Hills, Tulsa despite a threat to his life. This was conveyed to him by USGA officials during the last round, but he decided to play on and eventually holed from 3 ft (0·90 m) to beat Lou Graham.

A record seven players tied the first-round lead. Twelve players were within 2 strokes of the lead as the last round began.

Entry 4726. Prize-money $284 990.

1978 Andy North beat Dave Stockton and J C Snead by one stroke at Cherry Hills, but nobody beat par for the championship. North returned a 1 over par 285.

1979 Second victory for Hale Irwin. At Inverness, Toledo he won by 2 strokes with a final round of 75, the highest last round by a champion since 1949. Not since 1935 had there been anything higher, a 76.

Gary Player finished tied second with a final round of 68, his highest position since he won in 1965. Jack Nicklaus also finished with a 68, but only made the cut by 1 stroke. Tom Watson, the leading money-winner at the time, failed to make the cut.

Prize-money $330 400.

DETAILED RECORDS

Most victories
4, Willie Anderson, 1901-03-04-05
Bobby Jones, 1923-26-29-30
Ben Hogan, 1948-50-51-53
Jack Nicklaus, 1962-67-72-80

Most times runner-up or joint runner-up
4, Sam Snead, 1937-47-49-53
Bobby Jones 1922-24-25-28
Arnold Palmer 1962-63-66-67

Oldest winner
Ted Ray, 43 years 4 months 16 days, 1920
Julius Boros, 43 years 3 months 20 days, 1963

Youngest winner
John J McDermott, 19 years 10 months 14 days, 1911
Francis Ouimet, 20 years 4 months 11 days, 1913
Gene Sarazen, 20 years 4 months 16 days, 1922

Biggest margin of victory
11 strokes, Willie Smith, 1899
9 strokes, Jim Barnes 1921
7 strokes, Fred Herd, 1898; Alex Smith, 1906; Tony Jacklin, 1970

Lowest winning aggregate
272 (63, 71, 70, 68), Jack Nicklaus, Baltusrol, 1980

Lowest aggregate by runner-up
274 (68, 68, 68, 70) Isao Aoki, Baltusrol, 1980

Lowest aggregate by an amateur
282 (71, 71, 69, 71), Jack Nicklaus, Cherry Hills, 1960

Lowest individual round
63, Johnny Miller, fourth round, Oakmont, 1973. Tom Weiskopf, first round, Baltusrol, 1980. Jack Nicklaus, first round, Baltusrol, 1980.

Lowest individual round by an amateur
65, James B McHale, St Louis, 1947
65, Jim Simons, Merion, 1971

Lowest first round
63, Tom Weiskopf and Jack Nicklaus, Baltusrol, 1980

Lowest second round
64, Tommy Jacobs, Congressional CC, 1964; Rives McBee, Olympic CC, 1966

Lowest third round
65, James B McHale, St Louis, 1947; Jim Simons, Merion, 1971, Hubert Green, Baltusrol, 1980

Lowest fourth round
63, Johnny Miller, Oakmont, 1973

Lowest first 36 holes
134 (63, 71) Jack Nicklaus, Baltusrol, 1980

Lowest second 36 holes
136 (70, 66), Gene Sarazen, Fresh Meadow, 1932
136 (68, 68), Cary Middlecoff, Inverness, 1957
136 (66, 70), Ken Venturi, Congressional CC, 1964
136 (68, 68), Tom Weiskopf, Atlanta Athletic Club, 1976
136 (68, 68) Lou Graham, Southern Hills, 1977

Lowest first 54 holes
204 (63, 71, 70), Jack Nicklaus, and (68, 68, 68), Isao Aoki, Baltusrol, 1980

Lowest final 54 holes
204 (67, 72, 65), Jack Nicklaus, Baltusrol, 1967

Lowest 9 holes
30, James B McHale, first 9, third round, St Louis, 1947; Arnold Palmer; first 9, fourth round, Cherry Hills, 1960; Ken Venturi, first 9, third round, Congressional CC, 1964; Bob Charles, first 9, fourth round, Merion, 1971; Tom Shaw, first 9, first round, Merion, 1971

Biggest span between first and last victories
18 years, Jack Nicklaus, 1962–80
11 years, Julius Boros, 1952–63

Successive victories
3, Willie Anderson, 1903–05
2, J J McDermott, 1911–12; Bobby Jones, 1929–30; Ralph Guldahl, 1937–38; Ben Hogan, 1950–51

Victories by amateurs
4, Bobby Jones, 1923-26-29-30
1, Francis Ouimet, 1913; Jerome D Travers, 1915; Chick Evans, 1916; John G Goodman, 1933

Winner of US Open and Amateur on the same course
Jack Nicklaus, Pebble Beach, Amateur (1961); Open (1972)

Highest number of top ten finishes
16, Walter Hagen
15, Ben Hogan
14, Jack Nicklaus
13, Arnold Palmer
12, Sam Snead

First player to break 70
Dave Hunter, 68, first round, Englewood, New Jersey, 1909; Tom McNamara, 69, second round, Englewood, New Jersey, 1909

Outright leader after every round
Walter Hagen, 1914; Jim Barnes, 1921; Ben Hogan, 1953; Tony Jacklin, 1970

Hot sequences
1922–1930: Bobby Jones's finishes were = 2nd, 1st, 2nd, 2nd 1st, = 11th, 2nd, 1st, 1st

In twelve successive appearances from 1940 to 1956 (he did not play in 1949), Ben Hogan's worst placing was tied for 6th place

Left-handed champions
None

Bespectacled champions
Willie Macfarlane, 1925; Hale Irwin, 1974–1979

Unusual champions
Tommy Armour, 1927, lost an eye in World War I; Ed Furgol, 1954, had a withered left arm—the result of a childhood playground accident

Play-offs
26, 1901-03-08-10-11-13-19-23-25-27-28-29-31-39-40-46-47-50-55-57-62-63-65-66-71-75

By comparison, the British Open has produced only 12 play-offs in 108 championships

Lowest round in a play-off
68, Byron Nelson, 1939; Craig Wood, 1939; Lee Trevino, Merion, 1971
69, Lew Worsham, St Louis, 1947; Ben Hogan, Merion, 1950; Jack Fleck, Olympic CC, 1955; Billy Casper, Olympic CC, 1966

First American-born champion
Johnny McDermott, 1911

Record leads (since 1898)
After 18 holes:
5 strokes, Tommy Armour, 1933
After 36 holes:
5 strokes, Willie Anderson, 1903
After 54 holes:
7 strokes, Jim Barnes, 1921

Champions with each round lower than previous one
Ben Hogan, 1951, Oakland Hills, 76, 73, 71, 67

Champions with four rounds the same
None

Biggest variation between rounds of a champion
13 strokes, Johnny Miller, Oakmont, 1973, third round 76 fourth round 63
10 strokes, Bobby Jones, Winged Foot, 1929, first round 69 fourth round 79
10 strokes, Gene Sarazen, Fresh Meadow, 1932, second round 76 fourth round 66
10 strokes, Johnny Goodman, Glen View, 1933, second round 66 fourth round 76

Best comebacks by champions
After 18 holes:
Jack Fleck, 1955, 9 strokes behind

After 36 holes:
Lou Graham, 1975, 11 strokes behind
After 54 holes:
Arnold Palmer, 1960, 7 strokes behind
After 63 holes:
Billy Casper, 1966, 7 strokes behind

Champions with four rounds under 70
Lee Trevino, 1968, Oak Hill, Rochester (69, 68, 69, 69)
Ben Hogan, 1948; Billy Casper, 1966; Jerry Pate, 1976, had three rounds under 70. In 1966, Casper had a fourth round under 70 in the play-off. Isao Aoki, runner-up, had three under 70 in 1980.

Best finishing round by a champion
63, Johnny Miller, Oakmont, 1973
65, Arnold Palmer, Cherry Hills, 1960; Jack Nicklaus, Baltusrol, 1967

Worst finishing round by a champion since 1919
79, Bobby Jones, Winged Foot, 1929
(All-time worst: 84, Fred Herd, 1898)

Worst opening round by a champion since 1919
78, Walter Hagen, Brae Burn, 1919; Tommy Armour, Oakmont, 1927
(All-time worst: 94, Horace Rawlins, Newport, 1895; Worst since 1946: 76, Ben Hogan, Oakland Hills, 1951 and Jack Fleck, Olympic CC, 1955

Best opening round by a champion
63, Jack Nicklaus, Baltusrol, 1980

Championship with highest number of rounds under 70
Southern Hills, 1977, 35 rounds

Championship since 1946 with fewest rounds under 70
Oakland Hills, 1951 and Oakmont, 1953, two rounds

Continuity of appearances
Gene Sarazen teed off in 31 successive Opens from 1920—a record. He also played right through 22 successive Opens from 1920 to 1941
Sam Snead played through 27 Opens between 1937 and 1973, a record

Champions who led outright after three rounds (1898–1980)
A total of 32 champions out of 77:
Fred Herd, 1898; Willie Smith, 1899; Harry Vardon, 1900; Laurie Auchterlonie, 1902; Willie Anderson, 1903; Alex Smith, 1906; Walter Hagen, 1914; Jerome Travers, 1915; Chick Evans, 1916; Jim Barnes, 1921; Bobby Jones, 1923; Willie Macfarlane, 1925; Bobby Jones, 1929; Bobby Jones, 1930; Johnny Goodman, 1933; Lawson Little, 1940; Craig Wood, 1941; Lew Worsham, 1947; Ben Hogan, 1948; Cary Middlecoff, 1949; Julius Boros, 1952; Ben Hogan, 1953; Ed Furgol, 1954; Cary Middlecoff, 1956; Tommy Bolt, 1958; Billy Casper, 1959; Gary Player, 1965; Tony Jacklin, 1970; Jack Nicklaus, 1972; Hubert Green, 1977; Andy North, 1978; Hale Irwin, 1979

Longest course
Bellerive CC, St Louis, 1955, 7191 yd (6575 m)

Courses most often used (1895–1980)
Baltusrol, 6; Oakmont, 5; Myopia Hunt, Oakland Hills and Inverness, 4; Merion, Winged Foot, Philadelphia Cricket Club, 3

Lowest individual 18-hole score on Open courses since 1909

Merion	**64,** Lee Mackey, Jr, 1950
Oakmont	**63,** Johnny Miller, 1973
Atlanta Athletic	**67,** Michael Reid*; Butch Baird, 1976
Pebble Beach	**68,** Arnold Palmer; Lanny Wadkins, 1972
Medinah	**67,** Cary Middlecoff, 1949; Frank Beard, Tom Watson and Pat Fitzsimons, 1975
Winged Foot	**67,** Sam Snead, 1959; Hubert Green, 1974
Olympic	**64,** Rives McBee, 1966
Congressional	**64,** Tommy Jacobs, 1964
Southern Hills	**66,** Jerry McGee, Donald E Padgett II, 1977
Hazeltine National	**67,** Randy Wolff; Bob Charles, 1970
Champions, Houston	**66,** Bob Murphy, Bobby Mitchell, 1969
Oak Hill	**65,** John S Spray, 1968
Cherry Hills	**65,** Arnold Palmer, 1960
Baltusrol	**63,** Jack Nicklaus, Tom Weiskopf, 1980
Bellerive	**68,** Ray Floyd, Kel Nagle, 1965
Country Club, Brookline	**69,** Arnold Palmer, Bob Gajda, Dow Finsterwald, 1963
Oakland Hills	**66,** Jimmy Thomson, 1937
Inverness	**65,** Walter Burkemo, 1957
Northwood, Dallas	**68,** Julius Boros, Al Brosch, Johnny Bulla, 1952
Riviera, Los Angeles	**67,** Ben Hogan, Lew Worsham, 1948
St Louis	**65,** James McHale,* 1947
Canterbury, Ohio	**67,** Sam Snead 1940; Chick Harbert, Chandler Harper, 1946

Colonial	68, Ben Hogan, 1941
Philadelphia CC	66, Clayton Heafner, 1939
North Shore, Illinois	66, Johnny Goodman,★ Walter Hagen, 1933
Fresh Meadow	66, Gene Sarazen, 1932
Olympia Fields	68, Ed Dudley, 1928
Scioto	68, Bill Mehlhorn, Macdonald Smith, 1926
Worcester CC	67, Willie Macfarlane, 1925
Interlachen	68, Bobby Jones, 1930★
Inwood, New York	70, Jock Hutchison, 1923
Skokie, Illinois	68, Gene Sarazen, Walter Hagen, 1922
Columbia CC	69, Jim Barnes, Alfred Hackbarth, 1921
Brae Burn	72, Charles Hoffner, 1919
Minikhada	68, Jock Hutchison, 1916
Midlothian	68, Walter Hagen, 1914
CC of Buffalo	69, Tom McNamara, 1912
Chicago GC, Wheaton	72, John McDermott, Fred McLeod, 1911
Englewood, New Jersey	68, Dave Hunter, 1909
Philadelphia Cricket Club	70, Fred McLeod, 1910

★ Amateur.

PRIZE-MONEY

Year	Total $	First prize $
1926	2145	500
1929	5000	1000
1936	5000	1000
1940	6000	1000
1946	8000	1500
1953	20400	5000
1958	35000	8000
1960	60720	14400
1965	131690	26000
1970	203500	30000
1972	202400	30000
1974	227700	35000
1976	268000	42000
1977	284990	45000
1978	310200	45000
1979	330400	50000
1980	350000	55000

RESULTS

1895 Newport GC, Rhode Island

Horace Rawlins, Newport	45	46	41	41	173
Willie Dunn, Shinnecock Hills	43	46	44	42	175
James Foulis, Chicago	46	43	44	43	176
★A W Smith, Toronto	47	43	44	42	176
W F Davis, Newport	45	49	42	42	178
W Campbell, Brookline	41	48	42	48	179

1896 Shinnecock Hills GC, New York

James Foulis, Chicago	78	74	152
Horace Rawlins, Sadequada	79	76	155
G Douglas, Brookline	79	79	158
★A W Smith, Toronto	78	80	158
John Shippen, Shinnecock Hills	78	81	159
★H J Whigham, Onwentsia	82	77	159

1897 Chicago GC, Illinois

Joe Lloyd, Essex	83	79	162
Willie Anderson, Watch Hill	79	84	163
James Foulis, Chicago	80	88	168
Willie Dunn, New York	87	81	168
W T Hoare, Pittsburgh	82	87	169
A Ricketts, Albany	91	81	172
Bernard Nicholls, Lenox	87	85	172

1898 Myopia Hunt Club, Massachusetts

Fred Herd, Washington Park	84	85	75	84	328
Alex Smith, Washington Park	78	86	86	85	335
Willie Anderson, Baltusrol	81	82	87	86	336
Joe Lloyd, Essex County	87	80	86	86	339
Willie Smith, Shinnecock Hills	82	91	85	82	340
W V Hoare, Dayton	84	84	87	87	342

1899 Baltimore CC, Maryland

Willie Smith, Midlothian	77	82	79	77	315
George Low, Dyker Meadow	82	79	89	76	326
Val Fitzjohn, Otsego	85	80	79	82	326
W H Way, Detroit	80	85	80	81	326
Willie Anderson, New York	77	81	85	84	327
J Park, Essex County	88	80	75	85	328

1900 Chicago GC, Illinois

Harry Vardon, Ganton (England)	79	78	76	80	313
J H Taylor, Richmond (England)	76	82	79	78	315
David Bell, Midlothian	78	83	83	78	322
Laurie Auchterlonie, Glen View	84	82	80	81	327
Willie Smith, Midlothian	82	83	79	84	328
George Low, Dyker Meadow	84	80	85	82	331

1901 Myopia Hunt Club, Massachusetts

Willie Anderson, Pittsfield	84	83	83	81	331
Alex Smith, Washington Park	82	82	87	80	331
(Anderson won play-off 85 to 86)					
Willie Smith, Midlothian	84	86	82	81	333
Stewart Gardner, Garden City	86	82	81	85	334
Laurie Auchterlonie, Glen View	81	85	86	83	335
Bernard Nicholls, Boston	84	85	83	83	335

1902 Garden City GC, New York

Laurie Auchterlonie, Chicago	78	78	74	77	307
Stewart Gardner, Garden City	82	76	77	78	313
★Walter J Travis, Garden City	82	82	75	74	313
Willie Smith, Chicago	82	79	80	75	316
John Shippen, New York	83	81	75	79	318
Willie Anderson, Montclair	79	82	76	81	318

1903 Baltusrol GC, New Jersey

Willie Anderson, Apawamis	149	76	82	307
David Brown, Wollaston	156	75	76	307
(Anderson won play-off 82 to 84)				
Stewart Gardner, Garden City	154	82	79	315
Alex Smith, Nassau	154	81	81	316
Donald J Ross, Oakley	158	78	82	318
Jack Campbell, Brookline	159	83	77	319

1904 Glen View Club, Illinois

Willie Anderson, Apawamis	75	78	78	72	303
Gilbert Nicholls, St Louis	80	76	79	73	308
Fred Mackenzie, Onwentsia	76	79	74	80	309
Laurie Auchterlonie, Glen View	80	81	75	78	314

Bernard Nicholls, Elyria, Ohio 80 77 79 78 314
Robert Simpson, Riverside, Illinois 82 82 76 76 316
P F Barrett, Lambton, Ontario 78 79 79 80 316
Stewart Gardner, Garden City 75 76 80 85 316

1905 Myopia Hunt Club, Massachusetts
Willie Anderson, Apawamis 81 80 76 77 314
Alex Smith, Nassau 81 80 76 79 316
Peter Robertson, Oakmont 79 80 81 77 317
P. F. Barret, Canada 81 80 77 79 317
Stewart Gardner, Garden City 78 78 85 77 318
Alex Campbell, The Country Club 82 76 80 81 319

1906 Onwentsia Club, Illinois
Alex Smith, Nassau 73 74 73 75 295
Willie Smith, Mexico 73 81 74 74 302
Laurie Auchterlonie, Glen View 76 78 75 76 305
James Maiden, Toledo 80 73 77 75 305
Willie Anderson, Onwentsia 73 76 74 84 307
Alec Ross, Brae Burn 76 79 75 80 310

1907 Philadelphia Cricket Club, Pennsylvania
Alec Ross, Brae Burn 76 74 76 76 302
Gilbert Nicholls, Woodland 80 73 72 79 304
Alex Campbell, The Country Club 78 74 78 75 305
John Hobens, Englewood 76 75 73 85 309
Peter Robertson, Oakmont 81 77 78 74 310
George Low, Baltusrol 78 76 79 77 310
Fred McLeod, Midlothian 79 77 79 75 310

1908 Myopia Hunt Club, Massachusetts
Fred McLeod, Midlothian 82 82 81 77 322
Willie Smith, Mexico 77 82 85 78 322
(McLeod won play-off 77 to 83)
Alex Smith, Nassau 80 83 83 81 327
Willie Anderson, Onwentsia 85 86 80 79 330
John Jones, Myopia 81 81 87 82 331
Jack Hobens, Englewood 86 81 85 81 333
Peter Robertson, Oakmont 89 84 77 83 333

1909 Englewood GC, New Jersey
George Sargent, Hyde Manor 75 72 72 71 290
Tom McNamara, Wollaston 73 69 75 77 294
Alex Smith, Wykagyl 76 73 74 72 295
Isaac Mackie, Fox Hills 77 75 74 73 299
Willie Anderson, St Louis 79 74 76 70 299
Jack Hobens, Englewood 75 78 72 74 299

1910 Philadelphia Cricket Club, Pennsylvania
Alex Smith, Wykagyl 73 73 79 73 298
John J McDermott, Merchantville 74 74 75 75 298
Macdonald Smith, Claremont 74 78 75 71 298
(Alex Smith won play-off 71 to 75 to 77)
Fred McLeod, St Louis 78 70 78 73 299
Tom McNamara, Boston 73 78 73 76 300
Gilbert Nicholls, Wilmington 73 75 77 75 300

1911 Chicago GC, Illinois
John McDermott, Atlantic City 81 72 75 79 307
Mike J Brady, Wollaston 76 77 79 75 307
George O Simpson, Wheaton 76 77 79 75 307
(McDermott won play-off 80 to 82 to 85)
Fred McLeod, St Louis 77 72 76 83 308
Gilbert Nicholls, Wilmington 76 78 74 81 309
Jock Hutchison, Allegheny 80 77 73 79 309

1912 Buffalo CC, New York
John J McDermott, Atlantic City 74 75 74 71 294
Tom McNamara, Boston 74 80 73 69 296
Alex Smith, Wykagyl 77 70 77 75 299
Mike J Brady, Wollaston 72 75 73 79 299
Alec Campbell, Brookline 74 77 80 71 302
George Sargent, Chevy Chase 72 78 76 77 303

1913 Brookline CC, Massachusetts
*Francis Ouimet, Woodland 77 74 74 79 304
Harry Vardon, England 75 72 78 79 304
Ted Ray, England 79 70 76 79 304
(Ouimet won play-off 72 to 77 to 78)
Walter Hagen, Rochester 73 78 76 80 307
Jim M. Barnes, Tacoma 74 76 78 79 307
Macdonald Smith, Wykagyl 71 79 80 77 307
Louis Tellier, France 76 76 79 76 307

1914 Midlothian Country Club, Illinois
Walter C Hagen, Rochester 68 74 75 73 290
*Charles Evans, Jr, Edgewater 76 74 71 70 291
George Sargent, Chevy Chase 74 77 74 72 297
Fred McLeod, Columbia 78 73 75 71 297
*Francis Ouimet, Woodland 69 76 75 78 298
Mike J Brady, Wollaston 78 72 74 74 298
James A Donaldson, Glen View 72 79 74 73 298

1915 Baltusrol GC, New Jersey
*Jerome D Travers, Upper Montclair 148 73 76 297
Tom McNamara, Boston 149 74 75 298
Robert G MacDonald, Buffalo 149 73 78 300
Jim M Barnes, Whitemarsh Valley 146 76 79 301
Louis Tellier, Canoe Brook 146 76 79 301
Mike J Brady, Wollaston 147 75 80 302

1916 Minikahda Club, Minnesota
*Charles Evans, Jr, Edgewater 70 69 74 73 286
Jock Hutchison, Allegheny 73 75 72 68 288
Jim M Barnes, Whitemarsh Valley 71 74 71 74 290
Wilfrid Reid, Wilmington 70 72 79 72 293
Gilbert Nicholls, Great Neck 73 76 71 73 293
George Sargent, Interlachen 75 71 72 75 293

1919 Brae Burn CC, Massachusetts
Walter Hagen, Oakland Hills 78 73 75 75 301
Mike J Brady, Oakley 74 74 73 80 301
(Hagen won play-off 77 to 78)
Jock Hutchison, Glen View 78 76 76 76 306
Tom McNamara, New York 80 73 79 74 306
George McLean, Great Neck 81 75 76 76 308
Louis Tellier, Brae Burn 73 78 82 75 308

1920 Inverness Club, Ohio
Ted Ray, England 74 73 73 75 295
Harry Vardon, England 74 73 71 78 296
Jack Burke, Town and Country 75 77 72 72 296
Leo Diegel, Lake Shore 72 74 73 77 296
Jock Hutchison, Glen View 69 76 74 77 296
*Charles Evans, Jr, Edgewater 74 76 73 75 298
Jim M Barnes, Sunset Hills 76 70 76 76 298

1921 Columbia CC, Maryland
Jim M Barnes, Pelham 69 75 73 72 289
Walter Hagen, New York 79 73 72 74 298
Fred McLeod, Columbia 74 74 76 74 298
*Charles Evans, Jr, Edgewater 73 78 76 75 302
*Bob T Jones, Jr, Atlanta 78 71 77 77 303
Emmett French, Youngstown 75 77 74 77 303
Alex Smith, Shennecossett 75 75 79 74 303

1922 Skokie CC, Illinois
Gene Sarazen, Highland, Pittsburgh 72 73 75 68 288
John L Black, Oakland, California 71 71 75 72 289
*Bob T Jones, Jr, Atlanta 74 72 70 73 289
Bill E Mehlhorn, Shreveport 73 71 72 74 290
Walter Hagen, New York 68 77 74 72 291
George Duncan, England 76 73 75 72 296

1923 Inwood CC, New York
*Bob T Jones, Jr, Atlanta 71 73 76 76 296

Bobby A Cruickshank, Shackamaxon

                    73 72 78 73 296

(Jones won play-off 76 to 78)
Jock Hutchison, Glen View   70 72 82 78 302
Jack Forrester, Hollywood, New Jersey

                    75 73 77 78 303
Johnny J Farrell, Quaker Ridge 76 77 75 76 304
Francis Gallett, Port Washington 76 72 77 79 304
*W M Reekie, Upper Montclair   80 74 75 75 304

1924 Oakland Hills CC, Michigan

Cyril Walker, Englewood   74 74 74 75 297
*Bob T. Jones, Jr, Atlanta   74 73 75 78 300
Bill E Mehlhorn, Normandy, Missouri

                    72 75 76 78 301
Bobby A Cruickshank, Shackamaxon

                    77 72 76 78 303
Walter Hagen, New York   75 75 76 77 303
Macdonald Smith, San Francisco 78 72 77 76 303

1925 Worcester CC, Massachusetts

Willie Macfarlane, Oak Ridge   74 67 72 78 291
*Bob T Jones, Jr, Atlanta   77 70 70 74 291
(Macfarlane won play-off 147 to 148)
Johnny Farrell, Quaker Ridge   71 74 69 78 292
*Francis Quimet, Woodland   70 73 73 76 292
Gene Sarazen, Fresh Meadow 72 72 75 74 293
Walter Hagen, Pasadena, Florida 72 76 71 74 293

1926 Scioto CC, Ohio

*Bob T Jones, Jr, Atlanta·   70 79 71 73 293
Joe Turnesa, Fairview   71 74 72 77 294
Bill E Mehlhorn, Chicago   68 75 76 78 297
Gene Sarazen, Fresh Meadow 78 77 72 70 297
Leo Diegel, Mountain View Farm 72 76 75 74 297
Johnny Farrell, Quaker Ridge   76 79 69 73 297

1927 Oakmont CC, Pennsylvania

Tommy Armour, Congressional 78 71 76 76 301
Harry Cooper, El Serreno   74 76 74 77 301
(Armour won play-off 76 to 79)
Gene Sarazen, Fresh Meadow 74 74 80 74 302
Emmett French, Southern Pines 75 79 77 73 304
Bill E Mehlhorn, New York   75 77 80 73 305
Walter Hagen, Pasadena, Florida 77 73 76 81 307

1928 Olympia Fields CC, Illinois

Johnny Farrell, Quaker Ridge   77 74 71 72 294
*Bob T Jones, Jr, Atlanta   73 71 73 77 294
(Farrell won play-off 143 to 144)
Roland Hancock, Wilmington, North Carolina

                    74 77 72 72 295
Walter Hagen, New York City   75 72 73 76 296
*George von Elm, Tam O'Shanter 74 72 76 74 296
Joe Turnesa, Elmsford   74 77 74 74 299
Gene Sarazen, Fresh Meadow 78 76 73 72 299
Henry Ciuci, Mill River, Connecticut 70 77 72 80 299
Waldo W Crowder, Cleveland 74 74 76 75 299
Bill Leach, Overbrook   72 74 73 80 299
Macdonald Smith, Lakeville   75 77 75 72 299
Densmore Shute, Worthington, Ohio 75 73 79 72 299
Ed Dudley, Unattached   77 79 68 75 299

1929 Winged Foot CC, New York

*Bob T Jones, Atlanta   69 75 71 79 294
Al Espinosa, Glencoe, Illinois   70 72 77 75 294
(Jones won play-off 141 to 164)
Gene Sarazen, Fresh Meadow 71 71 76 78 296
Densmore Shute, Worthington, Ohio 73 71 76 76 296
Tommy Armour, Tam O'Shanter 74 71 76 76 297
*George von Elm, Tam O'Shanter 79 70 74 74 297

1930 Interlachen CC, Minnesota

*Bob T Jones, Jr, Atlanta   71 73 68 75 287
Macdonald Smith, Lakeville   70 75 74 70 289
Horton Smith, Cragston   72 70 76 74 292
Harry Cooper, Glen Elyn, Illinois 72 72 73 76 293
Johnny Golden, Wee Burn   74 73 71 76 294
Tommy Armour, Tam O'Shanter 70 76 75 76 297

1931 Inverness Club, Ohio

Billy Burke, Round Hill   73 72 74 73 292
*George von Elm, Unattached 75 69 73 75 292
(Burke won play-offs 149/148 to 149/149)
Leo Diegel, Mexico   75 73 74 72 294
Wiffy Cox, Brooklyn   75 74 74 73 296
Bill E Mehlhorn, Pinewald, New Jersey

                    77 73 75 71 296
Gene Sarazen, Lakeville   74 78 74 70 296

1932 Fresh Meadow CC, New York

Gene Sarazen, Lakeville   74 76 70 66 286
Bobby A Cruickshank, Willowbrook, New York

                    78 74 69 68 289
Phil Perkins, Unattached   76 69 74 70 289
Leo Diegel, Mexico   73 74 73 74 294
Wiffy Cox, Brooklyn   80 73 70 72 295
José Jurado, Argentina   74 71 75 76 296

1933 North Shore GC, Illinois

*Johnny Goodman, Omaha   75 66 70 76 287
Ralph Guldahl, St Louis   76 71 70 71 288
Craig Wood, Hollywood   73 74 71 72 290
Walter Hagen, Unattached   73 76 77 66 292
Tommy Armour, Medinah   68 75 76 73 292
Mortie Dutra, Red Run   75 73 72 74 294

1934 Merion Cricket Club, Pennsylvania

Olin Dutra, Brentwood, California 76 74 71 72 293
Gene Sarazen, New York City 73 72 73 76 294
Wiffy Cox, Dyker Beach, New York 71 75 74 75 295
Bobby Cruickshank, Virginia CC 71 71 77 76 295
Harry Cooper, Glen Oak, Illinois 76 74 74 71 295
Billy Burke, Cleveland   76 71 77 72 296
Macdonald Smith, Nashville 75 73 78 70 296

1935 Oakmont CC, Pennsylvania

Sam Parks, Jr, South Hills, Pennsylvania

                    77 73 73 76 299
Jimmy Thomson, Lakewood, California

                    73 73 77 78 301
Walter Hagen, Detroit   77 76 73 76 302
Densmore Shute, Chicago   78 73 76 76 303
Ray Mangrum, Los Angeles   76 76 72 79 303
Henry Picard, Hershey   79 78 70 79 306
Gene Sarazen, Brookfield, Connecticut

                    75 74 78 79 306
Alvin Krueger, Beloit, Wisconsin 71 77 78 80 306
Horton Smith, Oak Park, Illinois 73 79 79 75 306

1936 Baltusrol GC, New Jersey

Tony Manero, Sedgefield, North Carolina

                    73 69 73 67 282
Harry E Cooper, Glen Oak, Illinois 71 70 70 73 284
Clarence Clark, Forest Hill Field, New Jersey

                    69 75 71 72 287
Macdonald Smith, Glendale, California

                    73 73 72 70 288
Henry Picard, Hershey, Pennsylvania 70 71 74 74 289
Wiffy Cox, Kenwood, Maryland 74 74 69 72 289
Ky Laffoon, Northmoor, Illinois 71 74 70 74 289

1937 Oakland Hills CC, Michigan

Ralph Guldahl, Chicago   71 69 72 69 281

Sam Snead, Greenbrier 69 73 70 71 283
Bobby Cruickshank, Virginia CC 73 73 67 72 285
Harry E Cooper, Chicago 72 70 73 71 286
Ed Dudley, Philadelphia 70 70 71 76 287
Al Brosch, Bethpage State Park, New York
74 73 68 73 288

1938 Cherry Hills Club, Colorado
Ralph Guldahl, Braidburn, New Jersey
74 70 71 69 284
Dick Metz, Mill Road Farm, Illinois 73 68 70 79 290
Harry Cooper, Chicopee 76 69 76 71 292
Tony Penna, Dayton, Ohio 78 72 74 68 292
Byron Nelson, Reading, Pennsylvania
77 71 74 72 294
Emery Zimmerman, Columbia-Edgewater, Oregon
72 71 73 78 294

1939 Philadelphia CC, Pennsylvania
Byron Nelson, Reading, Pennsylvania
72 73 71 68 284
Craig Wood, Winged Foot, New York
70 71 71 72 284
Densmore Shute, Huntington, West Virginia
70 72 70 72 284
(Nelson won play-off 138 to 141 Shute eliminated)
Marvin (Bud) Ward, Spokane, Washington
69 73 71 72 285
Sam Snead, Greenbrier 68 71 73 74 286
Johnny Bulla, Chicago 72 71 68 76 287

1940 Canterbury GC, Ohio
Lawson Little, Bretton Woods, New Hampshire
72 69 73 73 287
Gene Sarazen, Brookfield Center, Connecticut
71 74 70 72 287
(Little won play-off 70 to 73)
Horton Smith, Oak Park 69 72 78 69 288
Craig Wood, Winged Foot, New York
72 73 72 72 289
Ben Hogan, Century, New York 70 73 74 73 290
Ralph Guldahl, Chicago 73 71 76 70 290
Lloyd Mangrum, Oak Park 75 70 71 74 290
Byron Nelson, Inverness, Ohio 72 74 70 74 290

1941 Colonial Club, Texas
Craig Wood, Winged Foot, New York 73 71 70 70 284
Densmore Shute, Chicago 69 75 72 71 287
Johnny Bulla, Chicago 75 71 72 71 289
Ben Hogan, Hershey 74 77 68 70 289
Herman Barron, Fenway, New York 75 71 74 71 291
Paul Runyan, Metropolis, New York 73 72 71 75 291

1946 Canterbury GC, Ohio
Lloyd Mangrum, Los Angeles 74 70 68 72 284
Byron Nelson, Toledo, Ohio 71 71 69 73 284
Vic Ghezzi, Knoxville, Tennessee 71 69 72 72 284
(Mangrum won play-offs 72/72 to 72/73 to 72/73)
Herman Barron, Fenway, New York 72 72 72 69 285
Ben Hogan, Hershey 72 68 73 72 285
Jimmy Demaret, Houston 71 74 73 68 286
Porky Oliver, Jr, Wilmington, Delaware
71 71 74 70 286

1947 St Louis CC, Missouri
Lew Worsham, Oakmont 70 70 71 71 282
Sam Snead, Cascades, Virginia 72 70 70 70 282
(Worsham won play-off 69 to 70)
Bobby Locke, Vereeniging (South Africa)
68 74 70 73 285
Porky Oliver, Jr, Wilmington, Delaware
73 70 71 71 285

*Marvin (Bud) Ward, Spokane, Washington
69 72 73 73 287
Jim Ferrier, Chicago 71 70 74 74 289
Vic J Ghezzi, Victory Hills, Kansas 74 73 73 69 289
Leland Gibson, Blue Hills, Missouri 69 76 73 71 289
Ben Hogan, Hershey 70 75 70 74 289
Johnny Palmer, Badin 72 70 75 72 289
Paul Runyan, Annandale, California 71 74 72 72 289

1948 Riviera CC, California
Ben Hogan, Hershey 67 72 68 69 276
Jimmy Demaret, Houston 71 70 68 69 278
Jim Turnesa, Elmsford 71 69 70 70 280
Bobby Locke, Vereeniging (South Africa)
70 69 73 70 282
Sam Snead, Greenbrier 69 69 73 72 283
Lew Worsham, Oakmont 67 74 71 73 285

1949 Medinah CC, Illinois
Cary Middlecoff, Colonial, Tennessee
75 67 69 75 286
Clayton Heafner, Eastwood, North Carolina
72 71 71 73 287
Sam Snead, Greenbrier 73 73 71 70 287
Jim Turnesa, Briar Hall, New York 78 69 70 72 289
Bobby Locke, Vereeniging (South Africa)
74 71 73 71 289
Buck White, Greenwood, Mississippi
74 68 70 78 290
Dave Douglas, Newark, Delaware 74 73 70 73 290

1950 Merion GC, Pennsylvania
Ben Hogan, Hershey 72 69 72 74 287
Lloyd Mangrum, Tam O'Shanter 72 70 69 76 287
George Fazio, Woodmont, Maryland 73 72 72 70 287
(Hogan won play-off 69 to 73 to 75)
Dutch Harrison, St Andrews, Illinois 72 67 73 76 288
Joe Kirkwood, Jr, Kirkwood, California
71 74 74 70 289
Jim Ferrier, Chicago 71 69 74 75 289
Henry Ransom, St Andrews, Illinois 72 71 73 73 289

1951 Oakland Hills CC, Michigan
Ben Hogan, Hershey 76 73 71 67 287
Clayton Heafner, Eastwood, North Carolina
72 75 73 69 289
Bobby Locke, Ohenimuri (South Africa)
73 71 74 73 291
Lloyd Mangrum, Tam O'Shanter 75 74 74 70 293
Julius Boros, Mid Pines, North Carolina
74 74 71 74 293
Al C Besselink, Hillcrest, Michigan 72 77 72 73 294
Paul Runyan, Annandale, California 73 74 72 75 294
Fred E Hawkins, El Paso, Texas 76 72 75 71 294
Dave Douglas, Newark, Delaware 75 70 75 74 294

1952 Northwood Club, Texas
Julius Boros, Mid Pines, North Carolina
71 71 68 71 281
Porky Oliver, Jr, Cog Hill, Illinois 71 72 70 72 285
Ben Hogan, Tamarisk, California 69 69 74 74 286
Johnny Bulla, Westmoreland, Pennsylvania
73 68 73 73 287
George Fazio, Pine Valley, New Jersey
71 69 75 75 290
Dick Metz, Maple City, Kansas 70 74 76 71 291

1953 Oakmont CC, Pennsylvania
Ben Hogan, Tamarisk, California 67 72 73 71 283
Sam Snead, Greenbrier, West Virginia
72 69 72 76 289
Lloyd Mangrum, Tam O'Shanter 73 70 74 75 292
Pete Cooper, Century, New York 78 75 71 70 294

George Fazio, Pine Valley, New Jersey
                                   70 71 77 76 294
Jimmy Demaret, Concord, New York   71 76 71 76 294
Ted Kroll, New Hartford   76 71 74 74 295
Dick Metz, Maple City, Kansas   75 70 74 76 295

1954 Baltusrol GC, New Jersey

Ed Furgol, Westwood, Missouri   71 70 71 72 284
Gene Littler, Thunderbird, California 70 69 76 70 285
Dick Mayer, St Petersburg, Florida 72 71 70 73 286
Lloyd Mangrum, Tam O'Shanter   72 71 72 71 286
Bobby Locke, Ohenimuri CC (South Africa)
                                   74 70 74 70 288
Tommy Bolt, Memorial Park, Texas   72 72 73 72 289
Ben Hogan, Fort Worth, Texas   71 70 76 72 289
Shelley Mayfield, Sequin, Texas   73 75 72 69 289
Fred Haas, New Orleans   73 73 71 72 289
*Billy Joe Patton, Mimosa, North Carolina
                                   69 76 71 73 289

1955 Olympic CC, California

Jack Fleck, Davenport Municipal, Iowa
                                   76 69 75 67 287
Ben Hogan, Fort Worth, Texas   72 73 72 70 287
(Fleck won play-off 69 to 72)
Sam Snead, Greenbrier, West Virginia
                                   79 69 70 74 292
Tommy Bolt, Chattanooga   67 77 75 73 292
Julius Boros, Mid Pines, North Carolina
                                   76 69 73 77 295
Bob R Rosburg, Palo Alto, California 78 74 67 76 295

1956 Oak Hill Country Club, New York

Cary Middlecoff, Riverlake, Texas 71 70 70 70 281
Julius Boros, Mid Pines, North Carolina
                                   71 71 71 69 282
Ben Hogan, Fort Worth, Texas   72 68 72 70 282
Ed Furgol, Westwood, Missouri   71 70 73 71 285
Peter Thomson, Victoria (Australia) 70 69 75 71 285
Ted Kroll, Fort Lauderdale   72 70 70 73 285

1957 Inverness Club, Ohio

Dick Mayer, St Petersburg, Florida 70 68 74 70 282
Cary Middlecoff, Riverlake, Texas 71 75 68 68 282
(Mayer won play-off 72 to 79)
Jimmy Demaret, Concord International, New York
                                   68 73 70 72 283
Julius Boros, Mid Pines, North Carolina
                                   69 75 70 70 284
Walter Burkemo, Franklin Hills, Michigan
                                   74 73 72 65 284
Ken Venturi, California   69 71 75 71 286
Fred E Hawkins, El Paso, Texas   72 72 71 71 286

1958 Southern Hills CC, Oklahoma

Tommy Bolt, Paradise, Florida   71 71 69 72 283
Gary Player, Killarney (South Africa) 75 68 73 71 287
Julius Boros, Mid Pines, North Carolina
                                   71 75 72 71 289
Gene Littler, Singing Hills, California 74 73 67 76 290
Walter Burkemo, Franklin Hills, Michigan
                                   75 74 70 72 291
Bob R Rosburg, Silverado, California 75 74 72 70 291

1959 Winged Foot GC, New York

Billy Casper, Jr, Apple Valley   71 68 69 74 282
Bob R Rosburg, Palo Alto, California 75 70 67 71 283
Claude Harmon, Winged Foot, New York
                                   72 71 70 71 284
Mike Souchak, Grossinger, New York
                                   71 70 72 71 284
Doug Ford, Paradise, Florida   72 69 72 73 286
Ernie Vossier, Midland, Texas   72 70 72 72 286

Arnold Palmer, Laurel Valley, Pennsylvania
                                   71 69 72 74 286

1960 Cherry Hills CC, Colorado

Arnold Palmer, Laurel Valley, Pennsylvania
                                   72 71 72 65 280
*Jack Nicklaus, Scioto, Ohio   71 71 69 71 282
Dutch Harrison, Old Warson, Missouri
                                   74 70 70 69 283
Julius Boros, Mid Pines, North Carolina
                                   73 69 68 73 283
Mike Souchak, Grossinger, New York
                                   68 67 73 75 283
Ted Kroll, DeSoto Lakes, Florida   72 69 75 67 283
Jack Fleck, El Caballero, California 70 70 72 71 283
Dow Finsterwald, Tequesta, Florida 71 69 70 73 283

1961 Oakland Hills CC, Michigan

Gene Littler, Singing Hills, California 73 68 72 68 281
Bob Goalby, Paradise, Florida   70 72 69 71 282
Doug Sanders, Ojai, California   72 67 71 72 282
Mike Souchak, Grossinger, New York
                                   73 70 68 73 284
*Jack Nicklaus, Scioto, Ohio   75 69 70 70 284
Dow Finsterwald, Tequesta, Florida 72 71 71 72 286
Eric Monti, Hillcrest, California 74 67 72 73 286
Doug Ford, Tuckahoe, New York   72 69 71 74 286

1962 Oakmont CC, Pennsylvania

Jack Nicklaus, Tucson National, Arizona
                                   72 70 72 69 283
Arnold D Palmer, Miami   71 68 73 71 283
(Nicklaus won play-off 71 to 74)
Phil Rodgers, La Jolla, California 74 70 69 72 285
Bobby Nichols, Midland, Texas   70 72 70 73 285
Gay Brewer, Jr, Paradise, Florida 73 72 73 69 287
Tommy Jacobs, Bermuda Dunes, California
                                   74 71 73 70 288
Gary Player, Ponte Vedra, Florida 71 71 72 74 288

1963 The Country Club, Brookline, Massachusetts

Julius Boros, Mid Pines, North Carolina
                                   71 74 76 72 293
Jacky D Cupit, Mountain View, California
                                   70 72 76 75 293
Arnold Palmer, Laurel Valley, Pennsylvania
                                   73 69 77 74 293
(Boros won play-off 70 to 73 to 76)
Paul Harney, Sunset Oaks, California 78 70 73 73 294
Billy Maxwell, Tropicana, Nevada   73 73 75 74 295
Bruce Crampton, Sydney (Australia) 74 72 75 74 295
Tony Lema, San Leandro, California 71 74 74 76 295

1964 Congressional CC, Washington, D.C.

Ken Venturi, Paradise, Florida   72 70 66 70 278
Tommy Jacobs, Bermuda Dunes, California
                                   72 64 70 76 282
Bob J Charles, De Soto Lakes, Florida
                                   72 72 71 68 283
Billy Casper, Mountain View, California
                                   71 74 69 71 285
Gay Brewer, Jr, Dallas   76 69 73 68 286
Arnold Palmer, Laurel Valley, Pennsylvania
                                   68 69 75 74 286

1965 Bellerive CC, Missouri

Gary Player, Johannesburg (South Africa)
                                   70 70 71 71 282
Kel Nagle, Pymble (Australia)   68 73 72 69 282
(Player won play-off 71 to 74)
Frank Beard, Seneca, Kentucky   74 69 70 71 284
Julius Boros, Mid Pines, North Carolina
                                   72 75 70 70 287

Al Geiberger, Carlton Oaks, California
70 76 70 71 287
Raymond Floyd, St Andrews, Illinois 72 72 76 68 288
Bruce Devlin, Sydney (Australia) 72 73 72 71 288

1966 Olympic CC, California

Billy Casper, Jr, Peacock Gap, California
69 68 73 68 278
Arnold Palmer, Laurel Valley, Pennsylvania
71 66 70 71 278
(Casper won play-off 69 to 73)
Jack Nicklaus, Scioto, Ohio 71 71 69 74 285
Tony Lema, Marco Island, Florida 71 74 70 71 286
Dave Marr, Goodyear, Arizona 71 74 68 73 286
Paul Rodgers, La Jolla, California 70 70 73 74 287

1967 Baltusrol GC, New Jersey

Jack Nicklaus, Scioto, Ohio 71 67 72 65 275
Arnold Palmer, Laurel Valley, Pennsylvania
69 68 73 69 279
Don January, Dallas 69 72 70 70 281
Billy Casper, Jr, Bonita, California 69 70 71 72 282
Lee Trevino, Horizon Hills, Texas 72 70 71 70 283
Bob Goalby, Tamarisk, California 72 71 70 71 284
Deane R Beman, Bethesda, Maryland
69 71 71 73 284
Gardner Dickinson, Jr, Lost Tree, Florida
70 73 68 73 284

1968 Oak Hill CC, New York

Lee Trevino, Horizon Hills, Texas 69 68 69 69 275
Jack Nicklaus, Scioto, Ohio 72 70 70 67 279
Bert Yancey, Killearn, Florida 67 68 70 76 281
Bobby Nichols, Louisville, Kentucky 74 71 68 69 282
Don Bies, Seattle 70 70 75 69 284
Steve Spray, Cedar Rapids, Iowa 73 75 71 65 284

1969 Champions GC, Texas

Orville J Moody, Yukon, Oklahoma 71 70 68 72 281
Deane R. Beman, Bethesda, Maryland
68 69 73 72 282
Al Geiberger, Santa Barbara, California
68 72 72 70 282
Bob R Rosburg, Westwood, Missouri
70 69 72 71 282
Bob Murphy, Jr, Bartow, Florida 66 72 74 71 283
Miller Barber, Woodlawn, Texas 67 71 68 78 284
Bruce Crampton, Bahama Reef 73 72 68 71 284
Arnold Palmer, Laurel Valley, Pennsylvania
70 73 69 72 284

1970 Hazeltine GC, Minnesota

Tony Jacklin, The Cloisters, Georgia 71 70 70 70 281
Dave Hill, Evergreen, Colorado 75 69 71 73 288
Bob J Lunn, Haggin Oaks, California 77 72 70 70 289
Bob J Charles, Christchurch (New Zealand)
76 71 75 67 289
Ken Still, Fircrest, Washington 78 71 71 71 291
Miller Barber, Woodlawn, Texas 75 75 72 70 292

1971 Merion GC, Pennsylvania

Lee Trevino, El Paso, Texas 70 72 69 69 280
Jack Nicklaus, Scioto, Ohio 69 72 68 71 280
(Trevino won play-off 68 to 71)
Bob R. Rosburg, French Lick, Indiana
71 72 70 69 282
Jim J Colbert, Jr, Prairie Creek, Arkansas
69 69 73 71 282
*Jim Simons, Butler, Pennsylvania 71 71 65 76 283
Johnny L Miller, San Francisco GC 70 73 70 70 283
George Archer, Gilroy, California 71 70 70 72 283

1972 Pebble Beach, California

Jack Nicklaus, Scioto, Ohio 71 73 72 74 290
* Amateur.

Bruce Crampton, Australia 74 70 73 76 293
Arnold Palmer, Laurel Valley, Pennsylvania
77 68 73 76 294
Lee Trevino, El Paso, Texas 74 72 71 78 295
Homero Blancas, Houston, Texas 74 70 76 75 295
Kermit Zarley, Houston, Texas 71 73 73 79 296

1973 Oakmont CC, Pennsylvania

Johnny Miller, San Francisco GC 71 69 76 63 279
John Schlee, Preston Trails, Texas 73 70 67 70 280
Tom Weiskopf, Columbus, Ohio 73 69 69 70 281
Arnold Palmer, Laurel Valley, Pennsylvania
71 71 68 72 282
Lee Trevino, El Paso, Texas 70 72 70 70 282
Jack Nicklaus, Scioto, Ohio 71 69 74 68 282

1974 Winged Foot GC, New York

Hale Irwin, Boulder CC, California 73 70 71 73 287
Forest Fezler, Indian Wells CC, California
75 70 74 70 289
Lou Graham, Richland CC, Tennessee
71 75 74 70 290
Bert Yancey, Palm Aire CC, Florida 76 69 73 72 290
Arnold Palmer, Laurel Valley, Pennsylvania
73 70 73 76 292
Jim Colbert, Overland Pk, Kansas 72 77 69 74 292
Tom Watson, Kansas City CC 73 71 69 79 292

1975 Medinah CC, Illinois

Lou Graham, Richland CC, Nashville 74 72 68 73 287
John D Mahaffey, Jr, Champions GC, Houston, Texas
73 71 72 71 287
(Graham won play-off 71 to 73)
Bob Murphy, Delray Dunes, Florida 74 73 72 69 288
Hale Irwin, St Louis, Missouri 74 71 73 70 288
Ben Crenshaw, CC of Austin, Texas 70 68 76 74 288
Frank Beard, Hurstbourne CC, Kentucky
74 69 67 78 288

1976 Atlanta Athletic Club, Duluth, Georgia

Jerry Pate, Pensacola CC, Florida 71 69 69 68 277
Al Geiberger, Silver Lakes, California 70 69 71 69 279
Tom Weiskopf, Columbus, Ohio 73 70 68 68 279
Butch Baird, Miami Beach, Florida 71 71 71 67 280
John Mahaffey, Riverhill CC, Texas 70 68 69 73 280
Hubert Green, Bay Point CC, Florida 72 70 71 69 282

1977 Southern Hills CC, Tulsa, Oklahoma

Hubert M Green, Birmingham, Alabama
69 67 72 70 278
Lou Graham, Richland CC, Nashville, Tennessee
72 71 68 68 279
Tom Weiskopf, Columbus, Ohio 71 71 68 71 281
Tom Purtzer, Moon Valley CC, Arizona
69 69 72 72 282
Jay Haas, St Clair CC, Belleville 72 68 71 72 283
Gary Jacobson, Minnetonka, Minnesota
73 70 67 73 283

1978 Cherry Hills, Denver, Colorado

Andy North, Gainesville, Florida 70 70 71 74 285
Jesse C Snead, Hot Springs, Virginia 70 72 72 72 286
Dave Stockton, Westlake GC, California
71 73 70 72 286
Hale Irwin, St Louis, Missouri 69 74 75 70 288
Tom Weiskopf, Columbus, Ohio 77 73 70 68 288

1979 Inverness, Toledo, Ohio

Hale Irwin, St Louis, Missouri 74 68 67 75 284
Jerry Pate, Pensacola, Florida 71 74 69 72 286
Gary Player, South Africa 73 73 72 68 286
Larry Nelson, Kennesaw, Georgia 71 68 76 73 288
Bill Rogers, Texarkana, Texas 71 72 73 72 288
Tom Weiskopf, Columbus, Ohio 71 74 67 76 288

USPGA

First played 1916

The PGA championship is the oldest and most important of the events which make up the US professional tour. It has become known as one of the four championships comprising the modern Grand Slam, but is less publicised than the US and British Opens and the Masters.

This is because its emphasis is more domestic and entry to the championship as a player is based on qualification from events in America. Full membership of the American PGA is an essential. Life exemption from pre-qualifying for any PGA event is one of the benefits to the winner and it has now assumed a settled date in the calendar. For some time it was played opposite the British Open or in the week immediately following it. In 1953, Ben Hogan was prevented from playing in it after winning the Masters, US Open and British Open.

From the year of its inception until 1958, it was traditionally a matchplay event with a distinguished list of early champions including Jim Barnes, Walter Hagen, Gene Sarazen and Tommy Armour. Hagen won it five times, including four in a row. Starting in 1924, he won 22 consecutive matches against the best professional golfers in America.

As the modern dislike for matchplay among professionals grew in America, the championship fell victim to the supporters of strokeplay and the influence of television. Two rounds a day were also going out of fashion and in 1958 it became 72 holes of strokeplay just like all the other tournaments.

After Sam Snead won his third victory in 1951, nobody won more than once until Jack Nicklaus won his second victory in 1971, when the event was held in February, and Gary Player followed suit a year later. Nicklaus later won thrice more, but it remains a championship which Arnold Palmer never won.

MILESTONES

1916 First title won by Jim Barnes, an Englishman from Lelant in Cornwall, later both British and American Open champion. He defeated Jock Hutchison a 32-year-old Scotsman from St Andrews by 1 hole. Both Barnes and Hutchison lived in America.

1919 Second title for Barnes. In the final, he beat another Scottish-born professional, Fred McLeod, by 6 and 5. McLeod was US Open champion in 1908.

1920 Jock Hutchison (runner-up in 1916) beat J Douglas Edgar by 1 hole in the final. Edgar, Canadian Open Champion in 1919 and 1920, was killed some months later.

1921 Walter Hagen became the first American-born champion and began a remarkable period of dominance with Gene Sarazen. Between them they won from 1921 to 1927. In the final, Hagen beat Jim Barnes 3 and 2.

1922 Hagen did not defend and in his absence Sarazen, later to become his great rival, beat Emmet French 4 and 3 in the final at Oakmont, Pennsylvania. He is the youngest winner of the title.

1923 The only final involving Sarazen and Hagen produced the first extra hole victory for Sarazen. He won on the 38th, his second title in a row.

1924 First of an historic run of four victories for Walter Hagen. He scored his second victory in a final against Jim Barnes.

1925 Hagen needed 39 holes to beat Al Watrous and 40 to shake off Leo Diegel but, starting his final at Olympia Fields with an eagle, he beat Bill Mehlhorn by 6 and 5.

1926 Hagen won for the third time in a row. Having accounted for Johnny Farrell by 6 and 5 in the semi-final, he beat Leo Diegel by 5 and 3. At the 1st hole after lunch, Diegel's ball finished under Hagen's parked car.

1927 Hagen's record run extended to a fourth successive victory at Cedar Crest CC, Dallas, although he was behind for most of the final against Joe Turnesa. He finally squared at the 29th and went head at the 31st.

1928 Hagen took his run of victorious matches to 22 before he lost in the third round, but Leo Diegel, finalist in 1926, crowned a great week at Five Farms, Baltimore. It was he who beat Hagen; he then beat Gene Sarazen 9 and 8 and finally defeated Al Espinosa 6 and 5.

1929 Second successive victory for Leo Diegel. He won the final against Johnny Farrell, US Open champion, by 6 and 4. However, Diegel was only 1 up after 27 holes. Twice, subsequently, Farrell, set a stymie, putted Diegel's ball into the hole.

Leo Diegel, the man whose putting style was all elbows (US Golf Association)

1930 In a great final, Tommy Armour beat Gene Sarazen by 1 hole with a putt of 14 ft (4·3 m) on the 36th green. Sarazen was 1 up after 9, Armour 1 up after 18 holes and the match all square after 27 holes.

1931 Tom Creavy, one-time caddie for Gene Sarazen and Johnny Farrell, scored a surprise victory, the second winner aged 20. On his way to the final Creavy beat Jock Collins, Peter O'Hara, Cyril Walker and Sarazen; in the final, he beat Densmore Shute by 2 and 1. Illness later curtailed his tournament career.

1932 Olin Dutra caused something of a surprise on his way to the final where he beat Frank Walsh. In the semi-final, Walsh beat Bobby Cruickshank who, in an earlier round, beat Al Watrous after being 9 down with 12 to play. On the 24th green, Watrous conceded a 6 ft (1·8 m) putt for a half. In this same championship Johnny Golden beat Walter Hagen at the 43rd hole, the longest match in the history of the USPGA.

1933 Sarazen's third and last victory, eleven years after his first. He beat Willie Goggin by 5 and 4 in the final at Blue Mound CC, Milwaukee.

1934 Paul Runyan won the championship, beating his old teacher Craig Wood at the 38th, equalling the longest match played in the final.

1935 Johnny Revolta, a former caddie with the reputation of being a fine bunker player and putter, beat Tommy Armour by 5 and 4 to win the championship. In the final, he displayed a phenomenal short game, having beaten Walter Hagen in the first round.

1936 Densmore Shute, though heavily out-hit, beat Jimmy Thomson in the final.

1937 Shute became the last man to win the PGA title twice in succession. He won an extra-hole final at the 37th after Harold 'Jug' McSpaden has missed a shortish putt to win on the 36th, but McSpaden had led a bit of a charmed life. He won at the 38th in the first round and at the 39th in the 4th.

1938 After a welter of low scoring, Paul Runyan recorded his second victory. His margin of 8 and 7 over Sam Snead was the biggest in a final. Runyan had a first round of 67 and a 5-up lead.

Byron Nelson, some of whose records on the US tour will never be broken (US Golf Association)

1939 One of Byron Nelson's few defeats at this time. Having looked likely to beat Henry Picard in the final at Pomonok CC, New York, he lost at the 37th.

1940 Nelson soon atoned for his defeat in the previous final. Snead, despite going 1 up on the 32nd, lost by 1 hole. It was his second losing final in three years.

1941 Three down on the 28th tee, Vic Ghezzi came from behind in the final against Byron Nelson at Cherry Hills. It was Nelson's third final in a row.

1942 Sam Snead's first national championship. At Seaview CC, Atlantic City, he beat Jim Turnesa in the final by 2 and 1. Turnesa's victims included Hogan, McSpaden and Nelson.

1944 Nelson's third defeat in the final in five years. Bob Hamilton, his surprising conqueror, halved the 36th with a birdie when 1 up.

1945 Byron Nelson's fifth final in six years produced a clear-cut victory over Sam Byrd by 4 and 3 at Morraine CC, Dayton, Ohio. It was one of the peaks of his career.

1946 At Portland GC, Oregon, Ben Hogan won his first PGA title, virtually deciding his final with Ed 'Porky' Oliver by covering the first 9 holes after lunch in 30. It took him from 3 down to 2 up.

1947 Deadly putting and the odd stroke of luck enabled Australian-born Jim Ferrier to beat Chick Harbert by 2 and 1 in the final at Plum Hollow CC, Detroit.

1948 In the year in which he won his first US Open, Ben Hogan won his second PGA. After some devastating scoring in the earlier rounds, he beat Mike Turnesa by 7 and 6 despite being heavily outdriven.

1949 Sam Snead scored his second victory on a course, the Hermitage, Richmond, Virginia, in his own home territory. Well supported by the crowd, he beat Johnny Palmer in the final.

1950 Having beaten Lloyd Mangrum and Jimmy Demaret, Chandler Harper defeated Henry Williams by 4 and 3 in the final to record his only national success.

1951 Sam Snead followed Walter Hagen and Gene Sarazen by winning a third title; at 39, he was also the oldest winner at that time. In a one-sided final against Walter Burkemo at Oakmont, he won 5 of the first 6 holes.

1952 Jim Turnesa was also 39 when he won his title at the Big Spring CC, Louisville. Although the famous Turnesa family had many achievements—brother Joe was runner-up to Hagen in 1927—this was the best. In the final, Jim beat Chick Harbert having been 3 down at lunch.

1953 Walter Burkemo, beaten by Sam Snead in the final of 1951, won his greatest honour in golf in his home state of Michigan. He beat Felice Torza by 2 and 1 and completed an amazing recovery as Torza was 7 up at lunch. Burkemo had originally thought of becoming a professional boxer.

Six former champions fell in the first two rounds, a bad blow for those wedded to matchplay.

1954 Burkemo reached the final in defence of his title and won 3 of the first 4 holes but Chick Harbert, twice runner-up, was 8 under par for the remaining holes. He won 4 and 3.

1955 Doug Ford, noted for his great putting, scored a good victory in the final over Cary Middlecoff at Meadowbrook CC.

1956 The penultimate championship to be decided by matchplay produced the biggest field, 128. The new champion was Jack Burke who, showing great touch with his putter throughout, came from behind in the semi-final and final. In the final, he beat Ted Kroll.

1957 The end of an era. The last major professional matchplay event in America. Held at Miami Valley GC, Dayton, Ohio, it saw Lionel Hebert crowned as champion. It was his first tournament victory. His victim in the final was Dow Finsterwald.

1958 As frequently happens, the runner-up one year becomes champion the next and Finsterwald maintained the tradition in the first PGA championship to be decided by strokeplay. At Llanerch CC, Pennsylvania, he was ahead with a 67 on the first day but behind with a round to play. However, he went out in 31 in the final round, returned another 67 and beat Billy Casper by 2 strokes.

1959 Bob Rosburg, a graduate of Stanford, achieved his most outstanding success at Minneapolis. Amazingly enough, nine players shared the first round lead on 69, but it was Rosburg's final round of 66 which settled things. It enabled him to beat Doug Sanders and Jerry Barber, 6 and 7 strokes more in the last round, by 1 stroke. Barber's 36-hole total of 134 (69,65) has never been beaten in the PGA championship; nor has his 30 for the front 9 in his 65.

1960 The PGA is well known as the one major championship which Arnold Palmer never won. The year 1960 was as good a chance as he had. As the new Open champion, he opened with a 67, but he followed with 74 and 75 and the winner was Jay Hebert. He followed his brother, Lionel, champion in 1957.

1961 Jerry Barber rivalled Gene Sarazen as the

smallest champion. At 5 ft 5 in (1·65 m) and the wearer of spectacles, he was not long, but he was deadly on the greens, as he showed over the last three holes. He holed from 6, 12 and 20 yd (5·5, 11 and 18 m) at Olympia Fields to earn a play-off with Don January. This he won with 67 to 68, was voted Player of the Year and captained the Ryder Cup team in England.

1962 Gary Player, having already won the British Open and the Masters, registered his third major victory at Aronimink. He defeated Bob Goalby by 1 stroke with Jack Nicklaus, the new Open champion playing in his first PGA, equal third.

1963 Nicklaus, though he failed to qualify in defence of his Open title, won the Masters and did not have to wait long to add a third major title. In fierce heat in Dallas, he started the final round 3 strokes behind Bruce Crampton who had a third round 65, but a final 68 gave him victory by 2 strokes from Dave Ragan. By his victory, Nicklaus joined the company of Ben Hogan, Gene Sarazen and Byron Nelson as winner of the US Open, Masters and PGA; and Nicklaus had been a professional for less than two years.

1964 Bobby Nichols's greatest hour. He started with a 64 at the Firestone CC, Akron, Ohio, and led after every round. He held off Arnold Palmer and Jack Nicklaus who were second and third but for Palmer, the only player to break 70 in all four rounds (68,68,69,69), it was another disappointment. Nichols's total of 271 is the lowest recorded in any PGA championship.

1965 Victory for Dave Marr at Laurel Valley was the highlight of his career. Four even rounds (70,69,70,71) gave him victory over Billy Casper and Jack Nicklaus by 2 strokes after he had driven into a bunker at the final hole but saved his 4.

Arnold Palmer could not sustain a challenge on his own front door, but Nicklaus's share of second place meant that in his first four PGAs, he finished third, first, equal second and equal second.

1966 Al Geiberger recorded the biggest victory to date; 4 strokes from Dudley Wysong at Firestone CC. Wysong lost to Jack Nicklaus in the final of the 1961 US Amateur at Pebble Beach.

1967 Don January, the eventual winner, and Don Massengale tied with 281 at the Columbine CC, Denver. In 1961, January had lost a play-off to Jerry Barber and so was due a major win.

1968 The 50th championship produced the oldest winner in Julius Boros, 48, and another

Al Geiberger who returned a round of 59 in the 1977 Memphis Classic (Action Photos)

close call for Arnold Palmer at the Pecan Valley CC, Texas. At the final hole, Boros got up and down in two from a long way to beat Palmer and Bob Charles by 1 stroke.

1969 Gary Player, the target of some unruly local demonstrators who broke on to the course, just failed to deny the new champion, Raymond Floyd at the NCR course, Dayton, Ohio. He

Raymond Floyd who shares the record low aggregate in the Masters with Jack Nicklaus (Action Photos)

took a 5-stroke lead into the last round, but it was whittled down to one in a close finish.

1970 Dave Stockton, having lifted himself with a third-round 66 to take a 3-stroke lead, ended with 73 for a 2-stroke victory. Bob Murphy finished with a 66 to share second place with Arnold Palmer. It was Palmer's third second-place finish. He never came as close again.

1971 The first championship to be held in February and the first to be housed on the PGA National course at Palm Beach Gardens, Florida. It was appropriate, therefore, that a near neighbour, Jack Nicklaus, should record his second PGA success when he had 2 strokes

to spare over Billy Casper. His victory meant that he was the first player to win the US and British Opens, the PGA and the Masters twice.

1972 A championship won by a remarkable recovery stroke. At the 16th at Oakland Hills in the final round Gary Player, having dropped strokes at the 14th and 15th, pushed his drive, but hit a daring 9 iron over a host of trouble to within 4 ft (1·2 m) of the flag. He holed for a birdie and went on to his second title.

1973 Remembered not as the best PGA championship, but the one in which Nicklaus won his 14th major victory and went ahead of Bobby Jones. At Canterbury GC, Cleveland, he won by 4 strokes from Bruce Crampton, thus equalling the biggest margin of victory since the championship moved to strokeplay.

1974 Gary Player had a 64 in his second round at Tanglewood GC, one off the PGA record set the following year, but in a week of heavy rain the new champion was Lee Trevino. Nicklaus was second and Bobby Cole of South Africa, who went into the lead at the start of the last round, was third. Trevino's win followed his victories in the US and British Opens.

1975 Jack Nicklaus crept within one of Walter Hagen's record with his fourth win. It was his 16th major victory, but he had to contend with a brilliant spell from Bruce Crampton. On the long and demanding Firestone CC South course, Crampton had a second-round 63. This is the lowest round ever played in the PGA and his total of 134 equalled that held by Jerry Barber for 36 holes.

However, playing together in the third round, Nicklaus had a 67 to Crampton's 75 and though Crampton finished strongly in the last round, nobody could catch Nicklaus.

1976 A championship in which thunderstorms made a Monday finish necessary, brought a second victory for Dave Stockton. His total of 281 at Congressional equalled the highest winning aggregate at that time, but Stockton had to get down in 2 from off the last green holing from 10 ft (3 m) to prevent a play-off with Don January and Ray Floyd. 282 was the highest winning total.

Gil Morgan's 36-hole total of 134 (66, 68) equalled the lowest in a PGA championship.

1977 Pebble Beach's first PGA seemed to be destined for Gene Littler. He led from the first round, was still 5 ahead with 9 holes to play and was only headed on the 3rd hole of the sudden-death play-off. Lanny Wadkins, having won no event for almost four years, had two eagles on the front 9 of the final round and profited when Littler dropped strokes on 5 of the first 6 holes

One of the great workers of the ball—Lee Trevino (Action Photos)

on the back 9. Jack Nicklaus led after 15 holes, but he bogeyed the par-3 17th while Wadkins had a birdie at the par-5 18th.

Having had to hole from 20 ft (6 m) to stay in the play-off at the 1st hole, Wadkins won with a 4 to a 5 on the 3rd. It was the first time a sudden-death play-off had decided a major championship.

1978 A three-way tie resulting in the first major victory for John Mahaffey at Oakmont. It was the second sudden-death play-off in two years. Mahaffey won with a birdie on the 2nd extra hole from Tom Watson and Jerry Pate. Pate missed a short putt to win the championship on the 72nd hole, but Watson had been 4 ahead of Pate and 5 ahead of Mahaffey with 9 holes to play. However, after many setbacks, nobody begrudged Mahaffey his success.

1979 For the third year running, it needed a sudden-death play-off to decide the championship at Oakland Hills. David Graham and Ben Crenshaw were those involved and Graham holed from 6 yd (5·5 m) and 10 ft (3 m) on the first two sudden-death holes before winning on the 3rd with a 2 to a 4.

He thus became the first Australian winner since Jim Ferrier in 1947, but there was drama on the 72nd hole. Needing a 4 for a 2-stroke victory which would have set a new 72-hole record aggregate and equalled the lowest single round in the USPGA (63), he took 6. His drive was way right, his second through the green and he needed 2 chips and 2 putts.

Crenshaw who was down in 2 from a bunker at the 17th and from the back of the 18th, got into a play-off but, after the British Open a few weeks previously, he again suffered a disappointment when in sight of his first major championship win.

He was unluckily thwarted by Graham's 2 saving putts, but Graham's last round of 65 was remarkable despite taking 6 at the last. His total of 272 (69, 68, 70, 65) earned first prize of $30 000. Sam Snead finished 40th on 288, level fours, at the age of 67.

Crenshaw became only the second man to break 70 in all four rounds (69, 67, 69, 67). The first was Arnold Palmer at Columbus in 1964 (68, 68, 69, 69) but, like Crenshaw, he was second. Bobby Nichols won a record 271.

DETAILED RECORDS 1916–1980

Held by matchplay 1916 to 1957. Since 1958 held as strokeplay

Most victories
5, Walter Hagen, 1921-24-25-26-27; Jack Nicklaus, 1963-71-73-75-80
3, Gene Sarazen, 1922-23-33; Sam Snead, 1942-49-51

Most times runner-up or joint runner-up
3, Byron Nelson, 1939-41-44; Arnold Palmer, 1964-68-70; Billy Casper, 1958-65-71; Jack Nicklaus, 1964-65-74

Oldest winner
Julius Boros, 48 years 4 months 18 days, 1968

Youngest winner
Gene Sarazen, 20 years 5 months 20 days, 1922
Tom Creavy, 20 years 7 months 11 days, 1931

Biggest margin of victory
Matchplay (final): 8 and 7, Paul Runyan beat Sam Snead, 1938
Strokeplay: 7 strokes, Jack Nicklaus, 1980; 4 strokes, Al Geiberger, 1966, Jack Nicklaus, 1973

Lowest winning aggregate
271 (64, 71, 69, 67), Bobby Nichols, Columbus CC, Ohio, 1964
272 (69, 68, 70, 65), David Graham, Oakland Hills, 1979

Highest winning aggregate
282 (69, 71, 72, 70), Lanny Wadkins, Pebble Beach, 1977; after a play-off with Gene Littler

Lowest individual round
63, Bruce Crampton, second round, Firestone CC, Akron, 1975
64, Bobby Nichols, first round, Columbus CC, 1964; Jack Nicklaus, fourth round, Columbus CC, 1964; Gary Player, second round, Tanglewood GC, 1974

Lowest first round
64, Bobby Nichols, Columbus CC, 1964

Lowest second round
63, Bruce Crampton, Firestone CC, Akron, 1975

Lowest third round
65, Bruce Crampton, DAC CC, Dallas, 1963

Lowest fourth round
64, Jack Nicklaus, Columbus CC, 1964

Lowest 36-hole total
134 (69, 65), Jerry Barber, Minneapolis GC, 1959
134 (71, 63) Bruce Crampton, Firestone CC, 1975

134 (66, 68) Gil Morgan, Congressional CC, 1976

Lowest 54-hole total
202 (69, 66, 67), Raymond Floyd, NCR CC, Dayton, 1969

Lowest 9 holes
30, Art Wall, Jr, second 9, third round, Llanerch CC, 1958; Jerry Barber, first 9, second round, Minneapolis GC, 1959; Bob Rosburg, first 9, fourth round, Minneapolis GC, 1959; Jim Colbert, second 9, second round, Firestone CC, 1975

Biggest span between first and last victories
17 years, Jack Nicklaus, 1963–80

Successive victories
4, Walter Hagen, 1924-25-26-27
2, Jim Barnes, 1916-19; Gene Sarazen, 1922-23; Leo Diegel, 1928–29; Densmore Shute, 1936-37

Matchplay—most times in final
6, Walter Hagen, 1921-23-24-25-26-27
5, Sam Snead, 1938-40-42-49-51; Byron Nelson, 1939-40-41-44-45

Most consecutive finals
5, Walter Hagen, 1923–27

Most matches won
51, Gene Sarazen
42, Walter Hagen

Most consecutive matches won
22, Walter Hagen
14, Densmore Shute
13, Gene Sarazen

Longest final
38 holes: Gene Sarazen beat Walter Hagen, 1923; Paul Runyan beat Craig Wood, 1934; Vic Ghezzi beat Byron Nelson, 1941

Longest match
43 holes: Johnny Golden beat Walter Hagen, 1932

Best comeback
In a 36-hole match at Keller GC, St Paul, Minnesota, in 1932, Bobby Cruickshank beat Al Watrous at the 41st hole, having been 9 down with 12 holes to play. In the next round, Cruickshank lost to Frank Walsh who lost in the final to Olin Dutra.

Most extra hole matches in one championship
In 1937, Harold 'Jug' McSpaden won on the

38th in the first round, on the 39th in the fourth round and lost the final to Densmore Shute on the 37th.

In 1953, Dave Douglas won on the 20th in the first round, on the 19th in the second round and on the 37th in the third round. His opponents were Lew Worsham, Sam Snead and Jackson Bradley.

RESULTS

USPGA Championship Finals

1916 Siwanoy CC, New York
Jim M Barnes beat Jock Hutchison 1 up

1919 Engineers CC, New York
Jim M Barnes beat Freddy McLeod 6 and 5

1920 Flossmoor CC, Illinois
Jock Hutchison beat J D Edgar 1 up

1921 Inwood CC, New York
Walter Hagen beat Jim M Barnes 3 and 2

1922 Oakmont CC, Pennsylvania
Gene Sarazen beat Emmet French 4 and 3

1923 Pelham CC, New York
Gene Sarazen beat Walter Hagen at 38th

1924 French Lick CC, Indiana
Walter Hagen beat Jim M Barnes 2 up

1925 Olympia Fields CC, Illinois
Walter Hagen beat Bill Mehlhorn 6 and 5

1926 Salisbury GC, New York
Walter Hagen beat Leo Diegel 5 and 3

1927 Cedar Crest CC, Texas
Walter Hagen beat Joe Turnesa 1 up

1928 Baltimore CC Five Farms, Maryland
Leo Diegel beat Al Espinosa 6 and 5

1929 Hillcrest CC, California
Leo Diegel beat John Farrell 6 and 4

1930 Fresh Meadow, New York
Tommy Armour beat Gene Sarazen 1 up

1931 Wannamoisett CC, Rhode Island
Tom Creavy beat Densmore Shute 2 and 1

1932 Keller GC, Minnesota
Olin Dutra beat Frank Walsh 4 and 3

1933 Blue Mound CC, Wisconsin
Gene Sarazen beat Willie Goggin 5 and 4

1934 Park CC, New York
Paul Runyan beat Craig Wood at 38th

1935 Twin Hills CC, Oklahoma
Johnny Revolta beat Tommy Armour 5 and 4

1936 Pinehurst CC, North Carolina
Densmore Shute beat Jimmy Thomson 3 and 2

1937 Pittsburgh CC, Pennsylvania
Densmore Shute beat Harold McSpaden at 37th

1938 Shawnee CC, Pennsylvania
Paul Runyan beat Sam Snead 8 and 7

1939 Pomonok CC, New York
Henry Picard beat Byron Nelson at 37th

1940 Hershey CC, Pennsylvania
Byron Nelson beat Sam Snead 1 up

1941 Cherry Hills CC, Colorado
Vic Ghezzi beat Byron Nelson at 38th

1942 Seaview CC, New Jersey
Sam Snead beat Jim Turnesa 2 and 1

1944 Manito G & CC, Washington
Bob Hamilton beat Byron Nelson 1 up

1945 Morraine CC, Ohio
Byron Nelson beat Sam Byrd 4 and 3

1946 Portland GC, Oregon
Ben Hogan beat Porky Oliver 6 and 4

1947 Plum Hollow CC, Michigan
Jim Ferrier beat Chick Harbert 2 and 1

1948 Norwood Hills CC, Missouri
Ben Hogan beat Mike Turnesa 7 and 6

1949 Hermitage CC, Virginia
Sam Snead beat John Palmer 3 and 2

1950 Scioto CC, Ohio
Chandler Harper beat Henry Williams Jr 4 and 3

1951 Oakmont CC, Pennsylvania
Sam Snead beat Walter Burkemo 7 and 6

1952 Big Spring CC, Kentucky
Jim Turnesa beat Chick Harbert 1 up

1953 Birmingham CC, Michigan
Walter Burkemo beat Felice Torza 2 and 1

1954 Keller GC, Minnesota
Chick Harbert beat Walter Burkemo 4 and 3

1955 Meadowbrook CC, Michigan
Doug Ford beat Cary Middlecoff 4 and 3

1956 Blue Hill CC, Massachusetts
Jack Burke beat Ted Kroll 3 and 2

1957 Miami Valley GC, Ohio
Lionel Hebert beat Dow Finsterwald 2 and 1

1958 Llanerch CC, Pennsylvania
(Decided by strokeplay hereafter)

Dow Finsterwald	67	72	70	67	276
Billy Casper	73	67	68	70	278
Sam Snead	73	67	67	73	280
Jack Burke	70	72	69	70	281
Julius Boros	72	68	73	72	285
Tommy Bolt	72	70	73	70	285

1959 Minneapolis GC, Minnesota

Bob Rosburg	71	72	68	66	277
Jerry Barber	69	65	71	73	278
Doug Sanders	72	66	68	72	278
Dow Finsterwald	71	68	71	70	280
Mike Souchak	69	67	71	74	281
Bob Goalby	72	69	72	68	281
Ken Venturi	70	72	70	69	281

1960 Firestone CC, Ohio

Jay Hebert	72	67	72	70	281
Jim Ferrier	71	74	66	71	282
Sam Snead	68	73	70	72	283
Doug Sanders	70	71	69	73	283
Don January	70	70	72	72	284
Wesley Ellis	72	72	72	69	285
Arnold Palmer	67	74	75	70	286

1961 Olympia Fields CC, Illinois

Jerry Barber	69	67	71	70	277
Don January	72	66	67	72	277
(Barber won play-off 67 to 68)					
Doug Sanders	70	68	74	68	280
Ted Kroll	72	68	70	71	281
Arnold Palmer	73	72	69	68	282
Wesley Ellis	71	71	68	72	282
Johnny Pott	71	73	67	71	282
Doug Ford	69	73	74	66	282
Gene Littler	71	70	72	69	282
Art Wall	67	72	73	70	282

1962 Aronimink GC, Pennsylvania

Gary Player	72	67	69	70	278
Bob Goalby	69	72	71	67	279
Jack Nicklaus	71	74	69	67	281
George Bayer	69	70	71	71	281
Doug Ford	69	69	73	71	282
Bobby Nichols	72	70	71	70	283

1963 Dallas Athletic CC, Texas

Jack Nicklaus	69	73	69	68	279
Dave Ragan	75	70	67	69	281
Dow Finsterwald	72	72	66	72	282
Bruce Crampton	70	73	65	74	282
Al Geiberger	72	73	69	70	284
Billy Maxwell	73	71	69	71	284

1964 Columbus CC, Ohio

Bobby Nichols	64	71	69	67	271
Arnold Palmer	68	68	69	69	274
Jack Nicklaus	67	73	70	64	274
Mason Rudolph	73	66	68	69	276
Ken Venturi	72	65	73	69	279
Tom Nieporte	68	71	68	72	279

1965 Laurel Valley GC, Pennsylvania

Dave Marr	70	69	70	71	280
Billy Casper	70	70	71	71	282
Jack Nicklaus	69	70	72	71	282
Bo Winniger	73	72	72	66	283
Gardner Dickinson	67	74	69	74	284
Bruce Devlin	68	75	72	70	285

1966 Firestone CC, Ohio

Al Geiberger	68	72	68	72	280
Dudley Wysong	74	72	66	72	284
Billy Casper	73	73	70	70	286
Gene Littler	75	71	71	70	286
Gary Player	73	70	70	73	286

1967 Columbine CC, Colorado

Don January	71	72	70	68	281
Don Massengale	70	75	70	66	281
(January won play-off 69 to 71)					
Jack Nicklaus	67	75	69	71	282
Dan Sikes	69	70	70	73	282
Julius Boros	69	76	70	68	283
Al Geiberger	73	71	69	70	283

1968 Pecan Valley CC, Texas

Julius Boros	71	71	70	69	281
Bob Charles	72	70	70	70	282
Arnold Palmer	71	69	72	70	282
George Archer	71	69	74	69	283
Marty Fleckman	66	72	72	73	283
Frank Beard	68	70	72	74	284
Billy Casper	74	74	70	70	284

1969 NCR GC, Dayton, Ohio

Ray Floyd	69	66	67	74	276
Gary Player	71	65	71	70	277
Bert Greene	71	68	68	71	278
J Wright	71	68	69	71	279
Larry Ziegler	69	71	70	70	280
Miller Barber	73	75	64	68	280

1970 Southern Hills CC, Oklahoma

Dave Stockton	70	70	66	73	279
Bob Murphy	71	73	71	66	281
Arnold Palmer	70	72	69	70	281
Larry Hinson	69	71	74	68	282
Gene Littler	72	71	69	70	282
Jack Nicklaus	68	76	73	66	283
Bruce Crampton	73	75	68	67	283

1971 PGA National GC, Florida

Jack Nicklaus	69	69	70	73	281
Billy Casper	71	73	71	68	283
Tommy Bolt	72	74	69	69	284
Miller Barber	72	68	75	70	285
Gary Player	71	73	68	73	285
Dave Hill	74	71	71	70	286
Jim Jamieson	72	72	72	70	286
Gibby Gilbert	74	67	72	73	286

1972 Oakland Hills GC, Michigan

Gary Player	71	71	67	72	281
Tommy Aaron	71	71	70	71	283
Jim Jamieson	69	72	72	70	283
Billy Casper	73	70	67	74	284
Raymond Floyd	69	71	74	70	284
Sam Snead	70	74	71	69	284

1973 Canterbury Club, Ohio

Jack Nicklaus	72	68	68	69	277
Bruce Crampton	71	73	67	70	281
Mason Rudolph	69	70	70	73	282
Lanny Wadkins	73	69	71	69	282
Jesse C Snead	71	74	68	69	282
Dan Sikes	72	68	72	71	283
Tom Weiskopf	70	71	71	71	283
Don Iverson	67	72	70	74	283

1974 Tanglewood GC, North Carolina

Lee Trevino	73	66	68	69	276
Jack Nicklaus	69	69	70	69	277
Bobby Cole	69	68	71	71	279
Hubert Green	68	68	73	70	279
Dave Hill	74	69	67	69	279
Sam Snead	69	71	71	68	279

1975 Firestone CC, Akron, Ohio

Jack Nicklaus	70	68	67	71	276
Bruce Crampton	71	63	75	69	278
Tom Weiskopf	70	71	70	68	279

1976 Congressional CC, Maryland

Dave Stockton	70	72	69	70	281
Raymond Floyd	72	68	71	71	282
Don January	70	69	71	72	282

1977 Pebble Beach, California

Lanny Wadkins	69	71	72	70	282
Gene Littler	67	69	70	76	282
(Wadkins won sudden-death play-off at 3rd hole)					
Jack Nicklaus	69	71	70	73	283

1978 Oakmont CC, Pennsylvania

John Mahaffey	75	67	68	66	276
Jerry Pate	72	70	66	68	276
Tom Watson	67	69	67	73	276
(Mahaffey won sudden-death play-off at 2nd hole)					

1979 Oakland Hills, Michigan

David Graham	69	68	70	65	272
Ben Crenshaw	69	67	69	67	272
(Graham won sudden-death play-off at 3rd hole)					
Randy Caldwell	67	70	66	71	274

US MASTERS

First played 1934

This is the youngest of the world's four major championships. Unlike the other three (the British Open, the US Open and the USPGA), it is always played on the same course, the Augusta National in Georgia, and is an invitation only tournament, invitations being based on a formula laid down in advance and reviewed from time to time.

Both the Augusta course and the Masters tournament were the brainchild of Bobby Jones whose influence always dominated the event even after his death. Although he retired as a player in 1930, he took part in the first tournament in 1934 because the Club was short of money and it needed someone to draw the local public.

Jones had invited some of his old rivals to what, by modern standards, was an informal gathering and he finished in a tie for 13th place. However, a start had been made and the following year it received maximum publicity from the famous double eagle at the 15th in the

last round of the eventual winner, Gene Sarazen.

More recently, its fame has been spread by the televising of the event every April on a course, designed by Alister Mackenzie, which is spectacularly beautiful and always at its best in Masters week. Originally, it was a plantation that Baron Berckmans, a distinguished Belgian horticulturist, had developed into the South's first great nursery.

Another trend which the Masters set has been the advance booking of tickets and no admission on a casual daily basis. But the real difference between the Masters and other major tournaments is the absence of advertising or any form of commercialism.

Nowadays, the field comprises the leading American professionals and amateurs together with a few selected overseas players who meet prescribed qualifications. For many years, the Masters was guided by Jones and Clifford Roberts and, since their deaths, it continues to be run from within the Club. It consists of 72 holes of strokeplay.

MILESTONES

1934 First tournament in which Horton Smith finished birdie, par to beat Craig Wood by 1 stroke. First hole in one by Ross Somerville the Canadian amateur. There have been nine since. Full list:

4th hole: None

6th hole: Leland Gibson (1954), Billy Joe Patton (1954), Charles Coody (1972)

12th hole: Claude Harmon (1947), William Hyndman III (1959)

16th hole: Ross Somerville (1934), (Willie Goggin (1935), Ray Billows (1940), John Dawson (1949), Clive Clark (1968)

1935 One of golf's most famous strokes was played by Gene Sarazen at the par-5 15th hole in the last round. He holed a 220 yd (200 m) 4 wood shot for a double eagle 2. Three behind Craig Wood on the 15th tee, he finished the last 3 holes in par, tied and won the play-off by 5 strokes. It was the only 36-hole play-off.

Frank Walsh took 12 on the 8th.

1936 Craig Wood shot 88 in the first round, 67 in the second.

Horton Smith's second victory with a remarkable finish in extremely rainy conditions. He made up 6 strokes in the last two rounds on Harry Cooper; then went one ahead.

1937 Byron Nelson, the winner, picked up 6 strokes in the final round on Ralph Guldahl at the 12th and 13th. Nelson scored 2, 3 to Guldahl's 5, 6 and won by two. Nelson's first round 66 was the lowest to date.

1938 Henry Picard became the second winner by more than 1 stroke winning by 2. A final 70 beat Ralph Guldahl and Harry Cooper who tied second on 287. Ben Hogan's first Masters.

1939 Sam Snead appeared to be the winner until Ralph Guldahl shot 33 on the back 9 to win by 1 stroke. In June of the same year, Snead took 8 on the final hole of the US Open at the Philadelphia Country Club.

1940 Two notable records. Jimmy Demaret won by 4 strokes, the biggest margin until 1948. In the first round, he covered the second 9 holes in 30 thus equalling the all-time record on a championship course. Lloyd Mangrum, who finished second, opened with a 64, the lowest score in any of the four major championships

This miniature of the Augusta National's Club House serves as the permanent Masters Tournament Trophy. Designed by a firm of silversmiths in Chicago and built by hand in England, this trophy is comprised of 900 separate pieces of silver. On the band around the base of the trophy are the names of the past winners.

A small replica of this trophy will be presented each year to the winner of the Masters.

A much sought-after prize. A scale model of the Club House at the Augusta National Golf Club (Action Photos)

for many years. It was not matched at Augusta until 1965.

1941 Craig Wood's first major victory. The leader for three rounds, he was caught by Byron Nelson at the turn in the 4th, but came home in 34 to win by 3 strokes. Two months later, he also won the US Open.

1942 The first 18-hole play-off. In it, Byron Nelson gained 5 strokes on his fellow Texan Ben Hogan in a stretch of 11 holes although Hogan played them in one under par.

1946 Another chance for Hogan who took 3 putts on the 72nd green to finish runner-up for the second year running. A little earlier, Herman Keiser, the winner, also took 3 putts on the last green. Keiser had started the final round 5 strokes ahead of Hogan.

1947 Jimmy Demaret emulated Horton Smith and Byron Nelson as two-time winners of the Masters. Tied for the first-round lead with Nelson, he then went into the lead and stayed there.

Gene Sarazen and George Fazio, first off in the final round, completed the course in 1 hr 57 min. Sarazen scored 70.

1948 Claude Harmon was better known as a club professional, but he won the Masters by 5 strokes and equalled the record aggregate of 279. He covered the 6th, 7th and 8th in the final round in 2, 3, 3—4 under par.

1949 After high winds on the first two days, Sam Snead had two marvellous 67s to finish on 282. His total for the last two rounds was 14 strokes better than that for the first two rounds. They remained the best two finishing rounds until Jack Nicklaus scored 64, 69 in 1965.

In Snead's last round, he had more birdies (8) than pars (7).

1950 A 7-stroke swing on the last 6 holes enabled Jimmy Demaret to catch Jim Ferrier and beat him by 2 strokes. He thus became the first three-time winner.

Jimmy Demaret—first three-time winner of the Masters (US Golf Association)

Herman Barron took 11 on the par-3 16th.
1951 Having been close several times, Ben Hogan finally won with a final-round 68 for 280 and victory by 2 strokes over Skee Riegel who, in turn, was 4 ahead of those tied for third place.

Dow Finsterwald took 11 on the par-3 12th.
1952 Sam Snead who triumphed in high winds in 1949, did so again. This time, the winds came in the last two rounds. After gaining a 3-stroke lead at half-way (70, 67), Snead added a 77 and a 72 for a 4-stroke victory over Jack Burke, the only player to break 70 on the last day.
1953 Part one of Ben Hogan's *annus mirabilis*. He became the first player to have three rounds under 70 in the Masters, his last three rounds being 69, 66, 69 for a total of 274, a new low and victory by 5 strokes.

The Masters record book states Hogan's belief that his play at Augusta was the finest of his career.

There were 13 eagles on the 13th hole.
1954 The year in which the two best-known professionals, Sam Snead and Ben Hogan, contested a play-off, but were nearly defeated before they got there by a virtually unknown amateur playing his first Masters, Billy Joe Patton from North Carolina.

Patton led the field after 36 holes, was 5 strokes behind after 54 and lead again as late as the 12th hole in the final round, having been helped by holing in one at the 6th. However, a 7 at the 13th and a 6 at the 15th saved the professionals' pride. Patton finished 1 stroke behind Snead and Hogan. In the play-off Snead scored 70 to Hogan's 71.

Patton, who had a birdie on all four days at the par-4 9th, had a remarkable haul of prizes. Gold and silver cup for best amateur score; gold medal for best Amateur score; crystal vase for being the low scorer in the first round; crystal cup for a hole in one and a gold money clip for winning the pre-tournament long driving contest.
1955 Record 7-stroke victory for Dr Cary Middlecoff who had a 65 in the second round which, though equalled by Frank Beard in 1968, was not bettered in any second round until 1979, when Miller Barber had a second-round 64.

Ben Hogan and Sam Snead finished second and third.
1956 Jack Burke's winning score of 289 equalled the record highest, but he made up 8 strokes over the last 18 holes on the amateur Ken Venturi and beat him by one. Burke's final round was 71, Venturi's 80. Middlecoff, the holder, took 77 to finish third, 2 behind Burke. Gary Player's first Masters.
1957 A closing 66, the lowest final round at the time, brought victory for Doug Ford who holed out of a bunker at the 18th. He won by 3 strokes from Sam Snead who had started the last round 3 ahead.

No mistaking the man or his action—Arnold Palmer (Action Photos)

1958 Arnold Palmer's first Masters Victory. At 28, he was the youngest winner since Byron Nelson in 1937.

1959 Art Wall, the new champion, had 8 birdies in a final 66, 5 of them on the last 6 holes. He had started the final round 6 strokes behind Arnold Palmer, defending champion and Canadian, Stan Leonard.

1960 Second of Arnold Palmer's victories. He led the field at the end of every round but in the final round he was 1 stroke behind Ken Venturi with 2 holes to play. Palmer birdied both to win by 1 stroke. It was the second time in five years that Venturi finished second.

George Bayer and Jack Fleck went round in 1 hr 52 min. Bayer scored 72 and Fleck 74.

1961 Gary Player, 25, became the first foreign winner of the Masters. He won by 1 stroke from the amateur Charles Coe and defending champion Arnold Palmer. In a dramatic finish, Player made a 4 from a bunker at the 18th; Palmer took 6 from the same bunker.

Coe's total of 281 is the lowest ever returned by an amateur at the Masters.

1962 Revenge for Palmer over Player in the first triple tie. In the play-off, Palmer scored 68 (the lowest in a play-off) to Player's 71 and Dow Finsterwald's 77. Palmer came home in 31.

1963 First victory for Jack Nicklaus, the youngest champion at 23. In rough weather, he won by 1 stroke from Tony Lema who was playing in his first Masters.

1964 Record fourth victory for Arnold Palmer in a span of only seven tournaments. He won by 6 strokes from Dave Marr and Jack Nicklaus, but it was his last victory in any of the world's four major championships.

The qualifying score was 148, equalled four times subsequently, but not bettered until 1979.

1965 Jack Nicklaus, second winner to have three rounds under 70, lowered the record aggregate to 271 and equalled Lloyd Mangrum's record individual round with a third-round 64.

Arnold Palmer and Gary Player tied second on 280, the only occasion on which the Big Three finished 1,2,3 in a major championship.

1966 Second triple tie but Jack Nicklaus (70) held off Tommy Jacobs (72) and Gay Brewer (78) in a play-off that only just beat darkness to become the first champion to successfully defend his title. It is one of the Masters oddest records that he remains so.

Twelve amateurs made the cut. The qualifying was the highest, 153, although a record number of 64 qualified. The 10-stroke rule was invoked for the first time.

1967 Gay Brewer who had taken 5 at the 72nd the year before, defeated his playing partner Bobby Nichols in an exciting finish by 1 stroke.

Ben Hogan shot a third-round 66 at the age of 54, the lowest of the tournament.

Bobby Cole, 18, became the youngest player to survive the cut. He was still an amateur.

1968 The year Roberto de Vicenzo signed for a 4 on the 71st hole instead of a 3 and lost to Bob Goalby by 1 stroke.

Generally, the year of the best scores: 127 rounds of par or better were played during the four days compared with the next best of 94 in 1965.

During the final round, de Vicenzo, on his 45th birthday, played the first 3 holes in 4 under par, an all-time record. He began by holing his second at the par-4 1st hole, but little did anyone realise that the end would be so tragic.

1969 25 players led, or shared the lead, over the four days—a record—but George Archer (6 ft 6 in (1·98 m), the tallest champion, triumphed in the end. Billy Casper, the joint runner-up 2 strokes behind, went out in 40 in the final round.

1970 Compensation for the year before as Casper became champion after a play-off with another Californian, Gene Littler.

1971 Charles Coody separated himself from some distinguished pursuers by playing the last 4 holes in 2 under par to become champion. After the 68th hole Johnny Miller had been 2 ahead of Coody and Jack Nicklaus. Coody's finish was in contrast to that in 1969 when he lost the title on the last 3 holes.

1972 Nicklaus joined Palmer as a four-time champion in a slightly disappointing Masters if there is such a thing. His total of 286 was the only one under par. Charles Coody, defending champion, holed in one at the 6th in the first round then took 7 at the par-4 7th.

1973 The Masters lost a day's play for the first time. Saturday was washed out by storms and the finish postponed until Monday when the first Georgian, Tommy Aaron, won the Green Jacket. In a close finish he won by 1 stroke from J C Snead.

At 24, Britain's Peter Oosterhuis became the youngest foreign player to lead the Masters at any point. He led after three rounds by 3 strokes, but he took a final 74 to finish in a triple tie for 3rd.

1974 Gary Player's second victory on a last day when six or seven others had a chance on the last 9 holes.

Sam Snead, 61 years 1 month and 8 days became the oldest player to make the cut.

Ralph Johnston became the first first-year player since Horton Smith in 1934 to complete four rounds of par or better.

Maurice Bembridge lowered the final round record with 64.

1975 Sometimes called the best Masters of all. Johnny Miller and Tom Weiskopf dominated the dramatic last day but could not prevent Jack Nicklaus from registering his record fifth victory. Weiskopf and Miller had chances of birdies at the 72nd hole to tie Nicklaus, but both failed. It was the fourth time Weiskopf finished second or joint second.

Hale Irwin had a final round of 64 to finish fourth, 5 strokes behind Weiskopf and Miller.

Miller had 6 birdies in a row from the 2nd in his record outward half of 30 in the third round.

1976 A championship dominated by Raymond Floyd. He led from start to finish; played the first 36 holes in a new record of 131(65,66); set another record for 54 holes (65,66,70), took an 8-stroke lead into the last round and equalled Jack Nicklaus's record aggregate of 271.

Floyd had a total of 21 birdies and 1 eagle.

1977 Tom Watson got the better of a terrific

Augusta National Golf Club, 10th green (Phil Sheldon)

Severiano Ballesteros fitted with his Masters jacket by deposed champion Fuzzy Zoeller (Phil Sheldon)

final day duel with Jack Nicklaus, who was playing just in front of him. A 67 for 276 gave Watson his first major championship victory, one he repeated in July over Nicklaus in the British Open.

Severiano Ballesteros, who celebrated his 20th birthday on the third day, became the youngest professional to take part in the Masters.

1978 Gary Player's third victory, 17 years after his first—a record span. Starting the last day 7 strokes behind the leader, Hubert Green, he had 7 birdies on the last 10 holes to win by 1 stroke. He came back in 30 to hoist a record last-round 64 by a winner.

Wally Armstrong finished equal 5th with 280, the lowest score ever by a player in his first Masters until Fuzzy Zoeller's win a year later.

Tsuneyuki Nakajima of Japan took 13 at the 13th. Three months later, he took 9 at the 17th in the British Open at St Andrews.

1979 Victory after the first sudden-death play-off in the Masters for Fuzzy Zoeller, the first player to win on his first Masters appearance (1934 excluded). He beat Ed Sneed and Tom Watson with a birdie 3 at the 11th (the play-off started at the 10th) after all three had missed birdie chances at the 10th. It was a Masters which Sneed lost. Having started poorly and then held his challenge together stoutly on the 11th, 12th, 13th, 14th and 15th, he dropped strokes on each of the last 3 holes. At the 18th, his 6 ft (1·8 m) winning putt hung on the lip.

Jack Nicklaus maintained his incredible run of consistency, but overran the 17th green downwind in the final round and took 5.

Earlier in the tournament, Miller Barber had equalled the lowest score with a second round of 64. Owing to the edge of a tornado hitting Augusta, it was a round which began on Friday and ended on Saturday morning.

The 36-hole cut was 145, the lowest ever.

First prize of $50 000.

1980 A Masters in which Severiano Ballesteros stole the show. Three strokes ahead after 36 holes and 7 ahead after 54, he was 10 strokes clear with 9 holes to play. Then 3 putts on the 10th, 5 at the par 3 12th and a 6 on the 13th gave Gibby Gilbert and Jack Newton a chance. It also meant that Ballesteros would not break the record winning margin, the record aggregate or become the first champion with four rounds under 70.

However, Ballersteros played the last 5 holes in 1 under par to become the youngest winner and the first European to win. With Jack Newton finishing equal 2nd, it was the first time two overseas players had finished so well. A third overseas player, David Graham, was 5th.

Tom Weiskopf took 13 on the 12th in the first round and 7 on the same hole in the second round.

WILLS'S CIGARETTES.

JAMES BRAID

WILLS'S CIGARETTES.

ARCHIE COMPSTON

WILLS'S CIGARETTES.

T. HENRY COTTON

WILLS'S CIGARETTES.

ARTHUR G. HAVERS

WILLS'S CIGARETTES.

GEORGE GADD

WILLS'S CIGARETTES.

HAROLD D. GILLIES

WILLS'S CIGARETTES.

WALTER J. HAGEN

WILLS'S CIGARETTES.

REX W. HARTLEY

WILLS'S CIGARETTES.

GEORGE DUNCAN

WILLS'S CIGARETTES.

ALEXANDER HERD

WILLS'S CIGARETTES.

C. O. HEZLET

WILLS'S CIGARETTES.

SIR E. W. E.
HOLDERNESS

WILLS'S CIGARETTES.

MISS CECIL LEITCH

WILLS'S CIGARETTES.

ARNAUD MASSY

WILLS'S CIGARETTES.

ABE MITCHELL

WILLS'S CIGARETTES.

R. H. DE MONTMORENCY

WILLS'S CIGARETTES.

T. P. PERKINS

WILLS'S CIGARETTES.

EDWARD RAY

WILLS'S CIGARETTES.

FREDERICK
ROBSON

WILLS'S CIGARETTES.

J. H. TAYLOR

WILLS'S CIGARETTES.

CYRIL J. H. TOLLEY

WILLS'S CIGARETTES.

HARRY VARDON

WILLS'S CIGARETTES.

MISS JOYCE WETHERED

WILLS'S CIGARETTES.

ROGER H. WETHERED

WILLS'S CIGARETTES.

C. A. WHITCOMBE

Aerial view of the most famous strip of golfing land in the world, St Andrews (Phil Sheldon)

Above: Stained-glass roundel at the base of the Crécy Window (*c* 1357) in Gloucester Cathedral showing a man swinging a club at a ball. (With kind permission of the Dean and Chapter of Gloucester. Photo by Peter Bateman)

Left: Golf's first 'holy' trinity. Harry Vardon (swinging), J H Taylor (sitting) and James Braid (Illustrated London News Pic. Lib.)

Above: Jack Nicklaus giving voice to his sentiments. Victory after a dramatic play-off at St Andrews 1970. The valiant loser, Doug Sanders, ponders what might have been. The presentation was made by the Captain of the Royal and Ancient Golf Club, the Rt Hon William Whitelaw (Action Photos)

Below: Gary Player, the most successful overseas golfer ever to play in America (All-Sport/Steve Powell)

Above: The ageless magic of Sam Snead, widely held to have the most classic of classic swings (All-Sport/Don Morley)

Above: Bobby Jones. A portrait of a man who had a profound and lasting influence on the game (Photograph by kind permission of Royal Lytham & St Annes Golf Club; from a painting by John A A Berrie)

Only the third Englishman to win the world's two most famous championships, Tony Jacklin (Photograph by courtesy of Dunlop Sports Co Ltd)

Left: Tom Watson who twice in 1977 had a head to head with Jack Nicklaus—and won (Action Photos)

Below: The greatest personal duel the British Open has seen, Tom Watson v Jack Nicklaus. Part of the historic scene. Turnberry 1977 (All Sport/Don Morley)

The greatest of all continental golfers, Severiano Ballesteros (Photograph by courtesy of Slazengers Ltd)

Right: The most successful Open champion of modern times and the best Australian of all time, Peter Thomson (Phil Sheldon)

Below: The most popular and best-loved golfer in post-war golf, Roberto de Vicenzo (Photograph by courtesy of Dunlop Sports Co Ltd)

LEADER BOARD

HOLES	+PAR-	PLAYER	SCORE
36	=9	WEISKOPF	135
36	=6	MILLER	138
34	=4	YANCLAUS	69
34	=5	NICKEY	69
32	=3	OCONNOR	73
31	■=2	GALLACHER	73
36	=1	COLES	143
36	=1	BUTLER	143
34	=1	BARNES	76
36	E	WADKINS	1■4
26	E	HUISH	74

Nickey Yanclaus. A 1973 British Open scoreboard which couldn't quite keep pace with events (All-Sport/Don Morley)

1976, the hottest summer and the hottest British Open. Royal Birkdale (All Sport/Don Morley)

Below: Johnny Miller, the man who became US Open champion at Oakmont in 1973 with the lowest round ever played in that championship (All-Sport/Don Morley)

Right: Hubert Green, the 1977 US Open champion who triumphed over a distinguished field and a threat on his life (Photograph by courtesy of Dunlop Sports Co Ltd)

A typically dashing picture of Arnold Palmer, founder of golf's richest golden age (Action Photos)

DETAILED RECORDS

Most victories
5, Jack Nicklaus, 1963-65-66-72-75
4, Arnold Palmer, 1958-60-62-64

Most times runner-up or joint runner-up
4, Ben Hogan, 1942-46-54-55; Tom Weiskopf, 1969-72-74-75

Oldest winners
Gary Player, 42 years 5 months 9 days, 1978
Sam Snead, 41 years 11 months 15 days, 1954

Youngest winners
Severiano Ballesteros, 23 years 4 days, 1980
Jack Nicklaus, 23 years 2 months, 1963

Biggest margin of victory
9 strokes, Jack Nicklaus, 1965
8 strokes, Raymond Floyd, 1976
7 strokes, Cary Middlecoff, 1955

Lowest winning aggregate
271 (67, 71, 64, 69), Jack Nicklaus, 1965
271 (65, 66, 70, 70) Raymond Floyd, 1976

Highest winning aggregate
289 (72, 71, 75, 71), Jack Burke, Jr, 1956;
289 (74, 73, 70, 72) Sam Snead, 1954

Lowest aggregate by runner-up
277 (75, 71, 65, 66), Johnny Miller, 1975;
277 (69, 72, 66, 70), Tom Weiskopf, 1975

Lowest aggregate by an amateur
281 (72, 71, 69, 69), Charles Coe, 1961

Lowest individual round
64, Lloyd Mangrum (32, 32), first round, 1940;
Jack Nicklaus (31, 33), third round, 1965;
Maurice Bembridge (34, 30), fourth round,
1974; Hale Irwin (32, 32), fourth round, 1975;
Gary Player (34, 30), fourth round, 1978; Miller
Barber (31, 33), second round, 1979

Lowest first round
64, Lloyd Mangrum, 1940

Lowest second round
64, Miller Barber, 1979

Lowest third round
64, Jack Nicklaus, 1965

Lowest fourth round
64, Maurice Bembridge, 1974; Hale Irwin, 1975; Gary Player, 1978

Lowest first 36 holes
131 (65, 66), Raymond Floyd, 1976

Lowest middle 36 holes
133 (68, 65), Dow Finsterwald, 1962

Lowest final 36 holes
131 (65, 66), Johnny Miller, 1975

Lowest first 54 holes
201 (65, 66, 70), Raymond Floyd, 1976

Lowest final 54 holes
202 (71, 65, 66), Johnny Miller, 1976

Lowest 9 holes
30, second 9: Jimmy Demaret, 1940; Gene Littler, 1966; Ben Hogan, 1967; Miller Barber, 1970; Maurice Bembridge, 1974; Gary Player, 1978
30, first 9: Johnny Miller, 1975

Most rounds under 70
27, Jack Nicklaus

Biggest span between first and last victories
17 years, Gary Player, 1961-78. Player also won in 1974

Successive victories
2, Jack Nicklaus, 1965–66
Two defenders, Ben Hogan, 1954, and Gary Player, 1962, lost in a play-off

Victories by amateurs
None. Ken Venturi finished second in 1956; Frank Stranahan (1947) and Charles Coe (1961) tied for second. Billy Joe Patton finished third in 1954, 1 stroke behind Ben Hogan and Sam Snead, who tied. Patton led with 6 holes to play

Highest number of top five finishes
13, Jack Nicklaus
9, Sam Snead, Ben Hogan, Arnold Palmer

First player to break 70
Ed Dudley 69, second round, 1934

Outright leader after every round
Craig Wood, 1941; Arnold Palmer, 1960; Jack Nicklaus, 1972; Raymond Floyd, 1976

Led or tied for lead from start to finish
Horton Smith, 1934; Herman Keiser, 1946; Jimmy Demaret, 1947; Arnold Palmer, 1964; Severiano Ballesteros, 1980

Play-offs
1935-42-54-62-66-70-79

Lowest round in a play-off
68, Arnold Palmer, 1962. Sudden death introduced in 1979

Overseas winners
Gary Player, 1961-74-78; Severiano Ballesteros, 1980

Record leads
After 18 holes: 5 strokes, Craig Wood, 1941
After 36 holes: 5 strokes, Herman Keiser, 1946; Jack Nicklaus, 1975; Raymond Floyd, 1976
After 54 holes: 8 strokes, Raymond Floyd, 1976

Biggest variation between rounds of a champion
10 strokes, Sam Snead, 1952, second round 67 third round 77

9 strokes, Byron Nelson, 1937, first round 66 third round 75

9 strokes, Arnold Palmer, 1962, second round 66 fourth round 75

Best comebacks by champions
After 18 holes: Jack Burke, 1956, and Gay Brewer, 1967, 6 strokes behind leader

After 36 holes: Jack Burke, 1956, 8 strokes behind the leader

After 54 holes: Jack Burke, 1956, 8 strokes behind the leader (made up 9 to win)

Champions with four rounds under 70
None. Ben Hogan, 1953; Gary Player, 1961; Arnold Palmer, 1964; Jack Nicklaus, 1965; Jack Nicklaus, 1975 and Severiano Ballesteros, 1980 had three rounds under 70

Best finishing round by a champion
64, Gary Player, 1978

Worst finishing round by a champion
75, Arnold Palmer, 1962 (after a play-off)

Best opening round by a champion
65, Raymond Floyd, 1976

Worst opening round by a champion
74, Horton Smith, 1936; Sam Snead, 1954; Jack Nicklaus, 1963

Winners at first attempt
Horton Smith, 1934; Gene Sarazen, 1935; Fuzzy (Frank Urban) Zoeller, 1979

Record number of appearances
39, Sam Snead, 1937–78

RESULTS

US Masters Tournament at Augusta National, Georgia

1934
Horton Smith	70	72	70	72	284
Craig Wood	71	74	69	71	285
Billy Burke	72	71	70	73	286
Paul Runyan	74	71	70	71	286
Ed Dudley	74	69	71	74	288
Willie Macfarlane	74	73	70	74	291

1935
Gene Sarazen	68	71	73	70	282
Craig Wood	69	72	68	73	282
(Sarazen won play-off 144 to 149)					
Olin Dutra	70	70	70	74	284
Henry Picard	67	68	76	75	286
Densmore Shute	73	71	70	73	287
Lawson Little, Jr	74	72	70	72	288

1936
Horton Smith	74	71	68	72	285
Harry Cooper	70	69	71	76	286
Gene Sarazen	78	67	72	70	287
Bobby Cruickshank	75	69	74	72	290
Paul Runyan	76	69	70	75	290
Lloyd Mangrum	76	73	68	76	293
Ed Dudley	75	75	70	73	293
Ky Laffoon	75	70	75	73	293

1937
Byron Nelson	66	72	75	70	283
Ralph Guldahl	69	72	68	76	285
Ed Dudley	70	71	71	74	286
Harry Cooper	73	69	71	74	287
Ky Laffoon	73	70	74	73	290
Jimmy Thomson	71	73	74	73	291

1938
Henry Picard	71	72	72	70	285
Ralph Guldahl	73	70	73	71	287
Harry Cooper	68	77	71	71	287
Paul Runyan	71	73	74	70	288
Byron Nelson	73	74	70	73	290
Ed Dudley	70	69	77	75	291
Felix Serafin	72	71	78	70	291

1939
Ralph Guldahl	72	68	70	69	279
Sam Snead	70	70	72	68	280
Billy Burke	69	72	71	70	282
Lawson Little, Jr	72	72	68	70	282
Gene Sarazen	73	66	72	72	283
Craig Wood	72	73	71	68	284

1940
Jimmy Demaret	67	72	70	71	280
Lloyd Mangrum	64	75	71	74	284
Byron Nelson	69	72	74	70	285
Ed Dudley	73	72	71	71	287
Harry Cooper	69	75	73	70	287
Willie Goggin	71	72	73	71	287

1941
Craig Wood	66	71	71	72	280
Byron Nelson	71	69	73	70	283
Sam Byrd	73	70	68	74	285
Ben Hogan	71	72	75	68	286
Ed Dudley	73	72	75	68	288
Sam Snead	73	75	72	69	289
Vic Ghezzi	77	71	71	70	289

1942
Byron Nelson	68	67	72	73	280
Ben Hogan	73	70	67	70	280
(Nelson won play-off 69 to 70)					
Paul Runyan	67	73	72	71	283
Sam Byrd	68	68	75	74	285
Horton Smith	67	73	74	73	287
Jimmy Demaret	70	70	75	75	290

1946
Herman Keiser	69	68	71	74	282
Ben Hogan	74	70	69	70	283
Bob Hamilton	75	69	71	72	287
Ky Laffoon	74	73	70	72	289
Jimmy Demaret	75	70	71	73	289
Jim Ferrier	74	72	68	75	289

1947
Jimmy Demaret	69	71	70	71	281
Byron Nelson	69	72	72	70	283

Frank Stranahan	73	72	70	68	283
Ben Hogan	75	68	71	70	284
Harold McSpaden	74	69	70	71	284
Henry Picard	73	70	72	71	286
Jim Ferrier	70	71	73	72	286

1948

Claude Harmon	70	70	69	70	279
Cary Middlecoff	74	71	69	70	284
Chick Harbert	71	70	70	76	287
Jim Ferrier	71	71	75	71	288
Lloyd Mangrum	69	73	75	71	288
Ed Furgol	70	72	73	74	289
Ben Hogan	70	71	77	71	289

1949

Sam Snead	73	75	67	67	282
Johnny Bulla	74	73	69	69	285
Lloyd Mangrum	69	74	72	70	285
Johnny Palmer	73	71	70	72	286
Jim Turnesa	73	72	71	70	286
Lew Worsham, Jr	76	75	70	68	289

1950

Jimmy Demaret	70	72	72	69	283
Jim Ferrier	70	67	73	75	285
Sam Snead	71	74	70	72	287
Ben Hogan	73	68	71	76	288
Byron Nelson	75	70	69	74	288
Lloyd Mangrum	76	74	73	68	291

1951

Ben Hogan	70	72	70	68	280
Skee Riegel	73	68	70	71	282
Lloyd Mangrum	69	74	70	73	286
Lew Worsham, Jr	71	71	72	72	286
Dave Douglas	74	69	72	73	288
Lawson Little, Jr	72	73	72	72	289

1952

Sam Snead	70	67	77	72	286
Jack Burke, Jr	76	67	78	69	290
Al Besselink	70	76	71	74	291
Tommy Bolt	71	71	75	74	291
Jim Ferrier	72	70	77	72	291
Lloyd Mangrum	71	74	75	72	292

1953

Ben Hogan	70	69	66	69	274
Porky Oliver, Jr	69	73	67	70	279
Lloyd Mangrum	74	68	71	69	282
Bob Hamilton	71	69	70	73	283
Tommy Bolt	71	75	68	71	285
Chick Harbert	68	73	70	74	285

1954

Sam Snead	74	73	70	72	289
Ben Hogan	72	73	69	75	289
(Snead won play-off 70 to 71)					
Billy Joe Patton	70	74	75	71	290
Dutch Harrison	70	79	74	68	291
Lloyd Mangrum	71	75	76	69	291
Jerry Barber	74	76	71	71	292
Jack Burke, Jr	71	77	73	71	292
Bob Rosburg	73	73	76	70	292

1955

Cary Middlecoff	72	65	72	70	279
Ben Hogan	73	68	72	73	286
Sam Snead	72	71	74	70	287
Bob Rosburg	72	72	72	73	289
Mike Souchak	71	74	72	72	289
Julius Boros	71	75	72	71	289

1956

Jack Burke, Jr	72	71	75	71	289
Ken Venturi	66	69	75	80	290
Cary Middlecoff	67	72	75	77	291
Lloyd Mangrum	72	74	72	74	292
Sam Snead	73	76	72	71	292
Jerry Barber	71	72	76	75	294
Doug Ford	70	72	75	77	294

1957

Doug Ford	72	73	72	66	283
Sam Snead	72	68	74	72	286
Jimmy Demaret	72	70	75	70	287
Harvie H Ward, Jr	73	71	71	73	288
Peter Thomson	72	73	73	71	289
Ed Furgol	73	71	72	74	290

1958

Arnold Palmer	70	73	68	73	284
Doug Ford	74	71	70	70	285
Fred Hawkins	71	75	68	71	285
Stan Leonard	72	70	73	71	286
Ken Venturi	68	72	74	72	286
Cary Middlecoff	70	73	69	75	287
Art Wall, Jr	71	72	70	74	287

1959

Art Wall, Jr	73	74	71	66	284
Cary Middlecoff	74	71	68	72	285
Arnold Palmer	71	70	71	74	286
Dick Mayer	73	75	71	68	287
Stan Leonard	69	74	69	75	287
Charlie R Coe	74	74	67	73	288

1960

Arnold Palmer	67	73	72	70	282
Ken Venturi	73	69	71	70	283
Dow Finsterwald	71	70	72	71	284
Billy Casper, Jr	71	71	71	74	287
Julius Boros	72	71	70	75	288
Walter Burkemo	72	69	75	73	289
Ben Hogan	73	68	72	76	289
Gary Player	72	71	72	74	289

1961

Gary Player	69	68	69	74	280
Arnold Palmer	68	69	73	71	281
Charlie Coe	72	71	69	69	281
Tommy Bolt	72	71	74	68	285
Don January	74	68	72	71	285
Paul Harney	71	73	68	74	286

1962

Arnold Palmer	70	66	69	75	280
Gary Player	67	71	71	71	280
Don Finsterwald	74	68	65	73	280
(Palmer won play-off 68 to 71 to 77)					
Gene Littler	71	68	71	72	282
Mike Souchak	70	72	74	71	287
Jimmy Demaret	73	73	71	70	287
Jerry Barber	72	72	69	74	287
Billy Maxwell	71	73	72	71	287

1963

Jack Nicklaus	74	66	74	72	286
Tony Lema	74	69	74	70	287
Julius Boros	76	69	71	72	288
Sam Snead	70	73	74	71	288
Dow Finsterwald	74	73	73	69	289
Ed Furgol	70	71	74	74	289
Gary Player	71	74	74	70	289

1964

Arnold Palmer	69	68	69	70	276
Dave Marr	70	73	69	70	282
Jack Nicklaus	71	73	71	67	282
Bruce Devlin	72	72	67	73	284
Billy Casper, Jr	76	72	69	69	286
Jim Ferrier	71	73	69	73	286
Paul Harney	73	72	71	70	286
Gary Player	69	72	72	73	286

1965

Jack Nicklaus	67	71	64	69	271
Arnold Palmer	70	68	72	70	280
Gary Player	65	73	69	73	280
Mason Rudolph	70	75	66	72	283
Dan Sikes	67	72	71	75	285
Gene Littler	71	74	67	74	286
Ramon Sota	71	73	70	72	286

1966

Jack Nicklaus	68	76	72	72	288
Tommy Jacobs	75	71	70	72	288
Gay Brewer	74	72	72	70	288
(Nicklaus won play-off 70 to 72 to 78)					
Arnold Palmer	74	70	74	72	290
Doug Sanders	74	70	75	71	290
Don January	71	73	73	75	292
George Knudson	73	76	72	71	292

1967

Gay Brewer	73	68	72	67	280
Bobby Nichols	72	69	70	70	281
Bert Yancey	67	73	71	73	284
Arnold Palmer	73	73	70	69	285
Julius Boros	71	70	70	75	286
Paul Harney	73	71	74	69	287
Gary Player	75	69	72	71	287

1968

Bob Goalby	70	70	71	66	277
Roberto de Vicenzo	69	73	70	66	278
Bert Yancey	71	71	72	65	279
Bruce Devlin	69	73	69	69	280
Frank Beard	75	65	71	70	281
Jack Nicklaus	69	71	74	67	281

1969

George Archer	67	73	69	72	281
Tom Weiskopf	71	71	69	71	282
George Knudson	70	73	69	70	282
Billy Casper	66	71	71	74	282
Charles Coody	74	68	69	72	283
Don January	74	73	70	66	283

1970

Billy Casper	72	68	68	71	279
Gene Littler	69	70	70	70	279
(Casper won play-off 69 to 74)					
Gary Player	74	68	68	70	280
Bert Yancey	69	70	72	70	281
Tommy Aaron	68	74	69	72	283
Dave Hill	73	70	70	70	283
Dave Stockton	72	72	69	70	283

1971

Charles Coody	66	73	70	70	279
Johnny Miller	72	73	68	68	281
Jack Nicklaus	70	71	68	72	281
Don January	69	69	73	72	283
Gene Littler	72	69	73	69	283
Gary Player	72	72	71	69	284

Tom Weiskopf	71	69	72	72	284
Ken Still	72	71	72	69	284

1972

Jack Nicklaus	68	71	73	74	286
Tom Weiskopf	74	71	70	74	289
Bruce Crampton	72	75	69	73	289
Bobby Mitchell	73	72	71	73	289
Bruce Devlin	74	75	70	71	290
Jerry McGee	73	74	71	72	290
Homero Blancas	76	71	69	74	290
Jerry Heard	73	71	72	74	290
Jim Jamieson	72	70	71	77	290

1973

Tommy Aaron	68	73	74	68	283
Jesse C. Snead	70	71	73	70	284
Peter Oosterhuis	73	70	68	74	285
Jim Jamieson	73	71	70	71	285
Jack Nicklaus	69	77	73	66	285
Johnny Miller	75	69	71	73	288
Bob Goalby	73	70	71	74	288

1974

Gary Player	71	71	66	70	278
Dave Stockton	71	66	70	73	280
Tom Weiskopf	71	69	70	70	280
Jack Nicklaus	69	71	72	69	281
Hale Irwin	68	70	72	71	281
Jim Colbert	67	72	69	73	281

1975

Jack Nicklaus	68	67	73	68	276
Johnny Miller	75	71	65	66	277
Tom Weiskopf	69	72	66	70	277
Hale Irwin	73	74	71	64	282
Bobby Nichols	67	74	72	69	282
Billy Casper	70	70	73	70	283

1976

Ray Floyd	65	66	70	70	271
Ben Crenshaw	70	70	72	67	279
Jack Nicklaus	67	69	73	73	282
Larry Ziegler	67	71	72	72	282
Charles Coody	72	69	70	74	285
Hale Irwin	71	77	67	70	285
Tom Kite	73	67	72	73	285

1977

Tom Watson	70	69	70	67	276
Jack Nicklaus	72	70	70	66	278
Tom Kite	70	73	70	67	280
Rik Massengale	70	73	67	70	280
Hale Irwin	70	74	70	68	282
David Graham	75	67	73	69	284
Lou Graham	75	71	69	69	284

1978

Gary Player	72	72	69	64	277
Rod Funseth	73	66	70	69	278
Hubert Green	72	69	65	72	278
Tom Watson	73	68	68	69	278
Wally Armstrong	72	70	70	68	280
Billy Kratzert	70	74	67	69	280

1979

Fuzzy Zoeller	70	71	69	70	280
Tom Watson	68	71	70	71	280
Ed Sneed	68	67	69	76	280
(Zoeller won play-off at 2nd extra hole)					
Jack Nicklaus	69	71	72	69	281
Tom Kite	71	72	68	72	283
Bruce Lietzke	67	75	68	74	284

1980

Severiano Ballesteros	66 69 68 72 275
Gibby Gilbert	70 74 68 67 279
Jack Newton	68 74 69 68 279
Hubert Green	68 74 71 67 280
David Graham	66 73 72 70 281

Augusta's roll of honour (Phil Sheldon)

AUSTRALIAN OPEN CHAMPIONSHIP

First played 1904

Most victories
7, Gary Player, 1958-62-63-65-69-70-74.
6, Jack Nicklaus, 1964-68-71-75-76-78.
5, Ivo Whitton, 1912-13-26-29-31

Oldest winner
Peter Thomson, 43 years, 1972

Youngest winner
Ivo Whitton, 19 years, 1912

Lowest aggregate
264 (62, 71, 62, 69), Gary Player, Kooyonga GC, Adelaide, 1965

Lowest Individual round
62 (twice), Gary Player, Kooyonga GC, Adelaide, 1965

Biggest margin of victory
8 strokes, Jack Nicklaus, Royal Hobart, 1971
7 strokes, Gary Player, Royal Melbourne, 1968

Amateur winners
Hon. Michael Scott, 1904-07; C Pearce, 1908; C Felstead, 1909; I Whitton, 1912-13-26-29-31. A Russell, 1924; M Ryan, 1932; J Ferrier, 1938-39; B Devlin, 1960

Biggest span between victories
19 years, Ivo Whitton, 1912–31

Prize-money
1948, $500; 1978, $220 000

Bruce Devlin, winner of the Australian Open as an amateur and later a highly successful professional in America (Action Photos)

RESULTS

Year	Winner	Venue	Score
1904	Hon Michael Scott*	The Australian (Botany)	315
1905	D Soutar	Royal Melbourne	330
1906	Carnegie Clark	Royal Sydney	322
1907	Hon Michael Scott*	Royal Melbourne	318
1908	Clyde Pearce*	The Australian	311
1909	C Felstead*	Royal Melbourne	316
1910	Carnegie Clark	Royal Adelaide	306
1911	Carnegie Clark	Royal Sydney	321
1912	Ivo Whitton*	Royal Melbourne	321
1913	Ivo Whitton*	Royal Melbourne	302
1920	Joe Kirkwood	The Australian	290
1921	A Le Fevre	Royal Melbourne	295
1922	C Campbell	Royal Sydney	307
1923	T Howard	Royal Adelaide	301
1924	A Russell*	Royal Melbourne	303
1925	F Popplewell	The Australian	299
1926	Ivo Whitton*	Royal Adelaide	297
1927	R Stewart	Royal Melbourne	297
1928	F Popplewell	Royal Sydney	295
1929	Ivo Whitton*	Royal Adelaide	309
1930	F Eyre	Metropolitan	306
1931	Ivo Whitton*	The Australian	301
1932	M J Ryan*	Royal Adelaide	296
1933	M L Kelly	Royal Melbourne	302
1934	W J Bolger	Royal Sydney	283
1935	F McMahon	Royal Adelaide	293

1936	Gene Sarazen	Metropolitan	282		1963	Gary Player	Royal Melbourne	278
1937	G Naismith	The Australian	299		1964	Jack Nicklaus	The Lakes	287
1938	Jim Ferrier*	Royal Adelaide	283		1965	Gary Player	Kooyonga	264
1939	Jim Ferrier*	Royal Melbourne	285		1966	Arnold Palmer	Royal Queensland	276
1946	Ossie Pickworth	Royal Sydney	289		1967	Peter Thomson	Commonwealth	281
1947	Ossie Pickworth	Royal Queensland	285		1968	Jack Nicklaus	Lake Karrinyup	270
1948	Ossie Pickworth	Kingston Heath	289		1969	Gary Player	Royal Sydney	288
1949	Eric Cremin	The Australian	287		1970	Gary Player	Kingston Heath	280
1950	Norman von Nida	Kooyonga	286		1971	Jack Nicklaus	Royal Hobart	269
1951	Peter Thomson	Metropolitan	283		1972	Peter Thomson	Kooyonga	281
1952	Norman von Nida	Lake Karrinyup	278		1973	Jesse Snead	Royal Queensland	280
1953	Norman von Nida	Royal Melbourne	278		1974	Gary Player	Lake Karrinyup	279
1954	Ossie Pickworth	Kooyonga	280		1975	Jack Nicklaus	Australian	279
1955	Bobby Locke	Gailes	290		1976	Jack Nicklaus	Australian	286
1956	Bruce Crampton	Royal Sydney	289		1977	David Graham	Australian	284
1957	Frank Phillips	Kingston Heath	287		1978	Jack Nicklaus	Australian	284
1958	Gary Player	Kooyonga	271		1979	Jack Newton	Metropolitan	288
1959	Kel Nagle	The Australian	284					
1960	Bruce Devlin*	Lake Karrinyup	282		*Amateur.			
1961	Frank Phillips	Victoria	275					
1962	Gary Player	Royal Adelaide	281					

CANADIAN OPEN CHAMPIONSHIP

First played 1904

Most victories
4, Leo Diegel, 1924-25-28-29

Oldest winner
Kel Nagle, 43 years, Pinegrove, Quebec, 1964

Youngest winner
Albert H· Murray, 20 years 10 months, Montreal, 1908

Lowest 72-hole aggregate
263, John Palmer (USA), St Charles CC, Winnipeg, 1952

Lowest individual round
63, Jerry Pate (USA) fourth round, Windsor, Essex, 1976
64, Jack Nicklaus (USA) fourth round, Windsor, Essex, 1976

Amateur winner
Doug Sanders, Beaconsfield GC, Montreal, 1956·

Biggest margin of victory
16 strokes, John Douglas Edgar, Hamilton, 1919.
He defeated Bobby Jones and Karl Keffer with a total of 278. Edgar won again in 1920, but was killed in 1921, it was said in a street gang fight in Atlanta before he could try for three in a row.

Brothers as champion
Charles and Albert Murray both won the title twice. Charles in 1906 and 1911 and Albert, the elder by 7 years in 1908 and 1913.

Sponsorship
Seagram's began sponsorship in 1936 with a purse of $3000. It reached $25 000 in 1957; $100 000 in 1965 and in 1967; for one year only, it went to $200 000 ($100 000 of which came from the City of Montreal).

In 1971 Peter Jackson, a division of Imperial Tobacco, took over at $150 000. By 1979, it was $350 000, both Peter Jackson and the Royal Canadian Golf Association contributing to the purse.

Tom Weiskopf, British Open champion 1973 (Action Photos)

RESULTS

Year	Winner	Venue	Score
1904	J H Oke	Montreal	156
1905	George Cumming	Toronto	146
1906	Charles R Murray	Ottawa	170
Increased to 72 holes from 1907			
1907	Percy Barrett	Toronto	300
1908	Albert Murray	Montreal	300
1909	Karl Keffer	Toronto	309
1910	D Kenny	Toronto	303
1911	Charles R Murray	Ottawa	314
1912	George Sargent	Toronto	299
1913	Albert Murray	Montreal	295
1914	Karl Keffer	Toronto	300
1919	J Douglas Edgar	Hamilton	278
1920	J Douglas Edgar	Ottawa	298
1921	William Trovinger	Toronto	293
1922	Al Watrous	Montreal	303
1923	Clarence Hackney	Toronto	295
1924	Leo Diegel	Montreal	285
1925	Leo Diegel	Toronto	295
1926	Macdonald Smith	Montreal	283
1927	Tommy Armour	Toronto	288
1928	Leo Diegel	Toronto	282
1929	Leo Diegel	Montreal	274
1930	Tommy Armour	Hamilton	277
1931	Walter Hagen	Toronto	292
1932	Harry Cooper	Ottawa	290
1933	Joe Kirkwood	Toronto	282
1934	Tommy Armour	Toronto	287
1935	G Kunes	Montreal	280
1936	Lawson Little	Toronto	271
1937	Harry Cooper	Toronto	285
1938	Sam Snead	Toronto	277
1939	Jug McSpaden	Saint John, New Brunswick	282
1940	Sam Snead	Toronto	281
1941	Sam Snead	Toronto	274
1942	Craig Wood	Toronto	275
1943–44	No championship.		
1945	Byron Nelson	Toronto	280
1946	George Fazio	Montreal	278
1947	Bobby Locke	Toronto	268
1948	C Congdon	Vancouver, British Columbia	280
1949	Dutch Harrison	Toronto	271
1950	Jim Ferrier	Montreal	271
1951	Jim Ferrier	Toronto	273
1952	Johnny Palmer	Winnipeg	263
1953	Dave Douglas	Toronto	273
1954	Pat Fletcher	Vancouver	280
1955	Arnold Palmer	Toronto	265
1956	Doug Sanders*	Montreal	273
1957	George Bayer	Kitchener	271
1958	Wes Ellis, Jr	Edmonton	267
1959	Doug Ford	Montreal	276
1960	Art Wall	Toronto	269
1961	Jack Cupit	Winnipeg	270
1962	Ted Kroll	Montreal	278
1963	Doug Ford	Toronto	280
1964	Kel D G Nagle	Montreal	277
1965	Gene Littler	Toronto	273
1966	Don Massengale	Vancouver	280
1967	Billy Casper	Montreal	279
1968	Bob Charles	Toronto	274
1969	Tommy Aaron	Montreal	275
1970	Kermit Zarley	London, Ontario	279
1971	Lee Trevino	Montreal	275
1972	Gay Brewer	Ridgeway, Ontario	275
1973	Tom Weiskopf	Quebec	278
1974	Bobby Nichols	Mississauga, Toronto	270
1975	Tom Weiskopf	Royal Montreal	274
1976	Jerry Pate	Essex, Windsor	267
1977	Lee Trevino	Glen Abbey, Oakville, Ontario	280
1978	Bruce Lietzke	Glen Abbey, Oakville, Ontario	283
1979	Lee Trevino	Glen Abbey, Oakville, Ontario	281
1980	Bob Gilder	Royal Montreal	274

*Amateur.

JAPANESE OPEN CHAMPIONSHIP

First played 1927

Most victories
6, Tomekichi Miyamoto, 1929-30-32-35-36-40

Oldest winner
Tomekichi Miyamoto, 39 years, 1940

Youngest winner
Severiano Ballesteros, 20 years 6 months, 1977

Lowest winning score
278, Takashi Murakami, Kasugai CC, 1975

Lowest individual round
66, Takashi Murakami, Kasugai CC, 1975

Overseas winners
Hang Chang Sang (Korea) 1972; Ben Arda (Philippines) 1973; Severiano Ballesteros (Spain) 1977 and 1978; Kuo Chie Hsiung (Taiwan) 1979.

First non-Asian winner
Severiano Ballesteros (Spain) 1977

Amateur winner
Rokuro Akaboshi, **309**, Hodogaya, 1927

Total prize-money
1978: 65 000 000 Yen (approximately US $325 000)

There were no championships between 1942 and 1950

RESULTS

Year	Winner	Venue	Score
1927	R Akahoshi*	Hodogaya	309
1928	R Asami	Tokio	301

1929	T Miyamoto	Ibaraki	298	1959	Chen Ching-Po	Sagamihara	298
1930	T Miyamoto	Ibaraki	287	1960	H Kobari	Hirono	296
1931	R Asami	Hodogaya	281	1961	K Hosoishi	Takanodai	289
1932	T Miyamoto	Ibaraki	298	1962	T Sugihara	Chiba	287
1933	K Nakamura	Kasumigaseki	294	1963	T Toda	Yokkaichi	283
1934	No Championship owing to typhoon disaster.			1964	H Sugimoto	Tokio	288
1935	T Miyamoto	Asaka	293	1965	T Kitta	Miyoshi	284
1936	T Miyamoto	Inagawa	296	1966	S Sato	Sodegaura	285
1937	Chin Sei Sui	Sagami	284	1967	T Kitta	Hirono	282
1938	R M Fuku	Fujisawa	294	1968	T Kono	Sobu	284
1939	T Toda	Hirono	287	1969	H Sugimoto	Ono	284
1940	T Miyamoto	Asaka	285	1970	M Kitta	Musashi	282
1941	En Toku Shun	Hodogaya	290	1971	Y Fujii	Aichi	282
1942–49	No Competition.			1972	H Chang Sang	Iwai City	278
1950	Y Hayashi	Abiko	288	1973	B Arda	Osaka	278
1951	Son Shi Kin	Inagawa	284	1974	M Ozaki	Central	279
1952	T Nakamura	Kawana	278	1975	T Murakami	Kasugai	278
1953	Son Shi Kin	Takarazuka	299	1976	K Shimada	Central	288
1954	Y Hayashi	Tokio	291	1977	S Ballesteros	Narashino	284
1955	K Ono	Hirono	293	1978	S Ballesteros	Yokohama	281
1956	T Nakamura	Kasumigaseki	281	1979	Kuo Chie-Hsiung	Hino GC, Kyoto	285
1957	H Kobari	Aichi	285				
1958	T Nakumura	Takanodai	288				

* Amateur.

The most powerful of the Orientals, Jumbo Ozaki of Japan (Action Photos)

JAPANESE PGA RECORDS

| Leading money-winners | | |
Year	Winner	Yen
1969	Takaaki Kono	7 980 000
1970	Takaaki Kono	11 800 000
1971	Masashi Ozaki	17 143 906
1972	Masashi Ozaki	27 519 618
1973	Masashi Ozaki	48 859 000
1974	Masashi Ozaki	49 024 108
1975	Takashi Murakami	44 173 550
1976	Isao Aoki	41 960 801
1977	Masashi Ozaki	35 932 608
1978	Isao Aoki	79 258 200
1979	Isao Aoki	61 348 211

Over-all leading money-winner
Isao Aoki, 326 345 140 Yen at December 1979

Record official prize-money for one calendar year
62 987 200 Yen Isao Aoki, 1978 (unofficial)
79 258 200 Yen 1978

Most tournaments won in one year
10, Masashi Ozaki, 1972

Lowest aggregates
72 holes:
265 (23 under par), Masashi Ozaki, Seto-Naikai Circuit (Hiroshima CC, Happongi, Club), 1971
54 holes:
197 (19 under par), Isao Aoki, Kanto District Professional championship (Isogo CC), 1972
36 holes:
129 (13 under par), Lu Liang Huan, Sanpo Classic (Chiba Asahi CC), 1976
18 holes:
61 (7 under par), Takashi Murakami, Kanto Professional championship (Isogo CC), 1972
9 holes:
28 (7 under par), Takashi Murakami, Kanto Professional championship (Isogo CC), second 9, third round, 1972

Biggest margin of victory
11 strokes, C H Kuo, Dunlop International, 1979. Winning score 265

Most over-all victories
38, Masashi Ozaki

NEW ZEALAND OPEN

First played 1907 (since 1959 sponsored by BP New Zealand Ltd)
No championships 1915–18 and 1940–45

Most victories
9, Peter Thomson (Australia) 1950-51-53-55-59-60-61-65-71
7, Kel Nagle (Australia) 1957-58-62-64-67-68-69; A J Shaw 1926-29-30-31-32-34-36

Oldest winner
Kel Nagle, 48 years 11 months, 1969

Youngest winner
Bob Charles, 18 years 7 months (then an amateur), 1954

Lowest aggregate
266, Kel Nagle, Christchurch GC, 1964. (1907 championship played over 36 holes.)

Biggest margin of victory
18 strokes, A J Shaw, Manawatu GC, Palmerston North, 1930

Amateur winners
H W Berwick (Australia), 1956
R J Charles, 1954
A D S Duncan, 1907-10-11
R H Glading, 1946-47
J P Hornabrook, 1937-39
E M Macfarlane, 1925
S Morpeth, 1928

Lowest individual round
63, Peter Thomson, Wanganui, 1963

Consecutive victories
4, A J Shaw, 1929-30-31-32
3, E S Douglas, 1913-14-19; Peter Thomson, 1959-60-61; Kel Nagle, 1967-68-69
2, J A Clements, 1908-09; A D S Duncan, 1910-11; A Brooks, 1922-23; R H Glading, 1946-47; Peter Thomson, 1950-51; Kel Nagle, 1957-58

Unusual records
In 1930, Andy Shaw led by 15 strokes after 36 holes. He won by 18 strokes. His aggregate was 10 strokes better than the previous best. He achieved all this despite rain and strong winds. He was born near Troon, Scotland in 1898.

The first champion in 1907, A D S Duncan,

finished leading amateur 28 years later at the age of 60.

In 1954, competing in his second championship, Bob Charles led after every round. Peter Thomson finished third, 4 months after winning his first British Open title.

B M Silk finished leading amateur in 1934 and did so again (for the fourth time) in 1963, aged 53

Total prize-money
Year
1907   £25 for the winner, £10 for the runner-up or the two leading professionals

$

1953	470
1958	800
1963	2000
1968	5000
1973	16 000
1978	50 000

The spectacular increase in recent years is attributable to the sponsorship of BP New Zealand Ltd, who took over in 1969

RESULTS

One of professional golf's globetrotters—the ever-popular Kel Nagle (Action Photos)

Year	Winner	Venue	Score
1907	Mr A D S Duncan*	Napier	159
1908	J A Clements	Otago	333
1909	J A Clements	Auckland	324
1910	Mr A D S Duncan*	Christchurch	295
1911	Mr A D S Duncan*	Wanganui	319
1912	J A Clements	Wellington	321
1913	E S Douglas	Otago	303
1914	E S Douglas	Auckland	313
1919	E S Douglas	Napier	327
1920	J H Kirkwood	Hamilton	304
1921	E S Douglas	Christchurch	302
1922	A Brooks	Manawatu	308
1923	A Brooks	Wanganui	312
1924	E J Moss	Auckland	301
1925	E M Macfarlane*	Christchurch	308
1926	A J Shaw	Miramar	307
1927	E J Moss	Hamilton	300
1928	S Morpeth*	Otago	303
1929	A J Shaw	Wanganui	299
1930	A J Shaw	Manawatu	284
1931	A J Shaw	Christchurch	287
1932	A J Shaw	Wellington	289
1933	E J Moss	Titirangi	300
1934	A J Shaw	Wanganui	288
1935	A Murray	Christchurch	286
1936	A J Shaw	New Plymouth	292
1937	J P Hornabrook*	Hamilton	299
1938	Bobby Locke	Otago	288
1939	J P Hornabrook*	Miramar	291
1946	R H Glading*	Manawatu	306
1947	R H Glading*	New Plymouth	291
1948	A Murray	Otago	294
1949	James Galloway	Hastings	283
1950	Peter Thomson	Christchurch	280
1951	Peter Thomson	Titirangi	288
1952	A Murray	Wanganui	293
1953	Peter Thomson	Otago	295
1954	Bob Charles*	Wellington	280
1955	Peter Thomson	Auckland	280
1956	H W Berwick*	Christchurch	292
1957	Kel Nagle	Manawatu	294
1958	Kel Nagle	Hamilton	278
1959	Peter Thomson	Paraparaumu	287
1960	Peter Thomson	Invercargill	281
1961	Peter Thomson	New Plymouth	267
1962	Kel Nagle	Titirangi	281
1963	Bruce Devlin	Wanganui	273
1964	Kel Nagle	Christchurch	266
1965	Peter Thomson	Auckland	278
1966	Bob Charles	Paraparaumu	273
1967	Kel Nagle	Hamilton	275
1968	Kel Nagle	Christchurch	272
1969	Kel Nagle	Wanganui	273
1970	Bob Charles	Auckland	271
1971	Peter Thomson	Dunedin	276

1972	Bill Dunk	Paraparaumu	279
1973	Bob Charles	Palmerston North	288
1974	R Gilder	Christchurch	283
1975	Bill Dunk	Hamilton	272
1976	Simon Owen	Wellington	284
1977	Bob Byman	Auckland	290
1978	Bob Shearer	Wanganui	277
1979	Stuart Ginn	Dunedin	278

* Amateur.

SOUTH AFRICAN OPEN

First played 1909

Most victories
12, Gary Player, 1956-60-65-66-67-68-69-72-75-76-77-79
9, Bobby Locke, 1935-37-38-39-40-46-50-51-55

Youngest winner
Bobby Locke, 17 years, 1935

Oldest winner
Sid Brews, 53 years, 1952

Lowest aggregate
272, Bobby Cole, Royal Johannesburg, 1974

Hugh Baiocchi, South African Open champion 1978 (By courtesy of Slazengers Ltd)

Lowest individual round
63, Gary Player, Royal Johannesburg, 1977
(This was accomplished five months after Mark Hayes lowered British Open record to 63)

Amateur winners (since 1930)
Bobby Locke, 1935 and 1937
C E Olander, 1936
R W Glennie, 1947
M Janks, 1948
J R Boyd, 1953
R C Taylor, 1954
A A Stewart, 1958
D Hutchinson, 1959

Total prize-money
1978 R45 000

Unusual records
At the age of 15, Wayne Player, Gary Player's son, led the pre-qualifying round with a 65. Then, at the 1st hole of the championship proper at Royal Johannesburg in 1977, he holed a 3-iron shot for an albatross 2

RESULTS

After 1908—72 holes played

1899, Walter Day (Kimberley); 1902, Professional match (3 competitors)—Final: W Day (Kimberley) beat J Johnson (Port Elizabeth); 1903, L B Waters (Johannesburg); 1904, L B Waters (Johannesburg); 1905, A Gray (Port Elizabeth); 1906, A Gray (Port Elizabeth).

Year	Winner	Venue	Score
1907	Lawrence Waters	Kimberley	147
1908	George Fotheringham	Johannesburg	163
1909	John Fotheringham	Potchefstroom	306
1910	George Fotheringham	Wynberg	315
1911	George Fotheringham	Durban	301
1912	George Fotheringham	Potchefstroom	305
1913	J A W Prentice*	Kimberley	304
1914	George Fotheringham	Wynberg	299
1919	W H Horne	Durban	320
1920	L B Waters	Johannesburg	302
1921	J Brews	Port Elizabeth	316
1922	F Jangle	Port Alfred	310
1923	J Brews	Royal Cape	305
1924	B H Elkin	Durban	316
1925	Sid F Brews	Johannesburg	295
1926	J Brews	Port Elizabeth	301
1927	Sid F Brews	Maccauvlei	301
1928	J Brews	Durban	297
1929	A Tosh	Royal Cape	315
1930	Sid F Brews	East London	297
1931	Sid F Brews	Port Elizabeth	302
1932	C McIlvenny	Mowbray	304
1933	Sid F Brews	Maccauvlei	297
1934	Sid F Brews	Port Elizabeth	319

The sign says no cameras, but somebody got a good shot of Bob Charles, the best left-hander in history (Action Photos)

1935	Bobby Locke*	Johannesburg	296
1936	C E Olander*	Royal Cape	297
1937	Bobby Locke*	East London	288
1938	Bobby Locke	Maccauvlei	279
1939	Bobby Locke	Royal Durban	279
1940	Bobby Locke	Port Elizabeth	293
1946	Bobby Locke	Royal Johannesburg	285
1947	R W Glennie*	Mowbray, Cape Town	293
1948	M Janks*	East London	298
1949	Sid F Brews	Maccauvlei	291
1950	Bobby Locke	Durban	287
1951	Bobby Locke	Houghton	275
1952	Sid F Brews	Humewood	300
1953	J R Boyd*	Royal Cape	302
1954	Reg C Taylor*	East London	289
1955	Bobby Locke	Zwartkop	283
1956	Gary Player	Durban	286
1957	Harold Henning	Humewood	289
1958	A A Stewart*	Bloemfontein	281
1959	Denis Hutchinson*	Johannesburg	282
1960	Gary Player	Mowbray	288
1961	Retief Waltman	East London	289
1962	Harold R Henning	Johannesburg	285
1963	Retief Waltman	Durban	281
1964	Alan Henning	Bloemfontein	278

1965	Gary Player	Cape Town	273
1966	Gary Player	Johannesburg	274
1967	Gary Player	East London	279
1968	Gary Player	Houghton	278
1969	Gary Player	Durban	273
1970	Tommy Horton (Britain)	Royal Durban	285
1971	Simon Hobday	Mowbray, Cape Town	276
1972	Gary Player	Royal Johannesburg	274
1973	Bob Charles (NZ)	Durban	282
1974	Bobby Cole	Royal Johannesburg	272
1975	Gary Player	Mowbray, Cape Town	278
1976	Dale Hayes	Houghton	287
	(with alteration in timing played twice in 1976)		
1976	Gary Player	Durban	280
1977	Gary Player	Royal Johannesburg	273
1978	Hugh Baiocchi	Mowbray	285
1979	Gary Player	Houghton	279

* Amateur.

The Professionals

USPGA TOUR

The tournament circuit—the tour—is a remarkable piece of organisation. As long ago as 1899 there was a Western Open, but even in the 1920s when Gene Sarazen, Walter Hagen, Jim Barnes and Jock Hutchison were the main performers, there was little continuity.

Later, under the management of Bob Harlow and Fred Corcoran, the schedule grew with players like Ben Hogan, Sam Snead and Byron Nelson to adorn the shopwindow. Resorts, hotels and Chambers of Commerce soon realised the value of professional golf in promoting their interests and, even if it did involve many players in a lot of travelling, it enabled them to follow the sun.

By 1938, there were 38 events and a purse of $158 000. By 1952, there was almost $500 000 to play for, but by the late fifties, the tour really took off.

Television brought the game to a new public; TV rights brought a huge increase in prize money and a new generation of professionals, led by Arnold Palmer, entered a rich era. There was a tournament somewhere nearly every week. There was the establishment of the PGA School, stern rules about qualification and a satellite tour. In 1968, the tournament players separated from the PGA, formed their own organisation known as the Tournament Players' Division and appointed Joe Dey as Commissioner.

Such rapid expansion brought its problems but, though the tournament schedule has been cut back to enable American players to play elsewhere at the end of the year, total prizemoney in 1981 is likely to reach $14 million. The present commissioner is Deane Beman.

DETAILED RECORDS

Most consecutive victories
11, Byron Nelson, from Miami Four Ball, 8–11 March 1945 to Canadian Open, 2–4 August 1945
The other nine victories were Charlotte Open, Greensboro Open, Durham Open, Atlanta Open, Montreal Open, Philadelphia Inquirer Invitational, Chicago Victory National Open, PGA championship, Tam O'Shanter Open. (Nelson won a twelfth victory, but it was unofficial. Its $2500 purse was below the PGA $3000 minimum.)
4, Jackie Burke, Jr, 1952
3, Byron Nelson, 1944, 1945-46; Sam Snead, 1945; Ben Hogan, 1946; Bobby Locke, 1947; Jim Ferrier, 1951; Billy Casper, 1960; Arnold Palmer, 1960-62; Johnny Miller, 1974; Hubert Green, 1976; Gary Player, 1978

Most consecutive victories in the same event
4, Walter Hagen, 1924-27, PGA Championship
3, Willie Anderson, 1903-05, US Open; Ralph Guldahl, 1936-38, Western Open; Gene Littler, 1955-57, Tournament of Champions; Billy Casper, 1959-61, Portland Open; Arnold Palmer, 1960-62, Texas Open, 1961-63, Phoenix Open; Jack Nicklaus, 1971-73, Disney World Golf Classic; Johnny Miller, 1974-76, Tucson Open

Most consecutive rounds under 70
19, Byron Nelson, 1945
Most official tournament victories in one calendar year
18, Byron Nelson, 1945
13, Ben Hogan, 1946
11, Ben Hogan, 1948
10, Sam Snead, 1950
8, Arnold Palmer, 1960; Johnny Miller 1974
7, Sam Snead, 1938; Arnold Palmer, 1962-63; Jack Nicklaus, 1972-73

Most career victories (PGA co-sponsored and/or approved tournaments only)
84, Sam Snead
66, Jack Nicklaus
62, Ben Hogan
61, Arnold Palmer
54, Byron Nelson
51, Billy Casper

Most consecutive tournaments in the money
113, Byron Nelson, 1940s
105, Jack Nicklaus, November 1970 to September 1976

Leading money-winner most often in a year
8, Jack Nicklaus
5, Ben Hogan

Above: Severiano Ballesteros tells all. Winner of
the Greensboro Open 1978 (Action Photos)

Right: Mike Souchak, holder of the lowest 72-hole
aggregate on the US tour (Associated Press)

Below: Not the sort of setting in which a champion
likes to be seen, but nothing that Tom Watson
cannot handle (Action Photos)

Most total money won in one calendar year
$462 636 by Tom Watson, 1979

Best Vardon Trophy scoring averages
69.23 Sam Snead, 1950
69.30 Ben Hogan, 1948
69.37 Sam Snead, 1949

Widest winning margin
16 strokes, Bobby Locke, Chicago Victory National, 1948
14 strokes, Ben Hogan, Portland Invitational, 1945; Johnny Miller, Phoenix Open, 1975
13 strokes, Byron Nelson, Seattle Open, 1945
12 strokes, Arnold Palmer, Phoenix Open, 1962

Most consecutive birdies
8, Bob Goalby, Pasadena GC, Florida, St Petersburg Open, 1961, fourth round
8, Fuzzy Zoeller, Oakwood CC, Illinois, Quad Cities Open, 1976, first round
Al Geiberger had six birdies and one eagle in his round of 59 during the 1977 Memphis Classic at Colonial CC, second round

Most first-time winners in one calendar year
12 in 1968, 1969 and 1979

Fewest putts
18 holes:
18, Sam Trahan, Whitemarsh Valley CC, fourth round IVB, Philadelphia Golf Classic, 1979
19, Bill Nary, El Paso CC, third round El Paso Open, 1952
19, Bob Rosburg, Pensacola CC, Florida, third round, Pensacola Open, 1959
19, Randy Glover, Keller GC, St Paul, Minnesota, fourth round, St Paul Open, 1965
19, Deane Beman, Mesa Verde CC, California, first round, Haig Open, 1968
9 holes:
8, Jim Colbert, Deerwood Club, Jacksonville, first 9 holes, last round, Greater Jacksonville Open, 1967
8, Sam Trahan, Whitemarsh Valley CC, second 9 holes, fourth round IVB, Philadelphia Golf Classic, 1979
72 holes:
99, Bob Menne, Sawgrass, Florida, Tournament Players championship, 1977
102, Bert Yancey, Portland GC, Oregon, Portland Open, 1966

Oldest winner
Sam Snead, 52 years 10 months, Greater Greensboro Open, 1965

Youngest winner
Gene Sarazen, 20 years 4 months, 1922 US Open

Horton Smith, 20 years 5 months, 1928 Oklahoma City Open
Ray Floyd, 20 years 6 months, 1963 St Petersburg Open
Severiano Ballesteros, 20 years 11 months, 1978 Greater Greensboro Open

Best scoring performances
72 holes:
257 (60, 68, 64, 65), Mike Souchak, 1955 Texas Open Brackenridge Park, San Antonio, 27 under par
259 (62, 68, 63, 66) Byron Nelson, Broadmoor GC, Seattle, Washington, 1945 Seattle Open, 21 under par
259 (70, 63, 63, 63) Chandler Harper, Texas Open, Brackenridge Park, 1954, 25 under par
54 holes:
192 (60, 68, 64) Mike Souchak, Brackenridge Park, Texas, Texas Open, 1955
(Chandler Harper had a 54-hole total of 189 (63, 63, 63) in the 1954 Texas Open at Brackenridge, but for the last three rounds
36 holes:
125 for last two rounds
(63, 62) Ron Streck, Oak Hills CC, Texas Open, 1978
126 (64, 62) Tommy Bolt, Cavalier Yacht and Country Club, Virginia, in Virginia Beach Open, 1954. First and second rounds
126 for second and third rounds
(63, 63), Chandler Harper, at Brackenridge Park, Texas Open, 1954
(60, 66), Sam Snead, at Glen Lakes, Dallas, Dallas Open, 1957
126 for third and fourth rounds
(62, 64), Johnny Palmer, El Rio CC, Tucson, Tucson Open, 1948
(63, 63), Sam Snead, Brackenridge Park, Texas Open, 1950
18 holes:
59, Al Geiberger, Colonial CC, Memphis, Tennessee, second round, Memphis Classic, 1977
60, Al Brosch, Brackenridge Park, third round, Texas Open, 1951
60, Bill Nary, El Paso CC, Texas, third round, El Paso Open, 1952
60, Ted Kroll, Brackenridge Park, third round, Texas Open, 1954
60, Wall Ulrich, Cavalier Yacht and CC, Virginia, second round, Virginia Beach Open, 1954
60, Tommy Bolt, Wethersfield CC, Connecticut, second round, Insurance City Open, 1954
60, Mike Souchak, Brackenridge Park, Texas, first round, Texas Open, 1955

60, Sam Snead, Glen Lakes CC, Dallas, second round, Dallas Open, 1957

9 holes:
27, Mike Souchak, second 9 Brackenridge Park, San Antonio, Texas, first round, Texas Open, 1955
27, Andy North, En-Joie GC, Endicott, New York, second 9 first round, B C Open, 1975

Player beating his age
In the Quad Cities Open played in July 1979 at the Oakwood CC, Coal Valley, Illinois, Sam Snead became the first player in the history of the USPGA tour to shoot his age. He equalled his age with a round of 67 and beat it with a 66.

GROWTH OF TOUR PURSES

Year	No of Events	Total Prize-money $
1938	38	158 000
1939	28	121 000
1940	27	117 000
1941	30	169 200
1942	21	116 650
1943	3	17 000
1944	22	150 500
1945	36	435 380
1946	37	411 533
1947	31	352 500
1948	34	427 000
1949	25	338 200
1950	33	459 950
1951	30	460 200
1952	32	498 016
1953	32	562 704
1954	26	600 819
1955	36	782 010
1956	36	847 070
1957	32	820 360
1958	39	1 005 800
1959	43	1 225 205
1960	41	1 335 242
1961	45	1 461 830
1962	49	1 790 320
1963	43	2 044 900
1964	41	2 301 063
1965	36	2 848 515
1966	36	3 704 445
1967	37	3 979 162
1968	45	5 077 600
1969	47	5 465 875
1970	55	6 751 523
1971	63	7 116 000
1972	71	7 596 749
1973	75	8 657 225
1974	57	8 165 941
1975	51	7 895 450
1976	49	9 157 522
1977	48	9 688 977
1978	48	10 337 332
1979	46	12 801 200

PAST LEADING MONEY-WINNERS

Year	Winner	Prize-money $
1934	Paul Runyan	6 767.00
1935	Johnny Revolta	9 543.00
1936	Horton Smith	7 682.00
1937	Harry Cooper	14 138 69
1938	Sam Snead	19 534.49
1939	Henry Picard	10 303.00
1940	Ben Hogan	10 655.00
1941	Ben Hogan	18 358.00
1942	Ben Hogan	13 143.00
1943	No Statistics Compiled	
1944	Byron Nelson (War Bonds)	37 967.69
1945	Byron Nelson (War Bonds)	63 335.66
1946	Ben Hogan	42 556.16
1947	Jimmy Demaret	27 936.83
1948	Ben Hogan	32 112.00
1949	Sam Snead	31 593.83
1950	Sam Snead	35 758.83
1951	Lloyd Mangrum	26 088.83
1952	Julius Boros	37 032.97
1953	Lew Worsham	34 002.00
1954	Bob Toski	65 819.81
1955	Julius Boros	63 121.55
1956	Ted Kroll	72 835.83
1957	Dick Mayer	65 835.00
1958	Arnold Palmer	42 607.50
1959	Art Wall	53 167.60
1960	Arnold Palmer	75 262.85
1961	Gary Player	64 540.45
1962	Arnold Palmer	81 448.33
1963	Arnold Palmer	128 230.00
1964	Jack Nicklaus	113 284.50
1965	Jack Nicklaus	140 752.14
1966	Billy Casper	121 944.92
1967	Jack Nicklaus	188 998.08
*1968	Billy Casper	205 168.67
1969	Frank Beard	164 707.11
1970	Lee Trevino	157 037.63
1971	Jack Nicklaus	244 490.50
1972	Jack Nicklaus	320 542.26
1973	Jack Nicklaus	308 362.10
1974	Johnny Miller	353 021.59
**1975	Jack Nicklaus	298 149.17
1976	Jack Nicklaus	266 438.57
1977	Tom Watson	310 653.16
1978	Tom Watson	362 428.93
1979	Tom Watson	462 636.00

*Total money listed beginning in 1968 through 1974.
**Official money listed beginning in 1975.

MILLION DOLLAR WINNERS

Name	Date/Event/Position	First Money	Time Elapsed	Wins
1 Arnold Palmer	21 July 1968 PGA Championship Tied 2nd	29 May 1955 Fort Wayne Open Tied 25th—$145.00	13 years 2 months	52
2 Billy Casper	11 January 1970 Los Angeles Open Winner	26 June 1955 Western Open Tied 30th—$33.33	14 years 7 months	43
3 Jack Nicklaus	25 January 1970 Bing Crosby 2nd	8 January 1962 Los Angeles Open Tied 50th—$33.33	8 years	30
(2nd million)	1 December 1973 Disney World Winner	25 January 1970 Bing Crosby 2nd—$11 840.83 towards 2nd million	3 years 11 months	21
(3rd million)	22 May 1977 Memorial Winner	1 December 1973 Disney World Winner—$12 068.09 towards 3rd million	3 years 5 months	12
4 Lee Trevino	20 May 1973 Memphis Classic Tied 2nd	20 June 1966 US Open Tied 54th—$600.00	6 years 11 months	15
(2nd million)	24 June 1979 Canadian Open Winner	20 May 1973 Memphis Classic Tied 2nd—$16187	6 years 1 month	7
5 Bruce Crampton	1 July 1973 Western Open Tied 4th	25 February 1957 Houston Open Tied 13th—$693.75	16 years 5 months	14
6 Gary Player	14 April 1974 Masters Winner	31 March 1957 Azalea Open Tied 25th—$16.16	17 years 1 month	17
7 Tom Weiskopf	25 August 1974 Westchester Classic 3rd	9 August 1964 Western Open Tied 30th—$487.50	10 years	9
8 Gene Littler	1 September 1974 Tournament Players Championship 4th	1 August 1954 Kansas City Open Tied 2nd—$1 950.00	20 years 1 month	25
9 Johnny Miller	8 February 1976 Bob Hope Classic Winner	11 May 1969 Texas Open Tied 23rd—$810.00	6 years 9 months	17

MILLION DOLLAR WINNERS

Name	Date/Event/Position	First Money	Time Elapsed	Wins
10 Miller Barber	29 February 1976 Tournament Players Championship Tied 43rd	20 September 1959 El Paso Open Tied 26th—$77.78	6 years 5 months	9
11 Dave Hill	15 August 1976 PGA Championship Tied 22nd	30 August 1959 Miller Open Tied 15th—$780.00	17 years	13
12 Hale Irwin	5 September 1976 World Series of Golf 2nd	30 June 1968 Cleveland Open Tied 39th—$457.41	8 years 3 months	7
13 Al Geiberger	3 April 1977 Greater Greensboro Tied 8th	24 January 1960 Bing Crosby Tied 42nd—$100.00	17 years 3 months	10
14 Julius Boros	17 July 1977 Pleasant Valley Tied 59th	10 June 1950 US Open 9th—$300.00	27 years 1 month	18
15 Ray Floyd	17 July 1977 Pleasant Valley Winner	17 March 1963 St Petersburg Open Winner—$3500.00	14 years 4 months	10
16 Hubert Green	26 March 1978 Heritage Winner	28 November 1970 Sea Pines Open Tied 13th—$540.00	7 years 4 months	14
17 Tom Watson	7 May 1978 Byron Nelson Winner	24 October 1971 Kaiser Open Tied 28th—$1065.00	6 years 7 months	9
18 Dave Stockton	18 June 1978 US Open Tied 2nd	1 November 1964 Almaden Open Tied 10th—$875.00	13 years 7 months	11
19 Frank Beard	18 February 1979 Tucson Tied 21st	18 November 1962 Mobile Sertoma Open Tied 15th—$270	16 years 3 months	11
20 Don January	20 May 1979 Colonial Tied 2nd	12 February 1956 Tucson Open Tied 4th—$700	22 years 3 months	12
21 Lou Graham	29 July 1979 Philadelphia Winner	25 October 1964 Mount View Open Tied 11th—$1110	14 years 9 months	6
22 J C Snead	19 August 1979 Westchester Tied 7th	30 June 1968 Cleveland Open Tied 39th—$457	11 years 2 months	6

Left to right: Miller Barber (Phil Sheldon), Dave Stockton (Phil Sheldon), Frank Beard (Action Photos), Dave Hill (Phil Sheldon)

BRITISH AND EUROPEAN TOURS

(Incorporating the continental championships, co-ordinated by the British PGA, beginning in 1972)

The professional tour in Britain and Europe is not as fortunate as its counterpart in America. Even allowing for the fact that the season is longer in southern Europe, the weather limits the number of tournaments that are possible in a year. However, this works in its favour since players can make themselves available for other circuits in Japan, Australia, South Africa and New Zealand.

Today, the European season lasts 25 weeks (April–October), prize-money totals over £1 615 500 and it is a real alternative to the tour in America. It is perfectly possible to make a sizeable fortune without going near America.

This is something new. For the first 30 years or so of its existence, the PGA, founded in 1901, looked after the interests of the club professional. There were tournaments, but most tournament players had a club job as well.

Things changed rapidly with the appointment as Secretary in 1933 of Commander Charles Roe. He realised the potential of the tournament side of golf and stoked the PGA into a far more active role.

In the 25 years that he was at the head of affairs, the tournament programme developed extensively but, ironically, it was after his retirement that the great golf boom occurred.

Nevertheless, under his training, the PGA was more ready than it would have been. It organised itself better, but it was not until the 1970s that the real impact was felt. Television was a major factor in encouraging sponsors and prize-money reflected their interest. Like the Americans, special qualification rules were introduced to sift out the enormous increase in professionals seeking to try their hand and in 1975 a Tournament Players' Division was formed quite separate from the rest of the PGA.

At the beginning of 1977, they became the European Players' Division, the European Opens and other events became part of the European tour; and in 1979 the Ryder Cup played America as a European team as distinct from a British one.

DETAILED RECORDS

Most victories (excluding British Open)
26 Neil Coles; **24,** Christy O'Connor; **22,** Bernard Hunt; **20,** Dai Rees; Peter Thomson

Most consecutive victories
4, Alf Padgham, 1935 *News of the World* matchplay (Royal Mid Surrey) 10–13 September; 1936 *Daily Mail* (Bramshot), total 284, 31 March–3 April; Silver King (Moor Park), total 280, 22–24 April; Dunlop Southport (Hesketh and Southport and Ainsdale), total 282, 4–8 May

Padgham was ninth in the next tournament, the Yorkshire Open (Templenewsam) 10–13 June, but then won the Open championship (Hoylake), total 287, 22–26 June. In those days, there was only about one tournament a month.
3 out of 4, Norman von Nida, 1947
First North British, Harrogate (21–25 July); first Lotus, Hollinwell (6–8 August); equal third *News Chronicle*, Hollingbury Park (19–21 August); equal first Penfold, Stoke Poges (3–5 September). In all, he won, or was equal first, in seven tournaments in 1947.

Oldest winner
Sandy Herd, 58 years, *News of the World* matchplay championship, 1926

Youngest winner
Severiano Ballesteros, 19 years 4 months, Dutch Open, 1976
Nick Faldo, 20 years 10 months, Colgate PGA championship, 1978

Most victories in one season (or joint victories)
7, Norman von Nida, 1947. Dunlop-Southport, *Star*, North British-Harrogate, Lotus, Penfold (tied), *Yorkshire Evening News* (tied) and the Brand Lochryn
5, Bernard Hunt, 1963. Dunlop Masters, Gevacolor, Swallow-Penfold, Carrolls and Smart Weston (36-hole event)

Winner of the Harry Vardon Trophy most often
4, Peter Oosterhuis, 1971-72-73-74
3, Severiano Ballesteros, 1976-77-78; Bernard Hunt 1958-60-65; Bobby Locke 1946-50-54

Biggest margin of victory
15 strokes, Peter Thomson, *Yorkshire Evening News*, Sand Moor, 1957. Total 264 (65, 67, 64, 68).

Most money won in a single year
£54 348, Severiano Ballesteros, 1978

Lowest 72-hole aggregate
260, (64, 65, 66, 65), Kel Nagle, Irish Hospitals, Woodbrook, 1961
262 (71, 63, 62, 66), Lu Liang Huan, French Open, Biarritz, 1971
262 (66, 63, 66, 67), Bernard Hunt, Piccadilly strokeplay tournament, Wentworth (East course), 1966

Lowest 18 holes
60, Baldovino Dassu, Swiss Open, Crans sur Sierre, 1971
61, Tom Haliburton, Spalding, Worthing, 1952
61, Tony Coop and Hugh Boyle, Senior Service, Dalmahoy (East course), 1965
61, Peter Butler, Bowmaker, Sunningdale (Old), 1967
61, Peter Townsend, Swiss Open, Crans sur Sierre, 1971

Lowest 9 holes
27 (4, 3, 2, 3, 3, 3, 2, 3, 4), José Maria Canizares, third round, Swiss Open, Crans sur Sierre, 1978 (he finished the round in 64)
28, John Panton, North British-Harrogate, 1952
28, Bernard Hunt, Spalding, Worthing, 1953
28, Peter Mills, Bowmaker, Sunningdale (Old), 1958

Lowest 36 holes
126, Tom Haliburton, Spalding, Worthing, 1952
127, Peter Alliss, Irish Hospitals, Woodbrook, 1961

Lowest 54 holes
194, John Lister, Gallaher, Ulster Open, Shandon Park, Belfast, 1970
194, Vicente Fernandez, Benson and Hedges, Fulford, 1975
195, Kel Nagle, Irish Hospitals, Woodbrook, 1961
195, Bernard Hunt, Piccadilly Tournament, Wentworth (East), 1966

Fewest putts in 18 holes
22, Bill Large, qualifying round for Benson and Hedges matchplay championship, Moor Park, 1972

Most consecutive birdies
11, José Maria Canizares, Swiss Open, Crans sur Sierre, 1978. He had 5 to finish his second round and 7 to begin his third round
7, Peter Thomson, Dunlop, 1958
7, Bernard Hunt, Daks, 1958
7, Angel Miguel, Daks, 1960
7, Peter Butler, Benson and Hedges, 1971
7, Peter Townsend, Viyella PGA, 1974

The courtly Flory van Donck of Belgium (Action Photos)

POST-WAR COMPOSITE MONEY-WINNING LEADERS as at December 1979
(1978 table position in brackets)

Players	£	Seasons
Neil Coles (1)	209 918	25
Severiano Ballesteros (2)	195 608	6
Brian Barnes (4)	157 095	15
Tony Jacklin (3)	152 736	16
Dale Hayes (10)	136 835	7
Gary Player (6)	133 752	24
Christy O'Connor (5)	127 239	25
Bernard Gallacher (11)	120 404	12
Graham Marsh (12)	119 915	10
Tommy Horton (8)	119 650	16
Bob Charles (9)	119 364	16
Peter Oosterhuis (7)	111 830	11
Hugh Baiocchi (15)	109 120	8
Brian Huggett (14)	103 637	19
Peter Butler (13)	100 511	22
Manuel Pinero (16)	94 120	8
Peter Townsend (18)	91 811	12
Eddie Polland (17)	87 854	11
Mark James (—)	85 940	4
Jack Nicklaus (20)	81 331	18

Dai Rees, a perennial favourite in British golf (Action Photos)

The smile of the first £1000 winner in British golf, 1962. Neil Coles, all-time leading money-winner in Europe at the end of 1979 (Action Photos)

Right: Peter Oosterhuis, winner of the Harry Vardon Trophy in Britain four years in a row, from 1971–74 (By courtesy of Slazengers Ltd)

LEADING PGA MONEY-WINNERS 1964–1978

Year	Winner	£
1964	Neil Coles	7 890
1965	Peter Thomson	7 011
1966	Bruce Devlin	13 205
1967	Gay Brewer	20 235
1968	Gay Brewer	23 107
1969	Billy Casper	23 483
1970	Christy O'Connor	31 532
1971	Gary Player	11 281
1972	Bob Charles	18 538
1973	Tony Jacklin	24 839
1974	Peter Oosterhuis	32 127
1975	Dale Hayes	20 507
1976	Severiano Ballesteros	39 504
1977	Severiano Ballesteros	46 436
1978	Severiano Ballesteros	54 348
1979	Sandy Lyle	49 232

HARRY VARDON TROPHY

The Harry Vardon Trophy is awarded annually by the PGA to the leading player in the Order of Merit.

Year	Winner	Club/Country
1937	Charles Whitcombe	Crews Hill
1938	Henry Cotton	Royal Mid-Surrey
1939	Reg Whitcombe	Parkstone
1940–45	*in abeyance*	
1946	Bobby Locke	South Africa
1947	Norman von Nida	Australia
1948	Charlie Ward	Little Aston
1949	Charlie Ward	Little Aston
1950	Bobby Locke	South Africa
1951	John Panton	Glenbervie
1952	Harry Weetman	Croham Hurst
1953	Flory van Donck	Belgium
1954	Bobby Locke	South Africa
1955	Dai Rees	South Herts
1956	Harry Weetman	Croham Hurst
1957	Eric Brown	Buchanan Castle
1958	Bernard Hunt	Hartsbourne
1959	Dai Rees	South Herts
1960	Bernard Hunt	Hartsbourne
1961	Christy O'Connor	Royal Dublin
1962	Christy O'Connor	Royal Dublin
1963	Neil Coles	Coombe Hill
1964	Peter Alliss	Parkstone
1965	Bernard Hunt	Hartsbourne
1966	Peter Alliss	Parkstone
1967	Malcolm Gregson	Dyrham Park
1968	Brian Huggett	Betchworth Park
1969	Bernard Gallacher	Ifield
1970	Neil Coles	Coombe Hill
1971	Peter Oosterhuis	Dulwich & Sydenham
1972	Peter Oosterhuis	Pacific Harbour, Fiji
1973	Peter Oosterhuis	Pacific Harbour, Fiji
1974	Peter Oosterhuis	Pacific Harbour, Fiji
1975	Dale Hayes	St. Pierre and South Africa
1976	Severiano Ballesteros	Spain
1977	Severiano Ballesteros	Spain
1978	Severiano Ballesteros	Spain
1979	Sandy Lyle	Hawkstone Park

Sandy Lyle—perhaps the best of Britain's younger generation of professionals (By courtesy of Dunlop Sports Company Ltd)

RYDER CUP

MILESTONES

The Ryder Cup came into being slightly by chance. If Samuel Ryder, a boy from Manchester, had persuaded his father, a seed merchant, to sell flower seeds in penny packets, he would never have moved south to start his own business at St Albans in Hertfordshire.

There, late in life, he took up golf under the skilled and watchful eye of Abe Mitchell and, whether at Mitchell's suggestion or not, presented a cup for competition between the professionals of America and Britain.

In an earlier unofficial match Britain won 13½–1½ at Wentworth, but in the first official match in 1927, five years after the start of the Walker

Cup, Britain quickly learned the lesson about the formidable nature of American golfers.

1927 Britain, captained by Ted Ray, travelled to Worcester, Massachusetts where America, under Walter Hagen, captured the trophy 9½–2½. America won three of the four 36-hole foursomes and then took six of the singles. Charles Whitcombe won a notable half with Gene Sarazen while George Duncan won Britain's only single against Joe Turnesa, runner-up the same year to Hagen in the USPGA championship. It was Hagen's fourth victory in succession. In the Ryder Cup he won his foursome with Johnny Golden and his single against Arthur Havers.

1929 Immediate revenge for Britain at Moortown and defeat for Walter Hagen in the singles battle of the captains. He lost 10 and 8 to George Duncan, a victory that helped to turn the tables after America had again won the foursomes. It is the biggest 36-hole singles margin in the history of the event. The victory of Charles Whitcombe by 8 and 6 over Johnny Farrell, 1928 US Open champion, was followed by wins for Archie Compston, Aubrey Boomer and a youthful Henry Cotton.

1931 The Americans underlined their supremacy in their own country. At Scioto, Ohio, they lost only one foursome and two singles. They had five victories by 7 and 6 or more.

1933 One of the more famous matches which Britain won at Southport and Ainsdale, victory coming in the last match on the course. It was the most exciting finish to a team match seen up until then and one watched by enormous crowds. The British, captained by J H Taylor, went for a run on the sands at 6.30 each morning and underwent other forms of physical training unheard of before or since.

How much it contributed to their victory was never known but, for the first time, Britain gained a foursomes lead and hung on in the singles. Eventually, everything depended on Syd Easterbrook and Densmore Shute, the 1933 British Open champion. They came to the last all square. Easterbrook putted dead for his four but Shute, characteristically for an American, knocked his winning putt past the hole and then, uncharacteristically for an American, missed the return.

Britain, without Henry Cotton who had gone to Brussels, had won but the match very nearly did not take place. Hagen did not keep the appointed meeting with Taylor to exchange orders beforehand—or a second appointed meeting. A third hour was named with Taylor issuing an ultimatum that, if Hagen defaulted

again, he would call the match off and the world should know why. This time, Hagen kept his appointment and all was well.

1935 Under Hagen's captaincy of America for the fifth time, Britain never recovered from their defeat in the foursomes at Ridgewood, New Jersey. All they gained were two victories by 1 hole and two halves.

1937 History did not repeat itself at Southport and Ainsdale. The British pairing of Henry Cotton and Alf Padgham was very much a case of putting the two best eggs in the same basket. Byron Nelson and Ed Dudley cracked them and America never looked back. Cotton won his single, but the outstanding achievement was the victory of Dai Rees over Nelson. It was the first of many appearances by Rees, but the last as American Captain by Hagen.

1939 The match did not take place although the Americans picked a side.

1947 Britain went to Portland, Oregon, although the fact that the Ryder Cup was resumed so soon after the war owed a great deal to Robert Hudson, a Portland businessman who more or less financed the expedition and played host to the British.

The benevolence, however, was centred off the course. The Americans won the first eleven matches, a whitewash being prevented by Sam King winning the final single against Herman Keiser.

It was the biggest victory margin in the history of the event. Porky Oliver and Lew Worsham equalled the biggest 36-hole foursome win, by 10 and 9, in the history of the event.

1949 America, captained by Ben Hogan who was still recovering from his terrible car accident, lost the foursomes 3–1. However, they staged a typical comeback in the singles. Dutch Harrison set the example by leading off in the singles with five straight 3s against Max Faulkner and his victory was followed by five others. The match was played at Ganton and the score was 7–5.

1951 Another heavy defeat for the British who won only one foursome and one single, although both involved Arthur Lees.

Played at Pinehurst, North Carolina with Ben Hogan, Sam Snead (Captain), Jimmy Demaret and Lloyd Mangrum in the American side. All four won their singles. It was Demaret's sixth and last game. His 100 per cent record covers more games than anybody else with a 100 per cent record.

The American side included Clayton Heafner whose son, Vance, played in the Walker

Above: Fred Daly holing the winning putt in his Ryder Cup foursomes of 1953 (Action Photos). *Right:* Christy O'Connor who has played in more Ryder Cup teams than anyone on either side (The Associated Press Ltd). *Below:* A rare sight: the crowd greeting victory for Britain and Ireland in the Ryder Cup. Lindrick 957 (Action Photos)

Cup match in 1977. They are the only father and son to play in the Ryder and Walker Cup.

1953 One of the best matches of the series at Wentworth, the result hinging on the missing of two shortish putts by the youngest British players in the singles. It was, nevertheless, a fine recovery by the British to get that close. They lost the foursomes 3–1, but had the edge in the singles. Harry Weetman beat Sam Snead after being 4 down with 6 to play.

1955 The match ventured into the Californian desert for the first time. The margin of the American victory was 8–4, but it was closer than that scoreline suggests. Most notable for two victories by John Jacobs in his only Ryder Cup match.

1957 First British victory for 34 years and, as it proved, the last. At Lindrick before huge crowds, Britain came back after losing the foursomes 3–1. They won six singles by convincing margins and lost only one. Dai Rees who captained the side, won both his matches as did Ken Bousfield. It was the first time since 1933 that no American won twice. In 1933, Ed Dudley and Billy Burke won the only American point in the foursomes but did not play in the singles.

1959 The year in which the British party had a narrow escape when their plane met a storm while travelling from Los Angeles to Palm Desert. After that, the Americans won $8\frac{1}{2}$–$3\frac{1}{2}$ but Eric Brown, the only British singles winner, preserved his 100 per cent singles record in his fourth and final match. He won all four singles and lost all four foursomes.

1961 Change to four series of 18-hole matches, foursomes the first day at Royal Lytham and singles the next. America, with Arnold Palmer in the team for the first time, won the foursomes 6–2, but there was only one point in the singles. It was also the first appearance of Billy Casper who set a record for the number of individual matches played. He was helped by the change of format.

1963 Introduction of fourballs, play being extended over three days. It was done to try and further interest in the matches in America, but served merely to emphasise American superiority. They won easily in Atlanta. Britain managed only one fourball victory out of eight.

1965 A closer match at Royal Birkdale although the day of fourballs ended in the dark. The first day of foursomes was halved, America winning the fourballs 4–2 and the singles 10–5. Peter Alliss won both his singles for Britain against Billy Casper and Ken Venturi.

1967 America's biggest win in Houston, $23\frac{1}{2}$–$8\frac{1}{2}$,

since the match was contested over six rounds. Britain scored no victories in the eight fourballs.

1969 After Tony Jacklin's victory in the Open championship earlier in the summer, the most exciting match of the whole series ended in a half.

The last day began with the scores even and ended the same way. Jacklin scored a 4 and 3 victory over Nicklaus on the last morning and was involved in the deciding game, again against Nicklaus, in the afternoon. Just ahead of them, Brian Huggett got a courageous half

British Walker and Ryder Cup captains in 1971— Michael Bonallack and Eric Brown (Action Photos)

HRH Princess Alexandra presenting the Ryder Cup to the American Captain, Dow Finsterwald, at Lytham, 1977 (Action Photos)

against Billy Casper. At the time that Huggett holed from 5 ft (1·5 m) on the 18th, Jacklin holed a huge putt on the 17th to get back to square.

Huggett thought that his putt might be to win the whole contest, but not so. Jacklin and Nicklaus, all square with one to play, halved the 18th in 4, although Nicklaus generously conceded Jacklin's final putt of about two and a half feet after he had holed an awkward one himself.

To underline the closeness of the three days, 18 of the 32 matches finished on the 18th green. The teams became 12 a side.

1971 After the excitement of Birkdale, 1971 produced the best performance by a British side in America. This score was 18½–13½ at St Louis, the five-point difference coming in the fourballs in which the British never fared well. It was an encouraging match for some of the young British players including Peter Oosterhuis, Peter Townsend, Harry Bannerman, Bernard Gallacher, Maurice Bembridge and Brian Barnes. The final two days consisted of a foursome and fourball not a day of each.

1973 In the first match to be played in Scotland, Britain led at lunchtime on the second day at Muirfield, but America won the singles 11–5, although four were halved and six went to the 17th green or beyond.

1975 Played in Arnold Palmer country at Laurel Valley, Pennsylvania, America won 21–11, a result that was always assured after winning all four foursomes on the first morning. The singles were, for the most part, close and Brian Barnes beat Jack Nicklaus twice on the last day.

1977 At Royal Lytham, only 18 holes were played each day; it was an experiment that was not a success and not popular among the players. There were five foursomes on the first day, five fourballs on the second day and ten singles on the third.

America led 7½–2½ after two days, but Hale Irwin, Tom Watson and Jack Nicklaus all lost their singles. Nicklaus's defeat meant that he had won only one of his last five singles in the Ryder Cup.

1979 For the first time, a European side was selected to play the Americans at the Greenbrier Club at White Sulphur Springs. Antonio Garrido and Severiano Ballesteros, British Open champion, won their places, although they only won one match.

The form of play was altered yet again. There were two days when eight foursomes and eight fourballs were played, the final day being devoted to twelve singles matches. However, Gil Morgan and Mark James were not fit enough to play in the singles, it being agreed by the captains to call it a half to both sides. It was the first time this had happened.

The European team, captained by John Jacobs, came back well on the second day after trailing 5½–2½ on the first. They entered the final day trailing by one, but they lost the singles 8½–3½, although four matches which they lost finished on the last green.

For the Americans, captained by Billy Casper, Larry Nelson had a 100 per cent record from five games.

Tom Watson withdrew from the American side a few days before the match to be with his wife and newly born child. His place went to Mark Hayes.

Peter Oosterhuis's singles defeat by Hubert Green was his first in eight games.

Lee Elder became the first black golfer to take part in the Ryder Cup.

DETAILED RECORDS

Most appearances
10, Christy O'Connor, Sr (Great Britain and Ireland), 1955–73
9, Sam Snead (US), 1937–59, excluding 1957. No matches were played in 1939 and 1941, but the United States picked a team and Snead's total includes these two occasions

Most consecutive appearances
10, Christy O'Connor, Sr

Biggest margin of victory in individual matches
Over 36 holes (1927–59)
Foursomes: **10 and 9,** Ed Oliver and Lew Worsham (United States), 1947. Walter Hagen and Densmore Shute (United States), 1931
Singles: **10 and 8,** George Duncan (Great Britain), 1929
Over 18 holes (from 1961)
Foursomes: **6 and 5,** David Thomas and George Will (Great Britain and Ireland), 1965; Dave Marr and Arnold Palmer (United States), 1965; Bobby Nichols and Johnny Pott (United States), 1967; Jack Nicklaus and Arnold Palmer (United States), 1973
Singles: **7 and 6,** Miller Barber (United States), 1969; Lee Trevino (United States), 1971
Fourball: **7 and 6,** Tom Kite and Hale Irwin (United States), 1979; **5 and 4,** Arnold Palmer and Dow Finsterwald (United States), 1963; Dave Marr and Arnold Palmer (United States), 1965; Arnold Palmer and Gardner Dickinson (United States), 1971; Brian W Barnes and Bernard Gallacher (Great Britain and Ireland), 1973

Largest winning margin by team
36-hole matches, 1947: the United States won 11–1
18-hole matches (3 days), 1967: the United States won 23½–8½

Best team recovery
In 1957, Great Britain and Ireland lost the foursomes 3–1, but won the singles 6½–1½ for over-all victory

Most consecutive team victories
7 by the United States, 1935–55

Course most often used
Britain: Southport and Ainsdale, Royal Lytham and Royal Birkdale, twice each
USA: No course has been used more than once

Oldest competitors
Britain: Ted Ray, 50 years 2 months 5 days, 1927
Christy O'Connor, Sr, 49 years 8 months 30 days, 1973
USA: Don January, 47 years 9 months 26 days, 1977
Julius Boros, 47 years 7 months 17 days, 1967

Youngest competitors
Britain: Nick Faldo, 20 years 1 month 28 days, 1977
USA: Horton Smith, 21 years 4 days, 1929

Form of the match
1927–59: Two days, 36-hole matches, four foursomes, eight singles
1961: Two days, first day, two series 18-hole foursomes. Second day, two series 18-hole singles
1963–71: Three days, one day each of two series of 18-hole foursomes, fourballs and singles
1973–75: Three days, first two days, 18-hole foursomes and fourballs. Third day two series of singles
1977: Three days, first day, 18-hole foursomes; second day, 18 holes fourballs; third day 18-hole singles
1979: Three days, first two days, four foursomes and four fourballs, third day twelve singles

Teams winning all the foursomes or fourballs
1947: the United States won the foursomes 4–0
1963: the United States won the second series of foursomes 4–0
1975: the United States won the first series of foursomes 4–0
1967: the United States won the first series of fourballs 4–0
1971: the United States won the first series of fourballs 4–0

Teams winning all the singles
None, but in 1963 the United States won 7½ out of 8 in the second series of singles

The United States have won 19 matches, Great Britain and Ireland 3 and 1 halved

OUTSTANDING INDIVIDUAL RECORDS
UNITED STATES
(Number of individual matches shown in brackets.)

Name	%
Jimmy Demaret (6)	100
Larry Nelson (5)	100
Billy Maxwell (4)	100
Ben Hogan (3)	100
Johnny Golden (3)	100

Billy Burke (3)	100
Wilfrid Cox (2)	100
Ralph Guldahl (2)	100
Chick Harbert (2)	100
Lew Worsham (2)	100
Bob Rosburg (2)	100
Jim Turnesa (1)	100
Gardner Dickinson (10)	90
Lanny Wadkins (8)	88.88
Jack Burke (8)	87.5
Clayton Heafner (4)	87.5
Horton Smith (4)	87.5
Mike Souchak (6)	83.3
Walter Hagen (9)	83.3
Tony Lema (11)	81.81
Hale Irwin (12)	79.16
Tom Weiskopf (10)	75
Lloyd Mangrum (8)	75
Tommy Bolt (4)	75
Ted Kroll (4)	75
Tommy Jacobs (4)	75
Henry Picard (4)	75
Ed Dudley (4)	75
Byron Nelson (4)	75
Hubert Green (3)	75
Tom Kite (4)	75
Other players of interest	
Gene Sarazen (12)	70.83
Arnold Palmer (32)	68.75
Julius Boros (16)	68.75
Gene Littler (27)	66.66
Billy Casper (37)	63.51
Jack Nicklaus (24)	60.41

Billy Casper's 37 matches is a record for America.

A total of 113 players have actually *played* for the United States.

OUTSTANDING INDIVIDUAL RECORDS GREAT BRITAIN AND IRELAND

(Number of individual matches shown in brackets)

Name	%
John Jacobs (2)	100
John Fallon (1)	100
Peter Mills (1)	100
Nick Faldo (7)	85.71
Abe Mitchell (6)	66.66
Sid Easterbrook (3)	66.66
Peter Oosterhuis (25)	62
Percy Alliss (6)	58.33
Bernard Gallacher (25)	56
Charles Whitcombe (10)	50
Ken Bousfield (10)	50
Harry Bradshaw (5)	50
Arthur Lees (8)	50
Arthur Havers (6)	50
W H Davies (4)	50
Norman Drew (1)	50
Aubrey Boomer (4)	50
Eric Brown (8) won in all 4 singles	50
Other players of interest	
Tony Jacklin (35)	48.57
Brian Huggett (24)	45.83
Brian Barnes (26)	44.23
Fred Daly (8)	43.75
Peter Alliss (30)	41.66
Dai Rees (18)	41.66
Neil Coles (40)	38.75
Christy O'Connor (36)	36.11
Henry Cotton (6)	33.33

Neil Coles's 40 matches is a record for the other side.

A total of 83 players have actually *played* for Great Britain and Ireland (and Europe).

RYDER AND WALKER CUP MATCHES

Golfers who have played in both
British: Norman Drew, Peter Townsend, Peter Oosterhuis, Howard Clark, Mark James, Clive Clark, Sandy Lyle, Michael King.
American: Fred Haas, Gene Littler, Ken Venturi, Jack Nicklaus, Tommy Aaron, Mason Rudolph, and Lanny Wadkins, Bob Murphy, Tom Kite.

Tommy Armour played for Britain against America in the forerunner to the Walker Cup in 1921 and for America against Britain as a professional in 1926.

Mark James and Sandy Lyle are the only players to have made the change from Walker to Ryder Cup in two years. James played in the Walker Cup of 1975 and the Ryder Cup of 1977, Lyle in the Walker Cup of 1977 and the Ryder Cup of 1979.

RYDER CUP

Year	Venue	Winners	USA Total	Great Britain and Ireland Total	Captains USA	Britain
1927	Worcester, Massachusetts	USA	9½	2½	Walter Hagen	Ted Ray
1929	Moortown, Leeds	Britain	5	7	Walter Hagen	George Duncan
1931	Scioto, Ohio	USA	9	3	Walter Hagen	Charles A Whitcombe
1933	Southport and Ainsdale, Lancashire	Britain	5½	6½	Walter Hagen	*J H Taylor
1935	Ridgewood, New Jersey	USA	9	3	Walter Hagen	Charles A Whitcombe
1937	Southport and Ainsdale, Lancashire	USA	8	4	*Walter Hagen	Charles A Whitcombe
1947	Portland, Oregon	USA	11	1	Ben Hogan	Henry Cotton
1949	Ganton, Scarborough, Yorkshire	USA	7	5	*Ben Hogan	*Charles A Whitcombe
1951	Pinehurst, North Carolina	USA	9½	2½	Sam Snead	*Arthur Lacey
1953	Wentworth, Surrey	USA	6½	5½	Lloyd Mangrum	*Henry Cotton
1955	Palm Springs, California	USA	8	4	Chick Harbert	Dai Rees
1957	Lindrick, Sheffield	Britain	4½	7½	Jack Burke	Dai Rees
1959	Palm Desert, California	USA	8½	3½	Sam Snead	Dai Rees
1961	Royal Lytham and St Annes, Lancashire	USA	14½	9½	Jerry Barber	Dai Rees
1963	Atlanta, Georgia	USA	23	9	Arnold Palmer	*Johnny Fallon
1965	Royal Birkdale, Lancashire	USA	19½	12½	*Byron Nelson	*Henry Weetman
1967	Houston, Texas	USA	23½	8½	*Ben Hogan	*Dai Rees
1969	Royal Birkdale, Lancashire	(tie)	16	16	*Sam Snead	*Eric C Brown
1971	St Louis, Missouri	USA	18½	13½	*Jay Hebert	*Eric C Brown
1973	Muirfield, East Lothian	USA	19	13	*Jack Burke	*Bernard J Hunt
1975	Laurel Valley, Pennsylvania	USA	21	11	*Arnold Palmer	*Bernard J Hunt
1977	Royal Lytham and St Annes, Lancashire	USA	12½	7½	*Dow Finsterwald	*Brian G C Huggett
1979	Greenbrier, White Sulphur Springs	USA	17	11	Billy Casper	*John Jacobs

*Non-playing captains

WORLD CUP
(formerly Canada Cup)

Unlike soccer, the World Cup at golf is not regarded as the most important international tournament. It was founded in 1953 as the Canada Cup by John Jay Hopkins, an American industrialist for 'the furtherance of good fellowship and better understanding among the nations of the world through the medium of international golf competition'.

It consists of two-man teams representing their countries, the competition taking the form of 72 holes of strokeplay, the combined score of both players producing a team total. For the first two years, it was a 36-hole event and in two other years it was decided over 63 and 54 holes. In 1963, fog in Paris meant curtailment by 9 holes and in 1972 at Royal Melbourne, heavy rain washed out a day's play.

One of the problems of organisation is in finding dates suitable to everyone in view of such expansion in the golfing fixtures over the last 25 years. Nowadays, the International Golf Association settle for the end of the year but, despite a succession of worries, the competition has managed to survive.

It has been held in several countries where golf is not widely played and has traded on goodwill, modest prize-money and long hours of play. With such a variety of standard, rounds can take five or six hours.

The individual award is secondary but gives players who may have weak partners some extra interest.

DETAILED RECORDS

Most victories
15, The United States
  3, Australia
  2, South Africa; Spain
Member of the most winning teams
6, Arnold Palmer and Jack Nicklaus (both United States)
Lowest winning team aggregate
544, Australia (Bruce Devlin and David

Graham) at Jockey Club, Buenos Aires, 1970
(In 1963 and 1972, the competition was reduced to three rounds owing to the weather.)

Highest winning team aggregate
591, Spain (Severiano Ballesteros and Antonio Garrido) Manila, Philippines, 1977

Lowest individual score
269, Roberto de Vicenzo (Argentina), Jockey Club, Buenos Aires, 1970

Most individual lowest scores
3, Jack Nicklaus (USA)

Most times runner-up (team)
4, The United States, Argentina and South Africa

Lowest 9-hole record—individual (29)
Juan Sereda, Uruguay (Buenos Aires, 1962)

Lowest 18-hole record—individual (63)
Jack Nicklaus, USA (Palm Beach, 1971)

Holes in one
Ake Bergkvist, Sweden, 12th hole, Portmarnock, 1960
Juan Sereda, Uruguay, 16th hole, Royal Kaanapali, Hawaii, 6 December 1964
Cees Cramer, Holland, 11th hole, Club de Campo, Madrid, 2 October 1965
Jean-Charles Rey, Monaco, 7th hole, Circolo Golf Olgiata, Rome, 15 November 1968
Dave Thomas, Wales, 12th hole, Bukit Course, Singapore Island Country Club, 3 October 1969
Henrik Lund, Denmark, 12th hole, Jockey Club, Buenos Aires, 12 November 1970
José Maria Canizares, Spain, 2nd hole, Lagunita Country Club, Caracas, 24 November 1974
Antonio Evangelista, Brazil, 13th hole, Navatanee Golf Course, Bangkok, 6 December 1975

Youngest competitor:
Marko Vovk, 15 years, Yugoslavia 1979 (Athens)
Ossie Gartenmaier, 17 years, Austria, 1965 (Madrid)

Oldest competitor:
Flory van Donck, Belgium, 67 years 1979 (Athens)
Juan Dapiaggi, 66 years, Uruguay, 1973 (Marbella)

Most number of appearances
Jean Garaialde (France) 23 in 1979
Mohamed Moussa (Egypt) 21 in 1979
Roberto de Vicenzo (Argentina) 19 in 1974
Gary Player (South Africa) 17 in 1977
Flory van Donck (Belgium) 19 in 1979

RESULTS

Year	Total
1953 Beaconsfield GC, Montreal, Canada, 2–3 June	
Argentina: Roberto de Vicenzo 147, Tony Cerda 140	287
Canada: Stan Leonard 144, Bill Kerr 153	297
Individual: Tony Cerda 70, 70	140
1954 Laval Sur Le Lac GC, Montreal, Canada, 19–22 August	
Australia: Peter Thomson 277, Kel Nagle 279	556
Argentina: Roberto de Vicenzo 283, Tony Cerda 277	560
Individual: Stan Leonard (Canada) 66, 68, 71, 70	275
1955 Columbia CC, Washington DC, USA 9–12 June	
United States: Chick Harbert 281, Ed Furgol 279	560
Australia: Peter Thomson 279, Kel Nagle 290	569
Individual: Ed Furgol 73, 70, 69, 67	279
1956 Wentworth GC, Surrey, England 24–26 June	
United States: Ben Hogan 277, Sam Snead 290	567
South Africa: Bobby Locke 285, Gary Player 296	581
Individual: Ben Hogan 68, 69, 72, 68	277
1957 Kasumigaseki GC, Tokyo, Japan 24–27 October	
Japan: Torakichi Nakamura 274, Koichi Ono 283	557
United States: Sam Snead 281, Jimmy Demaret 285	566
Individual: Torakichi Nakamura 68, 68, 67, 71	274
1958 Club de Golf Mexico, Mexico City, 20–23 November	
Ireland: Harry Bradshaw 286, Christy O'Connor 293	579
Spain: Angel Miguel 286, Sebastian Miguel 296	582
Individual: Angel Miguel 72, 73, 71, 70	286
1959 Royal Melbourne GC, Australia, 18–21 November	
Australia: Peter Thomson 275, Kel Nagle 288	563
United States: Sam Snead 281, Cary Middlecoff 292	573
Individual: Stan Leonard (Canada) 70, 66, 69, 70	275

1960 Portmarnock GC, Dublin, Eire 23–26 June
United States: Arnold Palmer 284, Sam Snead 281 565
England: Bernard Hunt 289, Harry Weetman 284 573
Individual: Flory van Donck (Belgium) 68, 71, 70 70 279
1961 Dorado Beach GC, Puerto Rico, 1–4 June
United States: Sam Snead 272, Jimmy Demaret 288 560
Australia: Peter Thomson 280, Kel Nagle 292 572
Individual: Sam Snead 67, 67, 70, 68 272
1962 Jockey Club, Buenos Aires, Argentina, 8–11 November
United States: Arnold Palmer 278, Sam Snead 279 557
Argentina: Boberto de Vicenzo 276, Fidel de Luca 283 559
Individual: Roberto de Vicenzo 71, 68, 69, 68 276
1963 St Nom La Breteche, Paris, France, 24–27 October
United States: Jack Nicklaus 237, Arnold Palmer 245 482
Spain: Sebastian Miguel 242, Ramon Sota 243 485
Individual: Jack Nicklaus 67, 72, 66, 32 (63 holes only) 237
1964 Royal Kaanapali GC, Maui, Hawaii, 3–6 December
United States: Arnold Palmer 278, Jack Nicklaus 276 554
Argentina: Roberto de Vicenzo 281, Leopoldo Ruiz 284 565
Individual: Jack Nicklaus 72, 69, 65, 70 276
1965 Club de Campo, Madrid, Spain, 30 September–3 October
South Africa: Gary Player 281, Harold Henning 290 571
Spain: Ramon Sota 285, Angel Miguel 294 579
Individual: Gary Player 70, 69, 68, 74 281
1966 Yomiuri GC, Tokyo, Japan, 10–13 November
United States: Jack Nicklaus 273, Arnold Palmer 275 548
South Africa: Harold Henning 276, Gary Player 277 553
Individual: George Knudson (Canada) 64, 68, 66, 74 272
1967 Club de Golf, Mexico, Mexico City, 9–12 November
United States: Arnold Palmer 276, Jack Nicklaus 281 557

New Zealand: Bob Charles 281, Walter Godfrey 289 570
Individual: Arnold Palmer 68, 70, 71, 67 276
1968 Olgiata GC, Rome, Italy, 14–17 November
Canada: Al Balding 274, George Knudson 295 569
United States: Lee Trevino 283, Julius Boros 288 571
Individual: Al Balding 68, 72, 67, 67 274
1969 Singapore Island CC, Singapore 2–5 October
United States: Lee Trevino 275, Orville Moody 277 552
Japan: Takaaki Kono 279, Haruo Yasuda 281 560
Individual: Lee Trevino 71, 70, 69, 65 275
1970 Jockey Club, Buenos Aires, Argentina, 12–15 November
Australia: David Graham 270, Bruce Devlin 274 544
Argentina: Roberto de Vicenzo 269, Vicente Fernandez 285 554
Individual: Roberto de Vicenzo 64, 67, 68, 70 269
1971 PGA National GC, Palm Beach, USA 11–14 November
United States: Jack Nicklaus 271, Lee Trevino 284 555
South Africa: Gary Player 278, Harold Henning 289 567
Individual: Jack Nicklaus 68, 69, 63, 71 271
1972 Royal Melbourne, Australia, 9–12 November
Taiwan: Hsieh Min Nam 217, Lu Liang Huan 221 438
Japan: Takaaki Kono 219, Takashi Murakami 221 440
Individual: Hsieh Min Nam 70, 69, 78 (54 holes only) 217
1973 Golf Nueva Andalucia, Marbella, Spain, 22–25 November
United States: Johnny Miller 277, Jack Nicklaus 281 558
South Africa: Gary Player 280, Hugh Baiocchi 284 564
Individual: Johnny Miller 73, 65, 72, 67 277
1974 Lagunita CC, Venezuela, 21–24 November
South Africa: Bobby Cole 271, Dale Hayes 283 554
Japan: Isao Aoki 283, Masashi Ozaki 276 559
Individual: Bobby Cole 66, 70, 67, 68 271
1975 Navatanee, Bangkok, Thailand, 4–7 December
United States: Lou Graham 279, Johnny Miller 275 554

Sam Snead, World Cup, 1956 at Wentworth (BBC Hulton Pic. Lib.)

World Cup winners Jack Nicklaus and Lee Trevino, the United States, 1971 (Action Photos)

The Fijian World Cup pair Bose Lutunatabua (in bunker) and Arun Kumar, 1979 (Phil Sheldon)

Above: Aerial distraction—World Cup, Athens, 1979 (Phil Sheldon)
Below: An outside agency, but a movable obstruction. Angel Gallardo and alligator; World Cup, Florida 1971 (Action Photos)

The Asia Golf Circuit

Comprising the Philippines, Hong Kong, Thailand, Indian, Malaysian, Singapore, Indonesian, Republic of China (Taiwan) and Korean Opens; also a tournament in Tokyo sponsored by the Sobhu Company

In 1980 they were played between 21 February and 27 April

DETAILED RECORDS

Oldest winner
Ben Arda, 49 years, Philippines Open, 1979

Youngest winner
Lu Liang Huan, 22 years, Hong Kong Open, 1959
Lu Hsi Chuen, 24 years, Singapore Open, 1979

Most victories since 1959
14 Hsieh Yung Yo (Taiwan). He won the Hong Kong Open five times.
Prior to 1959, Larry Montez won the Philippines Open 13 times between 1929 and 1954

Biggest margin of victory
9 strokes, Bruce Crampton, Philippines Open, 1959; Mark McNulty, Malaysian Open, 1980

Lowest winning aggregate
269, T Kono (Japan), Malaysian Open, Royal Selangor, 1971

Highest winning aggregate
291, Frank Phillips, Philippines Open, 1960
291, Ben Arda, Indian Open, 1969

Lowest individual round
62, Kel Nagle, Hong Kong Open, Royal Hong Kong (New course), 1961
62, David Graham, Singapore Open, Bukit course, 1968

Lowest 9 holes
28, F Gambetta (USA), Singapore Bukit course, 1979

Amateur winners
287 (73, 72, 73, 69), Luis F Silverio, Philippines Open, 1966
283 (74, 73, 69, 67) Hsu Sheng San, Philippines Open, 1967
On both occasions Celestino Tugot was second. In 1965 the first prize was withdrawn—causing great consternation among the professionals, but the following year Tugot received the first prize money.

Growth of prize-money
About US $5000 in the early stages, to $700 000 in 1979.

The foundation of what is today known as the Asia Golf Circuit was laid in 1959 when the late Eric Cremin, a former Australian Open champion, and the late Kim Hall, a Welsh international then serving in the Royal Air Force, had the idea of running a small tournament for eight Australian professionals who would be playing in the Philippines Open. In those days, the Philippines Open was the only truly 'Open' professional event played in Southeast Asia.

As things turned out, Cremin and Hall managed to produce 24 professionals including Kel Nagle, Bob Charles and Mr Lu, as he later became known. With these names and an offer of £1000 in prize-money, Hall approached the Royal Hong Kong GC who accepted a proposal to run the first Hong Kong Open.

Together with the Philippines Open, the Far East Circuit was started and in 1961 Peter Thomson convinced the Singapore golfers to join in with the Singapore Open. The following year, the Malaysian Open followed suit while the Yomiuri Country Club in Tokyo staged the first Japan Invitational tournament.

India, Taiwan and Thailand followed in quick succession and, with the inclusion of Korea in 1970 and Indonesia in 1974, the family circle was complete. The circuit became firmly established with ten tournaments.

In 1961, Hall retired from the Royal Air Force and returned to Hong Kong to become co-ordinator of the circuit. He continued until 1968 when he handed over to Leonardo 'Skip' Guinto, then President of the Philippines Golf Association.

Guinto did much to build up the prize-money and in 1977 the first $100 000 tournament was reached. This was the Tokyo event whose sponsorship had been taken over by the Sobhu Company. This is the only tournament on the circuit which is not a national title.

In the early 1970s the minimum prize-money for inclusion in the circuit, renamed the Asia Golf Circuit in 1970, was $15 000. This increased to $25 000 and in 1977 to $30 000.

However, in 1978 the various bodies got together and agreed to make a grand circuit prize of $100 000 to encourage more leading overseas competitors.

Unfortunately, this had only limited success, but by 1979 the Philippines, Hong Kong and Japan had all raised their prize-money to $100 000 and in the same year, there was a record total prize-money of $700 000.

Also in 1979, 'Skip' Guinto retired; Kim Hall returned as Circuit Director and it is thought that in the near future prize-money for the circuit will reach $1 million.

Entries normally cover 16 different countries, with support from young Americans who cannot gain entry to their own tour and from the increasing number of Japanese professionals.

In 1979, there were 1300 professionals in Japan and it became necessary to restrict entries to 30 professionals from any one country with pre-qualifying, known in Asia as the 'Monday tournament', becoming an essential part of the circuit.

More countries such as Papua, New Guinea and Okinawa made requests to join the circuit, but with ten tournaments fitted in between the end of the Australian circuit and the beginning of those in Japan and Europe, there was no room to accept any more prize-money.

In 1979, Lu Hsi Chuen won $43 670, four Taiwanese players finishing in the first five in the order of merit and seven in the first eleven.

THAILAND OPEN

Year	Winner	Country	Venue	Score
1965	Hsieh Yung Yo	Taiwan	Royal Thai Air Force	283
1966	Tadashi Kitta	Japan	Royal Thai Air Force	283
1967	Tomoo Ishii	Japan	Royal Thai Air Force	283
1968	Randall Vines	Australia	Royal Thai Air Force	285
1969	Hsieh Yung Yo	Taiwan	Royal Thai Air Force	277
1970	David Graham	Australia	Bangphra GC	286
1971	Lu Liang Huan	Taiwan	Royal Thai Air Force	278
1972	Hsieh Min Nam	Taiwan	Royal Thai Air Force	278
1973	Graham Marsh	Australia	Siam CC	286
1974	Toshihiro Hitomi	Japan	Bangphra GC	291
1975	Howard Twitty	United States	Bangphra GC	285
1976	Ben Arda	Philippines	Navatanee GC	270
1977	Yurio Akitomi	Japan	Siam CC	284
1978	Hsu Sheng San	Taiwan	Siam CC	280
1979	Mike Krantz	United States	Royal Thai Air Force	282
1980	Lu Hsi Chuen	Taiwan	Royal Thai Air Force	274

INDONESIA OPEN

Year	Winner	Country	Score
1974	Ben Arda	Philippines	
1975	Hsu Sheng San	Taiwan	
1976	Mya Aye	Burma	
1977	Gaylord Burrows	United States	
1978	Kuo Chi Hsiung	Taiwan	275
1979	Lu Hsi Chuen	Taiwan	272
1980	Lu Hsi Chuen	Taiwan	265

KOREA OPEN

Year	Winner					Score
1970	Hahn Chang Sang	71	72	76	70	289
1971	Hahn Chang Sang	68	71	71	71	281
1972	Hahn Chang Sang	74	65	70	67	276
1973	Kim Seung Hak	71	68	72	71	282
1974	Cho Tae Woon	70	75	72	69	286
1975	Kuo Chie Hsiung	74	70	69	71	284
1976	Kazunari Takahashi	71	73	70		214
1977	Ho Ming Chong	73	70	70	72	285
1978	Kim Seung Hak	70	69	67	71	277
1979	Shen Chung Shyan					289

HONG KONG OPEN

Year	Winner	Venue	Score
1959	Lu Liang Huan	Fanling	281
1960	Peter Thomson	Fanling	272
1961	Kel Nagle	Fanling	261
1962	Len Woodward	Fanling	271
1963	Hsieh Yung Yo	Fanling	272
1964	Hsieh Yung Yo	Fanling	269
1965	P W Thomson	Fanling	278
1966	F Phillips	Fanling	275
1967	P W Thomson	Fanling	273
1968	R Vines	Fanling	271
1969	T Sugihara	Fanling	274
1970	I Katsumata	Fanling	274
1971	O Moody	Fanling	266
1972	W Godfrey	Fanling	272
1973	F Phillips	Fanling	278
1974	Lu Liang Huan	Fanling	280
1975	Hsieh Yung Yo	Fanling	288
1976	Ming-Chung Ho	Fanling	279
1977	Hsieh Min Nam	Fanling	280
1978	Hsieh Yung Yo	Fanling	275
1979	G Norman	Fanling	273
1980	Kuo Chi-Hsiung	Fanling	274

TAIWAN OPEN

Year	Winner	Country	Score
1965	Hsu Chi San		290
1966	Lu Liang Huan		281
1967	Hsieh Yung Yo		277
1968	Hsieh Yung Yo		282
1969	Hideyo Sugimoto	Japan	284
1970	Chang Chung-Fa		215
1971	Chang Chung-Fa		286
1972	A Yasuda	Japan	284
1973	E Nival	Philippines	283
1974	Kuo Chi Hsiung		282
1975	Kuo Chi Hsiung		277
1976	Hsu Chi San		288
1977	Hsieh Min Nan		276
1978	Hsieh Yung Yo		283
1979	Lu Liang Huan		287
1980	Kuo Chi Hsiung		277

INDIA OPEN

Year	Winner	Country	Venue	Score
1963	P W Thomson	Australia	New Delhi	292
1965	P G Sethi (Am.)	India	Calcutta	282
1966	P W Thomson	Australia	Delhi	284
1968	K Hosoishi	Japan	New Delhi	285
1969	B Arda	Philippines	Royal Calcutta	291
1970	C Chung Chen	Taiwan	Royal Calcutta	279
1971	G Marsh	Australia	New Delhi	275
1972	B Jones	Australia	Royal Calcutta	282
1973	G Marsh	Australia	New Delhi	280
1974	Chie-Hsiung Kuo	Taiwan	Royal Calcutta	287
1975	T Ball	Australia	New Delhi	282
1976	P W Thomson	Australia	New Royal Calcutta	288
1977	B Jones	Australia	New Delhi	284
1978	B Brask	United States	Royal Calcutta	284
1979	G Burrows	United States	New Delhi	284
1980	Kurt Cox	United States	Tollygunge	286

MALAYSIAN OPEN

Year	Winner	Country	Venue	Score
1963	Billy Dunk	Australia	Kuala Lumpur	276
1964	T Ishii	Japan	Kuala Lumpur	282
1965	T Ishii	Japan	Kuala Lumpur	282
1966	H R Henning	South Africa	Kuala Lumpur	278
1967	I Legaspi	Philippines	Kuala Lumpur	286
1968	K Hosoishi	Japan	Kuala Lumpur	271
1969	T Kono	Japan	Kuala Lumpur	280
1970	B Arda	Philippines	Kuala Lumpur	273
1971	T Kono	Japan	Kuala Lumpur	269
1972	T Murakami	Japan	Kuala Lumpur	276
1973	Hideyo Sugimoto	Japan	Kuala Lumpur	277
1974	G Marsh	Australia	Ipoh	278
1975	G Marsh	Australia	Kuala Lumpur	276
1976	Hsu Sheng-San	Taiwan	Kuala Lumpur	279
1977	S Ginn	Australia	Kuala Lumpur	276
1978	B Jones	Australia	Kuala Lumpur	276
1979	Lu Hsi Chuen	Taiwan	Kuala Lumpur	277
1980	M McNulty	South Africa	Kuala Lumpur	270

SINGAPORE OPEN

Year	Winner	Runner-up	Venue	By
1957	H Knaggs	G. Balleine	Royal Island	3 and 2
1958	D W McMullen	R Craik		

Year	Winner	Club/Country	Venue	Score
1959	R C W Stokes		Royal Island	—
1961	F Phillips	Australia	Island Course	275
1962	Brian Wilkes	South Africa	Bukit Course	283
1963	A Brookes	South Africa	Island Course	276
1964	T Ball	Australia	Bukit Course	291

Year	Winner	Country	Venue	Score
1965	F Phillips	Australia	Bukit Course	279
1966	R Newdick	New Zealand	Bukit Course	284
1967	B Arda (after a tie)	Philippines	Bukit Course	282
1968	Hsieh Yung Yo	Taiwan	Bukit Course	275
1969	T Kamata	Japan	Bukit Course	278
1970	Hsieh Yung Yo	Taiwan	Bukit Course	276
1971	H Yasuda	Japan	Bukit Course	277
1972	T Kono	Japan	Bukit Course	279
1973	B Arda	Philippines	Bukit Course	284
1974	E Nival	Philippines	Bukit Course	275
1975	Y Suzuki	Japan	Singapore Island	284
1976	K Uchida	Japan	Bukit Course	273
1977	Chi-San Hsu	Taiwan	Bukit Course	277
1978	T Gale	Australia	Bukit Course	278
1979	Lu Hsi Chuen	Taiwan	Bukit Course	280
1980	Kurt Cox	United States	Bukit Course	276

PHILIPPINES OPEN

Year	Winner	Country	Venue	Score
1962	C Tugot	Philippines	Manila	284
1963	B Arda	Philippines	Manila	289
1964	P W Thomson	Australia	Manila	285
1965	Lu Liang-Huan	Formosa	Manila	288
1966	L Silverio (Am.)	Manila	Manila	287
1967	Hsu Sheng San	Formosa	Manila	283
1968	Hsu Chi San	Formosa	San Pedro	278
1969	Haruo Yasuda	Japan	Manila	279
1970	Hsieh Yung-Yo	Taiwan	Manila	282
1971	C Chien Chung	Taiwan	Manila	282
1972	H Sugimoto	Japan	Manila	286
1973	King Seung Hack	South Korea	Manila	289
1974	Lu Liang Huan	Taiwan	Manila	281
1975	Kuo Chie Hsiong	Taiwan	Manila	276
1976	Q Mancao	Philippines	Manila	281
1977	Hsieh Yung Yo	Taiwan	Manila	281
1978	Lu Liang Huan	Taiwan	Manila	278
1979	B Arda	Philippines	Manila	286
1980	Lu Hsi Chuen	Taiwan	Manila	287

Lu Hsi Chuen, Taiwan (Phil Sheldon)

Tsuneyuki Nakajima, Japan (Phil Sheldon)

The Amateurs

BRITISH AMATEUR CHAMPIONSHIP

MILESTONES

1885 First played 20 April to 23 April. Not recognised as the official start of the championship until much later. It was started by the Royal Liverpool Club as a 'tournament open to all amateur golfers' and the first champion at Hoylake was Allan F MacFie, a Scottish member of the home club.

However, it was unusual in that the tournament rules decreed that halved matches were not to be decided on an extra hole basis, but were simply replayed. Byes were not eliminated in the first round and, as there were 48 entries, three players reached the semi-final.

MacFie was the man in receipt of a bye into the final where he beat Horace Hutchinson by 7 and 6. If that part was fortunate, he also halved two matches in the fourth round with H W de Zoete and was only successful in the third meeting.

He won on the last green, but was helped by a hole in one at the 13th, the first recorded in the event.

1886 After the highly successful start, the championship was officially instituted at St Andrews and won by Horace Hutchinson, runner-up at Hoylake.

1887 Hutchinson won a second victory back at Hoylake against John Ball, the local player who was to become so famous. There were only 33 entries.

1887 to 1895 A period dominated by John Ball and Johnny Laidlay. They won the title alternately. Ball in 1888-90-92-94, and Laidlay in 1889-91. In addition, Laidlay was runner-up to Ball in 1888-90 and to Peter Anderson in 1893. Ball was runner-up in 1895. Ball won the Open in 1890 and shares the distinction with Bobby Jones of winning both the Open and Amateur titles in the same year.

In 1895, the winner was Leslie Balfour (afterwards Leslie Balfour-Melville) who won his last three matches at the 19th hole. His opponents were William Grey, Laurie Auchterlonie and John Ball who all hit their second shots into the Swilcan Burn at St Andrews. It was the last time the final was played over 18 holes except for 1966—due to adverse weather conditions.

Above: Horace Hutchinson, a famous early British Amateur champion and writer on golf (BBC Hulton Pic. Lib.)

Below: John Ball, Jr, the most prolific winner of the British Amateur championship (BBC Hulton Pic. Lib.)

Above: Freddie Tait, a fine all-round games player
(Badminton Library)

Below: James Robb (Badminton Library)

1896 Freddie Tait beat Harold Hilton at Sandwich in the first 36-hole final. It was Hilton's third defeat in the final. Tait was something of a bogyman to Hilton and had earlier beaten Charles Hutchings, Johnny Laidlay, John Ball and Horace Hutchinson in succession.

1897 Something of a surprise win for Jack Allan, a medical student at Edinburgh University who never touched a club until 1891. At the time, he was the youngest winner and seemed destined for a fine career, but he died of lung disease the following year after taking up a medical appointment at Lasswade, near Edinburgh.

1898 A second victory for Freddie Tait who two years later was killed in the South African War. Reports of his victory at Hoylake say he was sadly out of form in the early rounds, saving himself with remarkable recovery play, but he was at his best in the final against S Mure-Fergusson.

1899 Entry of over 100 for the first time. John Ball scored his fifth win, this time against the defending champion, Freddie Tait, at Prestwick. He won at the 37th in Tait's last championship.

1900 Victory for Harold Hilton after three previous defeats in the final.

1901 Hilton conducted a successful defence of his title, the first to do so since 1887 and the last until Lawson Little in 1935.

1902 Both Charles Hutchings and Sidney Fry, the two finalists, used the new Haskell ball at Hoylake. Hutchings, the winner, was 53. The Hon Michael Scott, the oldest winner ever, was 54.

1903 First of two victories for Robert Maxwell. He won both at Muirfield where he was a member.

1904 Title taken overseas for the first time by Walter J Travis, an Australian-born resident of America, famous for his black cigars and centre-shafted Schenectady putter. He beat James Robb, Harold Hilton, Horace Hutchinson and, in the final at Sandwich, Edward Blackwell.

1905 In a final remembered for consistent heavy rain A Gordon Barry defeated the Hon Osmund Scott by 3 and 2. It was felt that in these conditions Scott was at a considerable disadvantage with rubber grips. Two weeks later he had had them changed. Barry, 19, was a student at St Andrews University.

1906 James Robb, runner-up in 1897 and 1900, became champion at last.

1907 A record entry of 200 for the sixth victory

of John Ball, apparently more interested in his garden and motor cycle since his last win.

1908 A Yorkshireman, E A Lassen caused a surprise by winning at Sandwich, but he proved his worth and reached the final again in 1911. An earlier round produced the longest match in the championship's history; C A Palmer beat Lionel Munn at the 28th.

1907, 1910 and 1912 The final chapters in the remarkable record of John Ball. At Westward Ho! in 1912, he completed his eighth victory, a record that will surely stand for ever. Michael Bonallack has come nearest to it with five successes. In 1912, Ball defeated Abe Mitchell, later a celebrated professional, in the final. The final lasted 38 holes, the second longest in the championship's history. They met in the 1910 semi-final when Ball also won. In 1912 Ball was 5 down and 7 to play in the fifth round.

In 1910 Ball scored the first double-figure victory in the final against C Aylmer.

1909 Of Robert Maxwell's second victory at Muirfield against Cecil Hutchison, the golf-course architect, Bernard Darwin wrote: 'They produced a never to be forgotten match by those who saw it. The golf was so faultless, the speed at which it was played so great, that they seemed to be playing not a championship final but one of the friendly, almost casual games which they had often played together on the links of the Lothians.'

1911 and 1913 Confirmation of Harold Hilton's skill in something of a revival. When he won at Prestwick in 1911, 20 years had passed since his first appearance in the final and ten since his previous victory. Hilton was also American champion in 1911.

1914 The champion, J L C Jenkins, was the player of the year who would no doubt have done greater things but for an injury in the war.

1920 In the first championship final for six years Cyril Tolley defeated Bob Gardner, twice American champion and the second American to reach the final of the British. At Muirfield, Tolley was 3 up and 4 to play in the final, but Gardner, at one time world record holder for the pole vault and US rackets doubles champion, won the 33rd, 34th and 36th. However, Tolley won the 37th with a superb 2, the old 1st hole at Muirfield being a short one.

1921 Willie Hunter, the son of the professional at Deal, won his championship over a burned-up course at Hoylake. He was a player of no great length but putted finely on very fast greens and handed a double-figure defeat in the final to Allan Graham. Earlier Graham beat Bobby Jones 6 and 5 with a queer brass putter.

In the afternoon, he was still in such a daze, he had towards the end to ask his caddie to score. Later that year, Hunter beat Jones in the US Amateur. He then turned pro. Graham's father died the day before the final.

1922 At this time the amateur triumvirate of Tolley, Roger Wethered and Ernest Holderness were dominant. In 1922, Holderness, the epitome of steadiness, won his first title at Prestwick.

1923 Sandwiched between Holderness's two victories was one for Roger Wethered at Deal, two years after losing a play-off for the Open championship at St Andrews. Wethered played outstandingly in beating Robert Harris by 7 and 6 in the final.

1924 Holderness's second victory. In a very rainy final he beat Eustace Storey, then still an undergraduate at Cambridge.

1925 The second championship at Westward Ho! with the winner, Robert Harris, born in Dundee. Harris, however, runner-up to Harold Hilton in 1913 and Roger Wethered in 1923, was a redoubtable champion who, as a stock-broker in London, was an Anglo-Scot although he had learned his game at Carnoustie.

He was also a pre-war golfer and was 43 when he won the championship, but his victory was thoroughly deserved. In the final, he defeated Kenneth Fradgley by 13 and 12, a severe margin which has only been exceeded by Lawson Little in 1934.

1926 A second American, Jess Sweetser, won the championship and so set a pattern of American victories in a Walker Cup year in Britain. It was not broken until 1963 when Michael Lunt won.

A quarter-mile runner at Yale, Sweetser swept through the hardest part of the draw and, as often happens, was rewarded with a relatively easy match in the final. He defeated an Edinburgh golfer, A F Simpson and became the second American (and the third person) to win both the British and American titles.

1927 A championship won by Dr William Tweddell, a deceptively good player who was born in Durham, qualified at Aberdeen University and played most of his golf in the Midlands. In the final, he beat Eustace Landale, a useful Hoylake player, by 7 and 6.

1928 T Phil Perkins, a product of the Midlands, followed his victory in the English championship the previous year, by winning the British, beating Roger Wethered 6 and 4 in the final at Prestwick. Later in the summer, Perkins played well in America, but he had what was described as a 'severe dose of the Bobby Jones's'.

In the Walker Cup match, Jones beat him 13 and 12 and in the final of the American Amateur at Brae Burn Jones won again, this time by 10 and 9.

He later turned professional and was joint runner-up in the US Open of 1932 won by Gene Sarazen; however, the US Amateur final was the first time the reigning British and American champions had met in a major final and, apart from Harold Hilton, Perkins is the only British golfer to have reached the final in both championships. Jack McLean reached the American final in 1936.

1929 Cyril Tolley's second victory, a little less spectacular than his first, but no more than his ability merited.

1930 Part of the legendary Grand Slam chapter of Bobby Jones. It was the first leg, but it was significant because it was always the championship which he found hardest to win; and, indeed it was the only one which he won just once.

Fittingly, it took place at St Andrews, scene of some of Jones's brightest and darkest moments, but even 1930 had its dark moments. He disliked 18-hole matches and had one or two close calls notably against George Voigt who was 2 up and 5 to play in their semi-final, and against Cyril Tolley in the second round. Jones won at the 19th.

In the final, Jones, with room to manœuvre, beat Roger Wethered 7 and 6 and was never likely to be denied. It was the second defeat in the final for Wethered in three years.

1931 Surprise victory for Eric Martin Smith who, none the less, played and putted very consistently.

Some measure of the surprise at his success can be gauged by the telegram which he received on the morning of his final with John de Forest. From one who had played with him at Cambridge, it read, 'Quite ridiculous but keep at it.'

It was the last championship to be held at Westward Ho!

1932 John de Forest confirmed his full worth the following year by winning at Muirfield in a final with Eric Fiddian. It was the fourth time a player had reached the final one year and become champion the next. The final was played at a very slow pace partly because, at that time, de Forest was suffering from 'the waggling disease in its most exaggerated form'. In the semi-final de Forest beat Lionel Munn at the 26th hole, the longest semi-final on record.

1933 The year of the oldest winner on record, the Hon Michael Scott, at 54. He was a year older than Charles Hutchings who had won in 1902. Having just scrambled through his first-round match, Scott grew ever stronger. He beat the American George Dunlap in the semi-final and was too good for Dale Bourn in the final.

1934 Year of the biggest victory in the final: 14 and 13 by Lawson Little from Newport, Rhode Island over Jack Wallace. Wallace, a local West of Scotland golfer, was overwhelmed before many of his supporters could reach Prestwick.

However, he had plenty of excuse. Little, who had had one victory at the 19th, was round in 66 in the morning and after lunch played 4 of the remaining 5 holes of the match in 3 and the other in 4. Such scoring had never been approached in a final. In one round, J G Montgomery and his opponent hit 5 balls out of bounds at the 1st hole between them.

1935 Part two of Little's dominance, one which was not confined to the British championship. In 1934 and 1935, he won the British and American titles, a unique achievement.

However, in the final at Royal Lytham St Annes, he was given a terrific match by the 1927 champion, William Tweddell, who made up for being outgunned in the long game by his work round the greens. Three down and 10 to play, Tweddell took the match to the 36th green.

It was Lytham's first Amateur championship, but it was not at its best owing to a plague of leatherjackets.

1936 In the absence of Little who turned professional, Hector Thomson won for Scotland. It is a remarkable fact that since World War I, there have only been four Scottish champions; Thomson, Robert Harris in 1925, Alec Kyle in 1939 and Reid Jack in 1957. Thomson was the only one of these four to have won in Scotland.

In the final at St Andrews, Thomson beat Jim Ferrier by 2 holes. Ferrier was the first Australian to reach the final. Later, he turned professional, became an American citizen and won the USPGA championship. In the second round, J L Mitchell, later Captain of the Royal and Ancient, defeated Lionel Munn at the 26th hole. In 1908, Munn lost at the 28th, and in 1932 also at the 26th.

1937 Victory at Royal St George's for Robert Sweeny, an American who played much of his golf in Britain and Europe. He defeated Lionel Munn who knew Sandwich blindfold, by 3 and 2, but the championship marked the first appearance of a 17-year-old Irishman, James Bruen, who made a spectacular impact on amateur golf over a short period.

1938 A championship at Troon for the first time preceded the famous Walker Cup match at St

Troon's three British Amateur champions: Michael Bonallack (1968), Charlie Yates (1938) and John Beharrell (1956). Taken during the championship, 1978 when the Club became Royal Troon (Action Photos)

Andrews. All the American team took part, however, and the winner was the ever-popular Charlie Yates of Atlanta whose opponent in the final was the Irishman Cecil Ewing.

1939 Alec Kyle's championship at Hoylake, the last before World War II. A Scotsman resident in Yorkshire, he won a delightful final against Tony Duncan played at a brisk pace. They took $2\frac{1}{4}$ hours for the first 18 holes, generally held to be a record.

It is the only final since 1914 played between two golfers from home countries who were not English. Duncan was the first Welsh finalist.

The other fact about this championship is that it was the first at which a running commentary for radio was tried. It was also the last.

1946 Deprived of championship glory during the war years, James Bruen from Cork made amends with victory over the 1937 champion, Robert Sweeny. The championship was Royal Birkdale's first, a course which has since become a regular venue for British championships and international matches. The Open followed in 1954.

1947 The first all-American final, Willie Turnesa adding the British crown to the American title he won in 1938. At Carnoustie, another new course on the Amateur championship list, he defeated Dick Chapman by 3 and 2.

1948 Frank Stranahan, son of a millionaire and an obsessively devoted golfer, won the first of his two championships in three years. At Sandwich, he defeated Charlie Stowe, once a miner, in the final by 5 and 4. Stowe, one of the victorious British Walker Cup team in 1938, had lost the final of the English championship the previous year.

1949 The only championship to be played in the Republic of Ireland (Portmarnock) was won by Sam (or Max) McCready who was born in Belfast. He beat the 1947 champion, Willie Turnesa, 2 and 1 in the final.

1950 Frank Stranahan's second victory in the second all-American final although, as it happened, the first of three in a row. It was also the slowest on record, the first 18 holes taking $4\frac{1}{2}$ hours at St Andrews. The match, however, turned out to be one sided with Stranahan beating Dick Chapman by 8 and 6.

There was a record entry of 324, the first time that 300 had been exceeded.

1951 In his third final in five years, victory came at last for Dick Chapman. He is the only player to have won all the major amateur championships of the world, the American, British and Canadian. He also won the French, Italian and Portuguese titles.

In the first championship at Royal Porthcawl, he defeated Charlie Coe by 5 and 4.

1952 Prestwick's last major championship (the last Open was 1925), saw a third consecutive American winner and a third consecutive all-American final. In it, Harvie Ward beat Frank Stranahan by 6 and 5.

It was the second final between two players who subsequently became professionals. The others were 1938 (Hector Thomson and Jim

Charlie Coe congratulating Dick Chapman, British Amateur final 1951 (Action Photos)

Ferrier), 1966 (Bobby Cole and Ronnie Shade), 1967 (Bob Dickson and Ron Cerrudo) and 1971 (Steve Melnyk and Jim Simons).

1953 The beginning of the Joe Carr era. He became the first champion from Eire and put an end to the run of American victories. His victory in the final at Hoylake against the defending champion, Harvie Ward, probably the most formidable amateur in the world at the time, was considered by many to be his best.

Three up at lunch and all square after the 11th in the afternoon, Carr had the better of the closing holes but no champion ever had such a run of escapes in reaching the final. In his last three matches, he had to hole from 12 ft (3·6 m) on the 18th to avoid defeat; hole again from the same distance the next morning when his opponent missed from 6 ft (1·8 m) and in his semi-final with Cecil Beamish he was 2 down with 3 to play. Beamish then went out of bounds at the 16th and 19th, easy enough to do at Hoylake, and Carr was through.

1954 The bicentenary celebrations of the Royal and Ancient Golf Club brought the most international entry to the championship at Muirfield. Four different nationalities were represented in the semi-finals and the eventual champion was Doug Bachli, the first Australian to succeed. By a notable coincidence, the year also saw the first Australian winner of the British Open, Peter Thomson, who, even more remarkably, was a member of the same club as Bachli: the Victoria in Melbourne.

In the final, Bachli beat Bill Campbell, the popular and respected American, by 2 and 1. It was felt at the time that Campbell would win one day but, though he came again fairly regularly, he never did.

1955 Joe Conrad from Texas, played in the Walker Cup at St Andrews where he was one of only two Americans to lose his single; he then stayed on to win the championship at Lytham and came back in 1956 to finish leading amateur in the Open.

At Lytham, he beat Alan Slater, a Yorkshireman, by 3 and 2 in the final.

1956 A year when the experiment of playing the quarter finals, semi-finals and final over 36 holes was tried, produced a big surprise and the youngest winner.

John Beharrell, another Midlands golfer, won a month after his 18th birthday. On his way to the final, he beat Charles Lawrie, Ian Caldwell, Gene Andrews, Frank Deighton, Reid Jack and then Leslie Taylor, a local member of Troon. The margin was 5 and 4.

With the course playing easily, Beharrell hit very few poor shots and pitched and putted effortlessly. First appearance of Michael Bonallack.

1957 Formby's introduction to the list of championship courses confirmed the talent of Reid Jack who twice finished well up in the Open (1959 and 1960). It was a just and popular triumph. He defeated the American Staff Sergeant, Harold Ridgley, in the final. Ridgley

Doug Bachli, British Amateur champion 1954, with Joe Carr. Bachli is the only Australian winner of the title (Action Photos)

spent many years serving in Britain. He won his semi-final by 13 and 12.

1958 Only the semi-finals and final were played over 36 holes at St Andrews, but it did not stop a second victory for Joe Carr. Two years later, he might just possibly have won the Open on the same course had not the last round been washed out after he had started birdie, par.

In the final he beat Alan Thirlwell 3 and 2, one of the deciding strokes undoubtedly being a 4 iron on to the 13th green out of Walkinshaw's bunker in the afternoon. Having just holed across the green for a 2 at the 12th, it enabled him to remain 2 up.

Michael Bonallack made his first real mark on the championship by reaching the semi-final, where he lost to Carr.

1959 Victory at Sandwich after the Walker Cup at Muirfield went not to the more experienced Americans, or to Jack Nicklaus who won the St George's Grand Challenge Cup, but to Deane Beman.

He accounted for Bill Hyndman in the first of Hyndman's three finals by 3 and 2, Hyndman having taken a lot out of himself the previous day in knocking out an obdurate American serviceman, Bob McGee at the 38th.

1960 The summit of Joe Carr's career. At Portrush, he stood 10 up on Bob Cochran on the 27th tee of the final. His third victory was the first time a British or Irish golfer had performed such a feat since Harold Hilton, more than half a century before.

Farewell championship appearance of James Bruen. He withdrew with a wrist injury during his first match.

Like the Open (1951) Portrush has held only one Amateur championship.

1961 The emergence of Turnberry as a championship course and a new champion to match. Michael Bonallack scored the first of his five victories in the course of the next ten years. He began by defeating Jimmy Walker, a local Ayrshire golfer, by 6 and 4 in the final. The only time Bonallack had to play the 17th was on the morning of the final.

Only the final was 36 holes, the semi-finals reverting to 18.

1962 A surprising American winner in Richard Davies, a Californian; and a slightly surprising finalist in John Povall, only the second Welshman to survive that far. The other was Tony Duncan in 1939, also at Hoylake.

1963 Historic victory for Michael Lunt. It was the first time since Sweetser set the pattern in 1926 that a British player won in a Walker Cup year at home.

His final opponent, however, was not an American, but John Blackwell, 48, Captain of Royal St George's and in 1966 Captain of the Royal and Ancient. The other two semi-finalists, Dr Ron Luceti and Ed Updegraff were both American although Luceti was not a Walker Cup player.

1964 The longest final on record. It took 39 holes for Gordon Clark to come from behind and beat Michael Lunt, so close to a successful defence of his title.

A long tradition was broken by the choice of Ganton for the championship. It was the first time it was played on other than a seaside links.

1965 Porthcawl's second championship and Michael Bonallack's second victory. The final against Clive Clark was a replica of the final of the English championship the following month; and the pattern was similar. Bonallack was down at lunch although at Porthcawl he had been 6 down after 13 holes. His recovery is thus the best on record. He was also down at lunch in the English final.

1966 The first final over 18 holes since 1895. A sea mist, common at Carnoustie, caused the loss of half a day and led to a revision of the programme. It also produced the first South African champion in Bobby Cole and the joint youngest at 18 years and 1 month exactly. He defeated Ronnie Shade 3 and 2 with half

Reid Jack, British Amateur champion 1957 (Action Photos)

The most prolific British Amateur champion of modern times, Michael Bonallack (Action Photos)

Scotland supporting Shade. Henri de Lamaze was the first Frenchman to reach the semi-final. He lost to Cole.

1967 Bob Dickson clinched the first leg of his double at Formby; he later went on to win the US Amateur also, the first man to win both in one year since Lawson Little. At Formby he beat fellow American Ron Cerrudo by 2 and 1 in what was undoubtedly the fastest final between two Americans, 2 hr 40 min for the first 18 holes.

1968 Two outstanding amateurs, Joe Carr and Michael Bonallack, met in the final at Troon although Carr was a little past his best. Bonallack won 7 and 6 and so began the first of three successive wins.

1969 In Hoylake's centenary year, Bonallack beat Bill Hyndman for his second successive title. It was his fourth victory, equalling Harold Hilton, a local man. Only John Ball, another Hoylake golfer, won more (8).

1970 More records for Michael Bonallack after his third win in a row at Newcastle, Co Down, the only time the championship has been played there. He again beat Bill Hyndman in the only repeat final since 1890 and his three wins in a row is an outright record.

Hyndman also equalled a record of being most times runner-up (3 with Harold Hilton) but he had his chance. Two up after 13 holes and 1 up at lunch, he was in sight of becoming the oldest winner but, looking exhausted, as any man of 54 has a right to do, he lost 8 and 7.

1971 Another American monopoly in the championship despite their Walker Cup defeat at St Andrews the previous week. Peter Moody prevented all four semi-finalists being American, but in the final Steve Melnyk beat Jim Simons who, inside a month, had come close to winning the US Open at Merion. He did so as an amateur but, like Melnyk, later turned professional.

1972 A surprising winner in Trevor Homer, another Midlander, who had never previously won even his county championship. However, he played extremely well all week and, in the first round of the final, completed Royal St George's in 69. He beat Alan Thirlwell by 4 and 3. It was 13 years since Thirlwell's other final. Only Horace Hutchinson (1885 to 1903) can claim such a span as runner-up.

1973 Richard Siderowf became the 16th American winner. At Porthcawl, he beat Peter Moody, semi-finalist in 1971, 5 and 3.

1974 Trevor Homer's second win in three years. At Muirfield, he defeated the American Walker Cup player Jim Gabrielsen by 2 holes in the closest final for ten years. Homer won the 36th hole despite driving into a bunker and leaving it there, an unprecedented luxury for a champion.

1975 Snow marked the first day of the championship at Hoylake (2 June) but the final was played in shirtsleeves. The weather caused a number of odd results but Vinny Giles was a worthy champion. He became the sixth American since World War II to win both British and American titles. Two up at lunch on Mark James, he won 8 and 7. James, who played in the Walker Cup of 1975, was a member of the Ryder Cup team in 1977.

1976 Dick Siderowf's second championship and only the second extra-hole final since 1920. At St Andrews, he beat John Davies at the 37th where Siderowf holed from 5 ft (1·5 m) and

Davies missed from $3\frac{1}{2}$ ft (1 m). Davies lost the final of the English the same summer.

1977 Ganton's second championship produced the sixth Midland winner in Peter McEvoy. In the final, he beat Hugh Campbell, 39, the first Scottish finalist for eleven years.

1978 McEvoy became only the fifth player to successfully defend his title. The others were, Hutchinson, Hilton, Little and Bonallack.

In Troon's centenary year (they became Royal Troon during the week), he beat Paul McKellar, a Walker Cup golfer from the West of Scotland, by 4 and 3 in a final which saw McKellar drive the 1st green after lunch. It was a feat nobody could remember happening before.

In their second-round match, Gordon Macdonald and A Liddle had played 19 holes when darkness beat them. They resumed at 7.30 am with Macdonald winning at the 25th. In point of time, it is the longest match ever played in the championship.

1979 Peter McEvoy's three in a row bid ended.

Two American finalists confirmed the pattern so prominent in Walker Cup years in Britain. Eight days after the match at Muirfield, Jay Sigel defeated Scott Hoch by 3 and 2 in the first Amateur championship to be played at Hillside, Royal Birkdale's neighbour in Southport.

For the first time ever, no British player reached the semi-final. The other semi-finalists were Tony Gresham of Australia and Doug Roxburgh of Canada.

A new qualification rule imposed by the Royal and Ancient greatly reduced the number of American entries. They were required to have qualified for either the US Open or US Amateur in any of the previous five years.

The championship cup, part of Sigel's luggage, was lost for days at London Airport. It was later found and sent on to Sigel.

1980 First Welsh champion appropriately enough on a Welsh course, Royal Porthcawl. In the final, Duncan Evans beat David Suddards of South Africa by 4 and 3.

DETAILED RECORDS

Most victories
8, John Ball, 1888-90-92-94-99-1907-10-12
5, Michael Bonallack, 1961-65-68-69-70
4, Harold Hilton, 1900-01-11-13

Most times runner-up
3, Harold Hilton, 1891-92-96; William Hyndman III, 1959-69-70

Oldest winner
Hon Michael Scott, 54 years, 1933

Youngest winner
John Beharrell, 1956, and Bobby Cole, 1966; both 18 years 1 month to the day

Consecutive winners
3, Michael Bonallack, 1968-69-70
2, Horace Hutchinson, 1886-87; Harold Hilton, 1900-01; W Lawson Little, 1934-35; Peter McEvoy, 1977-78

Biggest span between first and last victories
24 years, John Ball, 1888-1912

First overseas winner
Walter Travis (USA), Sandwich, 1904

Longest final
39 holes: Gordon Clark beat Michael Lunt, Ganton, 1964

Longest match (18 holes)
C A Palmer beat Lionel Munn at the 28th, Sandwich, 1908

Biggest margin of victory
Final: **14 and 13,** W Lawson Little beat J Wallace, Prestwick, 1934
18 holes: **10 and 8;** Alexander Stuart beat John L Stewart, Prestwick, 1888; Captain E F Carter, Royal Portrush, beat F S Wheeler, USA, Muirfield, 1920

Most finals
10, John Ball
7, Harold Hilton, three losing followed by four winning

Identical finals
1888 and 1890: John Ball beat John Laidlay
1969 and 1970: Michael Bonallack beat Bill Hyndman

Most appearances
Harold Hilton

First player to win the British Open and Amateur
John Ball, Amateur, 1888; Open, 1890

Players who have won the Amateur and Open
Same year: John Ball, 1890; Bobby Jones, 1930
Different years: Harold Hilton (Amateur 1900-01-11-13; Open 1892 and 1897)

Record entry
488, St Andrews, 1958

Courses most often used
Hoylake, 16
St Andrews, 14
Champion on the same course
John Ball, 3 times at Hoylake, twice at Prestwick

RESULTS

1885 Hoylake
A F MacFie, Royal Liverpool
Semi-finals: H G Hutchinson beat W J Ball 2 holes; MacFie a bye
Final: MacFie beat Hutchinson 7 and 6

1886 St Andrews
H G Hutchinson, Royal and Ancient
Semi-finals: Hutchinson beat C Chambers 5 and 3; H A Lamb beat J Ball, Sr 7 and 6
Final: Hutchinson beat Lamb 7 and 6

1887 Hoylake
H G Hutchinson, Royal and Ancient
Semi-finals: J Ball, Jr beat J G Tait 3 and 1; Hutchinson beat Ball, Sr 1 hole
Final: Hutchinson beat Ball 1 hole

1888 Prestwick
J Ball, Jr, Royal Liverpool
Semi-finals: J E Laidlay beat L M Balfour Melville 6 and 5; Ball beat A Stuart 4 and 3
Final: Ball beat Laidlay 5 and 4

1889 St Andrews
J E Laidlay, Hon Company
Semi-finals: Laidlay beat J Ball Jr at 20th; L M Balfour Melville beat W S Wilson 5 and 4
Final: Laidlay beat Balfour Melville 2 and 1

1890 Hoylake
J. Ball, Jr, Royal Liverpool
Semi-finals: Ball beat L M Balfour Melville 6 and 4; J E Laidlay beat D Leitch 1 hole
Final: Ball beat Laidlay 4 and 3

1891 St Andrews
J E Laidlay, Hon Company
Semi-finals: H H Hilton beat W Ballingall 6 and 4; Laidlay beat T Gilroy 5 and 4
Final: Laidlay beat Hilton at 20th

1892 Royal St George's
J Ball, Jr, Royal Liverpool
Semi-finals: H H Hilton beat J E Laidlay 5 and 4; Ball beat L M Balfour Melville 1 hole
Final: Ball beat Hilton 3 and 1

1893 Prestwick
P C Anderson, St Andrews University
Semi-finals: J E Laidlay beat F G Tait at 19th; Anderson beat S Mure Fergusson 2 holes
Final: Anderson beat Laidlay 1 hole

1894 Hoylake
J Ball, Jr, Royal Liverpool
Semi-finals: Ball beat J E Laidlay 5 and 3; S Mure Fergusson beat F G Tait 4 and 3
Final: Ball beat Mure Fergusson 1 hole

1895 St Andrews
L M Balfour Melville, Royal and Ancient
Semi-finals: J Ball, Jr beat F G Tait 5 and 3; Balfour Melville beat L Auchterlonie at 19th
Final: Balfour Melville beat Ball at 19th

1896 Royal St George's
F G Tait, Black Watch GC
Semi-finals: Tait beat H G Hutchinson 3 and 2; H H Hilton beat J H Graham 4 and 3
Final: Tait beat Hilton 8 and 7

1897 Muirfield (36-hole final introduced)
A J T Allan, Edinburgh University
Semi-finals: J Robb beat J L Low at 21st; Allan beat L M Balfour-Melville 3 and 1
Final: Allan beat Robb 4 and 2

1898 Hoylake
F G Tait, Black Watch GC
Semi-finals: Tait beat J L Low at 22nd; S Mure Fergusson beat J Robb 1 hole
Final: Tait beat Mure Fergusson 7 and 5

1899 Prestwick
J Ball, Jr, Royal Liverpool
Semi-finals: Ball beat G C Whigham 8 and 7; F G Tait beat J M Williamson 3 and 1
Final: Ball beat Tait at 37th

1900 Royal St George's
H H Hilton, Royal Liverpool
Semi-finals: J Robb beat J A T Bramston 3 and 1; Hilton beat J Graham, Jr 7 and 5
Final: Hilton beat Robb 8 and 7

1901 St Andrews
H H Hilton, Royal Liverpool
Semi-finals: Hilton beat H G Hutchinson 2 and 1; J L Low beat J Graham, Jr 1 hole
Final: Hilton beat Low 1 hole

1902 Hoylake
C Hutchings, Royal Liverpool
Semi-finals: Hutchings beat J Robb 2 and 1; S H Fry beat R Maxwell 1 hole
Final: Hutchings beat Fry 1 hole

1903 Muirfield
R Maxwell, Tantallon
Semi-finals: Maxwell beat H W de Zoete at 19th; H G Hutchinson beat A McDonald 4 and 2
Final: Maxwell beat Hutchinson 7 and 5

1904 Royal St George's
W J Travis, USA
Semi-finals: E Blackwell beat J E Laidlay 2 and 1; Travis beat H G Hutchinson 4 and 2
Final: Travis beat Blackwell 4 and 3

1905 Prestwick
A G Barry, St Andrews University
Semi-finals: Barry beat J Graham, Jr 1 hole; Hon O Scott beat A R Aitken 2 and 1
Final: Barry beat Scott 3 and 2

1906 Hoylake
J Robb, Prestwick St Nicholas
Semi-finals: Robb beat H S Colt 3 and 2; C C Lingen beat E A Smirke 1 hole
Final: Robb beat Lingen 4 and 3

1907 St Andrews
J Ball, Jr, Royal Liverpool
Semi-finals: C A Palmer beat R Harris 2 and 1; Ball beat G Campbell 2 and 1
Final: Ball beat Palmer 6 and 4

1908 Royal St George's
E A Lassen, Royal Lytham and St Annes
Semi-finals: H E Taylor beat J Graham, Jr 4 and 3; Lassen
beat C E Dick 2 and 1
Final: Lassen beat Taylor 7 and 6

1909 Muirfield
R Maxwell, Tantallon
Semi-finals: C K Hutchison beat R Andrew 3 and 2;
Maxwell beat B Darwin 3 and 2
Final: Maxwell beat Hutchison 1 hole

1910 Hoylake
J Ball, Jr, Royal Liverpool
Semi-finals: C C Aylmer beat H H Hilton 4 and 3; Ball beat
A Mitchell 5 and 4
Final: Ball beat Aylmer 10 and 9

1911 Prestwick
H H Hilton, Royal Liverpool
Semi-finals: Hilton beat G Lockhart 4 and 3; E A Lassen
beat L B Stevens 2 holes
Final: Hilton beat Lassen 4 and 3

1912 Westward Ho!
J Ball, Jr, Royal Liverpool
Semi-finals: A Mitchell beat C B Macfarlane 4 and 3; Ball
beat A V Hambro 3 and 1
Final: Ball beat Mitchell at 38th

1913 St Andrews
H H Hilton, Royal Liverpool
Semi-finals: R Harris beat E P Kyle 3 and 2; Hilton beat C C
Aylmer 1 hole
Final: Hilton beat Harris 6 and 5

1914 Royal St George's
J L C Jenkins, Troon
Semi-finals: C O Hezlet beat R P Humphries 1 hole;
Jenkins beat E M Smith 2 and 1
Final: Jenkins beat Hezlet 3 and 2

1915–19 No Championship

1920 Muirfield
C J H Tolley, Rye
Semi-finals: R A Gardner beat Hon M Scott 2 holes; Tolley
beat G T Mellin 5 and 4
Final: Tolley beat Gardner at 37th

1921 Hoylake
W I Hunter, Walmer and Kingsdown
Semi-finals: A J Graham beat H S B Tubbs; Hunter beat B
Darwin 3 and 2
Final: Hunter beat Graham 12 and 11

1922 Prestwick
E W E Holderness, Walton Heath
Semi-finals: Holderness beat W I Hunter 2 and 1; J Caven
beat R Scott, Jr 1 hole
Final: Holderness beat Caven 1 hole

1923 Deal
R H Wethered, Worplesdon
Semi-finals: Wethered beat F Ouimet 2 and 1; R Harris beat
D Grant 5 and 4
Final: Wethered beat Harris 7 and 6

1924 St Andrews
E W E Holderness, Walton Heath
Semi-finals: E F Storey beat R H Wethered 2 holes;
Holderness beat W A Murray 3 and 2
Final: Holderness beat Storey 3 and 2

1925 Westward Ho!
R Harris, Royal and Ancient
Semi-finals: Harris beat E N Layton 1 hole; K F Fradgley

beat R H Hardman 2 holes
Final: Harris beat Fradgley 13 and 12

1926 Muirfield
J Sweetser, USA
Semi-finals: Sweetser beat Hon W Brownlow at 21st; A F
Simpson beat A Jamieson, Jr 2 and 1
Final: Sweetser beat Simpson 6 and 5

1927 Hoylake
W Tweddell, Stourbridge
Semi-finals: Tweddell beat R H Wethered 4 and 3; D E
Landale beat R H Jobson 1 hole
Final: Tweddell beat Landale 7 and 6

1928 Prestwick
T P Perkins, Castle Bromwich
Semi-finals: Perkins beat W Tulloch 6 and 5; R H Wethered
beat E B Tipping 4 and 3
Final: Perkins beat Wethered 6 and 4

1929 Royal St George's
C J H Tolley, Rye
Semi-finals: Tolley beat R Hartley 1 hole; J N Smith beat J
Dawson at 19th
Final: Tolley beat Smith 4 and 3

1930 St Andrews
R T Jones, Jr, USA
Semi-finals: Jones beat G J Voigt 1 hole; R H Wethered
beat L Hartley 2 and 1
Final: Jones beat Wethered 7 and 6

1931 Westward Ho!
E Martin Smith, Royal St George's
Semi-finals: J de Forest beat W Tulloch 1 hole; Martin
Smith beat J D MacCormack 1 hole
Final: Martin Smith beat de Forest 1 hole

1932 Muirfield
J de Forest, Addington
Semi-finals: de Forest beat L O M Munn at 21st; E W
Fiddian beat E A McRuvie 2 holes
Final: de Forest beat Fiddian 3 and 1

1933 Hoylake
Hon M Scott, Royal St George's
Semi-finals: Scott beat G T Dunlap, Jr 4 and 3; T A Bourn
beat C J H Tolley at 20th
Final: Scott beat Bourn 4 and 3

1934 Prestwick
W Lawson Little, USA
Semi-finals: J Wallace beat G T Dunlap, Jr 2 and 1;
Lawson Little beat L G Garnett at 19th
Final: Lawson Little beat Wallace 14 and 13

1935 Royal Lytham and St Annes
W Lawson Little, USA
Semi-finals: W Tweddell beat T A Torrance 2 and 1;
Lawson Little beat R Sweeny, Jr 3 and 1
Final: Lawson Little beat Tweddell 1 hole

1936 St Andrews
H Thomson, Williamwood
Semi-finals: Thomson beat C Ewing 4 and 3; J Ferrier beat
G A Hill 1 hole
Final: Thomson beat Ferrier 2 holes

1937 Royal St George's
R Sweeny, Jr, Royal and Ancient
Semi-finals: L O M Munn beat J de Forest 4 and 3; Sweeny
beat C Stowe 6 and 5
Final: Sweeny beat Munn 3 and 2

1938 Troon
C R Yates, USA
Semi-finals: C Ewing beat C Ross Somerville 2 holes;

Yates beat H Thomson at 19th
Final: Yates beat Ewing 3 and 2

1939 Hoylake
A T Kyle, Sand Moor
Semi-finals: Kyle beat W E Holt, Jr 2 and 1; A A Duncan beat C Stowe 3 and 2
Final: Kyle beat Duncan 2 and 1

1940–45 No Championship

1946 Royal Birkdale
J Bruen, Cork
Semi-finals: Bruen beat H E Walker 3 and 2; R Sweeny, Jr beat G H Micklem 5 and 3
Final: Bruen beat Sweeny 4 and 3

1947 Carnoustie
W P Turnesa, USA
Semi-finals: Turnesa beat J G Campbell 4 and 3; R D Chapman beat S L McKinlay 2 holes
Final: Turnesa beat Chapman 3 and 2

1948 Royal St George's
F R Stranahan, USA
Semi-finals: Stranahan beat D H R Martin 3 and 1; C Stowe beat W P Turnesa 1 hole
Final: Stranahan beat Stowe 5 and 4

1949 Portmarnock
S M McCready, *Sunningdale*
Semi-finals: W P Turnesa beat E P Millward 1 hole; McCready beat K G Thom at 20th
Final: McCready beat Turnesa 2 and 1

1950 St Andrews
F R Stranahan, USA
Semi-finals: R D Chapman beat J B McHale 1 hole; Stranahan beat C J H Tolley 4 and 3
Final: Stranahan beat Chapman 8 and 6

1951 Royal Porthcawl
R D Chapman, USA
Semi-finals: C R Coe beat A D Evans 4 and 2; Chapman beat J B Carr 4 and 3
Final: Chapman beat Coe 5 and 4

1952 Prestwick
E Harvie Ward, USA
Semi-finals: Harvie Ward beat J B Carr 2 and 1; F R Stranahan beat J R Cater 2 holes
Final: Harvie Ward beat Stranahan 7 and 5

1953 Hoylake
J B Carr, Sutton
Semi-finals: Carr beat C H Beamish at 19th; E Harvie Ward beat A H Perowne 6 and 5
Final: Carr beat Harvie Ward 2 holes

1954 Muirfield
D W Bachli, Australia
Semi-finals: W C Campbell beat J B Carr 3 and 2; Bachli beat W A Slark 3 and 2
Final: Bachli beat Campbell 2 and 1

1955 Royal Lytham and St Annes
J W Conrad, USA
Semi-finals: A Slater beat A H Perowne 3 and 2; Conrad beat P F Scrutton 5 and 4
Final: Conrad beat Slater 3 and 2

1956 Troon (Quarter finals, semi-finals and final played over 36 holes in 1956–57)
J C Beharrell, Little Aston
Semi-finals: Beharrell beat R Reid Jack 2 and 1; L G Taylor beat G G Henderson 6 and 5
Final: Beharrell beat Taylor 5 and 4

1957 Formby
R Reid Jack, Dullatur
Semi-finals: Reid Jack beat A F Bussell 3 and 2; H B Ridgley beat A Walker 13 and 12
Final: Reid Jack beat Ridgley 2 and 1

1958 St Andrews (Semi-finals and final only played over 36 holes)
J B Carr, Sutton
Semi-finals: Carr beat M F Bonallack 4 and 3; A Thirlwell beat T Holland 4 and 3
Final: Carr beat Thirlwell 3 and 2

1959 Royal St George's (Semi-finals and final played over 36 holes)
D Beman, USA
Semi-finals: W Hyndman III beat B Magee at 38th; Beman beat G B Wolstenholme 5 and 4
Final: Beman beat Hyndman 3 and 2

1960 Royal Portrush
J B Carr, Sutton
Semi-finals: Carr beat J Walker 2 holes; B Cochran beat G Huddy 3 and 2
Final: Carr beat Cochran 8 and 7

1961 Turnberry
M F Bonallack, Thorpe Hall
Semi-finals: J Walker beat R L Morrow 1 hole; Bonallack beat M J Christmas 3 and 2
Final: Bonallack beat Walker 6 and 4

1962 Hoylake
R D Davies, USA
Semi-finals: J D Povall beat B H G Chapman 1 hole; Davies beat R Foster 3 and 2
Final: Davies beat Povall 1 hole

1963 St Andrews
M S R Lunt, Moseley
Semi-finals: Lunt beat E Updegraff 1 hole; J G Blackwell beat R Luceti 3 and 2
Final: Lunt beat Blackwell 2 and 1

1964 Ganton
G J Clark, Whitley Bay
Semi-finals: M S R Lunt beat J Hall 4 and 3; Clark beat M J Christmas 2 holes
Final: Clark beat Lunt at 39th

1965 Royal Porthcawl
M F Bonallack, Thorpe Hall
Semi-finals: Bonallack beat R Foster 1 hole; C A Clark beat M J Christmas 1 hole
Final: Bonallack beat Clark 2 and 1

1966 Carnoustie
R Cole, South Africa
Final: R D B M Shade beat G B Cosh 2 and 1; Cole beat H de Lamaze 2 and 1
Final: Cole beat Shade 3 and 2 (Final played over 18 holes)

1967 Formby
R B Dickson, USA
Semi-finals: Dickson beat G J Clark 4 and 3; R Cerrudo beat M Fleckman at 19th
Final: Dickson beat Cerrudo 2 and 1

1968 Troon
M F Bonallack, Thorpe Hall
Semi-finals: J B Carr beat R L Glading 3 and 1; Bonallack beat G C Marks 3 and 2
Final: Bonallack beat Carr 7 and 6

1969 Hoylake
M F Bonallack, Thorpe Hall
Semi-finals: Bonallack beat W C Davidson 4 and 3; W

Hyndman III beat D Hayes 3 and 2
Final: Bonallack beat Hyndman 3 and 2

1970 Royal County Down
M F Bonallack, Thorpe Hall
Semi-finals: Bonallack beat B Critchley 2 and 1; W Hyndman III beat T B C Hoey 2 holes
Final: Bonallack beat Hyndman 8 and 7

1971 Carnoustie
S Melnyk, USA
Semi-finals: J Simons beat T Kite 1 hole; Melnyk beat P H Moody 4 and 3
Final: Melnyk beat Simons 3 and 2

1972 Royal St George's
T W B Homer, Walsall
Semi-finals: A Thirlwell beat M F Bonallack 2 and 1; Homer beat R Revell 4 and 3
Final: Homer beat Thirlwell 4 and 3

1973 Royal Porthcawl
R Siderowf, USA
Semi-finals: Siderowf beat H Ashby 6 and 5; P H Moody beat H K Clark 3 and 2
Final: Siderowf beat Moody 5 and 3

1974 Muirfield
T W B Homer, Walsall
Semi-finals: J Gabrielsen beat M A Poxon 5 and 4; Homer beat H B Stuart 1 hole
Final: Homer beat Gabrielsen 2 holes

1975 Hoylake
Marvin Giles III, USA
Semi-finals: Giles beat R Siderowf at 21st; M James beat G C Marks 3 and 2
Final: Giles beat James 8 and 7

1976 St Andrews
R Siderowf, USA
Semi-finals: J C Davies beat I Carslaw 1 hole; Siderowf beat A Brodie 2 and 1
Final: Siderowf beat Davies at 37th

1977 Ganton
P M McEvoy, Copt Heath
Semi-finals: H M Campbell beat M F Bonallack at 24th; McEvoy beat P J McKellar 2 and 1
Final: McEvoy beat Campbell 5 and 4

1978 Royal Troon
P M McEvoy, Copt Heath
Semi-finals: McEvoy beat D R Suddards 4 and 3; P M McKellar beat J C Davies 3 and 2
Final: McEvoy beat McKellar 4 and 3

1979 Hillside
Jay Sigel, USA
Semi-finals: S Hoch beat A Gresham 3 and 2; Sigel beat D Roxburgh 6 and 5
Final: Sigel beat S Hoch 3 and 2

1980 Royal Porthcawl
D Evans, Leek
Semi-finals: Evans beat A D Pierse 2 and 1; D R Suddards beat D Lindsay-Smith 2 and 1
Final: Evans beat Suddards 4 and 3

US AMATEUR CHAMPIONSHIP

Matchplay 1895–1964 and after 1972
Strokeplay 1965–72

MILESTONES

1895 First champion, Charles Blair Macdonald at Newport, Rhode Island. No qualifying.
1896 Qualifying introduced, H J Whigham being medallist (86, 77) and matchplay champion. Whigham, an Oxford man, learned his golf in England.
1898 A field of 120 brought a new method of 36 holes qualifying for 32 places.
1900 Victory for Walter J Travis, an Australian who took to the game at 35.
1901 Travis made a successful defence of his title using the new Haskell ball. The death of President McKinley led to the championship being postponed a week.
1902 Eighteen-hole qualifying for 64 places. The winner was Louis James, 19 years and 10 months old.
1903 Walter Travis's third and last victory; 128 players allowed to compete, all at matchplay.

1904 Fifty-four holes qualifying for 32 places.
1905 Thirty-six holes qualifying for 32 places. An all-Chicago final, H Chandler Egan defeating D E Sawyer 6 and 5.
1907 First of four triumphs for Jerome D Travers and first appearance of Charles 'Chick' Evans, Jr.
1909 Robert A Gardner became the youngest winner at 19 years and 5 months and remains so.
1911 Title won by the Englishman, Harold Hilton. Having been 6 up on Fred Herreshoff in the final, he eventually won at the 37th. At that hole Hilton's second shot with a spoon got a lucky break.
1912 Jerome Travers, last in the qualifying, went on to win his fourth victory, a record he shares with Bobby Jones.
1914 Travers again reached the final but was beaten by Francis Ouimet who the previous year had scored his legendary win in the US Open.
1916 Momentous year at Merion. Charles 'Chick' Evans became the first man to win the US Open and US Amateur in the same year. He won the Open in June and added the Amateur by defeating defending champion, Robert A Gardner in the final.

It was momentous for another reason; the

first appearance, aged 14, of Bobby Jones who won two rounds.

1919 When the championship was resumed after the war, S Davidson Heron, playing on his own course, Oakmont, was four under 4s in beating Bobby Jones in the final by 5 and 4.

The entry reached 150.

1920 A huge increase in the entry to 235 forced the use of two courses for the qualifying. The record entry stood for eleven years. Evans beat Ouimet for the title. Cyril Tolley and several other British players failed to qualify.

Chick Evans who played in 50 American Amateur championships and won the US Open 1916 (US Golf Association)

Jess Sweetser, a fine athlete and golfer (US Golf Association)

1921 Championship held west of the Mississippi for the first time.

1922 Triumph for Jess Sweetser at 20. He defeated defending champion, Jesse P Guilford, Willie Hunter, Bobby Jones and Charles Evans, Jr, in the final. Jones's defeat by 8 and 7 was the biggest he suffered in the US Amateur.

1924 Beginning of the Jones era and his first victory at Merion. In the semi-final he beat Ouimet 11 and 10 and in the final he accounted for George von Elm.

1925 Jones's second victory. He beat Watts Gunn, his friend and protégé in the final. It was the only time two finalists represented the same club, Atlanta Athletic Club's East Lake course.

There were 16 qualifiers with all matches at 36 holes, but it was unpopular.

1926 Reversion to the old system of 36 holes

qualifying for 32 places. Jones thwarted by George von Elm from achieving three victories in a row.

1927 Number three for Jones. Victory in the final against Charles Evans, Jr.

1928 For the first time, the United States champion met the British champion in the final. Jones beat Phil Perkins 10 and 9.

1929 First championship on the Pacific coast. Bobby Jones beaten in the first round for the only time. His conqueror was Johnny Goodman, a future champion who was then beaten by another future champion, Lawson Little.

1930 One of the most historic championships of all time. The ultimate in achievement; the Grand Slam for Bobby Jones. The dream came true on Merion's 11th green when he beat Eugene Homans by 8 and 7. It was Jones's last championship.

Records of a different kind were set by Maurice McCarthy. He played 10 extra holes before beating George von Elm in the second round. This followed a 19-hole match with Watts Gunn and a play-off match, all in one day. He made a hole in one to make a place in the play-off for the qualifying.

1931 Francis Ouimet won again after a 17-year gap, a record. He defeated Jack Westland who, 21 years later, won the title himself. That gap of 21 years between finals is also a record.

Sectional qualifying for an entry of 583 was played at 20 different locations.

1932 Ross Somerville took the title to Canada for the first time.

1933 The champion, George Dunlap, was among the twelve players who played off for the last eight places in the championship.

1934 New format with no qualifying at the course, but 36-hole semi-finals and final produced Lawson Little as champion. He emulated Jones by winning the British and American titles in the same year.

1935 The double for Lawson Little both as American and British champion, the only time it has ever been done.

Entry of 945.

1936 Following the Walker Cup match at Pine Valley, Jack McLean lost the final at Garden City to Johnny Fischer. Fischer, 1 down and 3 to play against the British player, saved the 34th with a dead stymie and won on the 37th.

1937 Championship held in Pacific Northwest for the first time. Qualifying held at the course in addition to sectional qualifying to determine the 64 matchplayers. The champion was Johnny Goodman who won the US Open in 1933.

Above: John Goodman, the last amateur to win the US Open, 1933 (US Golf Association)
Below: Lawson Little, US Open champion in 1940 and winner of the British and American championships in 1934 and 1935 (US Golf Association)

Charlie Coe, an American amateur champion good enough to finish second in the US Masters (Action Photos)

1938 Willie Turnesa, one of seven brothers, won at Oakmont despite being in bunkers on 13 of the 29 holes of the final.

1942–45 No championships.

1946 After regional qualifying, 150 played for 64 places. New qualifying record for Skee Riegel with 136 (69, 67).

1947 In order to accommodate a larger field, qualifying on the site was abandoned and 210 admitted to matchplay.

1948 Entry of 1220, the largest to date. After ten years, Willie Turnesa won again, beating Ray

Billows in the final. It was Billows's third final.

1949 Two of the best-known names in post-war American amateur golf, Charles Coe and Harvie Ward contested a memorable fifth-round match, Coe, 3 down with 5 to play, winning at the 19th. He then went on to inflict upon Rufus King the largest defeat, 11 and 10, in any final.

1950 Having had the shortest final the previous year, 1950 produced the longest on record. In it, Sam Urzetta, a former caddie, defeated Frank Stranahan at the 39th hole.

1951 A record field of 1416. Billy Maxwell outlasted all the Walker Cup team, only Charles Coe surviving as far as the last 8.

1952 In keeping with a record-breaking period of three or four years, Jack Westland, finalist in 1931, became the oldest winner of the championship at 47. He beat Al Mengert in the first all-Northwest final, Westland from Everett, Washington, and Mengert from Spokane, Washington.

The championship was preceded by the first match between America, Canada and Mexico.

1953 Gene Littler became champion while serving in the US Navy. In the final, Dale Morey squared the final with birdies at the 34th and 35th, but Littler closed him out with a birdie at the 36th. Littler, 23, turned professional a few months later.

1954 The year of another US Open champion-to-be, Arnold Palmer. In an excellent final he beat Robert Sweeny on the 36th green. Like Littler the previous year, Palmer turned professional shortly afterwards.

For the first time the fairways were roped off.

1955 Some compensation for previous disappointments awaited Harvie Ward, British Amateur champion in 1952. A morning round of 66 in the final enabled him to lunch 8 up on Bill Hyndman who eventually went down 9 and 8.

Entry of 1493. Hillman Robbins set a sectional qualifying scoring record with 132 (66, 66) at Memphis.

1956 Ward became the sixth player to defend his title successfully. Two down in the final to Charles 'Chuck' Kocsis, he was 5 under par for the last 13 holes. He was 11 under par for the entire week.

Entry of 1600.

1957 Before the championship, Harvie Ward was adjudged by the USGA to have forfeited his amateur status and was not, therefore, eligible for a second defence of his title. In a year in which both British and American Walker Cup teams took part, the title was won by

Hillman Robbins who beat Dr Frank Taylor by 5 and 4. Both played in the Walker Cup and the other two semi-finalists, Mason Rudolph and Rex Baxter, were also members of the American team. The most successful British player was Alan Thirlwell, beaten in the 5th round.

1958 Charles Coe won his second title when he defeated Tommy Aaron, later to play for his country as an amateur and a professional, by 5 and 4 over the Lake course of the Olympic Club, San Francisco.

Harvie Ward returned and reached the 5th round. Nearly all the members of the Americas Cup matches took part.

George Boutell, aged 14, was in the field along with Dick and Dixie Chapman, the first father and son pair since 1950.

1959 In his second championship, Jack Nicklaus became the second youngest champion after a captivating final with Charles Coe, the defending champion.

Coe completed the morning round in 69 to be 2 up but, having twice squared the match Nicklaus, all square on the 36th tee, sank an 8-ft (2·4-m) putt for a winning birdie. Both had played in the Walker Cup match in Britain earlier in the summer. One of the semi-finalists, Gene Andrews, was 46 years old.

Entry 1696—a record.

1960 Deane Beman, one of the new young players in the Walker Cup match the previous year, became the ninth player to win both British and American titles. He defeated Bill Hyndman in the British and at St Louis CC, he beat Robert Gardner 6 and 4.

Charles Lewis of Little Rock, Arkansas, playing in his first Amateur, accounted for Jack Nicklaus, the defending champion, in the fourth round. In the third round, Nicklaus was 7 under par for 13 holes.

Entry 1737—another record.

1961 Jack Nicklaus made a triumphant farewell in his last Amateur. He was 20 under par for the holes he played at Pebble Beach, was rarely extended and won his final against Dudley Wysong 8 and 6. He became the 14th player to win the title at least twice.

William C Campbell set a new qualifying record 131 (67, 64) at the Guyan Golf and Country Club, West Virginia.

1962 On Pinehurst's famous No 2 course measuring 7051 yd (6447 m), the longest for any USGA event, Labron Harris beat Downing Gray on the 36th hole of the final after being 5 down at lunch.

Charles Evans, Jr, made his record 50th appearance in the championship and President

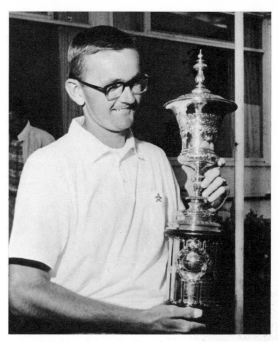

Bob Dickson, the first person since Lawson Little to win the British and American Amateur championships in the same summer, 1967 (US Golf Association)

Eisenhower was a spectator on the final afternoon.

1963 A second victory for Deane Beman. At the Wakonda Club, Iowa, he won his final against R H Sikes, the 1961 and 1962 Public Links champion by 2 and 1. For the second year running the champion had to come from behind in the final. Beman was 3 down after 14 holes.

1964 Years of trying at last bore fruit for William C Campbell. A semi-finalist in 1949 who reached the fifth round on five other occasions, he defeated Ed Tutwiler by 1 hole in the final. These two had met many times in West Virginia, Tutwiler winning six out of seven times.

A revision was made in the format: 150 players played two rounds on the championship course before the leading 64 advanced to matchplay.

1965 A major change from matchplay to medal play was made for this championship held at Southern Hills. After 72 holes, the winner was Robert Murphy, later a successful professional who beat Bob Dickson by 1 stroke with a total of 291. However, Dickson suffered the grave misfortune of a 4-stroke penalty for carrying a 15th club for the first 2 holes of the second round. To make matters worse, the club was not his and he did not use it although he was leading after 70 holes. He went 1 over par at each of the last 2 holes.

Charles Coe, the 54-hole leader, finished with an 80 to be 6 strokes behind Murphy.

1966 Gary Cowan became the second Canadian and the first foreign winner since 1932. He won after a play-off at Merion with Deane Beman who finished his fourth round with a 6. Ron Cerrudo might have tied with Beman and Cowan but missed a tiny putt on the last green.

The championship was televised nationally for the first time.

1967 Bob Dickson made up for his disappointment in 1965 by winning at Broadmoor a month or two after winning the British championship. Lawson Little was the last to achieve this feat and Bobby Jones the only other. Dickson won with a par 4 after missing the fairway on the 72nd hole and obtaining a free drop away from a television cable. He played back on to the fairway, hit his third shot to 7 ft (2 m) and holed the putt.

Bill Campbell, one of the most popular and most respected American amateurs (Frank Gardner)

Two rounds were played on the last day because heavy rain caused a day to be lost earlier in the week.

1968 Bruce Fleisher became the fourth youngest winner in his first championship. He scored 284 at Scioto and edged out Vinny Giles who had a final round of 65.

The entry was 2057—a record at the time.

1969 In a championship at Oakmont in which there were only four rounds under par and only six which equalled it, Steve Melnyk won by 5 strokes with a total of 286. This was convincing enough, but it was hard on Vinny Giles who finished runner-up for the third year in succession.

The entry increased to 2142.

1970 In a close finish, Lanny Wadkins just got the better of Tom Kite. His total of 279 was the lowest for the eight years during which the championship was decided by strokeplay.

1971 Canadian Gary Cowan won his second title with a dramatic finish at the Wilmington Country Club. One shot ahead of Eddie Pearce playing the 72nd hole, he drove into deep rough and was in some danger of dropping a stroke, but his 9 iron recovery finished in the hole for an eagle 2. This made his winning margin a rather more comfortable 3 strokes. Entry 2327.

1972 Deserved triumph for Vinny Giles at the Charlotte CC, North Carolina, when he beat Mark Hayes and Ben Crenshaw by 3 strokes. It was the last championship to be decided by strokeplay; in the eight years of this form, the only champions to remain as amateurs were Giles and Gary Cowan who did not defend his title.

1973 With matchplay restored, Craig Stadler defeated David Strawn at Inverness. Vinny Giles, having played in the Walker Cup, reached the semi-final in defence of his title where he lost to Stadler. In the other semi-final, Strawn beat William C Campbell, playing in his 30th championship at the age of 50.

1974 Jerry Pate won the championship at Ridgewood, New Jersey, two years before he added the US Open at Atlanta Athletic Club. He beat John Grace 2 and 1 in the final after being 3 down after 20 holes. It was the first time that Pate qualified for the championship.

Entry 2420.

1975 Fred Ridley defeated Keith Fergus in the final but Ridley's best performances were in beating Curtis Strange and Andy Bean on the way.

1976 In the final at Bel-Air CC, Bill Sander beat C Parker Moore by 8 and 6, the biggest victory margin since 1961.

Entry 2681.

1977 John Fought defeated Doug Fischesser by 9 and 8 in the final at Aronimink, the largest margin of victory since 1955. He won the last 4 holes of the morning round and the 1st hole after lunch to go 7 up.

In his 34th championship, Bill Campbell won his 52nd match over all.

1978 John Cook won the championship at Plainfield CC, New Jersey, with consistently good play. He beat Scott Hoch by 5 and 4 in the final but, for the first time, both semi-finals went to extra holes. Cook beat Michael Peck and Hoch beat Bob Clampett, both at the 20th.

1979 Cook was deposed as champion by Mark O'Meara, 22, the California State champion. O'Meara was persuaded to play by Cook and stayed during the championship at the Cook's condominium at the course. No champion has won back to back since Harvie Ward in 1956, but Cook started favourite in the final. He survived a long day on Friday, defeating Lennie Clements at the 8th extra hole and then accounting for Gary Hallberg. In the final, O'Meara lunched 4 up with a round of 70 and was 8 up after 26 holes.

DETAILED RECORDS

Most victories
5, Bobby Jones, 1924-25-27-28-30
4, Jerome D Travers, 1907-08-12-13
3, Walter J Travis, 1900-01-03

Most times runner-up or joint runner-up
3, Chick Evans, 1912-22-27; Ray Billows, 1937-39-48; Marvin Giles III, 1967-68-69

Oldest winner
Jack Westland, 47 years 8 months 9 days, 1952

Youngest winner
Robert A Gardner, 19 years 5 months, 1909
Jack Nicklaus, 19 years 8 months 29 days, 1959

Consecutive winners
2, Walter Travis, 1900-01; H Chandler Egan, 1904-05; Jerome D Travers, 1907-08, and 1912-13; Bobby Jones, 1924-25, and 1927-28; W Lawson Little, 1934-35; E Harvie Ward, 1955-56

Biggest span between first and last victories
17 years, Francis Ouimet, 1914–31

Biggest span between finals
21 years, Jack Westland, 1931–52

Overseas winners
Harold Hilton (England), 1911; C Ross Somerville (Canada), 1932; Gary Cowan (Canada), 1966 and 1971

Longest final
39 holes: Sam Urzetta beat Frank Stranahan, Minneapolis GC, 1950

Longest match (18 holes)
28 holes; Maurice McCarthy beat George von Elm, Merion, 1930

Most finals
7, Bobby Jones
5, Jerome D Travers and Chick Evans

Identical finals
None

Most appearances
50, Chick Evans, Jr
35, William C Campbell

Most golf in one day
63 holes, Maurice McCarthy, Jr, Merion, 1930. In the second qualifying round, he came to the 17th needing two birdies or an eagle to tie for the last qualifying place. He made a hole in one at the 17th to get the tie. Next morning, he won the play-off match lasting 16 holes, followed by a 19-hole match with Watts Gunn and in the afternoon beat George von Elm at the 28th, the longest 18-hole match ever played in the championship

First player to win the US Amateur and US Open
Francis Ouimet, Open 1913; Amateur, 1914

First player to win US Amateur and US Open the same year
Chick Evans, Jr, 1916, followed by Bobby Jones, 1930

Other amateur winners of both events
Jerome D Travers and John Goodman

Record entry
3916, Canterbury GC, Ohio, 1979

Youngest qualifier
Bobby Jones, 14 years 5½ months, 1916

Strokeplay—biggest margin of victory
5 strokes, Steve Melnyk, Oakmont, 1969

Lowest aggregate
279 (67, 73, 69, 70), Lanny Wadkins, Waverley CC, Oregon, 1970

Lowest individual round
65, Marvin Giles III, Scioto CC, 1968; Kurt

Cox, Waverley CC, Oregon, 1970
Courses most often used
The Country Club, Brookline,
Merion, Oakmont, Chicago GC, 4
Champion twice on same course
Bobby Jones, Merion, 1924 and 1930; Jerome
Travers, Garden City, 1908 and 1913

RESULTS

1895 Newport, Rhode Island
C B Macdonald, Chicago
Semi-finals: Macdonald beat C Claxton 8 and 7; C E Sands
beat F I Amory 3 and 2
Final: Macdonald beat Sands 12 and 11

1896 Shinnecock Hills, New York
J Whigham, Onwentsia
Semi-finals: Whigham beat A M Coats 8 and 6; J G Thorp
beat H P Toler 4 and 3
Final: Whigham beat Thorp 8 and 7

1897 Chicago, Illinois
H J Whigham, Onwentsia
Semi-finals: Whigham beat F S Douglas 6 and 5; W R Betts
beat C B Macdonald 1 up
Final: Whigham beat Betts 8 and 6

1898 Morris County, New Jersey
F S Douglas, Fairfield
Semi-finals: Douglas beat W J Travis 8 and 6; W B Smith
beat C B Macdonald 2 and 1
Final: Douglas beat Smith 5 and 3

1899 Onwentsia, Illinois
H M Harriman, Meadow Brook
Semi-finals: F S Douglas beat W J Travis 2 and 1; Harriman
beat C B Macdonald 6 and 5
Final: Harriman beat Douglas 3 and 2

1900 Garden City, New York
W J Travis, Garden City
Semi-finals: Travis beat A G Lockwood 11 and 10; F S
Douglas beat H M Harriman 4 and 3
Final: Travis beat Douglas 2 up

1901 Atlantic City, New Jersey
W J Travis, Garden City
Semi-finals: W E Egan beat C H Seeley 11 and 10; Travis
beat F S Douglas at 38th
Final: Travis beat Egan 5 and 4

1902 Glen View, Illinois
L N James, Glen View
Semi-finals: E M Byers beat D P Fredericks 4 and 3; James
beat F O Reinhart 2 and 1
Final: James beat Byers 4 and 2

1903 Nassau, New York
W J Travis, Garden City
Semi-finals: Travis beat F O Reinhart 5 and 4; E M Byers
beat B Smith 5 and 4
Final: Travis beat Byers 5 and 4

1904 Baltusrol, New Jersey
H C Egan, Exmoor
Semi-finals: F Herreshoff beat W T West 6 and 5; Egan beat
D P Fredericks 2 and 1
Final: Egan beat Herreshoff 8 and 6

1905 Chicago, Illinois
H C Egan, Exmoor
Semi-finals: D E Sawyer beat H C Fownes 2 up; Egan beat
H Weber 7 and 5
Final: Egan beat Sawyer 6 and 5

1906 Englewood, New Jersey
E M Byers, Allegheny
Semi-finals: G S Lyon beat E Knowles 5 and 4; Byers beat
W J Travis 4 and 3
Final: Byers beat Lyon 2 up

1907 Euclid, Ohio
J D Travers, Montclair
Semi-finals: Travers beat E M Byers 6 and 5; A Graham
beat H C Fownes 4 and 3
Final: Travers beat Graham 6 and 5

1908 Garden City, New York
J D Travers, Montclair
Semi-finals: Travers beat W J Travis 2 up; M Behr beat F
Herreshoff 37th
Final: Travers beat Behr 8 and 7

1909 Chicago, Illinois
R A Gardner, Hinsdale
Semi-finals: H C Egan beat C Evans 1 up; Gardner beat M E
Phelps 2 up
Final: Gardner beat Egan 4 and 3

1910 The Country Club, Brookline, Massachusetts
W C Fownes, Jr, Oakmont
Semi-finals: Fownes beat C Evans 1 up; W K Wood beat W
R Tukerman 2 up
Final: Fownes beat Wood 4 and 3

1911 Apawamis, New York
H H Hilton, Royal Liverpool
Semi-finals: Hilton beat C W Inslee 8 and 6; F Herreshoff
beat C Evans 3 and 2
Final: Hilton beat Herreshoff 37th

1912 Chicago, Illinois
J D Travers, Upper Montclair
Semi-finals: Travers beat H K Kerr 7 and 5; C Evans beat W
K Wood 4 and 3
Final: Travers beat Evans 7 and 6

1913 Garden City, New York
J D Travers, Upper Montclair
Semi-finals: J G Anderson beat C Evans 2 and 1; Travers
beat F Herreshoff 5 and 4
Final: Travers beat Anderson 5 and 4

1914 Ekwanok, Vermont
F D Ouimet, Woodland
Semi-finals: J D Travers beat W J Travis 5 and 3; Ouimet
beat W C Fownes 1 up
Final: Ouimet beat Travers 6 and 5

1915 Detroit CC, Michigan
R A Gardner, Hinsdale
Semi-finals: Gardner beat M Marston 37th; J G Anderson
beat S Sherman 2 and 1
Final: Gardner beat Anderson 5 and 4

1916 Merion, Pennsylvania
C Evans, Edgewater
Semi-finals: R A Gardner beat J P Guilford 4 and 3; Evans
beat D C Corkran 3 and 2
Final: Evans beat Gardner 4 and 3

1919 Oakmont, Pennsylvania
S D Herron, Oakmont
Semi-finals: R T Jones, Jr beat W C Fownes 5 and 3;
Herron beat J W Platt 7 and 6
Final: Herron beat Jones 5 and 4

1920 Engineers, New York
C Evans, Jr, Edgewater
Semi-finals: Evans beat E P Allis 10 and 8; F Ouimet beat R
T Jones, Jr 6 and 5
Final: Evans beat Ouimet 7 and 6

1921 St Louis CC, Missouri
J P Guilford, Woodland
Semi-finals: Guilford beat C Evans, Jr 5 and 4; R A Gardner
beat W I Hunter 6 and 5
Final: Guilford beat Gardner 7 and 6

1922 The Country Club, Brookline, Massachusetts
J W Sweetser, Siwanoy
Semi-finals: Sweetser beat R T Jones, Jr, 8 and 7; C Evans,
Jr beat R E Knepper 11 and 9
Final: Sweetser beat Evans 3 and 2

1923 Flossmoor, Illinois
M R Marston, Pine Valley
Semi-finals: J W Sweetser beat R A Gardner 8 and 7;
Marston beat F Ouimet 3 and 2
Final: Marston beat Sweetser at 38th

1924 Merion, Pennsylvania
R T Jones, Jr, Atlanta
Semi-finals: Jones beat F Ouimet 11 and 10; G Von Elm
beat M R Marston 7 and 6
Final: Jones beat Von Elm 9 and 8

1925 Oakmont, Pennsylvania
R T Jones, Jr, Atlanta
Semi-finals: W Gunn beat R A Jones 5 and 3; Jones beat G
Von Elm 7 and 6
Final: Jones beat Gunn 8 and 7

1926 Baltusrol, New Jersey
G Von Elm, Rancho
Semi-finals: Von Elm beat G Dawson 11 and 10; R T Jones
beat F Ouimet 5 and 4
Final: Von Elm beat Jones 2 and 1

1927 Minikahda Club, Minnesota
R T Jones, Jr, Atlanta
Semi-finals: C Evans, Jr beat R Mackenzie at 37th; Jones
beat F Ouimet 11 and 10
Final: Jones beat Evans 8 and 7

1928 Brae Burn CC, Massachusetts
R T Jones, Jr, Atlanta
Semi-finals: T P Perkins beat G J Voigt 6 and 4; Jones beat
P Finlay 13 and 12
Final: Jones beat Perkins 10 and 9

1929 Del Monte CC, California
H R Johnston, White Bear
Semi-finals: O F Willing beat H C Egan 4 and 3; Johnston
beat F Ouimet 6 and 5
Final: Johnston beat Willing 4 and 3

1930 Merion, Pennsylvania
R T Jones, Jr, Atlanta
Semi-finals: E V Homans beat C H Seaver 1 hole; Jones
beat J W Sweetser 9 and 8
Final: Jones beat Homans 8 and 7

1931 Beverly CC, Illinois
F Ouimet, Woodland
Semi-finals: Ouimet beat B Howell 2 and 1; J Westland
beat M J McCarthy, Jr 3 and 2
Final: Ouimet beat Westland 6 and 5

1932 Baltimore CC, Maryland
C Ross Sommerville, London (Canada)
Semi-finals: Sommerville beat J P Guilford 7 and 6; J
Goodman beat F Ouimet 4 and 2
Final: Sommerville beat Goodman 2 and 1

1933 Kenwood CC, Ohio
G T Dunlap, Pomonok
Semi-finals: M R Marston beat J Munger 6 and 5; Dunlap
beat W Lawson Little 4 and 3
Final: Dunlap beat Marston 6 and 5

1934 The Country Club, Brookline, Massachusetts
W Lawson Little, Jr, Presidio
Semi-finals: D Goldman beat Reynolds Smith 4 and 2;
Lawson Little beat D Armstrong 4 and 3
Final: Lawson Little beat Goldman 8 and 7

1935 The Country Club, Cleveland, Ohio
W Lawson Little, Jr, Presidio
Semi-finals: Lawson Little beat J Goodman 4 and 3; W
Emery beat J P Lynch 4 and 3
Final: Lawson Little beat Emery 4 and 2

1936 Garden City GC, New York
J W Fischer, Highland
Semi-finals: Fischer beat J Goodman 2 and 1; J McLean
beat G J Voigt 8 and 7
Final: Fischer beat McLean at 37th

1937 Alderwood CC, Oregon
J W Goodman, Omaha
Semi-finals: R Billows beat J W Fischer 6 and 5; Goodman
beat M Ward 1 hole
Final: Goodman beat Billows 2 holes

1938 Oakmont CC, Pennsylvania
W P Turnesa, Briar Hills
Semi-finals: B P Abbott beat R D Chapman 5 and 4;
Turnesa beat E C Kingsley 4 and 3
Final: Turnesa beat Abbott 8 and 7

1939 North Shore CC, Illinois
M Ward, Spokane
Semi-finals: R Billows beat D Schumacher 6 and 5; Ward
beat A L Doering 2 and 1
Final: Ward beat Billows 7 and 5

1940 Winged Foot GC, New York
R D Chapman, Winged Foot
Semi-finals: Chapman beat W Wehrle 3 and 2; W
McCullogh beat R Billows 5 and 3
Final: Chapman beat McCullogh 11 and 9

1941 Omaha Field, Nebraska
M Ward, Spokane
Semi-finals: Ward beat R H Riegel 9 and 8; B P Abbott beat
T Bishop 1 hole
Final: Ward beat Abbott 4 and 3

1946 Baltusrol GC, New Jersey
S E Bishop, Norfolk
Semi-finals: S L Quick beat A F Kammer, Jr 3 and 1;
Bishop beat R W Willits 10 and 9
Final: Bishop beat Quick at 37th

1947 Pebble Beach GL, California
R H Riegel, California
Semi-finals: J W Dawson beat J H Selby 5 and 4; Riegel
beat F Torza 2 and 1
Final: Riegel beat Dawson 2 and 1

1948 Memphis CC, Tennessee
W P Turnesa, Knollwood
Semi-finals: R E Billows beat C R Coe 6 and 5; Turnesa
beat E Dahlbender 8 and 6
Final: Turnesa beat Billows 2 and 1

1949 Oak Hill CC, New York
C R Coe, Oklahoma City
Semi-finals: R King beat W P Turnesa 2 and 1; Coe beat W
C Campbell 8 and 7
Final: Coe beat King 11 and 10

1950 Minneapolis GC, Minnesota
S Urzetta, Irondequoit
Semi-finals: Urzetta beat R W Knowles, Jr 6 and 5; F R Stranahan beat J P Ward 1 hole
Final: Urzetta beat Stranahan at the 39th

1951 Saucon Valley CC, Pennsylvania
B Maxwell, Odessa
Semi-finals: J F Gagliardi beat K T Jacobs, Jr 6 and 5; Maxwell beat J C Benson 10 and 9
Final: Maxwell beat Gagliardi 4 and 3

1952 Seattle GC, Washington
J Westland, Everett
Semi-finals: A Mengert beat D Cherry 3 and 2; Westland beat W C Mawhinney 5 and 4
Final: Westland beat Mengert 3 and 2

1953 Oklahoma City CC, Oklahoma
G Littler, La Jolla
Semi-finals: D Morey beat D Albert 5 and 4; Littler beat B Cudd 10 and 8
Final: Littler beat Morey 1 hole

1954 Detroit CC, Michigan
A D Palmer, Pine Ridge
Semi-finals: Palmer beat E L Meister at the 39th; R Sweeny beat T N Lenczyk 5 and 4
Final: Palmer beat Sweeny 1 hole

1955 Virginia CC, Virginia
E H Ward, San Francisco
Semi-finals: W Hyndman III beat H Robbins 4 and 3; Ward beat W A Booe 4 and 2
Final: Ward beat Hyndman 9 and 8

1956 Knollwood Club, Illinois
E H Ward, San Francisco
Semi-finals: C Kocsis beat G J Magee 4 and 2; Ward beat J Campbell 2 and 1
Final: Ward beat Kocsis 5 and 4

1957 The Country Club, Brookline, Massachusetts
H Robbins, Colonial
Semi-finals: F M Taylor beat E M Rudolph 5 and 4; Robbins beat R Baxter, Jr 2 holes
Final: Robbins beat Taylor 5 and 4

1958 Olympic CC, California
C R Coe, Oklahoma City
Semi-finals: Coe beat R T McManus 3 and 2; T D Aaron beat D Foote 10 and 9
Final: Coe beat Aaron 5 and 4

1959 Broadmoor GC, Colorado
J W Nicklaus, Scioto
Semi-finals: C R Coe beat D Wysong 6 and 4; Nicklaus beat G Andrews 1 hole
Final: Nicklaus beat Coe 1 hole

1960 St Louis CC, Minnesota
D R Beman, Bethesda
Semi-finals: R W Gardner beat C F Lewis 2 and 1; Beman beat J Farquhar 5 and 4
Final: Beman beat Gardner 6 and 4

1961 Pebble Beach GL, California
J W Nicklaus, Scioto
Semi-finals: H D Wysong beat J B Carr 2 holes; Nicklaus beat M C Methvin 9 and 8
Final: Nicklaus beat Wysong 8 and 6

1962 Pinehurst CC, North Carolina
L E Harris, Jr, Oakwood
Semi-finals: Harris beat W J Patton 3 and 1; Downing Gray beat C Coody 3 and 2
Final: Harris beat Gray 1 hole

1963 Wakonda, Iowa
D R Beman, Bethesda
Semi-finals: Beman beat G W Archer 5 and 4; R H Sikes beat C R Coe 2 and 1
Final: Beman beat Sikes 2 and 1

1964 Canterbury GC, Ohio
W C Campbell, Guyan
Semi-finals: Campbell beat J M Hopkins 3 and 1; E Tutwiler beat D Eichelberger 3 and 2
Final: Campbell beat Tutwiler 1 hole

Strokeplay introduced

1965 Southern Hills CC, Oklahoma

R J Murphy, Jr, Long Palm	73	69	76	73	291
R B Dickson, Muskogee	71	75	72	74	292
D C Allen, Rochester CC	70	74	76	73	293
C Sanudo, Carlton Oaks	71	76	72	74	293

1966 Merion GC, Pennsylvania

G Cowan, Westmount (Canada)	74	72	72	67	285
D R Beman, Bethesda	71	67	76	71	285
(Cowan won play-off 75 to 76)					
J W Lewis, Florence CC	73	69	75	69	286
R Cerrudo, California GC	70	75	70	71	286
A Downing Gray, Pensacola	74	72	68	72	286

1967 Broadmoor GC (West), Colorado

R B Dickson, McAlester	71	71	74	69	285
M M Giles III, Boonsboro	76	69	72	69	286
R Cerrudo, California GC	75	73	73	68	289
A D Gray, Pensacola	75	72	70	73	290

1968 Scioto CC, Ohio

B Fleisher, Miami CC	73	70	71	70	284
M M Giles III, Boonsboro	75	72	73	65	285
J Bohmann, Chaparral	74	73	74	67	288
H M Green, Birmingham CC	72	71	73	73	289

1969 Oakmont CC, Pennsylvania

S N Melnyk, Brunswick	70	73	73	70	286
M M Giles III, Boonsboro	72	75	72	72	291
A L Miller, Pensacola	77	69	73	74	293
R I Zender, Evanston	75	78	72	70	295

1970 Waverley CC, Oregon

L Wadkins, Meadowbrook	67	73	69	70	279
T Kite, Jr, Austin CC	69	67	72	73	280
G Cowan, West Mount	69	70	73	72	284
J R Gabrielsen, Peachtree	75	67	69	73	284
J B Simons, Butler	69	72	69	74	284

1971 Wilmington CC, Delaware

G Cowan, West Mount (Canada)	70	71	69	70	280
E Pearce, Temple Terrace	70	69	73	71	283
M M Giles III, Virginia CC	74	73	68	69	284
J C McLean, Rainier	72	67	73	73	285

1972 Charlotte CC, North Carolina

M M Giles III, Virgina CC	73	68	72	72	285
M S Hayes, Twin Hills	73	72	69	74	288
B Crenshaw, Austin	71	75	71	71	288
M R West III, Columbia	73	71	73	72	289

Reverted to Matchplay

1973 Inverness, Illinois
C Stadler, La Jolla
Semi-finals: D Strawn beat W C Campbell 6 and 5; C Stadler beat M M Giles III 3 and 1
Final: Stadler beat Strawn 6 and 5

1974 Ridgewood CC, New Jersey
J Pate, Pensacola CC
Semi-finals: J P Grace beat G Koch 2 and 1; Pate beat C

Strange 3 and 1
Final: Pate beat Grace 2 and 1

1975 CC of Virginia, Richmond, Virginia
Fred S Ridley, Winter Haven, Florida
Semi-finals: Ridley beat Andy Bean 2 and 1; Keith Fergus beat Henri de Lozier 3 and 2
Final: Ridley beat Fergus 2 holes

1976 Bel-Air CC, Los Angeles, California
Bill Sander, Kenmore, Washington
Semi-finals: C Parker Moore, Jr beat Stan K M Souza at 19th; Sander beat James T Mason 8 and 7
Final: Sander beat Parker Moore, Jr 8 and 6

1977 Aronimink GC, Newtown Square, Pennsylvania
John Fought, Portland, Oregon

Semi-finals: Doug H. Fischesser beat Ralph L Landrum 1 hole; Fought beat Jay Sigel 2 holes
Final: Fought beat Fischesser 9 and 8

1978 Plainfield CC, New Jersey
John Cook, Upper Arlington, Ohio
Semi-finals: Cook beat Michael Peck at 20th hole; Scott Hoch beat Bob Clampett at 20th hole
Final: Cook beat Hoch 5 and 4

1979 Canterbury GC, Cleveland, Ohio
Mark O'Meara, Mission Viejo CC, California
Semi-finals: O'Meara beat Joe Rassett 3 and 1; J Cook beat Cecil Ingram 5 and 3
Final: O'Meara beat Cook 8 and 7

WALKER CUP

MILESTONES

The Walker Cup was 'born' in the years after World War I when the leading British and American amateur golfers were seeking to win each other's championships. In addition, the USGA were invited to confer with the Royal and Ancient Golf Club over the rules and among the American delegation was George Herbert Walker of the National Golf Links of America on Long Island, USGA President in 1920.

On his return from St Andrews, the possibility of international team matches was discussed by the USGA executive committee and the idea so appealed to Mr Walker that he submitted a plan and offered to present an International Challenge Trophy. When the news was published, the newspapers called it the Walker Cup and the name stuck.

In 1921, the USGA invited all countries to send teams to compete for the Trophy, but none accepted. Desperate for competition, Mr William C Fownes, Jr who had twice assembled teams to play against Canada, rounded up a third team and this time took it to Hoylake, England where, in an informal match, they defeated a British team by 9 matches to 3 on the day before the Amateur championship.

The members of this informal American team were Charles Evans, Jr, William Fownes, Jesse Guilford, Paul Hunter, Bobby Jones, Francis Ouimet, J Wood Platt and Frederick J Wright, Jr. They were opposed by Cyril Tolley, J L C Jenkins, J Gordon Simpson, Ernest Holderness, Roger Wethered, R H de Montmorency, C C Aylmer and Tommy Armour who, five years later, played for America against Britain in the forerunner to the Ryder Cup.

If there had been any doubts that the Americans might not provide adequate opposition, they soon vanished and there have been none since. The following spring, the Royal and Ancient sent a team to compete for the Walker Cup in the United States. The match was held every two years after 1924 and is played alternately in Britain and America.

1922 Played at the National Golf Links, it proved most notable for the fact that Bernard Darwin, sent to cover the match for *The Times*, was called in to replace the British Captain, Robert Harris, who fell ill, and won his single.

In the first single, Hooman's match with Sweetser went to extra holes before anyone could stop them. Hooman won at the 37th and the result stood, but it is the only match ever to have played an extra hole. Ever since, halved matches have stood.

1923 A return match was soon settled at St Andrews in which the British side fared very much better. They won three of the four foursomes and led in most of the singles at one point, but the first of many disappointments for British teams followed. The Americans made a remarkable recovery and won the match 6–5 with one match halved. Ouimet halved after being 2 down and 3 to play to Wethered; George Rotan, 6 down after 14, won 11 of the next 12 holes and Frederick Wright won the 34th, 35th and 36th holes to beat Holderness.

1924 A comfortable victory for the Americans at the Garden City Golf Club by 9–3, although the biggest of their wins was 4 and 3. It was felt that

T.D.ARMOUR.   GORDON SIMPSON.   R.H.WETHERED   R.H. de MONTMORENCY.
E.W.E.HOLDERNESS.   J.L.C.JENKINS.   C.J.H.TOLLEY.   C.C.AYLMER.
GREAT BRITAIN.

FIRST INTERNATIONAL MATCH, HOYLAKE, 1921.
GREAT BRITAIN v. THE UNITED STATES OF AMERICA.   G.B.3.   U.S.A.9.

Informal start of the Walker Cup matches. First British and American teams; unofficial match at

an annual match was too much and thereafter the sides agreed to meet in alternate years.

1926 Another narrow victory for the Americans at Muirfield, the highlight being the 12 and 11 victory of Bobby Jones over Cyril Tolley. Jess Sweetser began the long sequence of victories in the Amateur championship in Walker Cup years in Britain.

1928 A heavy defeat (11–1) for Britain and the beginning of a lean period. Bobby Jones beat Phil Perkins at the Chicago Golf Club by 13 and 12, the biggest margin in the history of the Walker Cup. Tony Torrance won Britain's lone point, a 1-hole victory over Chick Evans.

1930 At Royal St George's, Sandwich, the United States won 10–2. In his Grand Slam year, Bobby Jones beat Roger Wethered 9 and 8 and preserved his 100 per cent record in his fifth and last single, but the most notable victory was that of Donald K Moe. He was 7 down with 13

to play but won with a birdie on the last hole. He was round in 67.

1932 Francis Ouimet took over the captaincy from Bobby Jones, appropriately enough on his own course, the Country Club, Brookline where he had won the US Open in 1913. He was Captain until 1949 although in a non-playing role after 1934.

The British had the brothers, Rex and Lister Hartley playing together in the first foursome, but they won only one match, that in which Leonard Crawley defeated George Voigt. He also dented the Walker Cup with an overstrong second at the 18th in the morning, the Cup being on display.

1934 The Americans won their eighth successive victory at St Andrews. Michael Scott

Hoylake, 1921 (By courtesy of Royal Liverpool Golf Club)

became the oldest participant at 56, but the British won only one foursome and one single. The singles winner was Tony Torrance who won three and halved one of his last four singles.
1936 The first and only time that Britain failed to win a match. It meant that they had only won two foursomes and four singles in the five matches from 1928. At Pine Valley, a complete whitewash was avoided by 2 half points in the foursomes. In the fourth foursome, Alec Hill and Cecil Ewing were 7 down to George Voigt and Harry Givan with 11 holes to play. They squared on the 35th and the Americans had to hole an awkward putt on the 36th to gain a half.
1938 In two years, Britain went from their worst result to their best. Prior to the Walker Cup, Charlie Yates had won the Amateur

championship at Troon but at St Andrews, amid scenes of wild delight, Britain won the foursomes 2½–1½ and the singles 5–3. It was only the second time that Britain had won a series of singles and they were not to do so again until 1963.
1947 Because of post-war conditions, a two-year gap resulted and the Americans agreed to come to Britain although it was Britain's turn to go to America. St Andrews was once again the venue but this time there was a comfortable American victory. Bud Ward was the only survivor of 1938 in the American team; Leonard Crawley, Alec Kyle and Cecil Ewing for Britain and Ireland. The match, however, saw the introduction of several outstanding players: Joe Carr, Ronnie White, Frank Stranahan and Dick Chapman.
1949 A one-sided contest at Winged Foot, but encouragement for Britain in the golf of Ronnie

Ronnie White, a remarkable singles record in the Walker Cup (Action Photos)

The outstanding single was that in which Ronnie White, 3 down after 30 holes, beat Dick Chapman by 1 hole. He had 3 birdies in the last 6 holes and so won his fourth successive single—a British record. John Morgan won both his matches for Britain.

1955 Back at St Andrews, America won all four foursomes and six of the eight singles; even Ronnie White suffered his first defeat for Britain in the singles. The American Captain, Bill Campbell, did not play himself although he was one of their best players and had reached the final of the British Amateur at Muirfield the previous summer.

1957 One of the best British sides and one of the best matches at Minikhada, but still a victory ($8\frac{1}{2}$–$3\frac{1}{2}$) for America. Still, Charlie Coe, the American Captain, commented at the presentation that he thought during the afternoon the Walker Cup was half-way back across the Atlantic!

He referred to the moment when three crucial singles were all square with 6, 5, and 2 holes to play, but America won them all. The best recovery was that of Billy Joe Patton, 5 down at lunch, who was round in 68 in the afternoon to beat Reid Jack, British champion, on the last green.

1959 Another big disappointment for the British side at Muirfield. They lost all four foursomes, but the Americans, who included the young Jack Nicklaus, fielded what many regard as their best team ever.

1961 The matches were held for the first time on the west coast, at Seattle where the Americans equalled their record victory margin (11—1) in 1928. Martin Christmas, the youngest member of the British side, was their only winner.

1963 A change in the form of the match took place at Turnberry, 18-hole matches being introduced for the first time. Foursomes and singles were played each day and at the end of the first day, Britain led $7\frac{1}{2}$–$4\frac{1}{2}$. They lost the foursomes and then won only their second series of singles since the matches began.

However, despite promising to win at least two of the second series of foursomes, they lost them all—the 16th hole proving enormously costly. Suitably reprieved, America then won five singles in the afternoon.

1965 The only halved match in the history of the series, America making a dramatic recovery on the last afternoon and then Clive Clark having to hole from 30 ft (9 m) to prevent a British defeat. Britain had a lead of five matches going into the last afternoon at Five Farms, Baltimore, but America made an historic rally.

White who won both his foursome (with Joe Carr) and single.

1951 Britain led in three foursomes and were square in the fourth after 18 holes on the first day, but they failed to win any of them. The best they could manage was two halves.

This was one of many disappointments over the years but in the singles, Ronnie White, playing on his home course, Royal Birkdale, beat Charlie Coe, Joe Carr beat Frank Stranahan and Alec Kyle beat Willie Turnesa.

1953 Notable for the incident on the first morning when James Jackson, paired with Gene Littler, discovered that he was carrying 16 clubs. In those days, the penalty was disqualification, but the British, captained by Tony Duncan, refused to accept victory in that way. The penalty was therefore modified to the loss of 2 holes. As the incident occurred on the 2nd hole, America, having lost the 1st at Kittansett, they were 3 down on the fourth tee where the match resumed. Jackson and Littler were still 3 down at the turn, but they lunched 2 up and went on to win 3 and 2.

1967 Not even the cold May weather at Royal St George's, Sandwich, could deter the Americans. They had the match well won on the first day and though Britain won three foursomes on the second morning, there were no dramatic recoveries, as there had been in Baltimore. Bill Campbell won four matches for America. Last match for Joe Carr who was picked for a record ten teams.

1969 A fine, close match at Milwaukee Country Club, Britain staging an effective rally after America had won the first day 8–4. On the second day, America won only three matches, but they held on to win 10–8 with six halved.

1971 A second victory for Great Britain and Ireland at St Andrews, the scene of their first in 1938. It was the 50th anniversary of the first informal match in 1921 and was made possible by their winning six of the final afternoon's singles. They lost the second series of foursomes 2½–1½ to go 2 points behind, but they got the better of six close singles, two on the 17th green and four on the last green. The deciding point was supplied by David Marsh who hit a 3 iron to the famous 17th to go dormie 1 on Bill Hyndman.

The British and Irish side included Roddy Carr, son of Joe. It is the only instance of a father and son winning Walker Cup honours.

1973 A good defence of the Cup by Britain at the Country Club, Brookline. Having managed only a half on the first morning, they won five singles, but again on Saturday the foursomes were their undoing. They went down 14–10 without winning one foursomes match. It was the last appearance of Michael Bonallack whose 25 individual matches is a record.

1975 Steady control for the Americans at St Andrews, the eighth time the match has been played over the Old course.

They were four points clear on the first day, shared the second series of foursomes and won the final singles 5½–2½.

1977 Great Britain and Ireland travelled to Shinnecock Hills with obvious hopes of victory, but they were destroyed on the first day by a new, young American side who led 9–3 at the end of it. Only Dick Siderowf had played in a previous match. Britain did better on the second day, but it was too late.

1979 Another young American side went to Muirfield although it was not at full strength owing to a clash with the National Collegiate championship which deprived them of Bob Clampett, Gary Hallberg and John Cook. It was a close match, America gaining a 1 point lead on the first day and preserving it on the second morning.

Britain made the better start in the last series of singles and, at one stage, were down in only one. However, in the end, they won only one. America won by the margin of 15½–8½.

DETAILED RECORDS

Most appearances
10, Joe Carr (for Great Britain and Ireland). In addition he was Captain in 1965 but did not play

Most consecutive appearances
9, Joe Carr, 1947–63
8, Francis Ouimet 1922–34. In addition, he was Captain in 1934–36–38–47–49. Michael Bonnallack, 1959–73. He was a member of the 1957 side, but did not play

Biggest margin of victory in individual matches
Over 36 holes (1922–61)
Foursomes: **9 and 8,** E Harvie Ward and Jack Westland, 1953; Billy Joe Patton and Charles Coe, 1959, both for the United States
Singles: **13 and 12,** Bobby Jones, 1928.
Over 18 holes
Foursomes: **7 and 5,** Marvin Giles and G Koch (United States) 1973;

Singles: **9 and 7,** Scott Hoch 1979; **8 and 7,** Douglas Clarke 1979; **7 and 6,** Scott Simpson 1977 (all United States)

Largest winning margin by team
11–1, United States, 1928 and 1961

Outstanding individual records
William C Campbell won seven singles, halved one and never lost. He also won six foursomes, lost three and halved one.

Bobby Jones won all his five singles matches and four of his five foursomes.

Best team recovery
The United States trailed by 3–1 after the foursomes in 1923, but won 6–5. In 1963, they trailed 6–3 after the first day and won 12–8. In 1965 they were 8–3 down on the first day and 10–5 down at lunch on the second day; and earned a halved match.

Brothers

In 1932, Rex and Lister Hartley played in the British side and were paired together in the foursomes.

Most consecutive team victories

9, United States 1922–36, 1947–63

Courses most often used

Britain: St Andrews, 8
America: The Country Club, Brookline, 2

Oldest competitor

Hon Michael Scott (Great Britain and Ireland) 56 years, 1934

Youngest competitor

James Bruen (Great Britain and Ireland) 18 years 25 days, 1938
John Langley (Great Britain and Ireland) 18 years 4 months 7 days, 1936
Peter Oosterhuis (Great Britain and Ireland) 19 years 2 weeks, 1967

Team winning all the foursomes

United States: 1928-32-55-59-61. They also won the second series of foursomes in 1963. Great Britain and Ireland won 4–0 in the first series of foursomes in 1971

Team winning all the singles

None, but the United States won 7½ out of 8 in 1936 at Pine Valley.

Form of the match

Foursomes and singles. From 1922 until 1961, there were four foursomes matches and eight singles—all played over 36 holes.

From 1963, one series of foursomes and one series of singles have taken place each day, all the matches being over 18 holes.

In all cases, halved matches count; the exception was in 1922 when Hooman and Sweetser played 37 holes before anyone could rectify the mistake. The result, victory for Hooman, was allowed to stand.

Unusual facts

In 1930, Jack Stout of Britain was 7 up with 13 holes to play on Donald Moe. However, when Moe had completed the second 18 in 67 at Sandwich, he had recovered to win on the last green.

In 1936, George Voigt and Harry Givan were 7 up with 11 holes to play in their foursomes match at Pine Valley. However, the British pair Alec Hill and Cecil Ewing squared on the 35th and halved the match—the Americans holing an awkward putt on the last green.

In 1971, Cecil Ewing and Frank Pennink, both members of Britain's first winning side in

1938, were selectors on the occasion of Britain and Ireland's second victory.

Up to and including 1979, the United States have won 24 matches, Great Britain and Ireland two, with one halved.

OUTSTANDING INDIVIDUAL RECORDS UNITED STATES

(Number of individual matches played shown in brackets)
Over 30 players have a 100% record. They include:

Name	%
E Harvie Ward (6)	100
Don Cherry (5)	100
Jack Nicklaus (4)	100
G T Moreland (4)	100
Skee Riegel (4)	100
O F Willing (4)	100
Watts Gunn (4)	100
Sam Urzetta (4)	100
Danny Edwards (4)	100
John Fought (4)	100
L Miller (4)	100
Scott Hoch (4)	100
Jay Haas (3)	100
Dr Frank Taylor (3)	100
Gene Littler (2)	100
Ken Venturi (2)	100
Other players of interest	
Jay Sigel (7)	92.85
Bobby Jones (10)	90
Charlie Yates (4)	87.50
Johnny Fischer (4)	87.50
Curtis Strange (4)	87.50
James B McHale (3)	83.3
H R Johnston (6)	83.3
Ed Tutwiler (6)	83.3
Douglas Clarke (3)	83.3
Roland R Mackenzie (5)	80.0
Jack Westland (5)	80
Billy Joe Patton (14)	78.57
Bill Hyndman (9)	77.77
R A Gardner (8)	75
George von Elm (6)	75
Deane Beman (11)	72.72
Vinny Giles (15)	70
William C Campbell (18)	66.66
Jess Sweetser (12)	62.50
Francis Ouimet (16)	62.5
Dick Chapman (5)	60
Charlie Coe (13)	57.69

Bill Campbell whose total of 18 matches is a record, won seven and halved one of his eight singles. Bobby Jones won all five of his singles matches.

A total of 138 competitors have played for the United States.

OUTSTANDING INDIVIDUAL RECORDS GREAT BRITAIN AND IRELAND

(Number of individual matches shown in brackets)

Name	%
John Wilson (2)	100
Robert Scott, Jr (1)	100
Roddy Carr (4)	87.5

Mark James (4)	75	David Sheahan (4)		50
Peter Townsend (4)	75	G Godwin (4)		50
Clive Clark (4)	75	B Marchbank (4)		50
Gordon Cosh (4)	75	A E Shepperson (3)		50
Allan Brodie (8)	68.75	Alan Bussell (2)		50
Gordon Peters (4)	62.50	**Other players of interest**		
Roger Wethered (9)	61.11	Sandy Saddler (10)		40
Ronnie White (10)	60	Tony Torrance (9)		38.88
Ian Hutcheon (12)	50	Michael Bonallack (25)		38
Leonard Crawley (6)	50	Cyril Tolley (12)		33.33
Bernard Darwin (2)	50	Joe Carr (20)		25
Hon Michael Scott (4)	50			
Hector Thomson (4)	50			
C C Aylmer (2)	50			
Laddie Lucas (2)	50			
Charlie Stowe (4)	50			
Frank Pennink (2)	50			
Ronnie Shade (14)	50			

Michael Bonallack's 25 matches are a record.

Ronnie White won four of his five singles matches. His opponents were A Frederick Kammer, Willie Tunesa, Charles Coe and Dick Chapman.

A total of 129 competitors have played for Great Britain and Ireland.

WALKER CUP

Year	Venue	US Winners	Total	Great Britain and Ireland Total	Captains USA	Britain
1922	National Links, Long Island, New York	USA	8	4	William C Fownes, Jr	Robert Harris
1923	St Andrews, Scotland	USA	6½	5½	Robert A Gardner	Robert Harris
1924	Garden City, New York	USA	9	3	Robert A Gardner	Cyril J H Tolley
1926	St Andrews, Scotland	USA	6½	5½	Robert A Gardner	Robert Harris
1928	Chicago GC, Wheaton, Illinois	USA	11	1	Robert T Jones, Jr	Dr William Tweddell
1930	Royal St George's, Sandwich	USA	10	2	Robert T Jones, Jr	Roger H Wethered
1932	Brookline, Massachusetts	USA	9½	2½	Francis D Ouimet	Tony A Torrance
1934	St Andrews, Scotland	USA	9½	2½	Francis D Ouimet	Hon Michael Scott
1936	Pine Valley, New Jersey	USA	10½	1½	*Francis D Ouimet	Dr William Tweddell
1938	St Andrews, Scotland	GB & I	4½	7½	*Francis D Ouimet	John B Beck
1947	St Andrews, Scotland	USA	8	4	*Francis D Ouimet	John B Beck
1949	Winged Foot, New York	USA	10	2	*Francis D Ouimet	Percy B 'Laddie' Lucas
1951	Royal Birkdale, Lancashire	USA	7½	4½	*William P Turnesa	Raymond Oppenheimer
1953	Kittansett, Club, Massachusetts	USA	9	3	*Charles R Yates	*Lt-Col Tony Duncan
1955	St Andrews, Scotland	USA	10	2	*William C Campbell	*G Alec Hill
1957	Minikhada Club, Minnesota	USA	8½	3½	*Charles R Coe	*Gerald H Micklem
1959	Muirfield, Scotland	USA	9	3	Charles R Coe	*Gerald H Micklem
1961	Seattle, Washington	USA	11	1	*Jack Westland	*Charles D Lawrie
1963	Ailsa Course, Turnberry, Scotland	USA	14	10	*Richard S Tufts	*Charles D Lawrie
1965	Baltimore, Maryland	(tie)	12	12	*John W Fischer	*Joe B Carr
1967	Royal St George's, Sandwich	USA	15	9	*Jess W Sweetser	Joe B Carr
1969	Milwaukee, Wisconsin	USA	13	11	*Billy Joe Patton	Michael Bonallack
1971	St Andrews, Scotland	GB & I	11	13	*John M Winters, Jr	Michael Bonallack
1973	Brookline, Massachusetts	USA	14	10	*Jess W Sweetser	Dr David Marsh
1975	St Andrews, Scotland	USA	15½	8½	*Dr Ed R Updegraff	*Dr David Marsh
1977	Shinnecock Hills, New York	USA	16	8	*Lou W Oehmig	*Sandy C Saddler
1979	Muirfield, Scotland	USA	15½	8½	*Richard Siderowf	Rodney Foster

* Non-playing captains.

WORLD AMATEUR TEAM CHAMPIONSHIP

EISENHOWER TROPHY

The idea for this championship was put by the United States Golf Association to the Royal and Ancient Golf Club in March 1958. It was agreed that the two governing bodies should join forces in running the event which was first played in October 1958 and has since been held every other year. A handsome trophy was presented bearing the name of President Eisenhower and the inscription, 'To foster friendship and sportsmanship among the Peoples of the World'.

The form of the tournament is strokeplay for teams of four, the best three scores to count for the four rounds played. The lowest aggregate of the four daily totals constitutes the winner.

1958 Played appropriately at St Andrews, the first championship was one of the best and certainly the closest. It produced a tie (the only tie so far) between Australia and the United States with Great Britain and Ireland 1 stroke behind in third place. It is the only time that 1 stroke has divided three teams.

Australia set the target of 918 thanks largely to Bruce Devlin, later such a well-known professional. In the first round, all four Australians took over 80 and they finished 17 strokes behind Britain.

On the last day, the United States, captained by Bobby Jones, looked out of it but Bill Hyndman had a 72, the lowest of all the fourth-round scores. He even had a 3 at the 17th to force the tie.

In the play-off, the Australians, with Devlin again leading the way, won by 2 strokes with a total of 222.

1960 The championship in which the Americans set all sorts of records at Merion which may never be broken. Led by Jack Nicklaus whose four rounds of 66, 67, 68, 68 for an 11 under par 269 is easily a record, they won by 42 strokes—another record.

Yet a further record was their team total of 834. No other championship has ever been so completely dominated by one team.

Thirty-two teams took part, three more than in 1958.

1962 At the Fuji Golf Course, Kawana, Japan, the United States gained their second title. Deane Beman was the only survivor of Merion (Jack Nicklaus had turned professional, win-

The best Eisenhower Trophy team ever—the United States team, Merion, 1960. *From left to right:* **Deane Beman, Robert Gardner, Bill Hyndman, Jack Nicklaus and non-playing Captain: Totton P Heffelfinger (US Golf Association)**

ning the US Open in 1962) but they held off Canada for whom Gary Cowan was the star. He won the individual title with 280. In the final round, after Billy Joe Patton had opened with an 81, Beman had 66, Richard Sikes 69 and Labron Harris 70. They had started the last round 2 behind Canada. Great Britain and Ireland were third for the third time.

1964 In rainy and blustery weather, Great Britain and Ireland won their first victory at Olgiata, Rome. Again Canada were the runners-up and on the last afternoon, Keith Alexander caused a terrible fright among the British and Irish by almost completing a miracle. Needing 5 birdies to tie the British total of 895, he got 4 of them, but bunkered his second to the 18th and took 5.

The lowest individual score was 294 by Hsieh Min Nam of the Republic of China. It was the first example of the strength of players from that country.

1966 Australia won their second victory at the Club de Golf, Mexico in Mexico City. Having built a good lead on the first day, they eventually won by 2 strokes from the United States. There were only four rounds under 70: one by Kevin Hartley of Australia in the first round, one by Deane Beman in the final round for America and two by Ronnie Shade of Great Britain and Ireland whose total of 283 was the lowest of all.

1968 On the composite course of Royal Melbourne, the United States had a great battle with Great Britain and Ireland who began the last round with a 7-stroke lead. At one point in the final round, Britain led by 11 strokes, but the United States made up the deficit. On the final hole, Ronnie Shade missed from 6 ft (1·8 m) and Dick Siderowf holed from a yard to give America a 1-stroke victory.

Michael Bonallack and Vinny Giles had the lowest individual totals, Bonallack's third-round 66 equalling the championship record previously held by Jack Nicklaus.

1970 At the Club de la Puerta de Hierro in Madrid, the United States successfully defended their title despite Tom Kite being ill on the last day and unable to play. By then, however, their victory was not in doubt. Over the four days, a 74 was their highest score; and on the first two days, the 73s of Vinny Giles did not count to the team total. They eventually won by 15 strokes from New Zealand.

Victor Regalado of Mexico had the best individual score—280.

1972 Third successive victory for the United States, but they did it the hard way at the Olivos Golf Club in Buenos Aires. They were 9 behind after the first round, 7 behind after the second round and 3 strokes back with 18 holes to play. A 68 in the last round by Ben Crenshaw led the way to a 5-stroke victory over Australia. Crenshaw had a third round of 69. Tony Gresham of Australia had the lowest individual aggregate.

Spain finished fourth, Argentina fifth and Japan ninth.

1974 A late switch of venue from Royal Selangor in Kuala Lumpur to the Cajuiles Golf Club, La Romana in the Dominican Republic brought the fourth successive victory for the United States and their sixth in nine championships. A fine new but difficult course posed many problems and the winning score of 888 was the highest since 1964.

However, America led after every round and finished 10 strokes ahead of Japan with Brazil third. The best score of the week was 70.

1976 Second victory for Great Britain and Ireland who were never behind at Penina, Portugal. They led by 2 strokes after the third round, but it needed an outstanding round under enormous pressure by Ian Hutcheon to see them through. His 71 gave them 2 strokes to spare over Japan, second for the second time in a row, and Australia.

The United States finished fifth, their worst placing since the championship began in 1958.

1978 The United States, 9 strokes ahead after the first round and 11 ahead after the second round, had their victory won long before the final day in Fiji. They took a 17-stroke lead into the last round, winning eventually by 13 strokes from Canada. Bob Clampett had the lowest score of the entire championship (287) but Doug Roxburgh of Canada was only 2 strokes worse, he and Clampett having the only rounds under 70. Clampett's came on the first day, Roxburgh's on the last.

Ian Hutcheon (Phil Sheldon)

DETAILED RECORDS

Most victories
7, United States
2, Great Britain and Ireland
2, Australia
Lowest winning aggregate
834, United States, at Merion 1960
Highest winning score
918, Australia (after play-off with the United States) at St Andrews, 1958
Lowest individual round
66, Jack Nicklaus, 1960; Ronnie Shade and Deane Beman, 1962; Michael Bonallack, 1968
Lowest individual aggregate
269 (66, 67, 68, 68), Jack Nicklaus, Merion, 1960
Lowest individual first round
66, Jack Nicklaus, Merion, 1960
Lowest individual second round
66, Ronnie Shade (Great Britain and Ireland) Fuji GC, Kawana, Japan, 1962
Lowest individual third round
66, Michael Bonallack, (Great Britain and Ireland) Royal Melbourne, 1968
Lowest individual fourth round
66, Deane Beman (United States) Merion, 1960
Largest lead, 18 holes
9 strokes, United States, Merion, 1960
Largest lead, 36 holes
20 strokes, United States, Merion, 1960
Largest lead, 54 holes
38 strokes, United States, Merion, 1960
Largest margin of victory
42 strokes, United States, Merion, 1960
Smallest margin of victory
Australia and the United States tied in 1958
Smallest lead, 18 holes
Great Britain and Ireland, and South Africa were tied at 219 in 1976
Smallest lead, 36 holes
Great Britain and Ireland, and South Africa were tied at 443 in 1976
Smallest lead, 54 holes
1 stroke, South Africa, 1966
Most teams to compete
38, Penina, Portugal, 1976
Lowest individual score not counted by team
69, Deane Beman, Merion, first round, 1960

Lowest 9-hole score
31, William Hyndman III, Merion, 1960
Play-off
1958, Australia and the United States
Oldest competitors
W J Gibb (Malaya) was 58 in 1958.
I S Malik (India) was 57 in 1960

RESULTS

1958 St Andrews, Scotland 8–11 and 13 October
Australia 918 (Doug Bachli, Peter Toogood, Bruce Devlin, Robert Stevens)
United States 918 (Charles Coe, Bill Hyndman, Billy Joe Patton, Frank Taylor)
  Play-off Australia 222; United States 224
1960 Merion Golf Club, Ardmore, Pennsylvania 28 September–1 October
United States 834 (Deane Beman, Jack Nicklaus, Bill Hyndman, Robert Gardner)
1962 Fuji GC, Kawana, Japan 10–13 October
United States 854 (Deane Beman, Labron Harris, Billy Joe Patton, Richard Sikes)
1964 Olgiata Golf Club, Rome 7–10 October
Great Britain and Ireland 895 (Michael Bonallack, Rodney Foster, Michael Lunt, Ronnie Shade)
1966 Mexico Golf Club, Mexico City 27–30 October
Australia 877 (Harry Berwick, Philip Billings, Kevin Donohoe, Kevin Hartley)
1968 Royal Melbourne Golf Club, Australia 9–12 October
United States 868 (Bruce Fleisher, Vinny Giles, Jack Lewis, Dick Siderowf)
1970 Real Club de la Puerta de Hierro, Madrid 23–26 September
United States 854 (Vinny Giles, Tom Kite, Allen Miller, Lanny Wadkins)
1972 Olivos Golf Club, Buenos Aires 18–21 October
United States 865 (Ben Crenshaw, Vinny Giles, Mark Hayes, Marty West)
1974 Campo de Golf Cajuiles, Dominica 30 Oct–2 Nov
United States 888 (George Burns, Gary Koch, Jerry Pate, Curtis Strange)
1976 Penina Golf Club, Algarve, Portugal 13–16 October
Great Britain and Ireland 892 (John Davies, Ian Hutcheon, Michael Kelley, Steve Martin)
1978 Pacific Harbour, Fiji, 18–21 October
United States 873 (Bob Clampett, John Cook, Scott Hoch, Jay Sigel)

Right: Lee Elder, first coloured golfer to win a tournament on the US circuit, and play in the Masters and the Ryder Cup (All-Sport/Steve Powell)

Below: The pleasant ceremony of fitting the Masters champion with his green jacket. Tom Watson, defending champion, doing the honours for Gary Player in 1978 (Phil Sheldon)

Above: The 13th hole, Augusta National (Phil Sheldon)

Above: Chako Higuchi, the first successful woman professional from the Far East (All Sport/Don Morley). Top right: Kathy Whitworth whose 80 victories on the US women's tour are only two short of the record held by Mickey Wright (All Sport/Don Morley). *Bottom left:* Donna Caponi Young, twice US Women's Open champion (All Sport/Tony Duffy). *Bottom right:* Judy Rankin, one of the most prolific money-winners in US women's golf (All Sport/Tony Duffy)

Oriental magic—Isao Aoki sizing up a putt (Frank Gardner)

Above: Caddie: 'Your Tee is ready, sir.' Absent-mind golfer: 'No thanks, I'll have a Guinness.' (Arthur Guinness Son and Company (Park Royal) Limited). *Top right:* 'The dream of the Golfer who forgot his Guinness a day' (Arthur Guinness Son and Company (Park Royal) Limited). *Bottom left:* 'Have a glass of Guinness when you're *Tired*.' (Arthur Guinness Son and Company (Park Royal) Limited). *Bottom right:* 'What should I take here, caddie?' 'I should take a Guinness, sir!' (Arthur Guinness Son and Company (Park Royal) Limited)

Left: Bing Crosby, a man who contributed to golf in a variety of ways (All Sport/Don Morley)

One of only two bespectacled US Open champions,
Hale Irwin, winner in 1974 and 1979 (Peter Dazeley)

In characteristically relaxed mood, Lee Trevino, twice British and twice American Open champion (Phil Sheldon)

A familiar scene at the Masters at Augusta. Different roles for player, caddie and rules marshal (Action Photos)

Women's Golf

LADIES' BRITISH OPEN AMATEUR CHAMPIONSHIP

DETAILED RECORDS

Most victories
4, Cecil Leitch, 1914-20-21-26. She won one victory in each of the four home countries; Joyce Wethered (later Lady Heathcoat-Amory), 1922-24-25-29.
3, Lady Margaret Scott, 1893-94-95; May Hezlet, 1899-1902-07; Enid Wilson, 1931-32-33; Jessie Valentine (*née* Anderson), 1937-55-58

Oldest winner
Jessie Valentine, 42 years 3 months, 1958

Youngest winner
May Hezlet, 17 years 1 week, 1899
Michelle Walker, 18 years 6 months 9 days, 1971

Biggest victory margin in final
9 and 7, Joyce Wethered beat Cecil Leitch, Princes, 1922

Longest final
39 holes, Moira Paterson beat Frances Stephens, Troon, 1952

Most finals
6, Cecil Leitch

Most times runner-up
3, Philomena Garvey and Belle Robertson (*née* McCorkindale)

Shortest 18-hole match
Ruth Porter beat Mrs A McCoy 10 and 8, first round, Royal Portrush, 1963

Longest 18-hole match
26 holes, Miss C Gerber (South Africa) beat Julia Greenhalgh, St Andrews, 1975

Consecutive winners
3, Lady Margaret Scott, 1893-94-95; Cecil Leitch, 1914-20-21; no championship 1915-19; Enid Wilson, 1931-32-33
2, Joyce Wethered, 1924-25; Marley Spearman, 1961-62; Elizabeth Chadwick, 1966-67; Michelle Walker, 1971-72

Longest span between victories
21 years, Jessie Valentine, 1937–58

Family records
In 1907, May Hezlet beat her sister, Florence Hezlet in the final. In 1897, Edith Orr beat her sister

Thought by many to be the best lady golfer of all time—Joyce Wethered (now Lady Heathcoat-Amory) (BBC Hulton Pic. Lib.)

First overseas winner
Mlle Thion de la Chaume (France), 1927

First American winner
Mildred 'Babe' Zaharias, 1947; Glenna Collett reached the finals of 1929 and 1930

Repeat finals
1893–94, Lady Margaret Scott beat Isette Pearson
1922 and 1925, Joyce Wethered beat Cecil Leitch; in 1921, Cecil Leitch beat Joyce Wethered

Club hosting most championships
7 each, Royal County Down (Northern Ireland) Newcastle, and Royal Portrush (Northern Ireland)

Winners of British and American championships
Dorothy Campbell, Gladys Ravenscroft, Pam Barton, 'Babe' Zaharias, Louise Suggs, Marlene Stewart, Barbara McIntire, Catherine Lacoste, Carol Semple, Anne Sander

Winners the same year
Dorothy Campbell, 1909; Pam Barton, 1936; Catherine Lacoste, 1969

LADIES' BRITISH OPEN AMATEUR CHAMPIONSHIP

Year	Winner	Runner-up	Venue	By
1893	Lady Margaret Scott	Isette Pearson	St Annes	7 and 5
1894	Lady Margaret Scott	Isette Pearson	Littlestone	3 and 2
1895	Lady Margaret Scott	Miss E Lythgoe	Portrush	3 and 2
1896	Amy Pascoe	Miss L Thomson	Hoylake	3 and 2
1897	Edith C Orr	Miss Orr	Gullane	4 and 2
1898	Miss L Thomson	Miss E C Neville	Yarmouth	7 and 5
1899	May Hezlet	Miss Magill	Newcastle, Co Down	2 and 1
1900	Rhona Adair	Miss E C Neville	Westward Ho!	6 and 5
1901	Miss Graham	Rhona Adair	Aberdovey	3 and 1
1902	May Hezlet	Miss E C Neville	Deal	19th hole
1903	Rhona Adair	Miss F Walker-Leigh	Portrush	4 and 3
1904	Lottie Dod	May Hezlet	Troon	1 hole
1905	Miss B Thompson	Miss M E Stuart	Cromer	3 and 2
1906	Mrs Kennion	Miss B Thompson	Burnham	4 and 3
1907	May Hezlet	Florence Hezlet	Newcastle, Co Down	2 and 1

An early Ladies' championship at Portrush (Mary Evans Pic. Lib.)

LADIES' BRITISH OPEN AMATEUR CHAMPIONSHIP

Year	Winner	Runner-up	Venue	By
1908	Miss M Titterton	Dorothy Campbell	St Andrews	19th hole
1909	Dorothy Campbell	Florence Hezlet	Birkdale	4 and 3
1910	Miss Grant Suttie	Miss L Moore	Westward Ho!	6 and 4
1911	Dorothy Campbell	Violet Hezlet	Portrush	3 and 2
1912	Gladys Ravenscroft	Miss S Temple	Turnberry	3 and 2
	(Final played over 36 holes after 1912)			
1913	Muriel Dodd	Miss Chubb	St Annes	8 and 6
1914	Cecil Leitch	Gladys Ravenscroft	Hunstanton	2 and 1
1915–18	No Championship owing to World War I.			
1919	Should have been played at Burnham in October, but abandoned owing to Railway Strike.			
1920	Cecil Leitch	Molly Griffiths	Newcastle, Co Down	7 and 6
1921	Cecil Leitch	Joyce Wethered	Turnberry	4 and 3
1922	Joyce Wethered	Cecil Leitch	Princes, Sandwich	9 and 7
1923	Doris Chambers	Miss A Macbeth	Burnham, Somerset	2 holes
1924	Jean Wethered	Mrs Cautley	Portrush	7 and 6
1925	Joyce Wethered	Cecil Leitch	Troon	37th hole
1926	Cecil Leitch	Mrs Garon	Harlech	8 and 7
1927	Miss Thion de la Chaume (France)	Miss Pearson	Newcastle, Co Down	5 and 4
1928	Nanette Le Blan (France)	Miss S Marshall	Hunstanton	3 and 2
1929	Joyce Wethered	Glenna Collett (USA)	St Andrews	3 and 1
1930	Diana Fishwick	Glenna Collett (USA)	Formby	4 and 3
1931	Enid Wilson	Wanda Morgan	Portmarnock	7 and 6
1932	Enid Wilson	Miss C P R Montgomery	Saunton	7 and 6
1933	Enid Wilson	Miss D Plumpton	Gleneagles	5 and 4
1934	Helen Holm	Pam Barton	Royal Porthcawl	6 and 5
1935	Wanda Morgan	Pam Barton	Newcastle, Co Down	3 and 2
1936	Pam Barton	Miss B Newell	Southport and Ainsdale	5 and 3
1937	Jessie Anderson	Doris Park	Turnberry	6 and 4
1938	Helen Holm	Elsie Corlett	Burnham	4 and 3
1939	Pam Barton	Mrs T Marks	Portrush	2 and 1
1946	Jean Hetherington	Philomena Garvey	Hunstanton	1 hole
1947	Babe Zaharias (USA)	Jacqueline Gordon	Gullane	5 and 4
1948	Louise Suggs (USA)	Jean Donald	Royal Lytham	1 hole
1949	Frances Stephens	Val Reddan	Harlech	5 and 4
1950	Vicomtesse de Saint Sauveur (France)	Jessie Valentine	Newcastle, Co Down	3 and 2
1951	Mrs P G MacCann	Frances Stephens	Broadstone	4 and 3
1952	Moira Paterson	Frances Stephens	Troon	39th hole
1953	Marlene Stewart	Philomena Garvey	Porthcawl	7 and 6
1954	Frances Stephens	Elizabeth Price	Ganton	4 and 3
1955	Jessie Valentine	Barbara Romack (USA)	Portrush	7 and 6
1956	Margaret Smith	Mary P Janssen	Sunningdale	8 and 7
1957	Philomena Garvey	Jessie Valentine	Gleneagles	4 and 3
1958	Jessie Valentine	Elizabeth Price	Hunstanton	1 hole
1959	Elizabeth Price	Belle McCorkindale	Ascot	37th hole
1960	Barbara McIntire (USA)	Philomena Garvey	Harlech	4 and 2
1961	Marley Spearman	Diane Robb	Carnoustie	7 and 6
1962	Marley Spearman	Angela Bonallack	Royal Birkdale	1 hole
1963	Brigitte Varangot (France)	Philomena Garvey	Newcastle, Co Down	3 and 1
1964	Carol Sorenson (USA)	Bridget Jackson	Prince's Sandwich	37th hole
1965	Brigitte Varangot (France)	Belle Robertson	St Andrews	4 and 3
1966	Elizabeth Chadwick	Vivien Saunders	Ganton	3 and 2
1967	Elizabeth Chadwick	Mary Everard	Harlech	1 hole
1968	Brigitte Varangot (France)	Claudine Rubin (France)	Walton Heath	20th hole
1969	Catherine Lacoste (France)	Ann Irvin	Portrush	1 hole
1970	Dinah Oxley	Belle Robertson	Gullane	1 hole
1971	Michelle Walker	Beverley Huke	Alwoodley	3 and 1
1972	Michelle Walker	Claudine Rubin (France)	Hunstanton	2 holes
1973	Ann Irvin	Michelle Walker	Carnoustie	3 and 2
1974	Carol Semple (USA)	Angela Bonallack	Royal Porthcawl	2 and 1
1975	Nancy Syms (USA)	Suzanne Cadden	St Andrews	3 and 2
1976	Cathy Panton	Alison Sheard (S Africa)	Silloth	1 hole
1977	Angela Uzielli	Vanessa Marvin	Hillside	6 and 5
1978	Edwina Kennedy (Australia)	Julia Greenhalgh	Notts	1 hole
1979	Maureen Madill	Jane Lock (Australia)	Nairn	2 and 1
1980	Anne Sander (USA)	Liv Wollin (Sweden)	Woodhall Spa	3 and 1

US WOMEN'S AMATEUR CHAMPIONSHIP

DETAILED RECORDS

Most victories

6, Glenna Collett Vare, 1922-25-28-29-30-35
5, JoAnne Gunderson Carner, 1957-60-62-66-68
3, Beatrix Hoyt; Margaret Curtis; Dorothy Campbell Hurd; Alexa Stirling; Virginia van Wie; Anne Quast (later Decker, later Welts, later Sander)

Oldest winner

Dorothy Campbell Hurd, 41 years 4 months, 1924

Youngest winner

Laura Baugh, 16 years 2 months 21 days, 1971; Beatrix Hoyt, 16 years 3 months 4 days, 1896

Peggy Conley reached the 1963 final at 16 years 2 months 2 weeks, and Roberta Albers reached the semi-final in 1961 aged 14 years 8 months.

Biggest margin of victory in final

14 and 13, Anne Quast beat Phyllis Preuss at Tacoma in 1961. Anne Quast was 12 up at lunch—also a record.

Longest final

41 holes, JoAnne Gunderson Carner beat Marlene Stewart Streit in 1966 at Sewickley Heights, Pennsylvania. This was the longest final in any USGA competition.

In 1954, the second 18 holes of the final was halted by storms and played on Sunday. It thus took 29 hours 15 minutes to complete.

US WOMEN'S AMATEUR CHAMPIONSHIP

Year	Winner	Runner-up	Venue	Score
1895	Mrs C S Brown	Miss N C Sargeant	Meadow Brook	132
Matchplay				By
1896	Beatrix Hoyt	Mrs Arthur Turnure	Morris County	2 and 1
1897	Beatrix Hoyt	Miss N C Sargeant	Essex CC	5 and 4
1898	Beatrix Hoyt	Maude Wetmore	Ardsley Club	5 and 3
1899	Ruth Underhill	Mrs Caleb Fox	Philadelphia CC	2 and 1
1900	Frances Griscom	Margaret Curtis	Shinnecock Hills	6 and 5
1901	Genevieve Hecker	Lucy Herron	Baltusrol	5 and 3
1902	Genevieve Hecker	Louisa Wells	The Country Club	4 and 3
1903	Bessie Anthony	Miss J A Carpenter	Chicago GC	7 and 6
1904	Georgianna Bishop	Mrs E F Sanford	Merion	5 and 3
1905	Pauline Mackay	Margaret Curtis	Morris County CC	1 hole
1906	Harriot Curtis	Mary Adams	Brae Burn CC	2 and 1
1907	Margaret Curtis	Harriot Curtis	Midlothian CC	7 and 6
1908	Catherine Harley	Mrs Polhemus	Chevy Chase Club	6 and 5
1909	Dorothy Campbell	Mrs R H Barlow	Merion	3 and 2
1910	Dorothy Campbell	Mrs G M Martin	Homewood CC	2 and 1
1911	Margaret Curtis	Lillian Hyde	Baltusrol	5 and 3
1912	Margaret Curtis	Mrs R H Barlow	Essex CC	3 and 2
1913	Gladys Ravenscroft	Marion Hollins	Wilmington CC	2 holes
1914	Mrs Arnold Jackson	Elaine Rosenthal	Glen Cove	1 hole
1915	Mrs C H Vanderbeck	Mrs W A Gavin	Owentsia Club	3 and 2
1916	Alexa Stirling	Mildred Caverly	Belmont Springs CC	2 and 1
1917–18	No Championship—World War I			
1919	Alexa Stirling	Mrs W A Garvin	Shawnee CC	6 and 5
1920	Alexa Stirling	Dorothy Hurd Campbell	Mayfield CC	5 and 4
1921	Marion Hollins	Alexa Stirling	Hollywood GC	5 and 4
1922	Glenna Collett	Mrs W A Gavin	Greenbrier CC	5 and 4
1923	Edith Cummings	Alexa Stirling	Westchester-Biltmore CC	3 and 2
1924	Dorothy Campbell Hurd	Mary Browne	Rhode Island CC	7 and 6
1925	Glenna Collett	Alexa Fraser Stirling	St Louis CC	9 and 8
1926	Mrs Henry Stetson	Mrs W D Goss, Jr	Merion	3 and 1
1927	Miriam Burns Horn	Maureen Orcutt	Cherry Valley Club	5 and 4
1928	Glenna Collett	Virginia van Wie	Hot Springs	13 and 12
1929	Glenna Collett	Leona Pressier	Oakland Hills CC	4 and 3
1930	Glenna Collett	Virginia van Wie	Los Angeles CC	6 and 5
1931	Helen Hicks	Glenna Collett Vare	CC of Buffalo	2 and 1
1932	Virginia van Wie	Glenna Collett Vare	Salem CC	10 and 8
1933	Virginia van Wie	Helen Hicks	Exmoor CC	4 and 3
1934	Virginia van Wie	Dorothy Traung	Whitemarsh Valley CC	2 and 1

Alexa Stirling, the leader of her time in American women's golf (US Golf Association)

Glenna Collett (now Mrs Vare), US Women's Amateur champion a record six times (US Golf Association)

Year				
1935	Glenna Collett Vare	Patty Berg	Interlachen CC	3 and 2
1936	Pamela Barton	Maureen Orcutt	Canoe Brook CC	4 and 3
1937	Mrs Julius A Page	Patty Berg	Memphis CC	7 and 6
1938	Patty Berg	Mrs Julius A Page	Westmoreland CC	6 and 5
1939	Betty Jameson	Dorothy Kirby	Wee Burn Club	3 and 2
1940	Betty Jameson	Jane Cothran	Del Monte G and CC	6 and 5
1941	Elizabeth Hicks Newell	Helen Sigel	The Country Club	5 and 3
1942–45	No Championships.			
1946	Mildred Zaharias	Clara Sherman	Southern Hills	11 and 9
1947	Louise Suggs	Dorothy Kirby	Franklin Hills CC	2 holes
1948	Grace Lenczyk	Helen Sigel	Del Monte G and CC	4 and 3
1949	Dorothy Germain Porter	Dorothy Kielty	Merion	3 and 2
1950				
	Beverly Hanson	Mae Murray	Atlanta AC, East Lake	6 and 4
1951	Dorothy Kirby	Claire Doran	Town and CC, St Paul	2 and 1
1952	Jacqueline Pung	Shirley McFedters	Waverley CC	2 and 1
1953	Mary Lena Faulk	Polly Riley	Rhode Island CC	3 and 2
1954	Barbara Romack	Mickey Wright	Allegheny CC	4 and 2
1955	Patricia Lesser	Jane Nelson	Myers Park CC	7 and 6
1956	Marlene Stewart	JoAnne Gunderson	Meridian Hills CC	2 and 1
1957	JoAnne Gunderson	Anne Casey Johnstone	Del Paso CC	8 and 6
1958	Anne Quast	Barbara Romack	Wee Burn CC	3 and 2
1959	Barbara McIntire	Joanne Goodwin	Congressional CC	4 and 3
1960	JoAnne Gunderson	Jean Ashley	Tulsa CC	6 and 5
1961	Anne Quast	Phyllis Preuss	Tacoma G and CC	14 and 13
1962	JoAnne Gunderson	Ann Baker	CC of Rochester	9 and 8
1963	Anne Quast	Peggy Conley	Taconic GC	2 and 1
1964	Barbara McIntire	JoAnne Gunderson	Prairie Dunes CC	3 and 2
1965	Jean Ashley	Anne Quast	Lakewood CC	5 and 4
1966	JoAnne Gunderson Carner	Marlene Stewart Streit	Sewickley Heights GC	41st hole
1967	Mary Lou Dill	Jean Ashley	Annandale GC	5 and 4
1968	JoAnne Gunderson Carner	Anne Quast	Birmingham CC	5 and 4
1969	Catherine Lacoste	Shelley Hamlin	Las Colinas CC	3 and 2
1970	Martha Wilkinson	Cynthia Hill	Wee Burn CC	3 and 2
1971	Laura Baugh	Beth Barry	Atlanta CC	1 hole
1972	Mary Anne Budke	Cynthia Hill	St Louis CC	5 and 4
1973	Carol Semple	Anne Quast	CC of Rochester	1 hole
1974	Cynthia Hill	Carol Semple	Broadmoor GC, Seattle	5 and 4
1975	Beth Daniel	Donna Horton	Brae Burn CC	3 and 2
1976	Donna Horton	Marianne Bretton	Del Paso CC	2 and 1
1977	Beth Daniel	Cathy Sherk	Cincinnati CC	3 and 1
1978	Cathy Sherk	Judith Oliver	Sunnybrook GC	4 and 3
1979	Carolyn Hill	Patty Sheehan	Memphis CC	7 and 6

'Babe' Zaharias (Action Photos)

Barbara McIntire, a champion of Britain and America (Action Photos)

Most times in the final
8, Glenna Collett Vare

Most times runner-up
3, Mrs William A Gavin, 1915-19-22; Anne Quast, 1965-68-73.

Longest 18-hole match
27 holes, Mae Murray beat Fay Crocker in the fourth round at East Lake, Atlanta in 1950.

Consecutive winners
3, Beatrix Hoyt, 1896-97-98; Alexa Stirling, 1916-19-20. No championship in 1917–18; Glenna Collett Vare, 1928-29-30; Virginia van Wie, 1932-33-34;
2, Genevieve Hecker, 1901-02; Dorothy Campbell, 1909-10; Margaret Curtis, 1911-12; Betty Jameson, 1939-40.

Family records
In 1907, the final was contested by the sisters Margaret Curtis and Harriot Curtis. Margaret won 7 and 6, succeeding Harriot as champion.

In 1962, Jean Trainor defeated her daughter Anne Trainor by 4 and 3 in the fourth round.

First to win American and British championships
Dorothy Campbell (later Dorothy Hurd), 1909

First American to win American and British championships
Mildred 'Babe' Didrikson Zaharias, 1946 and 1947.

Overseas winners
Dorothy Campbell; Gladys Ravenscroft; Pam Barton; Marlene Stewart; Catherine Lacoste

Winner of British and American championships the same year
Catherine Lacoste, 1969; Pam Barton, 1936; Dorothy Campbell, 1909

Longest span between victories
15 years, Dorothy Campbell, 1909-24.

Club hosting most championships
4 times, Merion, Pennsylvania.

Winners of British and American championships
'Babe' Zaharias; Gladys Ravenscroft; Pam Barton; Louise Suggs; Dorothy Campbell; Barbara McIntire; Marlene Stewart; Catherine Lacoste; Carol Semple; Anne Sander.

Winners of British, American and Canadian championships
Marlene Stewart and Dorothy Campbell Hurd.

Repeat finals
1928 and 1930, Glenna Collett Vare beat Virginia van Wie

CURTIS CUP

MILESTONES

An international match, involving the Curtis sisters Harriot and Margaret, was first played at Cromer, Norfolk, in 1905, but it was not until 1932 that the Cup bearing their name became the trophy for competition between America and Great Britain. In 1931, the USGA undertook to finance the American team while British arrangements were in the hands of the Ladies' Golf Union.

1932 The first match at Wentworth set a trend of American superiority that other matches

The Curtis sisters: Harriot (left) and Margaret. Both redoubtable golfers who presented the Curtis Cup, first played in 1932 (US Golf Association)

Glenna Collett Vare, driving during the Curtis Cup at Gleneagles 1936 (BBC Hulton Pic. Lib.)

followed. The British, with victories by the formidable trio of Joyce Wethered, Enid Wilson and Diana Fishwick, won the singles $3\frac{1}{2}$–$2\frac{1}{2}$, but a clean sweep by the Americans in the foursomes was the decisive factor. In the foursomes Glenna Collett Vare and Mrs Hill beat Wethered and Wanda Morgan by 1 hole, but in the singles Wethered beat Vare 6 and 4. They were incomparably the best players of their time. It was the only time that Wethered took part in the Curtis Cup.

1934 Chevy Chase Club, Chevy Chase, Maryland, was chosen for the first match on American soil and the British made a promising start by sharing the foursomes. The foursomes were played in a severe rainstorm, but the weather improved the next day when America won five of the six singles. Mrs J B Walker was the lone British winner. Mrs L D Cheney beat Pam Barton who, two years later, won the British and American Women's championship the same summer.

1936 The year of the first tie. At Gleneagles, the foursomes were again shared, but the real excitement came in the singles. Two last-green victories by Charlotte Glutting and Maureen Orcutt for America were countered by Helen Holm and Marjorie Ross Garon for Britain. Glenna Collett Vare had won the top match for America and so all depended on Mrs L D Cheney and Jessie Anderson (later Jessie Valentine), a 21-year-old who was born just down the road in Perth. In the first of a record seven appearances in the Curtis Cup, she became the British heroine, holing a putt of 20 ft (6 m) on the last green to win her match and tie the whole contest.

1938 At the Essex County Club, Massachusetts, a very British-sounding name, the British had high hopes of their first victory after winning the foursomes 2½–½, but they won only one single. The deciding match was between Nan Baird and Charlotte Glutting who won the last 3 holes for a 1-hole victory.

1948 After a gap of ten years because of World War II, the Americans resumed with a victory at Royal Birkdale. A newcomer, Jean Donald, won both her matches for Britain, but after her singles win and a half at the top from Philomena Garvey against Louise Suggs, who won the last 2 holes, America won the remaining four matches.

1950 Britain's defeat by 7½–1½ at the Country Club of Buffalo was the largest margin to date. There was never any doubt about the result, but there was encouragement for the British in the first appearance of Frances Stephens. She won her foursome with Elizabeth Price and halved the leading single with Dorothy Germain Porter.

1952 An historic first victory for Britain at the Honourable Company of Edinburgh Golfers, Muirfield, a club with no lady members and no provision for them. In cold blustery conditions, Britain won the foursomes by the odd match but they suffered a shock before winning three of the singles through Frances Stephens, Jeanne Bisgood and Elizabeth Price. Jean Donald, 5 up and 11 to play, lost on the 18th to Dorothy Kirby but, by then, Elizabeth Price had control of the bottom match with Grace DeMoss.

1954 Britain lost the Cup at Merion by losing all three foursomes by wide margins. However, they showed their strength by sharing the singles. In the top match, Frances Stephens beat Mary Lena Faulk by 1 hole. Mary Lena Faulk squared with a 2 at the 35th but Frances Stephens holed from 6 yd (5·4m) on the 36th for victory.

1956 Great Britain confirmed their strength throughout the fifties by winning again, this time at Princes, Sandwich, scene of Gene Sarazen's Open championship victory. They lost the foursomes 2–1, but they had three commanding victories in the singles; Mrs George Valentine beat Patricia Lesser 6 and 4, Angela Ward (later Mrs Michael Bonallack) won her first Curtis Cup on a course where she was a member by 4 and 3 against Mary Ann Downey; and Elizabeth Price beat Jane Nelson 7 and 6.

This left Frances Stephens Smith and Polly Riley in the deciding match, both players being undefeated in singles matches. Polly Riley squared on the 32nd and again on the 34th but, after a half at the 35th, Mrs Smith won the final hole.

1958 The second halved match of the series occurred at Brae Burn Country Club, Massachusetts. It was the first time that any British team in Walker, Ryder or Curtis Cup had avoided defeat in America, a feat which only the 1965 Walker Cup equalled subsequently.

As holders, the British side retained the Cup. They won the foursomes 2–1, but America had a slight edge in the singles. In the end, the whole match depended, as in 1956, on the match between Frances Smith and Polly Riley, this time playing in the last match. Mrs Smith, 1 up playing the 18th, won the hole to win by 2 holes.

1960 At Lindrick, Yorkshire, scene of Britain's Ryder Cup victory in 1957, America won the Curtis Cup for the first time since 1954. Since then, they have won all the matches. The Americans won the foursomes 2–1 and there was none of the excitement of the previous three matches. The Americans won 4½ singles.

Mrs Frances Stephens Smith's remarkable Curtis Cup career ended after the foursomes. She did not play in the singles in which she was unbeaten in five matches.

1962 A British team, with five new names in its midst, suffered their worst defeat, 8–1 at Broadmoor Golf Club, Colorado Springs. They lost all three foursomes and only Mrs Alistair Frearson won her single. She beat Judy Bell 8 and 7.

1964 A change to 18-hole matches produced a fine contest at Royal Porthcawl. Peggy Conley, 17, was the youngest competitor in the Curtis Cup at the time and she played a decisive part at the end of a close match.

After the first three singles on the last afternoon, the teams were level but Peggy Conley, Barbara Fay White and Carol Sorenson, who went on to win the British Women's championship, beat Bridget Jackson, Angela Bonallack and Ruth Porter to settle things for America. Mrs Marley Spearman halved both singles and won both foursomes with Angela Bonallack for the British side.

1966 A big victory by 13–5 for the Americans at Virginia Hot Springs. All the Americans had previous Curtis Cup experience compared to three of the British. On the second day, the British won only two matches.

1968 As in 1964, the result hung in the balance for a long time on the second day of the match held at Royal County Down, Newcastle, Northern Ireland. It was the first time that the Curtis, Walker or Ryder Cup had been held on the other side of the Irish Sea; it was a huge success in two days of glorious weather.

Ann Irvin was the outstanding British player,

but once again the last three American victories in the singles made the difference between the teams.

1970 Back at Brae Burn, Massachusetts, the Americans won 11½–6½, but the British began by winning the first foursomes series. However, they got only two points from the next nine matches which made all the difference.

1972 A match at Western Gailes, Ayrshire, notable for the play of the two young champions, Michelle Walker and Laura Baugh. The single between the two was halved; Walker won the foursome in which they were both involved, but they won their other matches, Walker dropping only that one half point in two days.

Over all, it was a match which swung in the Americans' favour on the first afternoon. They had lost the foursomes in the morning, but won the singles 4½–1½. The second day's play was halved.

1974 For the first time, the match was held on America's west coast at the San Francisco Golf Club. After the first morning's play was halved, the Americans gained and maintained a steady advantage. They won 13–5 with Mrs Anne Sander who played her first Curtis Cup match in 1958, winning all her three matches.

1976 An 11½–6½ victory for the United States was never seriously in doubt after they led 6½–2½ on the first day at Royal Lytham, St Annes. The American side included Nancy Lopez who, though winning her matches, played only twice.

1978 Britain made an encouraging start on the first morning at Apawamis, New York. They won the foursomes 2½–½, but thereafter were disappointing. They finished the first day behind at 5–4 and then lost all the second day's foursomes.

1980 A one-sided match at St Pierre, Chepstow, after the first morning. The Americans ran away on Friday afternoon and Saturday morning to win 13–5. The new British Professional tour had its effect upon the British. Jane Connachan was the youngest to take part in any Curtis Cup.

DETAILED RECORDS

Most appearances
7, Mrs George Valentine (Great Britain and Ireland)

6, Philomena Garvey (Great Britain and Ireland); Elizabeth Price (Great Britain and Ireland); Frances Smith (Great Britain and Ireland); Angela Bonallack (Great Britain and Ireland); Polly Riley (United States); Barbara McIntire (United States); Anne Quast Sander (United States); Mary McKenna (Great Britain and Ireland)

Most consecutive appearances
6, Elizabeth Price; Frances Smith; Angela Bonallack; Polly Riley

Biggest margin of victory
Over 36 holes (1932–62)
Foursomes: **8 and 7,** Jean Ashley and Lee Johnstone (United States) beat Mrs Alistair Frearson and Ruth Porter, 1962

Singles: **9 and 8,** Margaret 'Wiffi' Smith (United States) beat Philomena Garvey, 1956 Polly Riley (United States) beat Elizabeth Price, 1954

Over 18 holes (from 1964 onwards)
Foursomes: **8 and 7,** Carol Sorenson and Barbara Fay White (United States) beat Bridget Jackson and Susan Armitage, 1964

Singles: **7 and 5,** Jane Booth (United States) beat Julia Greenhalgh, 1974

Largest winning margin by team
13–5, United states over Great Britain and Ireland 1966, 1974 and 1980.

Prior to 1964, when 18 points became at stake, the largest winning score was 8–1 to the United States in 1962.

Ties
There have been two tied matches: in 1936 and 1958.

OUTSTANDING INDIVIDUAL RECORDS UNITED STATES (Number of individual matches shown in brackets.)	
Name	%
Debbie Massey (5)	100
Dorothy Kielty (4)	100
Claire Doran (4)	100
Clifford Ann Creed (2)	100
Beverly Hanson (2)	100
Nancy Lopez (2)	100
Barbara White Boddie (8)	93.75
Beth Daniel (8)	87.50
Virginia van Wie (4)	87.50
Mrs L D Cheney (6)	83.33
Carol Sorenson Elenniken (8)	81.25
Jane Bastenchury Booth (12)	75
Martha Wilkinson (4)	75
Charlotte Glutting (5)	70
JoAnne Gunderson Carner (10)	65
Glenna Collett Vare (7)	64.28

A total of 84 players have played for the United States in the 21 matches. The United States have won 17, Great Britain and Ireland two with two halved.

Best comebacks

In 1938, United States won 5½–3½ after trailing 2½–½ in the foursomes.

In 1956, Great Britain and Ireland won 5–4 after losing the foursomes 2–1.

Team winning all the foursomes

In 1932, 1954 and 1962 all by the United States

Team winning all the singles

None. The United States won 5½ out of 6 in 1950

Most consecutive victories

11, the United States, 1960–80

Youngest competitor

Jane Connachan, 16 years 3 months, 1980

OUTSTANDING INDIVIDUAL PERFORMANCES
GREAT BRITAIN AND IRELAND
(Number of individual matches played shown in brackets)

Name	%
Clarrie Tiernan (2)	100
Michelle Walker (4)	87.50
Marjorie Ross Garon (2)	75
Frances Smith (11)	68.18
Muriel Thomson (3)	66.66
Ita Burke (3)	66.66
Elizabeth Price (12)	62.50
A M Holm (5)	60
Ruth Porter (7)	50
Marley Spearman (6)	50
Jean Donald Anderson (6)	50
Joyce Wethered (2)	50
Enid Wilson (2)	50
Elsie Corlett (2)	50
Jacqueline Gordon (2)	50
Julia Greenhalgh (17)	47.05
Mary Everard (15)	46.60
Angela Ward Bonallack (15)	43.33
Mary McKenna (23)	41.30
Jessie Anderson Valentine (13)	30.76

Mrs Frances Stephens Smith was unbeaten in her five singles matches. She won four and halved one.

A total of 74 players have taken part in the 21 matches.

CURTIS CUP

Year	Venue	Winners	US Total	Great Britain and Ireland Total	Captains USA	Captains Britain
1932	Wentworth GC, Surrey England	USA	5½	3½	Marion Hollins	Joyce Wethered
1934	Chevy Chase Club, Maryland	USA	6½	2½	Glenna Collett Vare	Doris Chambers
1936	King's Course, Gleneagles, Scotland	(tie)	4½	4½	Glenna Collett Vare	Doris Chambers
1938	Essex CC, Massachusetts	USA	5½	3½	Frances Stebbins	Kathleen Wallace-Williamson
1948	Royal Birkdale, Lancashire, England	USA	6½	2½	Glenna Collett Vare	Doris Chambers
1950	Buffalo CC, New York	USA	7½	1½	Glenna Collett Vare	Diana Critchley
1952	Links of the Honourable Company of Edinburgh Golfers, Muirfield, Scotland	Britain	4	5	Aneila Goldthwaite	Lady Katherine Cairns
1954	Merion GC (East course), Pennsylvania	USA	6	3	Edith Flippin	Dorothy 'Baba' Beck
1956	Prince's GC, Sandwich, England	Britain	4	5	Edith Flippin	Zara Bolton
1958	Brae Burn GC, Massachusetts	(tie)	4½	4½	Virginia Dennehy	Daisy Ferguson
1960	Lindrick GC, Yorkshire, England	USA	6½	2½	Mildred Prunaret	Maureen Garrett
1962	Broadmoor GC, Colorado Springs	USA	8	1	Polly Riley	Frances Smith
1964	Royal Porthcawl GC, Wales	USA	10½	7½	Helen Hawes	Elsie Corlett
1966	Cascades Course, Hot Springs, Virginia	USA	13	5	Dorothy Porter	Zara Bolton
1968	Royal County Down GC, Newcastle, Northern Ireland	USA	10½	7½	Evelyn Monsted	Zara Bolton
1970	Brae Burn GC, Massachusetts	USA	11½	6½	Carol Cudone	Jeanne Bisgood
1972	Western Gailes, Scotland	USA	10	8	Jean Crawford	Frances Smith
1974	San Francisco GC, California	USA	13	5	Allison Choate	Belle Robertson
1976	Royal Lytham and St Annes, Lancashire	USA	11½	6½	Barbara McIntire	Belle Robertson
1978	Apawamis, New York	USA	12	6	Helen Sigel Wilson	Carol Comboy
1980	St Pierre, Chepstow, England	USA	13	5	Nancy Syms	Carol Comboy

WOMEN'S WORLD AMATEUR TEAM CHAMPIONSHIP FOR THE ESPIRITO SANTO TROPHY

MILESTONES

The championship was instituted by the French Golf Federation on a suggestion of the United States Golf Association. The inaugural event was held at the Saint-Germain Club in Paris in October 1964. Each team consists of three players, the two best each day making up the team's score. The sum of the four daily totals decides the winner.

1964 Appropriately, the first championship was won by France, the host country who, at that time, had three of the best players in the world, Claudine Cros, Catherine Lacoste and Brigitte Varangot.

They had a close duel with the United States who led by only 1 stroke after 54 holes. Lacoste had a final round of 73 and Cros 74, but the issue was decided when the American, Barbara McIntire, played the last 2 holes in 3 over par. France won by 1 stroke with a total of 588.

1966 A comfortable victory in Mexico City for the Americans despite losing the services of Mrs JoAnne Gunderson Carner. She was replaced by 17-year-old Shelley Hamlin who, after failing to count in the first two rounds, finished with two 72s, the best last 36-hole score by any player. The Americans won by 9 strokes from Canada and 17 from France, the holders.

1968 In a championship of high scoring, the United States won for the second time at the Victoria Golf Club, near Melbourne. After three rounds, America and Australia were level on 463, 1 ahead of France, but America won by 5 strokes.

1970 America won a desperate victory over France by a single stroke at the Club de Campo in Madrid. They had trailed after three rounds by 2 strokes but, with Martha Wilkinson, the US champion, paired with Catherine Lacoste, there were fluctuations in plenty before America squeezed home. The individual title was won by the South African, Sally Little.

1972 The United States won for the fourth time in a row at the Hindu Country Club, Buenos Aires. They won by 4 strokes from France who were 18 strokes behind America at the half-way.

Then Claudine Rubin and Brigitte Varangot had a 68 and a 71 to make up 14 strokes. Good finishing rounds of 72 and 73 by Laura Baugh and Jane Bastanchury Booth, whose 68 in the first round equalled the lowest round ever in the championship, saw America home.

1974 The United States made it five victories in a row at the Campo de Golf Cajuiles, Dominica, beating South Africa and Great Britain and Ireland into second place by a record 16 strokes. It was none the less, the highest winning total— 620. America were close to disaster on the first day—or so it seemed. Deborah Massey almost withdrew after 9 holes, having been heavily medicated, but in the end her score of 84 counted, because Carol Semple committed a breach of the rules and was disqualified. Cynthia Hill had 76, the lowest first round and one of the few under 80. They were only a stroke behind Italy and never looked back.

The lowest score of the championship was a 71 by Catherine Lacoste de Prado of France in the last round. The first six teams had only 25 rounds under 80 out of a possible 72.

1976 The United States yet again at Vilamoura, Portugal. They were never headed and steadily built up the record-winning margin of 17 strokes, 1 more than the previous championship. Nancy Lopez, whose 72 in the first round, was the lowest of the four days, had the best aggregate of all—297.

France, the only other country to have won, were second for the third time.

1978 First victory for Australia and the first time that the United States have finished outside the first two. They were tied fourth.

At Pacific Harbour, Fiji, Australia won by a single stroke in a desperate finish with Canada who started the final round 6 strokes behind. France had a good last day to finish third on 602, 6 strokes behind the winners.

DETAILED RECORDS

Most victories
6, United States
1, France
1, Australia

Lowest aggregate total
580, United States, 1966

Highest winning total
620, United States, 1974

Lowest individual round
68, Jane Bastenchury Booth, Marlene Stewart and Claudine Cros Rubin, all in 1972

Lowest individual aggregate
289 (74, 71, 70, 74) Marlene Stewart, Mexico City CC, 1966

Lowest individual first round
68, Marlene Stewart and Jane Bastenchury Booth, Hindu CC, Buenos Aires, 1972

Lowest individual second round
71, Catherine Lacoste, St Germain GC, Paris, 1964
71, Mrs Teddy Boddie and Marlene Stewart, Mexico City CC, 1966
71, Liv Forsell (Sweden) Hindu CC, Buenos Aires, 1972

Lowest individual third round
68, Claudine Cros Rubin, Hindu CC, Buenos Aires, 1972

Lowest individual fourth round
71, Claudine Cros Rubin and Isa Goldschmid, Hindu CC, Buenos Aires, 1972
71, Catherine Lacoste de Prado, Campo de Golf, Cajuiles, Dominican Republic, 1974

Largest lead after 18 holes
5 strokes, United States, 1972

Largest lead after 36 holes
13 strokes, United States, 1972

Largest lead after 54 holes
10 strokes, United States, 1974

Largest margin of victory
17 strokes, United States, 1976

Smallest lead after 18 holes
1 stroke, France in 1964; United States in 1966, Italy in 1974 and Great Britain and Ireland in 1978

Smallest lead after 36 holes
2 strokes, France in 1964 and 1968

Smallest lead after 54 holes
United States and Australia tied in 1968

Smallest margin of victory
1 stroke, France in 1964, the United States in 1970 and Australia in 1978

Most teams to compete
25 in 1964 and 1976

Youngest competitors
Maria de la Guardia and Silvia Corrie, both of the Dominican Republic, were both only 14 years old in 1974

RESULTS

Espirito Santo Trophy
1964 Saint-Germain GC, Paris 1–4 October
France 588 (Claudine Cros, Catherine Lacoste, Brigitte Varangot)
1966 Mexico City Country Club 20–23 October
United States 580 (Marjorie Boddie, Shelley Hamlin, Anne Welts)
1968 Victoria GC, Nr Melbourne, Australia 2–5 October
United States 616 (Jane Bastanchury, Shelley Hamlin, Anne Welts)
1970 Club de Campo, Madrid 30 September–3 October
United States 598 (Jane Bastanchury, Cynthia Hill, Martha Wilkinson)
1972 Hindu CC, Buenos Aires 11–14 October
United States 583 (Laura Baugh, Jane Bastanchury Booth, Mary Anne Budke)
1974 Campo de Golf Cajuiles, Dominica 22–25 October
United States 620 (Cynthia Hill, Deborah Massey, Carol Semple)
1976 Vilamoura GC, Algarve, Portugal 6–9 October
United States 605 (Donna Horton, Nancy Lopez, Deborah Massey)
1978 Pacific Harbour, Fiji 10–13 October Australia 596 (Lindy Goggin, Edwina Kennedy, Jane Lock)

US WOMEN'S OPEN

A championship started in 1946 and adopted by the United States Golf Association in 1953, it is the leading championship in women's golf. Unlike all the others, there is no sponsorship, but the popularity of women's golf has grown out of all recognition in recent years and in 1979, the Open was watched by crowds averaging 12 000 for the last three days. In addition, women's golf is high among the television ratings.

The championship is decided by 72 holes of strokeplay and is one of the very few occasions when amateurs and professionals compete together.

MILESTONES

1946 The first Women's Open produced one of the most famous players as winner. Patty Berg headed the qualifying field with 73, 72 for 145 at

Left: Mickey Wright, winner of a record 82 events on the American LPGA tour (US Golf Association). *Bottom left:* Louise Suggs (US Golf Association)

Spokane, Washington. In the matchplay section, she then beat Betty Jameson 5 and 4 in the final.

1947 Adoption of 72 holes of strokeplay. Betty Jameson, the previous year's runner-up, came back to win at Starmount Forest CC, Greensboro, North Carolina. She won by 6 strokes with a total of 295. Two amateurs were second.

1948 The great Mildred Zaharias, the 'Babe', triumphed with an even-par total of 300 at Atlantic City CC, New Jersey. In bad weather, she won by 8 strokes.

1949 Under the guidance of the Ladies' Professional Golf Association, Louise Suggs beat 'Babe' Zaharias by 14 strokes to register a total of 291—a record at that time.

1950 At the Rolling Hills CC, Wichita, Kansas, Mildred Zaharias wasted no time in equalling Louise Sugg's record of 291. She won by 9 strokes from the amateur Betsy Rawls, now Tournament Director of the LPGA.

1951 Betsy Rawls, now a professional, won the title at Druid Hills GC, Atlanta. Her score was 293, five better than Louise Suggs.

1952 Louise Suggs became champion for the second time with a record-breaking aggregate of 284 (70, 69, 70, 75) at the Bala GC, Philadelphia. Marilynn Smith set a low individual round record with 67 in the second round, but Marlene Bauer and Betty Jameson were joint runners-up on 291.

1953 A total of 37 entrants of whom 17 were professionals competed for the first championship to be run, at the request of the LPGA, by the USGA. It took place at the Country Club of Rochester, New York, and was won by Betsy Rawls after a play-off with Jacqueline Pung of Honolulu. Their 72-hole score was 302, Rawls winning the 18-hole play-off with 71 to 77.

1954 In a manner akin to Ben Hogan winning the US Men's Open after his terrible car crash, 'Babe' Zaharias ran away with the Women's championship at the Tam O'Shanter CC just over a year after her serious cancer operation. She won by 12 strokes from Betty Hicks, a victory which confirmed her as the leading American woman golfer of her time. It was her last appearance in the Open.

Mickey Wright, later one of the most famous names herself, was fourth and the leading amateur.

1955 Fay Crocker of Montevideo, Uruguay,

became the first foreign winner at the Wichita CC, Kansas. In high winds, she led after every round and won by 4 strokes with a total of 299. 'Babe' Zaharias was unable to defend owing to another operation just before the event.

1956 Kathy Cornelius defeated Barbara McIntire, later to become US Women's Amateur champion, after they had tied on 302 at Northland CC, Minnesota. 'Babe' Zaharias was too ill to take part and died later in the year.

1957 Betsy Rawls won her third title at Winged Foot with a total of 299 without it actually being the lowest score. That was the 298 of Jacqueline Pung. However, she signed and returned the card as kept by her marker on which the 6 she had taken at the 4th hole was shown as a 5. The total was correct, but Jacqueline Pung was disqualified since a player is solely responsible for his or her score at each hole. If the mistake had been in the addition, it would not have mattered.

It was a tragedy even worse than that befalling Roberto de Vicenzo at the 1968 Masters who was not disqualified—simply prevented by his error from taking part in a play-off. The members of Winged Foot promptly raised a collection for Jacqueline Pung which reached over $3000 and exceeded the first prize of $1800 which she lost. Total prize-money was $7200.

Competitors were asked to wear skirts not shorts in order to conform with a club rule.

1958 Start of a great burst of victories by Mickey Wright. She won three times in four years and four times in seven years.

Her first success at Forest Lake CC, Michigan, was by 5 strokes after she had led throughout. A total of 290 left her 5 strokes clear of Louise Suggs. It was a new record total for championships under the USGA's direction. At 23, she was also the youngest winner to date. The leading amateur was Anne Quast, 20.

1959 Mickey Wright lowered her record total to 287 and Louise Suggs again followed her home, this time only 2 strokes behind. To maintain the uniformity, Anne Quast was again leading amateur, her 299 being the first by an amateur under 300. At Churchill Valley CC near Pittsburgh, Mickey Wright sought advice on the telephone for her putting troubles from Paul Runyan.

1960 Betsy Rawls became the first four-time winner with a score of 292 at Worcester CC, Massachusetts. This Club housed the men's Open in 1925 and became the first to complete the double. Mickey Wright led for three rounds before posting a final 82. Joyce Ziske was second, 1 stroke behind Rawls.

Judy Torluemke, 15, finished leading amateur.

1961 Mickey Wright's third victory and one of her best over the Lower course at Baltusrol. The course measured 6372 yd (5826 m) and Wright's controlled power was seen to excellent advantage. She played the final 36 holes in 141 strokes and won by 6 strokes from Betsy Rawls with a total of 293.

1962 High scores and a surprising winner at the Dunes Golf and Beach Club, Myrtle Beach, South Carolina. Murle MacKenzie Lindstrom made up 5 strokes in the last round to win with 301. It was her first professional victory and she won by 2 strokes from Ruth Jessen and JoAnn Prentice. Her prize was $1800.

In contrast to the previous year, Mickey Wright scored 158 for the final 36 holes. The weather was bad throughout.

1963 Another winner, Mary Mills, scoring her first success in professional golf. Having set a record of 141 for the first two rounds, she won by 3 strokes with a total of 289 at Kenwood Country Club, Cincinnati. Mickey Wright did not play.

Prize-money totalled $9000 and the event was televised locally for the first time.

1964 Wright won her fourth title under USGA direction at her old home club, the San Diego CC, California, after a play-off with Ruth Jessen. They had tied on 290, but at the 72nd hole, Wright got down in 2 from a bunker whereas Jessen hit a wood to 3 ft (0.9 m) and made a birdie. In the play-off, Wright had 70 against 72.

1965 Carol Mann, 6 ft 3 in (1.88 m) tall, came back to win at Atlantic City CC, New Jersey, after an opening round of 78 which put her 7 strokes behind the leader, Cathy Cornelius. Cornelius had a closing round of 69 to finish on 292, 2 strokes behind Mann who had second and third rounds of 70.

Mickey Wright was unable to defend her title, but Catherine Lacoste was second amateur, 8 strokes behind Mrs Helen Sigel Wilson whose 296 set an amateur record.

The last two rounds were played over two days and the final round was televised nationally for the first time.

1966 Sandra Spuzich, 29, became yet another to celebrate her first professional victory in the national Open. At Hazeltine CC, Chaska, she defeated defending champion Carol Mann by 1 stroke with 297. The lowest round of the championship was an opening 71 by Mickey Wright.

1967 A famous victory by Catherine Lacoste of France at the Cascades course in Hot Springs, Virginia. She became the first amateur to win the title after leading at the half-way stage by 5 strokes. She preserved this lead in the third round and increased her lead to 7 at one point, but her play deteriorated and, in the end, she had only a couple of strokes to spare from Susie Maxwell and Beth Stone. At one stage, Louise Suggs, 9 behind after 54 holes, had made up 8 of them.

1968 A triumph from start to finish for Susie Maxwell Berning who married only seven weeks before the championship began at Moselem Springs, Pennsylvania. She won by 3 strokes from Mickey Wright with a total of 289, her 71 equalling the lowest last round by a champion. However, Wright's 68 was the lowest last round by any player.

There was a record entry of 104; first prize was $5000.

1969 Another first professional victory in the Open. Donna Caponi held off the challenge of Peggy Wilson to win by 1 stroke at the Scenic Hills CC, Pensacola, Florida.

She took the lead late on and was delayed 15 minutes by an electric storm as she waited to play the 18th. After taking shelter in the clubhouse, she then got a birdie for a round of 69, the best by a champion.

1970 Donna Caponi joined Mickey Wright as the only champion at that time to successfully defend her title. In so doing she also equalled Wright's record score of 287. At Muskogee CC, Oklahoma, she was almost caught by Sandra Haynie and Sandra Spuzich after being 4 ahead with a record 54-hole total of 210.

1971 A commanding win for JoAnne Carner at the Kahkwa Club, Pennsylvania. She led after every round and won by 7 strokes from Kathy Whitworth with a total of 288. She thus became the fourth player to have won the US Women's Amateur and Open championships; she won her last Amateur title in 1968.

Three amateurs finished in the first ten.

Prize-money totalled $34450.

1972 Susie Berning joined a select group of six who have won the Open at least twice. At Winged Foot, New York, she won with a score of 299, 1 stroke ahead of Judy Rankin, Pam Barnett and Kathy Ahern. However, after an opening 79, she did not look the likely

Catherine Lacoste, winner of the British and American championships, and the only amateur to win the US Women's Open (Frank Gardner)

Nancy Lopez, the current Queen of ladies' golf (All Sport/Tony Duffy)

champion. The defending champion JoAnne Carner also began with a 79, but despite the heavy rains that made 70 the best round of the week, Susie Berning's final round of 71 saw her home. In that round, she had a 2 at the 17th to Pam Barnett's 4.

Marilynn Smith finished 72 holes in her 20th consecutive Open—a record. Nine amateurs from the entry of 176 also completed 72 holes although the USGA set a limit of 150 competitors. Prize-money exceeded $38 000 with the winner claiming $6000—both records.

1973 Susie Berning successfully defended her title and so became only the third player to win the Open three times. At Rochester, New York, she won by 5 strokes from Shelley Hamlin and Gloria Ehret with a total of 290.

Marilynn Smith played through her 21st consecutive Open and the amateur Cynthia Hill set a new record with a first round of 68.

1974 Sandra Haynie of Texas had birdies on the last 2 holes of LaGrange CC, Illinois, to win by a single stroke from Carol Mann and Beth Stone. JoAnne Carner who led the field by 2 strokes with 9 holes to play, tied for 4th place on 297, 2 strokes behind Haynie.

Prize-money totalled $40 000.

1975 There were only two sub-par rounds all week in the 23rd championship at Atlantic City CC. One of these was a third round of 71 by Sandra Palmer who added a final par round of 72 to win by 4 strokes on 295. Among those who tied for 2nd place was Nancy Lopez, then still an amateur. It was the best finish by an amateur since Catherine Lacoste won in 1967.

1976 JoAnne Carner, champion in 1971, denied Sandra Palmer a successful defence of her title. After they had tied on 292, 8 over par, at Rolling Green GC, Pennsylvania, Carner won the play-off with 76 to 78, further indication of the difficulty of the course. It was the first play-off since 1964.

Miss Nancy Porter made a hole-in-one on the 16th (135 yd (123 m)) in the second round. It was only the fourth in the history of the championship, but two of the four have been by Nancy Porter.

Sectional qualifying was necessary for the first time. The entry reached 205.

1977 Hollis Stacy, 23, had a creditable victory at Hazeltine National GC, Chaska, Minnesota, scene of Tony Jacklin's US Open victory in 1970. She led after all four rounds and won by 2 strokes with a total of 292. Nancy Lopez and JoAnne Carner were 2nd and 3rd. All three were former Girls' Junior champions. It was Lopez's first tournament as a professional.

Prize-money totalled a record $75 000.

1978 Hollis Stacy joined the band of those who have successfully defended their titles. She is also the youngest to win twice. It was her fifth USGA title; she won three consecutive Girls' titles.

Sally Little set a new individual round record with 65.

1979 Jerilyn Britz chose a good moment to win her first tournament as a professional. She captured the 27th Women's Open at Brooklawn CC, Connecticut, by 2 strokes from Debbie Massey and Sandra Palmer. Her total of 284 (70, 70, 75, 69) was 3 strokes lower than any returned by a winner since the USGA took over the running of the event. Louise Suggs won with 284 in 1952, but the Bala course measured only 5460 yd (4993 m) compared with 6010 yd (5496 m) at Brooklawn.

Jerilyn Britz, who did not turn professional until she was 30 in 1973, left a position as a teacher of physical education at New Mexico State University to try her hand on the golf tour. Twenty-third in the money list in 1978, she led the 1979 LPGA championship with 7 holes to play, but it was obviously good experience.

Susie Berning's second-round 66 was the second lowest in the championship's history. Sally Little set the record in 1978.

DETAILED RECORDS

Most victories
4 Mickey Wright, 1958-59-61-64; Betsy Rawls, 1951-53-57-60

Oldest winner
Fay Crocker, 40 years 11 months, 1955

Youngest winner
Catherine Lacoste, 22 years and 5 days, 1967

Biggest margin of victory
12 strokes, Mildred 'Babe' Didrikson Zaharias, 1954

Lowest winning aggregate (after 1953)
280, Amy Alcott, Richland CC, 1980

Most times runner-up
4, Louise Suggs, 1955-58-59-63

Lowest single round
65, Sally Little, fourth round, Indianapolis CC, 1978
66, Susie Maxwell Berning, second round, Brooklawn CC, 1979

Lowest first round
68, Cynthia Hill, Rochester CC, New York, 1973 and Kathy Ahern, La Grange, Illinois, 1974

Lowest second round
66, Susie Maxwell Berring, Brooklawn CC, 1979

Lowest third round
67, Judy Bell, San Diego CC, 1964

Lowest fourth round
65, Sally Little, Indianapolis CC, 1978

Lowest first 36 holes
139, Donna Caponi and Carol Mann, Muskogee CC, 1970

Lowest last 36 holes
140, Mickey Wright, Churchill Valley CC, 1959

Lowest first 54 holes
210, Donna Caponi, 1970

Lowest last 54 holes
Carol Mann, 1965

Highest winning score
302, Betsy Rawls and Jacqueline Pung, Rochester CC, 1953 and Kathy Cornelius and Barbara McIntire, Northland CC, 1956

Largest span between victories
9 years, Betsy Rawls, 1951–60

Consecutive winners
2 Mickey Wright, 1958–59; Donna Caponi, 1969–70; Susie Maxwell Berning, 1972–73; Hollis Stacy, 1977–78

Amateur winner
Catherine Lacoste, 1967. Barbara McIntire lost a play-off to Kathy Cornelius in 1956

Overseas winners Fay Crocker, 1955; Catherine Lacoste, 1967

Play-offs
6, 1947-52-53-56-64-76

Poorest start by champion
79, Susie Maxwell Berning, 1972

Poorest finish by champion
79, Kathy Cornelius 1956; Catherine Lacoste 1967

Youngest leading amateur winner
Judy Torluemke was 15 years, 1960

Best comebacks by champions
After 18 holes: Susie Maxwell Berning in 1972 and Carol Mann in 1965 were 7 strokes behind
After 36 holes: in 1953, Betsy Rawls was 9 behind
After 54 holes: in 1962, Murle Lindstrom and in 1969, Donna Caponi were 5 behind.

In 1956, Barbara McIntire made up 8 strokes in the last round to tie Kathy Cornelius but lost the play-off.

Leaders' fate
Up until 1977, a player who has led after 18 holes has won 11 of the 25 Opens. A player who has led after 36 holes has won 12 times. A player who has led after 54 holes has won 19 times.

Champions who led outright all the way
Mildred Zaharias 1954; Fay Crocker 1955; Betsy Rawls 1957; Mickey Wright 1958 and 1964; Mary Mills 1963; Susie Maxwell Berning 1968; Donna Caponi 1970; JoAnne Gunderson Carner 1971; Hollis Stacy 1977

US WOMEN'S OPEN

Year	Winner	Venue	Score
1946	Patty Berg beat Betty Jameson 5 and 4	Spokane, Washington	
1947	Betty Jameson	Starmount Forest CC	295
1948	Mildred Zaharias	Atlantic City CC	300
1949	Louise Suggs	Prince Georges G and CC	291
1950	Mildred Zaharias	Rolling Hills CC	291
1951	Betsy Rawls	Druid Hills GC	293
1952	Louise Suggs	Bala GC	284
	Taken over by USGA		
1953	Betsy Rawls	CC of Rochester	302
1954	Mildred Zaharias	Salem CC	291
1955	Fay Crocker	Wichita CC	299
1956	Kathy Cornelius	Northland CC	302
1957	Betsy Rawls	Winged Foot	299
1958	Mickey Wright	Forest Lake CC	290
1959	Mickey Wright	Churchill Valley CC	287
1960	Betsy Rawls	Worcester CC	292
1961	Mickey Wright	Baltusrol GC (Lower)	293
1962	Murle Lindstrom	Dunes Golf and Beach Club	301
1963	Mary Mills	Kenwood CC	289
1964	Mickey Wright	San Diego CC	290
1965	Carol Mann	Atlantic City CC	290
1966	Sandra Spuzich	Hazeltine National GC	297
1967	Catherine Lacoste	Hot Springs, Virginia	294
1968	Susie Berning	Moselem Springs GC	289
1969	Donna Caponi	Scenic Hills CC	294
1970	Donna Caponi	Muskogee CC	287
1971	JoAnne Carner	Kahkwa Club	288
1972	Susie Berning	Winged Foot	299
1973	Susie Berning	CC of Rochester	290
1974	Sandra Haynie	La Grange CC	295
1975	Sandra Palmer	Atlantic City CC	295
1976	JoAnne Carner	Rolling Green GC	292
1977	Hollis Stacy	Hazeltine National	292
1978	Hollis Stacy	Indianapolis CC	289
1979	Jerilyn Britz	Brooklawn CC	284
1980	Amy Alcott	Richland CC	280

US LADIES PROFESSIONAL GOLF ASSOCIATION

DETAILED RECORDS

Most victories
82, Mickey Wright
80, Kathy Whitworth

Most consecutive victories
5, Nancy Lopez, 1978
4, Mickey Wright, 1962 and 1963; Kathy Whitworth 1969 and Shirley Englehorn 1970

Most victories in one calendar year
13, Mickey Wright, 1963

Most official money won in one calendar year
$197 488, Nancy Lopez, 1979. Her total prize-money in 1979 was $215 987.61

Biggest margin of victory
14 strokes, Louise Suggs, USGA Women's Open, 1949
12 strokes, Betsy Rawls, St Louis Women's Open, 1954
12 strokes, Mickey Wright, Memphis Women's Open, 1960
12 strokes, Kathy Whitworth, Milwaukee Jaycee Open, 1966

Lowest 72-hole aggregate
271 (68, 65, 69, 69), Hollis Stacy, Rail GC, Springfield, Illinois, Rail Muscular Dystrophy Classic, 1977

Lowest total 54 holes
200 (69, 65, 64), Ruth Jessen, Omaha JC Open, 1964
200 (66, 66, 68), Carol Mann, Lady Carling Open at Canongate CC, Palmetto, Georgia, 1968

Lowest total 36 holes
131 (66, 65), Kathy Martin, Green Valley CC, Birmingham, Alabama, in Birmingham Classic, 1976
131 (66, 65), Silvia Bertolaccini, Armitage GC Harrisburg, Pennsylvania, in Lady Keystone Open, 1977

Lowest 18 holes
62 (30, 32), Mickey Wright, Tall City Open, Hogan Park GC, Midland, Texas, 1964

Lowest 9 holes
29, Marlene Hagge, Raymond Memorial course, 1971

29, Carol Mann, Borden Classic at Riviera CC, 1975
29, Pat Bradley, Golden Lights championship, Calabasas Park CC, New York, 1978
29, Pat Bradley, Golden Lights championship, first round, Wykagyl CC, New York, 1979
29, Silvia Bertolaccini, Orange Blossom Classic, Pasadena GC, Florida 1979

All-time Career Money Winnings (to Dec 1978)
Kathy Whitworth $858 461.01 since 1959
Judy Rankin $761 130.10 since 1962
Jane Blalock $708 936.61 since 1969
JoAnne Carner $649 980.07 since 1970

Leading money-winner most often in a single year
8, Kathy Whitworth

Most official money won by a rookie
$161 235 by Nancy Lopez from 1 August 1977 to 31 July 1978. This is a record for both men and women

Most consecutive holes without a bogey
50, Donna Young, LPGA championship at Jack Nicklaus GC, King's Island, Ohio, 1979
41, Nancy Lopez, 1978, LPGA championship at Jack Nicklaus GC, Kings Island, Ohio

Most eagles in one round
3, Alice Ritzman, Colgate European Open, second round, Sunningdale GC, England, 1979

Most holes in one in one tournament
2, JoAnn Washam, 1979, second and fourth rounds Women's Kemper Open, Mesa Verde CC; the 16th and 7th holes.

Fewest putts in one round
19, Beverly Klass, second round, Women's International, Moss Creek Plantation, Hilton Head, 1978

Most birdies in one 18-hole round
10, Nancy Lopez, second round, Mary Kay Classic, Bent Tree CC, Dallas, 1979
8 and 1 eagle, Mickey Wright, Tall City Open, Hogan Park GC, Texas, 1964
9, JoAnne Carner, Lady Pepsi Open, Indian Hills, Marietta, Georgia, 1971
9, Kathy Martin, Birmingham Classic, Green Valley CC, 1976
9, Judy Rankin, Bent Tree Classic, Bent Tree Golf and Racquet Club, Florida, 1977
9, Laura Baugh, Borden Classic, Riviera CC, Dublin, Ohio, 1977

Most birdies in a row
7, Carol Mann on first 9 in first round, Borden Classic, Riviera CC, Dublin, Ohio, 1975

LEADING MONEY-WINNERS (1948–1979)

Year	Player	Amount $
1948	Babe Zaharias	3 400.00*
1949	Babe Zaharias	4 650.00*
1950	Babe Zaharias	14 800.00*
1951	Babe Zaharias	15 087.00*
1952	Betsy Rawls	14 505.00
1953	Louise Suggs	19 816.25
1954	Patty Berg	16 011.00
1955	Patty Berg	16 492.34
1956	Marlene Hagge	20 235.50
1957	Patty Berg	16 272.00
1958	Beverly Hanson	12 639.55
1959	Betsy Rawls	26 774.39
1960	Louise Suggs	16 892.12
1961	Mickey Wright	22 236.21
1962	Mickey Wright	21 641.99
1963	Mickey Wright	31 269.50
1964	Mickey Wright	29 800.00
1965	Kathy Whitworth	28 658.00
1966	Kathy Whitworth	33 517.50
1967	Kathy Whitworth	32 937.50
1968	Kathy Whitworth	48 379.50
1969	Carol Mann	49 152.50
1970	Kathy Whitworth	30 235.01
1971	Kathy Whitworth	41 181.75
1972	Kathy Whitworth	65 063.99
1973	Kathy Whitworth	82 864.25
1974	JoAnne Carner	87 094.04
1975	Sandra Palmer	76 374.51
1976	Judy T Rankin	150 734.28
1977	Judy T Rankin	122 890.44
1978	Nancy Lopez	189 813.83
1979	Nancy Lopez	197 488.61†

*Approximate figure
†Record

TOTAL PURSES (1956–1980)

Year	Amount $	Events
1956	140 447	26
1957	147 830	26
1958	158 600	25
1959	202 500	26
1960	186 700	25
1961	288 750	24
1962	338 450	32
1963	345 300	34
1964	351 000	33
1965	356 316	33
1966	509 500	37
1967	435 250	32
1968	550 185	34
1969	597 290	29
1970	435 040	21
1971	558 500	21
1972	988 400	30
1973	1 471 000	36
1974	1 752 500	35
1975	1 742 000	33
1976	2 527 000	32
1977	3 058 000	35
1978	3 925 000	37
1979	4 400 000	38
1980	5 000 000	39

MOST CAREER WINS

	Player	Wins	Unofficial Wins	Joined Tour
1	Mickey Wright	82		1955
2	Kathy Whitworth	80	2	1959
3	Betsy Rawls	55		1951
4	Louise Suggs	50		1949
5	Patty Berg	41		1948
6	Sandra Haynie	39		1961
7	Carol Mann	38		1961
8	Babe Zaharias	31		1948
9	Judy Rankin	26	2	1962
10	Jane Blalock	26	2	1969
11	Marlene Hagge	25		1950
12	JoAnne Carner	23	3	1970
13	Marilynn Smith	22		1949
14	Sandra Palmer	18	1	1964
15	Nancy Lopez	17	1	1977
16	Beverly Hanson	15		1951
17	Donna Caponi Young	14	2	1965
18	Susie Berning	11	1	1964
18	Fay Crocker	11		1954
18	Shirley Englehorn	11		1959
18	Ruth Jessen	11		1956
18	Clifford Ann Creed	11	1	1962
23	Mary Lena Faulk	10		1955

MOST VICTORIES IN A SEASON

Year	Player	Victories
1948	Patty Berg/Babe Zaharias	3
1949	Patty Berg/Louise Suggs	3
1950	Babe Zaharias	6
1951	Babe Zaharias	7
1952	Betsy Rawls/Louise Suggs	6
1953	Louise Suggs	8
1954	Louise Suggs/Babe Zaharias	5
1955	Patty Berg	6
1956	Marlene Hagge	8
1957	Patty Berg/Betsy Rawls	5
1958	Mickey Wright	5
1959	Betsy Rawls	10
1960	Mickey Wright	6
1961	Mickey Wright	10
1962	Mickey Wright	10
1963	Mickey Wright	13
1964	Mickey Wright	11
1965	Kathy Whitworth	8
1966	Kathy Whitworth	9
1967	Kathy Whitworth	8
1968	Kathy Whitworth/Carol Mann	10
1969	Carol Mann	8
1970	Shirley Englehorn	4
1971	Kathy Whitworth	5
1972	Kathy Whitworth/Jane Blalock	5
1973	Kathy Whitworth	7
1974	JoAnne Carner/Sandra Haynie	6
1975	Carol Mann/Sandra Haynie	4
1976	Judy T Rankin	6
1977	Judy T Rankin/Debbie Austin	5
1978	Nancy Lopez	9
1979	Nancy Lopez	8

Caught in the rain but still able to look elegant, Sally Little (*left*) of South Africa and Judy Rankin (Phil Sheldon)

ALL-TIME CAREER MONEY-WINNERS (Through 1979)

Rank	Name	Earnings $	Joined Tour
1	Kathy Whitworth	858 461.01	1959
2	Judy Rankin	761 130.10	1962
3	Jane Blalock	708 936.61	1969
4	JoAnne Carner	649 980.07	1970
5	Donna C Young	602 808.75	1965
6	Sandra Palmer	596 021.12	1964
7	Sandra Post	525 590.88	1968
8	Carol Mann	498 532.70	1961
9	Sandra Haynie	498 387.57	1961
10	Pat Bradley	452 617.30	1974
11	Nancy Lopez	410 440.77	1977
12	Marlene Hagge	372 252.11	1950
13	Mickey Wright	368 215.73	1955
14	Amy Alcott	366 435.04	1975
15	Jo Ann Prentice	358 299.87	1956
16	Sally Little	356 321.23	1971
17	Mary Mills	320 921.24	1962
18	Hollis Stacy	320 545.01	1974
19	Debbie Austin	319 461.26	1968
20	Betsy Rawls	302 664.63	1951
21	Jan Stephenson	302 537.88	1974
22	Marilynn Smith	294 273.91	1949
23	Betty Burfeindt	265 790.60	1969
24	Sandra Spuzich	263 335.14	1962
25	Clifford Ann Creed	262 298.82	1962

THE $100 000 CLUB

1976

Judy Rankin	150 734.28
Donna C. Young	106 553.94
JoAnne Carner	103 275.10

1977

Judy Rankin	122 890.44
JoAnne Carner	113 711.82
Kathy Whitworth	108 540.74
Jane Blalock	102 012.81

1978

Nancy Lopez	189 813.83
Pat Bradley	118 057.17
Jane Blalock	117 768.48
JoAnne Carner	108 092.92

1979

Nancy Lopez	197 488.61
Sandra Post	178 750.68
Amy Alcott	144 838.61
Pat Bradley	129 679.14
Donna C. Young	125 493.67
Sally Little	119 501.01
Jane Blalock	115 226.97
Judy Rankin	108 511.32

Great Golfing Achievements

RECORDS

Note—these records are taken from the *Guinness Book of Records*, Editor and Compiler Norris McWhirter, Sports Editor Stan Greenberg.

Club *Oldest*

The oldest club of which there is written evidence is the Gentlemen Golfers (now the Honourable Company of Edinburgh Golfers) formed in March 1744—ten years prior to the institution of the Royal and Ancient Club of St Andrews, Fife. The oldest existing club in North America is the Royal Montreal Club (1873).

Course *Highest*

The highest golf course (9-hole) in the world is the Tuctu Golf Club in Morococha, Peru, which is 14 335 ft (4369 m) above sea-level at its lowest point. Golf has, however, been played in Tibet at an altitude of over 16 000 ft (4875 m).

The highest 18-hole course is at La Paz Golf Club Bolivia, at an altitude of 13 500 ft (4115 m) above sea-level.

Course *Lowest*

The lowest golf-course in the world was that of the now defunct, Sodom and Gomorrah Golfing Society at Kallia (Qulya) on the northern shores of the Dead Sea, 1250 ft (380 m) below sea-level.

Currently the lowest is the 9-hole course of the Rotterdam GC at 26 ft (8 m) below sea-level.

Longest hole

The longest hole in the world is the 17th hole (par 6) of 745 yd (681 m) at the Black Mountain Golf Club, North Carolina. It was opened in 1964. In August 1927 the 6th hole at Prescott Country Club in Arkansas, measured 838 yd (766 m). The longest hole on a championship course in Great Britain is the 6th at Troon, Strathclyde, which stretches 580 yd (530 m).

Largest green

Probably the largest green in the world is the 5th green at International GC Bolton, Massachusetts, with an area greater than 28 000 ft^2 (2600 m^2).

Biggest bunker

The world's biggest bunker (called a trap in the USA) is Hell's Half Acre on the 7th hole of the Pine Valley course, New Jersey, built in 1912 and generally regarded as the world's most trying course.

Longest course

The world's longest course is at Dub's Dread GC, Piper, Kansas, and is a 78-par 8101 yd (7407 m). Floyd Satterlee Rood used the United States as a course, when he played from the Pacific surf to the Atlantic surf from 14 September 1963 to 3 October 1964 in 114 737 strokes. He lost 3511 balls on the 3397·7 mile (5468 km) trail.

Longest drives

In long-driving contests 330 yd (300 m) is rarely surpassed at sea-level. In officially regulated long-driving contests over level ground the greatest distance recorded is 392 yd (358 m) by William Thomas (Tommie) Campbell (Foxrock Golf Club) made at Dun Laoghaire, Co Dublin, in July 1964. On an airport runway Valentin Barrios (Spain) drove a Slazenger B51 ball 568½ yd (520 m) at Palma, Majorca on 7 March 1977. The greatest recorded drive on an ordinary course is one of 515 yd (471 m) by Michael Hoke Austin (b 17 February 1910) of Los Angeles, California, in the US National Seniors Open Championship at Las Vegas, Nevada, on 25 September 1974. Austin, 6 ft 2 in (1·88 m) tall and weighing 210 lb (92·250 kg) drove the ball to within a yard of the green on the par-4 450 yd (412 m) 5th hole of the Winterwood Course and it rolled 65 yd (59 m) past the flagstick. He was aided by an estimated 35 mph (56 km/h) tailwind.

A drive of 2640 yd (2414 m) (1½ miles) across ice was achieved by an Australian meteorologist named Nils Lied at Mawson Base, Antarctica,

Tuctu Golf Club in Morococha, Peru, at 14 335 ft (4369 m) the highest golf course in the world (Tuctu Golf Club)

Portrait of a long driver—George Bayer (The Associated Press Ltd)

in 1962. Arthur Lynskey claimed a drive of 200 yd (182 m) horizontal and 2 miles (3200 m) vertical off Pikes Peak, Colorado (14110 ft (4300 m) on 28 June 1968. On the Moon the energy expended on a mundane 300 yd (274 m) drive would achieve, craters permitting, a distance of 1 mile (1·6 km).

Longest hitter
The golfer regarded as the longest consistent hitter the game has ever known is the 6 ft 5 in (195 cm) tall, 17 st 2 lb (108·86 kg) George Bayer (USA), the 1957 Canadian Open Champion. His longest measured drive was one of 420 yd (384 m) at the 4th in the Las Vegas Invitational, Nevada, in 1953. It was measured as a precaution against litigation since the ball struck a spectator. Bayer also drove a ball pin high on a 426 yd (389 m) hole at Tucson, Arizona in 1955. Radar measurements show that an 87 mph (140 km/h) impact velocity for a golf ball falls to 46 mph (74 km/h) in 3 seconds.

Longest putt
The longest recorded holed putt in a major tournament was one of 86 ft (26 m) on the vast 13th green at the Augusta National, Georgia by Cary Middlecoff (b January 1921) (USA) in the 1955 Masters' Tournament. Robert Tyre (Bobby) Jones, Jr, (1902–71) was reputed to have holed a putt in excess of 100 ft (30 m) at the 5th green in the first round of the 1927 Open at St Andrews.

SCORES
Lowest 9 holes and 18 holes *Men*
The lowest recorded score on any 18-hole course with a par score of 70 or more is 55 (15 under bogey) first achieved by Alfred Edward Smith (b 1903) the Woolacombe professional, on his home course on 1 Jan 1936. The course measured 4248 yd (3884 m). The detail was 4, 2, 3, 4, 2, 4, 3, 4, 3 = 29 out, and 2, 3, 3, 3, 3, 3, 2, 5, 4, 1 = 26 in. At least three players are recorded to have played a long course (over 6000 yd (5846 m) in a score of 58. The lowest recorded score on a long course in Britain is 58 by Harry Weetman (1920–72) the British Ryder Cup golfer, for the 6171 yd (5642 m) Croham Hurst Course, Croydon, on 30 January 1956.

Nine holes in 25 (4, 3, 3, 2, 3, 3, 1, 4, 2) was

recorded by A J 'Bill' Burke in a round in 57 (32+25) on the 6389 yd (5842 m) par 71 Normandie course St Louis, Missouri, USA on 20 May 1970. The tournament record is 27 by: Jose Maria Canizares (Spain) (b 18 February 1947) for the first 9 of the third round in the 1978 Swiss Open on the 6811 yd (6228 m) Crans-Sur-Sierre course; Mike Souchak for second 9, first round of 1955 Texas Open; Andy North (b 9 March 1950) for second 9, first round of 1975 B.C. Open at En-Joie GC, Endicott, New York, USA.

Eclectic record
The lowest recorded eclectic (from the Greek *eklektikos*=choosing) score, ie the sum of a player's all-time personal low scores for each hole, for a course of more than 6000 yd (5486 m) is 33 by the club professional Jack McKinnon on the 6538 yd (5978 m) Capilano Golf and Country Club course, Vancouver, British Columbia, Canada. This was compiled over the period 1937–64 and reads 2, 2, 2, 1, 2, 2, 2, 2, 1 (16 out) and 2, 1, 2, 2, 1, 2, 2, 2, 3 (17 in)=33. The British record is 34 by John Harrowar (Jock) Morrison (b 3 October 1929) at West Kilbride GC, Strathclyde (6348 yd (5804 m)), from 1951 to 1978. This is made up of fourteen 2s, three aces and one 3.

Most shots for one hole
A woman player in the qualifying round of the Shawnee Invitational for Ladies at Shawnee-on-Delaware, Pennsylvania, in about 1912, took 166 strokes for the short 130 yd (118 m) 16th hole. Her tee shot went into the Binniekill River and the ball floated. She put out in a boat with her exemplary, but statistically minded husband at the oars. She eventually beached the ball 1½ miles (2.4 km) downstream but was not yet out of the wood. She had to play through one on the home run. In a competition at Peace-haven, Sussex, England in 1890, A J Lewis had 156 putts on one green without holing out.

Rounds fastest *Individual*
With such variations in lengths of courses, speed records, even for rounds under par, are of little comparative value. Bob Williams at Eugene, Oregon, completed 18 holes (6010 yd (5495 m)) in 27 min 48·2 sec in 1971 but this test permitted the striking of the ball while still moving. The record for a still ball is 30 min 10 sec by Dick Kimbrough (b 1931) (USA) at North Platte CC, Nebraska (6068 yd (5548 m)) on 8 August 1972, using only a 3 iron.

Rounds fastest *Team*
Forty-three players representing Borger High School, Texas, completed the 18-hole – 6109 yd

(5586 m) Huber Golf Course in 10 min 11.4 sec on 11 June 1976.

Rounds slowest
The slowest strokeplay tournament round was one of 6 hours 45 min taken by South Africa in the first round of the 1972 World Cup at the Royal Melbourne GC, Australia. This was a four-ball medal round, everything holed out.

Most rounds
The greatest number of rounds played on foot in 24 hours is 22 rounds and 5 holes (401 holes) by Ian Colston, 35, a top long-distance runner, at Bendigo GC Victoria (6061 yd (5542 m)) on 27–28 November 1971. The most holes played on foot in a week (168 hr) is 1102 by David Shepardson (USA) 17, at Maple Grove GC, Wisconsin in August 1976.

Most peripatetic golfer
George S Salter, of Carmel, California, has played in 116 different 'countries' round the world from 1964 to 1977.

Throwing the golf ball
The lowest recorded score for throwing a golf ball round 18 holes (over 6000 yd (5500 m)) is 82 by Joe Flynn, 21, at the 6228 yd (5694 m) Port Royal Course, Bermuda, on 27 March 1975.

Most club championships
D H R (Doug) Adams (b 16 October 1916) has won 29 club championships at the Port Pirie GC, South Australia, from 1939 to 1968, including 26 consecutively. The British record for amateur club championships is 20 consecutive wins (1937–39 and 1946–62) by Ronald Warner Hardy Taylor (1912–74) at the Dyke Golf Club, Brighton, East Sussex, who retired unbeaten in July 1963, and by Edward Christopher Chapman (b 9 April, 1909), who won the Tunbridge Wells GC Scratch Championship for 20 consecutive years from 1951 to 1971.

Largest tournament
The annual Ford Amateur Golf Tournament in Great Britain attracted a record 100 030 competitors in 1978.

Richest prizes
The greatest first-place prize-money was $100 000 (total purse $500 000) in the World Open played at Pinehurst, North Carolina, over 144 holes on 8–17 November 1973 won by Miller Barber (b 31 March 1931), of Texas. The World Series of Golf also carries a prize of $100 000. The highest British prize was £25 000 in the John Player Golf Classic at Hollinwell, Nottinghamshire on 3–6 September 1970 won by Christy O'Connor, Sr.

Biggest winning margin

The greatest margin of victory in a major tournament is 17 strokes by Randall Colin Vines (b 22 June 1945) of Australia, in the Tasmanian Open with 274 in 1968.

This was equalled by Bernhard Langer (West Germany) in winning the Cacharel World Under-25 tournament at Nîmes, France on 30 September 1979. His winning score was 274 (73, 67, 67, 67).

Shooting your age

In the Quad Cities Open played in July 1979 at the Oakwood CC, Coal Valley, Illinois, Sam Snead became the first player in the history of the USPGA tour to shoot his age. He equalled his age with a round of 67 then and beat it with a 66.

Previously, in a less important professional competition Sam Snead (USA) scored 64 at Onion Creek GC (6585 yd (6021 m), par 70), Austin, Texas, in April 1978 when one month short of his 66th birthday.

The oldest player to score under his age is C Arthur Thompson (1869–1975) of Victoria, British Columbia, Canada, who scored 103 on the Uplands course of 6215 yd (5682 m) aged 103 in 1973. The youngest player to score his age is Robert Leroy Klingaman (b 22 October 1914) who shot a 58 when aged 58 on the 5654 yd (5170 m) course at the Caledonia GC, Fayetteville, Pennsylvania, on 31 August 1973. Bob Hamilton shot 59, aged 59, on the 6233 yd (5699 m) Blue course, Hamilton GC, Evansville, Indiana, on 3 June 1975.

FACTS AND FEATS

The oldest club match in the world is that between Oxford University and Cambridge University. It was first played on 6 March 1878 on Wimbledon Common in London. Apart from the War Years, it has been played every year since.

1979 was the first year since he turned professional that Jack Nicklaus failed to win a tournament.

In the 1980 Memorial tournament at Muirfield Village, Ohio, George Burns had a third round of 74 which included a 10 at the par 5 7th hole.

In the final of the Suntory World matchplay championship at Wentworth in 1979, Bill Rogers beat Isao Aoki on the 36th green in a match in which neither player was ever more than 1 up.

In that same championship, Aoki holed in one on the 2nd in his match with David Graham thereby winning the apartment at Gleneagles which Bovis, the builders, offered as a prize for such an event.

In the Halford Hewitt competition at Deal in 1979, Ian Pilcher and Alan Scott-Miller, representing Hurstpierpoint, won their match against St Bees at the 19th hole without a single hole being halved.

Jack Nicklaus and Isao Aoki were paired in all four rounds of the 1980 US Open. They finished first and second. In the same championship, Severiano Ballesteros, US Masters champion, was disqualified for being late on the tee in the second round.

In the 1978 US Open championship at Cherry Hills, Robert Impaglia received a 2-stroke penalty for slow play.

Neil Coles is the first golfer to have won more than £200 000 on the British and European circuit.

In the final of the 1968 English Amateur championship at Ganton, Michael Bonallack holed the course in 61 during the first 18 holes. His figures were—Out: 3, 3, 3, 4, 3, 4, 4, 4, 4 = 32. In: 2, 3, 3, 3, 4, 4, 3, 3, 4 = 29. He went into lunch 11 up.

Jack Nicklaus won the 1978 Jackie Gleason Inverary Classic, his 64th victory on the US tour, by finishing with 5 birdies.

Sandy Lyle, winner of the Harry Vardon Trophy in 1979, won his first important professional victory in the 1978 Nigerian Open.

Lyle's total for the first 36 holes was 134 (61, 63) which is the lowest by any British professional.

In a Pro-Am prior to the 1973 Nigerian Open, David Jagger went round in 59.

Harry Weetman, the home professional, scored 58 in a round at Croham Hurst on 30 January 1956. The course measured 6171 yd (5643 m).

The 1938 British Open championship was scheduled for the Royal Cinque Ports GC, Deal. However, the sea invaded the course the previous winter (as it has done three times since) and the championship was transferred to neighbouring Royal St George's, Sandwich.

In 1957, it was transferred from Muirfield to St Andrews owing to a petrol shortage.

Gary Player's first professional victory was the 1955 Egyptian matchplay championship at the Gezira CC, Cairo. He beat Harold Henning in the final.

The first hole in one to be caught by the

Above: Arnold Palmer and Bob Hope pictured during the filming of *Call me Bwana* with the then Honorary Secretary of Denham Golf Club, F S Harrison (centre)

Below: Donald Steel, Pat Ward-Thomas, Bing Crosby and Bill Snideman photographed on the first tee at Cypress Point, California before the start of an eventful afternoon's golf in 1971

Top: Lee Kuan Yew, Prime Minister of Singapore, a keen golfer (High Commission for the Republic of Singapore)
Right: John Mahaffey, US PGA champion 1978 (Phil Sheldon)
Below: View of part of the Duchess course at Woburn taken about one month after seeding, 1979 (See page 213)

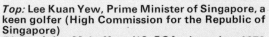

camera took place at Deal in the 1930s. Rather by accident, Lionel Munn, runner-up in the 1937 British Amateur championship was persuaded to pose for a picture taken at impact. As he was not playing a round, he borrowed a club from I V H Campbell and a ball from R H de Montmorency and, with his exhibition stroke holed in one at the 14th (199 yd (182 m)). The picture hangs in the Royal Cinque Ports GC clubhouse.

King Hassan II of Morocco has been a strong advocate of golf in his country. Helped by the need to attract tourists, Morocco now has a dozen courses. The best is Royal Rabat, completed in 1971 and designed by Robert Trent Jones to be 'fit for a king'. It is over 7400 yd (6767 m) long and is the scene of the annual Grand Prix International du Maroc.

Golf on Ascension Island in the South Pacific presents problems. At the One Boat GC, the terrain consists of extinct volcanoes, there is no grass and other hazards include wild goats.

In its earlier days, the Royal Hong Kong GC had its own Pullman Car in which breakfast was served to members travelling from the city. After breakfast, it was unhitched from the 'Taipo Belle' and members were run up to the club in rickshaws.

At the Dutch Open championship at Noordvijk in 1978, the European Tournament Players' Division decided that, owing to a dispute, none of its members should play in the championship. The strike took place but differences were resolved and a 54-hole event began a day late.

In his record-breaking round of 63 in the British Open at Turnberry on 7 July 1977 Mark Hayes's only 5 came at the 18th. He hit a 4 wood off the tee into a bunker and finally holed from 6 ft (1·8 m). His figures were—Out: 4, 3, 3, 3, 4, 3, 4, 4, 4=32. In: 4, 2, 3, 4, 4, 3, 3, 3, 5=31.

Pine Valley at Clementon, New Jersey, is renowned for the high scoring which takes place there. One exception was J Wood Platt, who started one round 3, 2, 1, 3; the 4th green is beside the clubhouse, he retired inside and never completed the round.

Miss Sue Prell of Chatswood GC, Australia, holed in one in a competition at the 13th (133yd (122 m)) and 14th (183 yd (167 m)). This is believed to be the first occasion on which a woman has achieved successive holes in one. The feat took place on 29 May 1977.

Mrs Paddy Martin had a hole in one in successive rounds on the 3rd hole (125 yd (114 m)) on the Rickmansworth Municipal course adjoining Moor Park in Hertfordshire. On

Good Friday and Easter Saturday 1960, she performed the feat using the same ball and club; and she repeated it on Easter Monday, again with the same ball and club.

In a four ball at Cypress Point, California in October 1971 involving Bing Crosby, Pat Ward-Thomas, Bill Snideman and Donald Steel, Steel holed a 3 wood for a double eagle at the par-5 5th; and at the 7th, Snideman holed in one (160 yd (146 m)).

Lew Worsham finished the Tam O'Shanter World championship at Chicago in dramatic fashion in 1953. He holed a wedge shot of some 135 yd (123 m) on the final hole to win by 1 stroke. The first prize was $25 000, then a fantastic sum.

In the President's Putter at Rye in 1937, Pat White finished his match with Leonard Crawley by holing in one at the 17th for a 2 and 1 victory. It is one of the few occasions that a hole in one finished an important match.

Harold Hilton, the only British golfer to win the British and American Amateur championships was the first editor of the magazine, *Golf Monthly*.

Prior to 1927, Bombay had three courses, one of them being 9 holes on a recreation ground where only morning play was permitted. They had canvas bunkers which were put out every morning and brought in at noon.

During the 1940s Byron Nelson played 113 consecutive events on the US tour without missing a cut. Jack Nicklaus played 105 events from November 1970 to September 1976, also without missing a cut.

In the 1957 Masters at Augusta, Nelson put his tee shot into the water on the 16th hole. Playing a fine 7-iron shot with his second ball, he hit the flagpole solidly about a foot above the cup and bounced back into the water.

In an earlier Masters at Augusta, Count John de Bendern, formerly John de Forest, British Amateur champion in 1932, found his ball on the bank of the brook on the 13th hole. Deciding the ball was playable, he took off his left shoe and sock and rolled his trouser above the knee. He then planted the bare foot on the bank and put his well-shod right foot into the water. The spectators no doubt found the Count's mistake more amusing than he did.

Harton S Semple, President of the United States Golf Association 1974–75, is the father of Carol Semple, former winner of the United States and British Women's Amateur championships. When she won the American title at the Montclair GC, New Jersey in 1973, she received the trophy from her father, then a Vice-President. The President, Lynford Lardner stepped aside in order that he could do this.

Frank (Sandy) D Tatum, Jr, President of the United States Golf Association in 1978–79, was National Collegiate champion in 1942. He also played for Oxford University in 1948 and 1949. He was a Rhodes Scholar.

John K Mahaffey, Jr, member of the USGA Executive Committee, is the father of John Mahaffey, well-known American professional and the 1978 USPGA champion.

When he died in 1973, aged 86, Henry Craske had served the Sheringham GC, Norfolk for 70 years. He started by caddying as a boy, helped his uncle, who was Secretary, because he had perfect handwriting; and was himself appointed Assistant Secretary in 1905. He became full Secretary in 1919 and held the post until his death.

Almost as long serving was Sheringham's professional, Ernest Riseboro. He held the post for 51 years until retiring in 1958.

Since 1892, Royal Ashdown Forest GC in Sussex, England, has had only two professionals, Jack Rowe and the present holder of the post, Hector Padgham. Padgham was first cousin of Alf Padgham, British Open champion in 1936 who died in 1966.

Orville Moody's only professional tournament victory in America has been the US Open championship of 1969.

In February 1914 when 11 holes had been completed at Pine Valley GC, Clementon, New Jersey, it was estimated that 22 000 tree-stumps had been removed. The holes were the first nine, the 10th and 18th. After that, it is said that George Crump, the architect, and his friends, stopped counting.

In the creation of the Duke's and Duchess courses at Woburn, Bedfordshire, it is estimated that 9000 mature trees were removed. No new courses in Britain have ever involved such a huge clearance operation. The Duke's was opened for play in 1976 and the Duchess in 1979.

When Jerilyn Britz won the 1979 US Women's Open championship at Brooklawn CC, Connecticut, it was her first victory in her five and a half years as a professional.

In 1849, Allan Robertson and Old Tom Morris of St Andrews beat the Dunn brothers of Musselburgh in a match for a stake of £400. The Dunns won the first leg on their own ground at Musselburgh by 13 and 12. Robertson and Morris levelled at St Andrews and won the third leg at North Berwick despite being 4 down with 8 holes to play.

Gary Player has competed in all but one of the World matchplay championships at Wentworth sponsored variously by Piccadilly, Penfold and Suntory. From 1964 to 1979, the only year in which he was absent from the select field was 1975.

He holds the record of five victories. In addition, he has three times defeated Tony Jacklin and twice defeated Peter Thomson, Jack Nicklaus, Arnold Palmer, Bob Charles and Neil Coles. One of his most outstanding successes was victory over Tony Lema in the semi-final of 1965 at the 37th hole having been 7 down on the 20th tee. The only golfer to have beaten him more than once is Hale Irwin. He lost to Irwin in the final of 1974 by 2 and 1 and in the semi-final the following year by 2 holes.

Baltusrol GC in Springfield, New Jersey is unique in that its two courses, the Upper and the Lower, have both been used for US Open championships. The Upper was used for the 1936 championship won by Tony Manero with a record score at that time (282) and the Lower used in 1954 and 1967 when Ed Furgol and Jack Nicklaus were champions. Nicklaus's score of 275 remains the lowest in the history of the event. The Opens of 1903 and 1915 were held at Baltusrol on a course that no longer exists.

In the 1972 US Women's Open, Shirley Englehorn, winner of the Ben Hogan Award in 1967, led after the first round with 72 and held her lead with a 75 for a total of 147 the following day. She had not played tournament golf for over a year following an operation to fuse ankle bones and had not walked 18 holes until the week before the championship.

On 29 November 1974, Gary Player had a second round of 59 in the Brazilian Open at Gavea Golf and Country Club, Rio de Janeiro. Out: 3, 4, 3, 3, 4, 2, 3, 3, 4 = 29. In: 2, 4, 3, 4, 4, 4, 2, 4, 3 = 30.

On 19 and 20 June 1968, the French Women's team defeated the United States Curtis Cup team in a match at Saint-Cloud GC in Paris. They led 5½–3½ after the first day and won the second day's play 5–4.

In the workshop at his home in Pennsylvania, Arnold Palmer has a collection of more than 4000 golf clubs. He has always been an inveterate tinkerer with his clubs, altering the lie and the loft and the weight even during a tournament. 'Some men go out in a fishing boat to find a place where they can get away from whatever is bothering them. I find it in my workshop.'

The best fastest round of golf on a regulation

A man who found golf easier on one leg than two. Trick shot specialist, Paul Hahn (Action Photos)

par-72 course was a 73 in 32 min and 12 sec by Jerry Volpe, professional at Crystal Lago CC, Pompano Beach, Florida on 30 May 1973.

Driven in what the Americans call a 'gas greens cart', he carried only seven clubs.

In an effort to raise money for the Muscular Dystrophy Association in 1975, ten golfers played golf in seven States in America in one day. The States they visited were Texas, New Mexico, Colorado, Utah, Arizona, California and Nevada; and the cities, El Paso, Albuquerque, Cortez, Montecello, Prescott, Needles and Las Vegas. They covered 1706 miles (2746 km) and raised $7500.

In June 1974, Joseph Johnson, Jr, played 423 holes over the Walhalla CC, Rexford, New York in a 24-hour period. He played from 6 am to 6 pm on 28 June and for the same period on 29 June. Joe was 16 years old at the time.

On 16 April 1972, David Ragaini holed in one at the 13th hole (207 yd (189 m)) of the Wykagyl CC, New Rochelle, New York from a kneeling position.

In 1954, Arnold Palmer succeeded Gene Littler as US Amateur champion. In 1961, it was Littler who succeeded Palmer as US Open champion.

On the first occasion that Francis Ouimet played golf at Sunningdale, he took 9 at the 1st hole.

Johnny Laidlay, British Amateur champion in 1889 and 1891, was taught by Bob Ferguson, British Open champion from 1880 to 1882. Ferguson was one of the Musselburgh professionals and Laidlay a boy at Loretto which was just beside the links. As golf was not part of the curriculum in those days, Laidlay and his friends would arrange to meet Ferguson on moonlit nights, having scrambled over the school wall.

Dr W G Grace, one of the greatest names in cricket, was an honorary member of Walton Heath GC in Surrey. In 1904 when Walton Heath was founded, Grace's first-class cricketing days were over but he had great enthusiasm for golf, James Braid making him a special club for the heather which Grace called his 'cleaver'.

Larry Nelson, who won all five of his matches in the 1979 Ryder Cup match and won his first PGA tournament the same year aged 32, did not take up golf until he was 21.

In the 1979 Carrolls Irish Open championship, Mark James returned a fourth round of 65 at Portmarnock. A fortnight later, he had a 64 at Turnberry in the third round of the European Open.

Jimmy Sheridan served Sunningdale Golf

Toots and Henry Cotton (Action Photos)

Club as caddie master for 56 years. He was made an honorary member in 1955, but he always maintained he was taken on for a trial period in 1911 and never confirmed in his post. He was known to kings, princes, great men of all walks of life and nearly all the famous golfers for half a century.

Mark McCumber won the 1979 Doral Open having failed to get his PGA player's card until his sixth attempt.

Both the 1978 and 1979 Greater Milwaukee Opens were won by black golfers, Lee Elder and Calvin Peete. On both occasions, Lee Trevino finished second.

Gertrude Lawrence, the actress, is thought to have holed in one with the first shot of the first round of golf she ever played.

Mrs Paul Dye who played for America in the 1970 Curtis Cup match is the wife of Pete Dye, one of the best-known American golf-course architects.

Mrs Henry Cotton as Madame de Moss won the 1937 Austrian Women's championship.

Seven hundred and fifty composite tickets for the 1980 British Open championship were all sold by the end of October 1979.

In the 1979 World Cup at Glyfada, Athens, the Fijian professional, Bose Lutunatabua had a second round of 92 and a fourth round of 71. Conditions were good on all four days.

After Robert Trent Jones, the well-known golf-course architect, had reshaped the par-3 4th hole at Baltusrol, New Jersey, scene of several US Open championships, there were comments that it was too difficult. The hole is over water and a new back tee was positioned.

Three officials of the club were playing one day with Jones; they all hit good tee shots but Jones went one better; he holed in one. At his best, Jones was a scratch golfer.

In his book, *The Golfer's Companion*, published by Dent in 1937, Peter Lawless mentions golf courses in Yugoslavia, at Agram, Belgrade and Zagreb; at Katowice and Warsaw in Poland; at Hankow, Hungjao and Shanghai in China and at Petrograd and Moscow in Russia. Nowadays, there is only one course in Yugo-

slavia and the start of one in Russia.

In his first professional tournament, the 1962 Los Angeles Open (5–8 January), Jack Nicklaus won $33·33. In the next 15 years, he won in excess of $3 million on the US tour.

Royal Troon, El Prat in Barcelona and Glyfada in Athens are all championship golf courses situated on the edge of international airports.

Lee Kuan Yew, Prime Minister of Singapore, is an ardent golfer.

Joe Kirkwood, the trick-shot specialist, once holed in one off the face of a watch at Cedar Rapids, Iowa, USA.

ST. ANDREWS AND CROWD PROBLEM

"Gate" Innovation Puts Course On Trial

TO-MORROW begins the historic and fateful experiment for St. Andrews — the home of golf. The gate-money innovation and the elaborate scheme of crowd-control which has been hammered out by months of thought and preparation will be put to their big test.

This British Open Championship is, I am certain, the cross roads for the Old Course big-golf connection.

By the operation of the control machinery the future of the Old Course will stand or fall, and though the Championship Committee have a belief in their plans, it is not shared by many who have had another close-up of the terrain upon which one of the greatest international struggles ever seen for the British title is about to take place.

It is felt that either the public will not pay for the restricted rights their gate money will give them, or they will pay and become absolutely unmanageable, especially in the later days of this week when the championship passes into its more hectic phases.

Times have swung over with a vengeance, and I am certain that the spectators this week will see a great deal less for their half-crowns than they used to see for nothing.

Extract from a newspaper article of 1933. Judging from the ticket sales for 1980 their fears were premature (See page 215) John Frost, Historical Newspaper Service

Since 1898 (apart from the War Years), the Country Club, Brookline, Boston has had an annual match with Royal Montreal, Canada. It is the oldest continuous match between clubs from different countries.

In a match in the 1978 Club championship at the Lincoln GC, Torksey, Harry Dunderdale had a run of 5, 4, 3, 2, 1. He had pars at the 504 yd (460 m) 3rd and 357 yd (326 m) 4th; birdies at the 285 yd (260 m) 5th and 144 yd (132 m) 6th; and a 1 at the 294 yd (269 m) 7th.

Lang Martin, 16, balanced six golf balls vertically without adhesive at Charlotte, North Carolina, on 10 July 1977.

After his victory in the British Open at Lytham in 1979, Severiano Ballesteros had a 110 gallon (500 l) cask of sherry dedicated to him by the city of Jerez. During a subsequent visit to the city, he was entertained to a week-long celebration of banquets and Flamenco fiestas as a guest of the Sherry Barons. Ballesteros's cask rests alongside those dedicated to Napoleon, Churchill and the Beatles.

Big victories
In the 1921 final of the Canadian Ladies' championship at Rivermead, Ottawa, Cecil Leitch defeated Mollie McBride by 17 and 15. Miss Leitch lost only 1 hole, the 9th. She was 14 up after 18 holes. Of the holes played, she won 18, lost 1 and halved 2. The Governor was coming to watch after lunch but though the match was over after 3 holes in the afternoon, Cecil Leitch was asked to continue playing.

The largest victory in a European championship was by Mlle Thion de la Chaume who beat Mrs Alex Johnston of England by 15 and 14 in the final of the French Ladies' Open championship at Le Touquet in 1927.

Outstanding records in important events
Michael Bonallack won the English Amateur championship a record five times (1962-63-65-67-68). He is also the only player to have won in succession twice. His four victories (one a joint victory) in the English Amateur strokeplay championship is another record.

The record in the Scottish Amateur championship is held by Ronnie Shade who won five years in a row (1963–67). When he was beaten in the fourth round in 1968, his winning sequence was 44 matches.

Joyce Wethered (Lady Heathcoat-Amory) won the English Ladies' championship five years in a row (1920–24).

In a space of four weeks in 1971, Lee Trevino won the United States, Canadian and British Open championships.

Old winners
Jack Cannon is the oldest winner of the Scottish Amateur championship (1969). He was 53 at the time.

Terry Shingler is the oldest winner of the English Amateur championship (1977). He was 41 years 11½ months. Gerald Micklem was just three months younger when winning in 1953.

Young winners
Sandy Lyle is the youngest winner of the English Open Amateur strokeplay championship (1975). He was 17 years 3 months.

Nick Faldo is the youngest winner of the English Amateur championship (1975). He was 18 years and 8 days.

Paul Downes was 18 years 10 months when he won the English Amateur championship (1978).

The finalists in 1978, Downes and Paul Hoad had a combined age of only 38.

Sandy Stephen is the youngest winner of the Scottish Amateur championship (1971). He was 17 years 6 months.

Jimmy Buckley is the youngest winner of the Welsh Amateur championship (1968). He was 17 years old.

May Hezlet won the Irish Women's championship on her 17th birthday in 1899.

Nancy Jupp was 13 years old when she won the British Girls' championship at Stoke Poges in 1934.

Mark Mouland was 15 years 4 months when he won the British Boys' championship at Sunningdale in 1976.

Elsie Kyle won the Scottish Women's championship in 1909, aged 18.

Pam Barton won the 1934 French Ladies' championship at the age of 17 and two years later won the British and American Women's championships at 19.

Jane Connachan won the Scottish Girls' Open strokeplay championship (age limit 21) when 14.

David Robertson is the youngest winner of the British Youths' championship (1974)—age limit under 22. He was 17 years and 7 weeks.

Donna Thomson won the Cumberland and Westmorland Women's county championship aged 13 in 1979.

Jimmy Buckley was 16 when representing Wales in the European team championship in 1967.

David Robertson is the youngest player to play for Scotland. He was 16 in 1973.

Paul Downes is the youngest player to play for England. He, too, was 16 in 1976.

HOLES IN ONE

To non-golfers, a hole in one is the ultimate achievement. To golfers, however, it is a delicious fluke that comes out of the blue, is frequently costly, bears no relation to players' ability and can be the result of a far from perfect stroke.

Holes in one come in all shapes, sizes and circumstances. They rarely make the difference between winning and losing and invariably form part of an otherwise undistinguished round. However, with the increase of television and the growth of professional golf, there have been some spectacular examples in recent times.

Gene Sarazen, aged 71, became the oldest competitor in a major championship to hole in one when he performed the feat at the 8th at Royal Troon in the British Open of 1973. Isao Aoki won a flat and its furnishings valued at £55 000 for holing in one on the 2nd at Wentworth during the Suntory world matchplay championship in 1979, and Tony Jacklin had a one in the final round of the Dunlop

Harold Henning with his cheque for £10 000 for holing in one, 1963 (Action Photos)

Masters in 1967. It came at the 16th at Royal St George's, Sandwich and put his victory beyond doubt.

Although Harold Henning's famous hole in one on the 18th at Moor Park (High) in 1963 earned him rather less than Aoki, £10 000 was an enormous sum at that time even if he had an arrangement with two fellow South Africans that summer that they pool all their winnings. In that particular tournament, the Esso Round Robin, the prize was on offer whether the 18-hole matches were finished or not. Both Henning's matches ended on the 17th (they played two matches at once) and he then holed his tee shot with an 8 iron.

Jacklin's was the first hole in one in Britain to be caught by the television cameras and was one of the very few achieved by a winner in the act of winning. Sarazen's at Troon was his sixth and, as he said at the time, 'the only one on film, Thank God. I can show it to Hagen, Armour and Jones when I go up there. I'll take the film with me.'

If Jacklin put his hole in one to good use, the unluckiest golfer in this respect must be Eric Fiddian. In the 36-hole final of the Irish Open Amateur championship at Royal County Down in 1933, he holed in one at the 7th (128 yd (117 m)) in the morning and at the 14th (205 yd (187 m)) in the afternoon; yet still lost the match to Jack McLean by 3 and 2.

Nowadays, it is perfectly usual for a Pro-Am or sponsored professional tournament to run a hole-in-one award varying from a motor car to an aeroplane, a house to a holiday. They are offered as an effective advertising platform and can be won by anybody.

It is remarkable that Harry Vardon, winner of the British Open more times than anyone else, had only 1 in his lifetime, whereas J H Taylor and James Braid, his two great contemporaries, had 10 and 16 respectively. What is more, Vardon's occurred during a period of convalescence on the 4th hole at Mundesley, a small 9-hole course in Norfolk.

This theme of contrast, however, can be developed further to include other contemporaries. For example, Ben Hogan has had 4, Sam Snead 24; Lee Trevino 1, Gary Player 9; Deane Beman 1, Jack Nicklaus 10; Ronnie White 1, Joe Carr 15; Brian Barnes 2, Bernard Gallacher 11; Walter Hagen 1, Gene Sarazen 7; and Percy Alliss 1, Henry Cotton 18. Peter Alliss admits that his father was reticent about counting his only hole in one as he is not sure that the ball fell in when the flagpole was removed.

Catherine Lacoste and Severiano Ballesteros

are among those still waiting for their first hole in one, but the accompanying list does show that the ladies have not been as successful as the men over all.

Joyce Wethered, whom many regard as the best lady golfer of all time, has had only 2 (the 10th at Worplesdon and the 17th at Swinley Forest). Marley Spearman Harris and Belle Robertson have had none and Angela Bonallack, Enid Wilson, Betsy Rawls, Patty Berg and Mary McKenna only 1 each. Glenna Collett Vare, the great American champion, has had 6, the leading lady being the late Frances Smith, one of whose 8 holes in one took place at the 5th in the final of the English championship at Woodhall Spa in 1954.

All these figures prove little, but there is still a fascination and amusement about them; and no small element of wonder, for instance, that Art Wall holds the world record with as many as 41. In broad terms, they represent one for every year of a professional career in which his only major championship victory was the 1959 Masters.

In Britain, Charles T Le Chevalier and Len Job, both club professionals, had 31 and 29 in their lifetimes but, if there is surprise but no doubt that Art Wall has had 41, there is no less surprise that Bobby Jones's tally was 2 and Ben Hogan's to date is just 4.

By popular agreement, Hogan hit more shots close to the flag for a period of time than anyone, with the possible exception of Sam Snead; it would be reasonable to suppose, therefore, that rather more than four tee shots at short holes would have gone in since the figures published are not confined to competition.

The four, however, are worth recording in detail; the 8th at the Z Boaz Municipal course in Fort Worth, Texas; the 10th at Brackenridge Park during the Texas Open—a course where many records fell; the 12th at Shady Oaks, Forth Worth; and the 4th during the Spokane Open, Washington, the only one achieved outside Texas, although Hogan cannot recall the number of the hole.

Moving away from the heat of major competition, many hole-in-one records belong to less exalted club golfers who have less opportunity to play particularly on other courses. Nevertheless, there are club golfers with rare claims to make. Dr Joseph O Boydstone of California has had 11 holes in one in one calendar year (1962) and Joseph Vitullo of Hubbard GC, Ohio, has holed the 16th hole in 1 stroke ten times. His tenth was on 26 June 1967, aged 63.

John Hudson who had two holes in one at successive holes in a professional tournament, the Martini Tournament, Royal Norwich 1971 (Action Photos)

There are over a dozen cases of golfers halving holes in one; several examples of golfers, apart from Eric Fiddian, holing in one twice in a day; and of achieving the feat with successive strokes.

The only time it has happened in full professional competition was on 11 June in the 1971 Martini tournament at Royal Norwich, Norfolk, England. The hero was John Hudson, then a 25-year-old attached to the Hendon Club in London. He holed out with a 4 iron at the 195 yd (178 m) 11th and, after a wait of 20 minutes, holed with a driver, at the downhill par-4 12th (311 yd (284 m)). Even so, his score for the round was a modest 72.

The other remarkable tale of holes in one in competition was set at Hunstanton, Norfolk in 1974. Bob Taylor, a member of the Leicestershire county team, holed in one at the 16th (188 yd (172 m)) on three successive days. The first was in practice on Friday with a 1 iron and the other two in earnest with a 6 iron on Saturday and Sunday. It is said that after his second, a member of the Leicestershire party offered a million to one in pennies against him doing a third the following day. Taylor told him he would stake ten pence, not one.

In a more leisurely atmosphere, Paddy Martin holed in one at the 3rd at Rickmansworth Municipal, next door to Moor Park, in successive rounds using the same club and the same ball each time. She performed the feat on Good Friday, Easter Saturday and Easter Monday, 1960.

N L Manley is the only person to have holed in one at successive par 4s, the 7th (330 yd (302 m)) and the 8th (290 yd (261 m)) at Del Valle Country Club, California in September 1964. They helped him to a new course record of 61 (par 71).

On 9 February 1975 at Ladhope, Galashiels, Scotland, Billy Taylor, 26 at the time, started his round in a four ball with holes in one at the 1st (296 yd (270 m)) and the 2nd (244 yd (223 m)). It must have been hard to live up to that standard for the rest of the round but, for all golfers' weird and wonderful achievements, there never will be the perfect round.

Even the dreams of Ben Hogan, who sought perfection with an intensity unrivalled by anyone, were foiled. He dreamt once that he had played a round with 17 ones and a two; and 'when I woke up', he said, 'I was mad'.

On Sunday morning, 28 October 1979, four players holed in one during the Monthly Medal at Daventry and District GC, Northamptonshire. Barry Highfield, Peter Grant and Roger Pickerin did so at the 2nd hole (100 yd (91 m)) and Harold Gorle at the 4th (170 yd (155 m)). It is a 9-hole course, the 2nd being uphill with the bottom of the flag out of sight from the tee. Only 35 players took part in the medal. It is the first time that 4 holes in one have been achieved at one club on the same day.

By coincidence Mrs Joyce Parker, the lady captain at Daventry, had a hole in one while playing away on the same day.

Jan Brostrom, a Swedish golfer who took up the game in 1977 at the age of 15, had 6 holes in one in the next 18 months. In the space of 370 days, he had 2 in 1978 and 4 in 1979. Nobody new to the game has had as many in such a short time, the feat being more remarkable in view of the fact that golf in Sweden is possible for only about half the year.

MILESTONES

1868 The earliest recorded hole in one was achieved in the 1868 Open championship by Young Tom Morris, the first great record-maker. He performed the feat at Prestwick's 8th hole.

1889 In the Open championship at Royal Musselburgh, an amateur, partnering Andrew Kirkaldy, holed the last hole in one. Remarkably, it was almost dark when he played the stroke, the green being scarcely discernible from the tee.

1906 R Johnston of North Berwick holed in one at the 14th at Muirfield during the Open championship using the adjustable-headed club which he used for every shot.

1930 Maurice McCarthy won the last place in a play-off for the United States Amateur championship at Merion having holed in one at the 17th. Subsequently in Bobby Jones's Grand Slam championship, McCarthy played the longest 18-hole match in the history of the championship. He defeated George von Elm at the 28th having beaten Watts Gunn at the 19th and won his qualifying play-off. His day's golf thus consisted of 63 holes, a world record in a major championship.

1933 In the 36-hole final of the Irish Open Amateur championship, Eric Fiddian holed in one both during the morning and afternoon round—and still lost. In the morning, he holed in one at the 7th and in the afternoon at the 14th. His opponent was the redoubtable Jack McLean who won 3 and 2.

1934 In the New Zealand Open championship at Wawganui, there were 3 holes in one. On the first day L B Gibson holed the 12th (135 yd (123 m)); on the second day, I Orr holed the 10th (176 yd (160 m)) and on the fourth day F Fryer also holed the 10th.

First hole in one at the US Masters by Ross Somerville, the 16th.

1948 Charles H. Ward became the first person to hole in one twice in the British Open. He had holed the 8th (163 yd (149 m)) at St Andrews in 1946 and repeated the feat at the 13th (153 yd (140 m)) at Muirfield.

1954 Frances Stephens holed in one during her English Ladies' championship final with Elizabeth Price, at the 5th (137 yd (125 m)) at Woodhall Spa. Miss Stephens won at the 37th hole.

1959 Patty Berg achieved the first hole in one in the US Women's Open, the 7th (170 yd (155 m)) at Churchill Valley CC, Pittsburgh.

1963 Harold Henning of South Africa won £10000 for holing in one at the 18th (156 yd (143 m)) on the High course at Moor Park near London. The prize was on offer during the Esso Golden Round Robin professional matchplay event. Even if their matches had finished, participants were still allowed to play the 18th.

1967 Tony Jacklin holed in one at the 16th (165 yd (150.8 m)) at Royal St George's, Sandwich during the last round of the Dunlop Masters. It

The key to the door: Isao Aoki receiving the key to the apartment he won for his hole in one at the 1979 Suntory matchplay championship (Peter Dazeley)

was watched by millions on television and was part of a round of 64. One of the rare occasions that a winner holed in one during a final round.

1971 John Hudson, the 25-year-old playing professional at Hendon, London had successive holes in one in the Martini professional tournament, a major British event. His miracle occurred at the 11th (195 yd (178 m)) and 12th (311 yd (284 m)) at Royal Norwich.

Lionel Platts holed in one during the Open championship at Royal Birkdale. He did so at the 4th (212 yd (194 m)), the first televised hole in one in the British Open.

1973 Peter Butler achieved the first hole in one in the Ryder Cup at the 16th (188 yd (172 m)) at Muirfield.

1974 Four holes in one were recorded at the Hong Kong Open.

Bob Taylor, 30, a former Leicestershire amateur champion, performed a unique feat in the Eastern Counties foursomes tournament at Hunstanton. In three consecutive rounds, the first a practice round on Friday, he holed in one at the 16th (188 yd (192 m)).

The other recorded occasion on which a hole in one was achieved at the same hole in three consecutive rounds was not in competition.

1976 Peter Dawson became the first left-handed golfer to hole in one in the British Open, the 4th (206 yd (188 m)) at Royal Birkdale.

This is an entirely random list of the number of holes in one achieved by well-known players. It refers to all holes in one, not just those in competition, and has been compiled solely for interest and amusement.

Art Wall	41	Bernard Gallacher	11
Sam Snead	24	J H Taylor	10
Sandy Herd	19	Horton Smith	10
Henry Cotton	18	Fred Daly	10
Bobby Locke	18	Guy Wolstenholme	10
James Braid	16	Jack Nicklaus	10
Joe Carr	15	Jimmy Demaret	9
Sid Scott	14	Bob Cruickshank	9
Harry Bradshaw	14	Arnold Palmer	9
Ken Bousfield	14	Ben Crenshaw	9
Arthur Lees	13	Tom Weiskopf	9
Peter Thomson	12	Gary Player	9
Roberto de Vicenzo	11	Dale Hayes	9
Dai Rees	11	Byron Nelson	8
Eric Brown	11	'Jug' McSpaden	8

Christy O'Connor	8	Pat Bradley	3
John Panton	8	Kathy Whitworth	3
Tommy Horton	8	Sandra Post	3
Tony Jacklin	8	Brian Huggett	3
Frances Smith	8	Sally Little	3
Gene Sarazen	7	Cecil Leitch	3
Michael Bonallack	7	Francis Ouimet	3
Mickey Wright	7	Cyril Tolley	3
Alan Thirlwell	7	Elizabeth Price Fisher	3
Flory van Donck	7	Harold Hilton	3
Johnny Farrell	7	Andrew Kirkaldy	3
Jean Garaialde	7	Arnaud Massy	3
Peter Alliss	7	Bill Rogers	3
Tom Watson	7	John Laidlay	2
Glenna Collett Vare	6	Hector Thomson	2
Laddie Lucas	6	Bobby Jones	2
John Jacobs	6	Joyce Wethered	2
David Thomas	6	Bill Campbell	2
Hon Michael Scott	6	Ben Sayers	2
Ted Ray	6	Lu Hsi-Chuen	2
Jane Blalock	6	Lawson Little	2
Brigitte Varangot	6	Willie Auchterlonie	2
Michael Lunt	6	Lionel Munn	2
Vicente Fernandez	6	Leonard Crawley	2
Jimmy Adams	6	Graham Marsh	2
Charlie Yates	5	Peter McEvoy	2
John Langley	5	Brian Barnes	2
Peter Oosterhuis	5	Lanny Wadkins	2
Sandra Palmer	5	Hollis Stacy	2
Gerald Micklem	5	Baldovino Dassu	2
Roger Wethered	5	Harry Vardon	1
Billy Casper	5	Lee Trevino	1
Isao Aoki	5	Walter Hagen	1
Dave Stockton	5	Jerry Pate	1
Isa Goldschmid	5	Simone Thion de la	
Antonio Garrido	5	Chaume	1
George Duncan	4	Fuzzy Zoeller	1
Ben Hogan	4	Betsy Rawls	1
David Graham	4	Patty Berg	1
Lally Sagard		Enid Wilson	1
(formerly Vicomtesse		Diana Critchley	1
de Saint-Sauveur)	4	Angela Bonallack	1
Neil Coles	4	Mary McKenna	1
Bob Charles	4	Deane Beman	1
Lu Liang Huan	4	John Ball	1
Judy Rankin	4	Ronnie White	1
Nancy Lopez	4	Percy Alliss	1
Laura Baugh	4	Amy Alcott	1
Donna Young	4	Victor Regalado	1
Jaime Gonzales	4	Tohru Nakamura	1
Ray Floyd	4	Anne Sander	1
Jumbo Ozaki	4	Catherine Lacoste	0
Hugh Baiocchi	4	Marley (Spearman)	
John Mahaffey	4	Harris	0
Hale Irwin	3	Belle Robertson	0
David Blair	3	Frank Pennink	0
Jack Newton	3	Severiano Ballesteros	0

Longest

The longest straight hole ever holed in one shot is the 10th (444 yd (406 m)) at Miracle Hills Golf Club, Omaha, Nebraska, by Robert Mitera (b 1944) on 7 October 1965. Mitera stands 5 ft 6 in (1·68 m) tall and weighs 165 lb (74·842 kg) (11 st 11 lb). He is a 2 handicap player who can normally drive 245 yd (224 m). A 50 mph (80 km/h) gust carried his shot over a 290 yd (265 m) drop-off. The longest 'dog-leg' hole achieved in one is the 480 yd (439 m) 5th at

Hope Country Club, Arkansas by L. Bruce on 15 November 1962. The feminine record is 393 yd (359 m) by Marie Robie on the 1st hole of the Furnace Brook Golf Club, Wollaston, Massachusetts, on 4 September 1949. The longest hole in one performed in the British Isles is the seventh (393 yd (359 m)) at West Lancashire Golf Club by Peter Parkinson in 1972.

In 1978 *Golf Digest* magazine recorded 28 576 'aces' which averages over 78 per day.

Consecutive

There are at least 15 cases of 'aces' being achieved in two consecutive holes of which the greatest was Norman L. Manley's unique 'double albatross' on the par-4 330 yd (301 m) 7th and par-4 290 yd (265 m) 8th holes on the Del Valle Country Club Course, Saugus, California, on 2 September 1964. The only woman to record consecutive 'aces' is Sue Prell, on the 13th and 14th holes at Chatswood Golf Club, Sydney, Australia on 29 May 1977.

There is no recorded instance of a golfer performing three consecutive holes in one. The closest to achieving it was by Dr Joseph Boydstone on the 3rd, 4th and 9th at Bakersfield G.C., California, on 10 October 1962, and by the Rev Harold Snider (b 4 July 1900) who aced the 8th, 13th and 14th holes of the par-3 Ironwood course, Arizona, on 9 June 1976.

Youngest and oldest

The youngest golfer recorded to have shot a hole-in-one was Coby Orr (5 years) of Littleton, Colorado on the 103 yd (94 m) 5th at the Riverside Golf Course, San Antonio, Texas in 1975. The oldest golfers to have performed the feat are 93-year-olds George Miller, on the 116 yd (106 m) 11th at Anaheim G.C., California on 4 December 1970 and Charles Youngman, at the Tam O'Shanter Club, Toronto in 1971.

ENTERTAINMENT

While there has only been one film which has dealt seriously with a golfing star and a golfing story, there have been a number which have either used the game as the basis of the storyline, albeit a flimsy one, or have been noted for a particular golfing scene.

The best golfing film was undoubtedly 'Follow the Sun', based on the life of Ben Hogan and starring Glenn Ford. It was released in 1951, the year Hogan successfully defended the US Open and two years after his terrible car accident. It was this recovery that gave the idea for the film.

An excellent light comedy called 'Pat and Mike' (1952) starred Katharine Hepburn and Spencer Tracy. Its many golfing sequences emanated from a story about a 'Babe' Zaharias-like woman athlete and her manager. The 'Babe' herself appeared in the film along with Patty Berg and other top women players.

One of the rather frenetic comedy films of Dean Martin and Jerry Lewis called 'The Caddie' (1953) had Martin playing on the US circuit with Lewis as his knowledgeable but accident-prone caddie. A number of notable golfers of the period played themselves in the film in which there were some quite good golfing sequences. However, some of the antics would not have done for the US tour.

W C Fields starred in a film 'The Golf Specialist' (1930) which, as its name suggests, had a definite golfing theme.

In 'Carefree' (1938), Fred Astaire included a golf-driving routine in which he danced to a number, 'Since they turned Loch Lomond into Swing'. The finale had him driving five balls in succession down the fairway in time to his routine.

Sid Field and Jerry Desmonde had a well-known stage golfing routine which was repeated in the British film, 'London Town'.

Arnold Palmer appeared with Bob Hope in 'Call me Bwana' in which Hope came across Palmer in the jungle. The film shots involving several wild animals were made at Denham Golf Club, close to Pinewood Studios and the old Denham Studios, in 1962.

One of the best golfing scenes was that in 'Goldfinger' in which James Bond had his famous match with Goldfinger, filmed at Stoke Poges GC, also close to Pinewood Studios. Its authenticity owed much to the fact that Ian Fleming was himself a keen golfer as, indeed, is Sean Connery who played Bond.

Fleming was a member of Royal St George's, Sandwich (hence the course Royal St Mark's in the book) and Connery is a member of the Royal and Ancient.

One of Bing Crosby's hits was a song entitled 'Straight down the middle'. Crosby was the first show-business personality to sponsor his own tournament on the US professional tour. It takes the form of a Pro-Am with a separate competition for the professionals going on at the same time.

In addition, there is now the Bob Hope Desert Classic, the Andy Williams San Diego Open, the Glen Campbell Los Angeles Open, the Jackie Gleason Inverrary Classic, the Sammy Davis, Jr, Greater Hartford Open and the Walt Disney World national team championship, all events on the US professional tour which illustrate the close links there are between golf and show business.

In the early twenties, Walter Hagen starred with Leo Diegel, Marge Beebe and Andy Clyde in a Hollywood production, 'Green Grass Widows', a film with plenty of golf.

In the 1930s, Henry Cotton appeared on stage at a London theatre (the Coliseum) giving a demonstration of golf including hitting soft balls into the audience. It was a very popular act.

FAMILY CONNECTIONS

FAMOUS GOLFERS WITH RELATIVES DISTINGUISHED IN OTHER SPORTS

René Lacoste, the champion French tennis-player has a wife and daughter who are champion golfers. His wife, as Simone Thion de la Chaume, became the first French woman to win the British Women's championship in 1927. In addition, she won the Open championship of France four times. She also won the French Women's Close championship six times in a row (1925–30).

Her daughter, Catherine is the only overseas golfer to win the US Women's Open (1967); she also won the US (1969) and British (1969) Women's Amateur championships, and several French titles.

Graham Marsh, winner of many professional tournaments all round the world, is the brother of Rodney, the Australian Test cricketer. Rodney has made more Test dismissals than any other Australian wicketkeeper reaching the 200 mark in the 1979/80 series against England.

John Lister, the New Zealander who won a tournament in 1976 on the US professional tour, and been a consistent player there, has a brother Tom who played rugby for the New Zealand All Blacks in 1968–71.

John Schroeder, a successful American touring professional, is the son of Ted Schroeder, the Wimbledon Lawn Tennis champion in 1949.

Frank Pennink's father Karel played soccer for Holland. Pennink, a Walker Cup player, was twice English Amateur champion.

Both the father and brother of **J Morton 'Morty' Dykes** (a Walker Cup player in 1936 and Scottish Amateur champion in 1951), played rugby football for Scotland. Morty Dykes himself was a reserve for Scotland at rugby football on 17 occasions.

Charles Dennehy, son of Virginia Dennehy, American Curtis Cup Captain in 1948, was a member of the American Olympic Equestrian team.

FAMILY ACHIEVEMENTS IN IMPORTANT COMPETITIONS

Father and Son

Willie Park, Sr (1860-63-66-75) and **Willie Park, Jr** (1889), both won the British Open championship.

The other father and son winners of the Open were **Old Tom Morris** (1861-62-64-67) and **Young Tom Morris** (1868-69-70-72)—the only occasion of son succeeding father as a major Open champion.

Percy Alliss and his son, **Peter**, both played for Great Britain in the Ryder Cup. Percy played three times and Peter eight.

Joe Carr and his son, **Roddy**, played in the Walker Cup. Joe established the record number of appearances by either side between 1947 and 1967; and Roddy was a member of only the second winning British and Irish team in 1971. Having halved his single with Bill Hyndman on the first afternoon, he won one of the crucial victories on the second day on the last green against Jim Simons.

Clayton Heafner played for the American Ryder Cup teams of 1949 and 1951; his son, **Vance**, played for the 1977 American Walker Cup team and, like his father before him, was unbeaten.

Stanley Lunt and his son, **Michael**, both won the English Amateur championship. Stanley in 1934 and Michael in 1966. In addition, Michael won the British Amateur in 1963 and was runner-up a year later. He was also runner-up to Michael Bonallack in the English final of 1962.

In 1952, the final of the Swiss Amateur championship was contested by **Antoine and André Barras**, father and son, the son winning.

Apart from the Lunts, two other fathers and sons have represented their countries in the Home Internationals: **Teddy** and **Michael Dawson** for Scotland; **James** and **Peter Flaherty** for Ireland.

Two fathers and sons have played for their countries in the same World Amateur team championship for the Eisenhower Trophy. In 1958 and 1960, **I S Malik** and **A S Malik**

played for India; and the **Visconde de Pereira Machado** and **Nuno Alberto de Brito e Cunha** for Portugal.

The most famous golfing father and son partnership in South America is **Mario and Jaimé Gonzales**. Mario, equal eleventh in the 1948 British Open, has been a regular winner of the Brazilian Open. His son, Jaimé, won the Brazilian Amateur championship four times before turning professional.

Brothers

In 1963, the brothers, **Bernard** and **Geoffrey Hunt** played for Great Britain and Ireland in the Ryder Cup in Atlanta. In 1953, they contested the final of the British Assistants' championship at Hartsbourne. Bernard won 2 and 1.

Willie and **Tony Torrance** played Walker Cup golf for Great Britain. Willie in 1922 and Tony in 1924-28-30-32 and 34.

In 1932, the brothers **Rex** and **Lister Hartley** played for great Britain in the Walker Cup match. They were paired together in the top foursome, but were beaten 7 and 6 by Jess Sweetser and George Voigt.

The brothers **Jay** and **Lionel Hebert** both played for the United States in the Ryder Cup, Lionel in 1957 and Jay in 1959 and 1961. They have also both won the USPGA championship, Lionel in 1957 and Jay in 1960.

In 1910, **Alex Smith** defeated his brother, **Macdonald**, in a play-off for the title in the US Open, which he had previously won in 1906. His victory followed that of another brother, **Willie**, in 1899.

Charles, Ernest and **Reg Whitcombe** all played in the Ryder Cup. In 1935, Charles and Ernest were paired together in the foursomes. Reg Whitcombe was British Open champion in 1938.

The seven **Turnesa** brothers (sons of the greenkeeper at Fairview CC) were equally famous. Six of them were professionals.

Joe Turnesa, runner-up to Walter Hagen (beaten 1 hole) in the USPGA championship of 1927, played in the Ryder Cup match of 1927 and 1929.

Jim Turnesa, the sixth son, won the USPGA championship in 1952 which earned him a place in the Ryder Cup of 1953; and **Willie**, the youngest, won the US Amateur championship in 1938 and again in 1948. He also won the British Amateur in 1947 and played in the Walker Cup, 1947-49-51.

Top left: Father congratulates son: Joe and Roddy Carr, Walker Cup 1971 (Action Photos)

Above: Wayne Player, giving advice to father (Action Photos)

Left: Miss Doris Park, member of one of golf's most famous families (John Frost, Historical Newspaper Service)

The Spanish professionals, **Angel** and **Sebastian Miguel** were leading players in Europe for a number of years before the European circuit was established. Both won the Spanish Open championship, Angel twice and Sebastian three times. In 1961 Angel succeeding Sebastian for the title.

In the 1958 World Cup competition in Mexico City, they were runners-up together for Spain and, additionally, in partnership with Ramón Sota, they each finished second— Sebastian in 1963 and Angel in 1965.

Harry and **Arnold Bentley** both won the English Amateur championship, the only brothers to achieve the feat. Harry won in 1936, the year in which he played in the Walker Cup at Pine Valley and halved his single, the only British success in the singles. He also played in the winning British team two years later. Arnold won the English title in 1939.

Alistair and **Walter McLeod**, and **Andrew** and **Allan Brodie** are brothers who played for Scotland in the Home International series. The McLeods played in the same team, the Brodies missed by a year.

In 1954, **Peter Toogood** won the final of the Australian Amateur championship with his brother, **John**, runner-up. Two years later, they finished first and third in the Tasmanian Open. In second place was their father Alfred.

More recently, **Severiano** and **Manuel Ballesteros** have succeeded the Miguels as the leading Spanish golfing brothers. Severiano, the best player ever to come out of Spain, has few peers and Manuel, though naturally overshadowed, is a good player in his own right. He has featured prominently in many European events. Incidentally, they are nephews of Ramón Sota.

In America, **Lanny** and **Bobby Wadkins** are the most notable golfing brothers. Lanny, a Walker and Ryder Cup player, was USPGA champion in 1977 and third in the money list; Bobby, the younger by about 20 months, has yet to win a big tournament in the States, but won the first European Open in London in October 1978.

The **Wilkes brothers, Trevor** and **Brian** of South Africa, were both successful tournament professionals in the late fifties and early sixties.

Siblings

Undoubtedly the most famous brother and sister combination were **Roger** and **Joyce Wethered** (later Lady Heathcoat-Amory). Joyce won the British Women's championship four times (1922-24-25-29) and the English five

times in a row (1920–24). Roger, British Amateur champion in 1923, tied for the British Open championship in 1921.

The Wethereds and the **Bonallacks** (**Michael** and **Sally**) were the only brothers and sisters to have played for Britain in the Walker and Curtis Cup, until the Moodys, Griff and Terri for America in 1979–80.

However, Charles Hezlet played in the Walker Cup and his sister, May, was British Women's champion on three occasions before the Curtis Cup started.

In 1906, the brothers, the **Hon Denys Scott** and the **Hon Osmund Scott** contested the final of the second Italian Open Amateur championship. Denys won 4 and 3. Their brother, the **Hon Michael Scott**, won the British Amateur of 1933, the oldest to do so, and played in the Walker Cup. Osmund was beaten in the 1905 final of the British Amateur by A G Barry.

Their sister, **Lady Margaret Scott**, won the first three British Women's championships (1893–95) and, to complete a remarkable golfing family, Osmund's son, **Kenneth Scott**, played for England in 1937 and 1938 while an undergraduate at Oxford University. Alas, he was killed in the war.

Claudine and **Patrick Cros**, brother and sister, were both champions of France in the same years, 1964 and 1965. She also won the French Women's Open on two occasions and Patrick the Men's Open, once. Claudine's older brother, **Jean Pierre Cros**, was French Close champion in 1959.

Franco Bevione and his sister, **Isa Goldschmid Bevione**, were national amateur champions of Italy; Franco 13 times (between 1946 and 1971) and Isa ten times (between 1952 and 1969). Franco was Italian Open Amateur champion three times.

Equally well known in Italy are **Baldovino Dassu** and his sister, **Federica**, lady champion of Italy in 1976. Baldovino, Professional and Amateur champion of Italy, won the Dunlop Masters in 1976.

In the United States, the best-known brother and sister in professional golf are **Raymond** and **Marlene Floyd**. Raymond, US Masters and USPGA champion, has been one of the leading players for a number of years. Marlene, though not as successful as her brother, is making her mark on the LPGA tour.

Another brother and sister combination on the PGA and LPGA tours is **Jack** and **Jane Renner**. Jack won the 1979 West Chester Classic.

Jack Graham, semi-finalist in the British Amateur championship on four occasions, was brother of **Molly Graham**, British Women's champion in 1901. Their cousin **Allan Graham** was runner-up in the British Amateur in 1921. They were all Hoylake players and Allan's son, **John**, was captain of the Royal Liverpool GC, Hoylake, in 1956.

Sisters

In 1897, **Edith Orr** defeated her sister in the final of the British Women's championship at Gullane. A third sister reached the fourth round.

It is said that when their father discovered that there had been betting on the outcome of the final involving his two daughters, he did not allow them to compete subsequently. They lived near by in North Berwick.

The other instance of sisters in a British final was in 1907 when **May Hezlet** defeated **Florence Hezlet**. They also contested the Irish finals of 1905, 1906 and 1908. May Hezlet won those also.

May is the youngest winner of the British championship. She was 16 when she won the Irish for the first time; the following week she won the British on the same course, County Down, and celebrated her 17th birthday during the week-end between the two events. In 1905 Florence, May and Violet Hezlet played first, second and third in the order for the Irish Ladies' team.

In the same year that the Hezlet sisters contested the final of the British (1907) the **Curtis** sisters, **Margaret** and **Harriot** contested the final of the US Women's Amateur. Margaret won 7 and 6, the other remarkable record being that she succeeded Harriot as champion.

Pam and **Mervyn Barton** were both English internationals. Mervyn, later Mrs Sutherland Pilch, was an England player, but Pam was the champion. She won the British and American Women's championships in the same year, 1936. Alas, she was killed on active service during World War II, aged 26.

Donna Caponi Young, twice US Women's Open champion, and one of the best players on the LPGA tour, has a sister **Janet Caponi LePera** who also competes on the LPGA tour.

Husband and wife

John Beharrell, the 1956 British Amateur champion, is married to **Veronica Anstey** who played in the 1956 Curtis Cup match.

Peter and **Pam Benka** played for Britain, Peter in the 1969 Walker Cup and Pam (formerly Pam Tredinnick) in two Curtis Cups.

Janette Robertson, a Curtis Cup player is married to **Innes Wright**, a former Scottish international, who turned professional and reached the semi-final of the matchplay championship in 1963.

John and **'Baba' Beck** were captain of the Walker Cup and Curtis Cup.

Father and daughter

One of the most famous father and daughter combinations is **André Vagliano**, a former French champion (1925) and **Lally Segard** (formerly the Vicomtesse de Saint-Sauveur). She was one of the best-known players in Europe, having also won the British Ladies' championship of 1950.

John Panton's daughter, **Cathy**, was British Women's Amateur champion in 1976. She later turned professional and headed the LPGA Order of Merit table after the first season of the women's professional tour in Britain. John Panton, one of the best-known Scottish professionals, played in the Ryder Cup and won the old *News of the World* matchplay championship in 1956 at Hoylake.

Mother and son

Diana Critchley (Fishwick), British Women's champion in 1930 and English champion in 1932, is the mother of **Bruce Critchley**, British and English international and a semi-finalist in the 1970 British Amateur championship at Royal County Down. Diana Critchley was the wife of Brigadier-General Alfred C Critchley, founder of the Greyhound Racing Association with Charles Munn. He was himself a scratch golfer.

Mother and daughter

Mme René Lacoste and **Catherine Lacoste** have both won the British Women's championship. Mme Lacoste (then Mlle Thion de la Chaume) was the first overseas player to win in 1927. Catherine was champion in 1969. Both won on Northern Irish courses—Mme Lacoste at Royal County Down, Newcastle, and Catherine at Royal Portrush.

Catherine also won the US Women's Amateur in the same year, 1969, and is the only amateur ever to have won the US Women's Open championship. She did so in 1967.

In 1962, **Jean Trainor** defeated her

daughter, Anne, by 4 and 3 in the second round of the US Women's Amateur.

Family

As a family, the achievements of the **Duncans** are unique. **John Duncan** was Welsh champion in 1905 and 1909; and runner-up in 1920. His wife was the Welsh Women's champion in 1922-27-28 and his sister, **Blanche**, was champion in 1906-07-08-09-12; she was also runner-up in 1905.

His brother, **J Hugh Duncan**, was a semi-finalist in 1908 and 1909; he just missed meeting John in the final. With Blanche winning the Ladies' championship in 1909, it was quite a year for the Duncans, but family traditions were faithfully carried on by John's sons, **Tony** and **George**.

Tony was Welsh champion in 1938-48-52-54, and runner-up in 1933. In addition, he reached the final of the British Amateur at Hoylake in 1939 and was non-playing Captain of the British Walker Cup team in 1953.

George's best year in the Welsh championship was 1956 when he lost a notable semi-final to Iestyn Tucker, but he played for Great Britain against Europe the same year and represented Wales many times.

A third brother, **John**, who was killed in the war, was a low-handicap golfer. **Derek**, son of Hugh, was equally good while **Michael Ivor Jones**, son of Blanche Duncan, won the British Seniors' championship in 1974.

In addition to **Willie Park, Jr** who won the Open championship, like his father, **Willie Park, Sr, Mungo Park**, brother of Willie, Sr, was Open champion in 1874. Although a little in the shadow of his brother and nephew, he might have been ever better if he had not been a sailor.

To complete the Park family, Willie Park, Jr, had a daughter, **Doris Park** (Mrs Aylmer Porter) who had a good record in ladies' international and championship golf.

J Lara Sousa e Mello, who has played for the continent of Europe against Britain, has been Portuguese champion four times. His mother **Maria** has also won the Women's championship (1953) while his father **José de Sousa e Mello** has represented his country in international competition.

In 1968, **Michael Bonallack** won the English Amateur championship in the same year that his sister, **Sally**, was English Women's champion. His wife, **Angela**, was twice English Women's champion (1958-63) and twice reached the final of the British Women's championship (1962-74). In one of

these years (1962), Michael was English champion. To complete the family's achievements, Angela's sister, **Shirley Ward**, won the English Girls' championship in 1964 while Michael's brother Tony was an Essex county player.

The **le Quellecs** of France were both international players. **Yan** was French champion in 1933 and his wife in 1948. Their nephew is Alexis Godillot, who has won the title four times.

Sue Hedges, runner-up in the English Women's championship in 1979, is the sister-in-law of **Peter Hedges**, the British Walker Cup player. Her husband, **David**, is also a low-handicap golfer.

Gary Player's brother-in-law is **Bobby Verwey**, a leading South African tournament professional.

Dave Marr, USPGA champion in 1965, is a cousin of **Jack Burke**, champion in 1956.

Jay Haas, a winner of the US professional tour and a former Walker Cup player, is a nephew of **Bob Goalby**, the 1968 US Masters champion.

Sam Snead and his nephew, **Jesse C Snead**, played for the United States in the Ryder Cup, Sam on seven occasions and Jesse on three.

Christy O'Connor, Sr, and his nephew **Christy O'Connor, Jr**, played in the Ryder Cup. Christy, Sr, on a record ten occasions and Christy, Jr, in 1975.

VERSATILITY

GOLFERS WITH OTHER SPORTING DISTINCTIONS

Leslie Balfur-Melville, 1895 British Amateur champion, played Rugby and Cricket for Scotland. He was also Scottish long jump, tennis and billiards champion.

'Babe' Zaharias, one of the most famous of women golfers, won two gold medals at the 1932 Olympic Games in Los Angeles. They were for the javelin and high hurdles. In each, she broke the existing world record. She was also second in the high jump.

As a golfer, she won the British and American Amateur championships and the American Women's Open three times.

Bob Falkenburg, Wimbledon tennis champion in 1948, was Brazilian Amateur golf champion three times (1959-60-61) and a regular competitor for a time in the British Amateur championship.

Leonard Crawley, English Amateur champion in 1931 and a Walker Cup player, played county cricket in England for Worcestershire and Essex; he scored nine first-class hundreds. He also toured the West Indies with the MCC in 1925. At lawn tennis he won the North of England doubles championship with his uncle.

George 'Pete' Bostwick, an American who won the 1964 French Amateur championship, was also the world champion at real tennis (1969-1972).

Charlotte Dod, British Ladies' champion in 1904, was a fine all-round athlete. She won the women's singles at Wimbledon five times; was an international hockey-player, a champion skater, a skilful archer (silver in the 1908 Olympics), fine billiards player and noteworthy member of the Alpine Club.

George Lyon did not take up golf until he was 38 yet, within two years, he had won the first of eight Canadian Amateur championships and was a versatile athlete. He excelled at cricket, baseball, tennis, football, curling and rowing. As a cricketer, he established the Canadian batting record of 238 not out.

In the 1904 Olympic Games, he won the golfing medal for Canada and at the dinner following the competition, walked the length of the dining-room on his hands.

Robert A Gardner, twice US Amateur champion and runner-up in the British Amateur in 1920 to Cyril Tolley, was a fine all-round athlete. At one time, he held the world record for the pole vault and, in addition, won the American double rackets championship. He was the first to vault over the then magic height of 13 ft (3·9 m) in winning the IC4A title on 1 June 1912. However his record only lasted seven days.

Ellsworth Vines, the famous American tennis star who won Wimbledon (1932) and Forest Hills (1931-32), later turned professional at golf and was good enough to become one of America's top 15 players.

In 1924, **Mary Kimball Browne** reached the final of the US Women's Amateur championship in the same year in which she reached the semi-final of the American Women's tennis championship at Forest Hills.

George Roberts played in the Home International golf matches for Scotland in 1937 and 1938 and also received five caps for Scotland at rugby football in 1938 and 1939.

Sam Roberts was a dual international for Wales at golf and hockey.

Above: Golf's most versatile athlete, 'Babe' Zaharias, *née* Mildred Didrikson, seen as a 19-year-old hurdler in 1932, the year she won two Olympic gold medals (The Associated Press Ltd)

Below: Cricketer turned golfer—W G Grace (from *The Memorial Biography of W G Grace* by Hawke, Harris and Gordon, published by Constable & Co Ltd)

George Crosbie, who played international golf for Ireland, was also an Olympic yachtsman.

Ted Dexter, a regular participant in major amateur events in Britain, played many times for England at cricket. He was captain and scored nine Test centuries.

Madame LeQuellec, French Ladies' Close champion in 1948, was also an international skier and hockey-player.

Philippe Washer of Belgium was a Davis Cup tennis-player for many years. In addition, he played golf for his country.

Sven Tumba played golf and ice hockey for Sweden and was capped once as centre-forward for the Swedish national soccer side.

Sune Malmstrom played in the Swedish Davis Cup tennis team and for his country at golf. He was Swedish matchplay champion in 1932-36-38.

Jess Sweetser, former British and American Amateur champion was a distinguished quarter-miler during his days at Yale. He was timed at a shade over 50 sec. Sweetser won the US Amateur in 1922 and the British in 1926.

Alfred J Evans (b 1.5.1889; d 18.9.1960), runner-up in the 1932 and 1935 President's Putters and a participant in major championships, played cricket for England in one test match against Australia in 1921. He also earned fame for his escapes from German prison camps in World War I when he served in the Royal Flying Corps.

Norman Stewart Mitchell Innes, Captain of Oxford University at golf, also played one test match for England at cricket while still an undergraduate.

Sidney Fry, runner-up in the British Amateur championship of 1902 was eight times English National Amateur champion in billiards between 1893 and 1925. In 1925, he was 57 years old. In 1899, he set a new championship record break of 168.

Former world record-holder for the pole vault and American Amateur golf champion, R A Gardner (US Golf Association)

He was also English National Amateur snooker champion. He was the first man to win both billiards and snooker championships, which he won in the same year, 1919.

Althea Gibson became a regular competitor on the American LPGA tour after retiring as a distinguished lawn tennis champion, winner of Forest Hills and Wimbledon, both 1957–58.

Tom Crow, Australian Amateur champion in 1961 and an international golfer, was also a leading player of Australian Rules football and a State class cricketer.

Bill Shankland, professional at Potters Bar, England, when Tony Jacklin joined him as assistant, played Rugby League for Australia.

Freddie Tait, twice British Amateur champion (1896 and 1898), was an expert rifle-shot and a first-class rugby player and cricketer. He was killed in the Boer War.

John Jacobs, British Ryder Cup player and Captain, and a well-known teacher in many countries, is also a keen fisherman. In 1978, he caught the most valuable salmon ever landed on the River Avon in Dorset. It weighed 27 lb (12 kg) and was sold to a local hotel for £130.

Jack Nicklaus is another skilled fisherman.

John S F Morrison (b 17.4.1892; d 28.1.1962), an England golfer in 1930, played football for the Corinthians and Sunderland. He also captained Cambridge University at cricket and represented Somerset. Later, he became a well known golf course architect.

Dr Reginald H B Bettington (b 24.2.1900; d 24.6.1969), Australian Amateur champion in 1932, was a cricketer of great note. A leg-spin bowler and attacking batsman, he was the first Australian to captain Oxford University in 1923. He won other Blues at golf and rugby; played cricket for the Gentlemen, Middlesex and was later captain of New South Wales in the year he won the NSW golf championship.

Charles Victor Lisle Hooman (b 3.10.1887; d 20.11.1969) who played in the first Walker Cup match and won the only game in the entire series which went to extra holes, also won a cricket Blue at Oxford, 1909–10. He helped Kent to win the County Championship and played for the Gentlemen in the same year that he played golf for England.

FAMOUS GOLFERS WITH DISTINCTIONS IN OTHER WALKS OF LIFE

Jack Westland, US Amateur champion in 1952 and runner-up in 1931, served as a US Congressman.

Bill Campbell, 1964 US Amateur champion and a member of several American Walker

Cup teams, has served as a member of the West Virginia State legislature. He is also a qualified pilot.

Gene Littler, US Amateur champion in 1953 and US Open champion in 1961, makes a hobby of collecting vintage cars—especially Rolls Royces.

He also made a marvellous recovery from a cancer operation in spring 1972.

Raymond Oppenheimer, British Walker Cup Captain (1951) and an English International, is the world's leading breeder of bull terriers and a world authority on the breed.

William Whitelaw, Home Secretary in the Rt Hon Mrs Thatcher's 1979 Government, is a former Captain of the Royal and Ancient Golf Club (1969) and a former Cambridge Blue.

Percy Belgrave 'Laddie' Lucas, a Walker Cup player and Captain, was a distinguished fighter pilot in World War II. He later became a Member of Parliament and Chairman of the Greyhound Racing Association.

Henry Longhurst (d 1978), the well-known British writer, television commentator and former German Amateur champion, served for a time as a Member of Parliament when Winston Churchill was Prime Minister.

Tom Blackwell, Captain of the Royal and Ancient Golf Club in 1963/64, was later twice Deputy Senior Steward of the Jockey Club.

Bing Crosby (d 1977) was a good enough golfer to have started 3, 3, in a British Amateur championship at St Andrews. He is also one of only two players to have holed in one at the

A man photographed in many guises, but only once as a golfer—Winston Churchill (Reproduced by permission of Ross-on-Wye Golf Club, who are fortunate in also possessing an early set of Churchill's golf clubs)

famous 16th at Cypress Point, California. The shot involves a carry of some 180 yd (165 m) across the edge of the Pacific Ocean.

He died suddenly on 14 October, after playing a round of golf in Madrid. His son **Nathaniel** continues to run the Bing Crosby tournament held in California in January.

Robin Cater, a Walker Cup player for Britain in 1955, later became Chairman of the Distillers' Company.

Guy Wolstenholme, well-known professional and former Walker Cup golfer, is a capable pianist.

Bobby Locke, four times British Open champion, flew as a bomber pilot with the South African Air Force during World War II.

Bernard Darwin, a semi-finalist in the British Amateur championship and winner of his Walker Cup single, when he was called in to replace the sick British captain, was an incomparable writer on golf. Grandson of Charles Darwin, he practised law on leaving Cambridge but decided on a life writing about golf. He was described by Herbert Asquith as 'the greatest living essayist in the English language' and was said by another eminent critic to be 'one of the six best essayists since Charles Lamb'. He was also a great authority on the works of Dickens.

Arnold Palmer and **Jerilyn Britz,** the 1979 US Women's Open champion, are qualified pilots.

The voice of golf—Henry Longhurst (Action Photos)

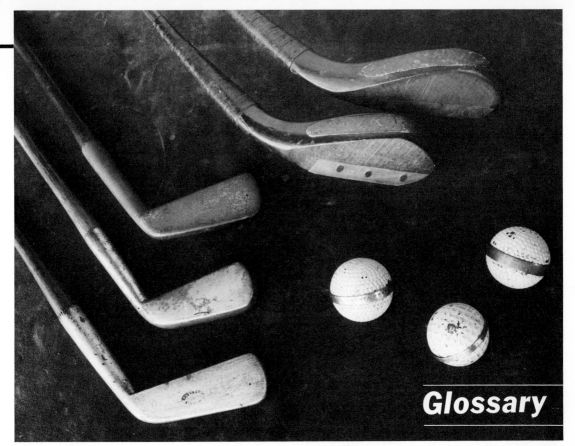

Glossary

A

Address The position which a player adopts in order to hit the ball. Used in the old sense of addressing oneself to a task.

A player is said to have 'addressed' the ball when he has taken up his stance and grounded his club. The exception is in a hazard when he is not allowed to ground his club.

Albatross The achievement of holing out in 3 below par on any individual hole: ie a 2 at a par-5 hole or a hole in one on a par-4. A rarity, hence albatross, an even rarer bird than an eagle which denotes 2 below par or the more common 'birdie', 1 below par. The Americans often refer to it as a double eagle.

Away 'Who's away' is a question enquiring 'whose ball is furthest from the hole'? It is most commonly used on the putting green in establishing whose turn it is to putt.

Alternate When a draw is made for a tournament or championship, the alternates are the reserves or substitutes. They make up the numbers when others withdraw. They would have been the next to qualify and are placed in order according to their qualifying score. It is rare if two or three alternates do not get into the British Open championship after the draw has been made.

Amateur Broadly speaking, a player who plays for the love of the game rather than any financial gain, although amateur prizes may now take the form of vouchers which can be used to pay bills.

Amateur status is carefully and rigidly defined by the Royal and Ancient Golf Club and the USGA. There is now a very much more liberal interpretation of these rules than formerly.

B

Birdie A hole completed in 1 under par, an improvement on the theoretical standard which allows a good golfer 2 putts on every hole to achieve his par.

The following is an account of the origin of the term, which became current between the two World Wars:

In 1899 at Atlantic City CC, Ab Smith tells the story. 'The second hole was a par 4 about 350 yards long. I was playing in a three-ball match with George A Crump (who incidentally planned Pine Valley layout) and my brother William P Smith. My drive of 185 yards was to the left giving me the diagonal of the green to play for. The green was guarded by a ditch and a cop bunker. I banged away with my second shot, and my ball—it was one of the new Haskells—came to rest within six inches of the cup. I said to George Crump "that was a bird of a shot and here I only get a paltry sum from each of you. Hereafter, I suggest that when one of us play a hole in one under par that he receive double compensation, and this goes for everyone in the match, including partners!" The other two both agreed and we began right away, just as soon as the next one came, to call it a "birdie." Naturally, "eagle" was the result when one scored two under par and then later came the double-eagle.'

Blaster A forerunner to the sand wedge: a lofted iron club principally used for bunker play and for recoveries from the rough.

Blind A hole is said to be blind when a player cannot see the target from where he stands. It can apply to a fairway or a green. Before the days when modern machinery made golf-course construction easier, there were more blind holes than there are today. If a sandhill got in the way, the golfer had to play over or round it; now it is more likely to be removed.

Bogey In days gone by, the term 'bogey' referred in Britain to the number of strokes in which a good player was expected to complete a hole. In America, it has come to mean a hole played in 1 stroke over par.

Nowadays in Britain, bogey has been replaced by par, but 'Colonel Bogey' was an invention of a golf-club secretary who thought that bogey implied a theoretical standard by which golfers could judge themselves.

It has other more realistic meanings such as a bogey hole—one at which disaster strikes in some form. Then 'Colonel Bogey' becomes the 'Bogey Man'.

Borrow The aim-off necessary on a putt to compensate for the natural rolls on the putting green. The amount of borrow on, say a curly 4 ft (1 m) putt depends upon the speed at which the putt is hit.

Bunker A hole or crater in the ground filled with sand; derived from a Scottish word for a storage place or receptacle—as in a domestic coal-bunker. A bunker is defined as a hazard in which a golfer may not ground his club.

Originally, bunkers were formed naturally; places in the sand-dunes where sheep may have sheltered. Their golfing intention is to catch a

Hell's Half Acre, the world's biggest bunker (called a trap in the USA) Pine Valley course, New Jersey, USA (Pine Valley Golf Club)

stray shot. The Americans refer to bunkers as 'traps'.

C

Caddie The golfer's companion, a man or, in some countries, a woman, skilled in the game who, for a fee, carries a player's clubs and offers advice.

Caddies are recognised by the Rules of Golf as part of the 'side'.

The word 'caddie' is the Scots form of the French *cadet*, a term applied, for example, to the younger sons of French noble families who went to Edinburgh in the train of Mary Queen of Scots. After being accepted as the Scottish spelling of the French *cadet*, meaning a little chief, it was applied with Scottish sarcasm to the hangers-on who ran errands in the Edinburgh streets in the 18th century. Thus 'caddie' came to mean a porter, although it was some time before it was restricted to a porter who carried golf clubs. Nevertheless, caddies were common as golfers' companions long before that. They probably became recognised during the latter half of the 17th century.

Carry The distance that a ball flies through the air. Some holes require that the ball *must* be hit in the air in order to clear the intervening trouble. In that case, the word is used in the sense of succeeding in 'making the carry'.

Casual water Any accumulation of water which is not permanent. The most common cause is flooding after heavy rain. It must be visible either before or after a player takes his stance.

Cocking Cocking the wrists is the sideways bend or break in the wrist necessary to impart force into a shot.

A 'Royal and Ancient' Caddie, 1914. *After A W Dendy Sadler, 1854–1923* (The Fotomas Index)

A Japanese caddie champion, 'Bullet Head' in 1905 (Illustrated London News Pic. Lib.)

Concede In matchplay the term applies to a situation whereby a player concedes a hole to his opponent without requiring him to hole out. It can occur, for instance, after hitting three balls out of bounds.

On the putting green, it relates to the concession of a putt which, in the player's opinion, cannot be missed. The American term is a Gimmie.

Croquet putting A method of putting similar in style to the act of hitting a croquet ball. It is usually adopted by players who, for various reasons, cannot make more conventional methods work.

A change in the rules declared it illegal, although now there are variations on it; a good example is the side-saddle method employed by Sam Snead. The new rule forbids the player to stand astride the line of the putt or to have the shaft of the putter at right angles to the head.

Cup Another name for the hole cut on the putting green.

Cut A type of spin imparted to the ball causing it to fly to the right. It is a little more exaggerated than the fade, but a little less so than a slice.

It is more commonly used in referring to the cut-off point in a tournament, whereby the field is reduced in numbers—usually after 36 or 54 holes or both.

The successful players are said to have 'made the cut'. In professional golf, it is an important landmark, often providing a future exemption from pre-qualifying for another circuit tournament; and unsuccessful players rarely receive prize-money.

Leonard Crawley demonstrating the now prohibited 'croquet' putting style (Action Photos)

Lightning makes a 'Hole in One' and leaves its imprint in a golf green (John Frost, Historical Newspaper Service)

D

Divot The strip of turf removed, accidentally or intentionally, in the process of hitting a shot. Divots are more commonly taken with iron shots than woods; and with the more lofted rather than less lofted irons.

Dogleg Golf holes which are curved in the shape of a dog's leg. The hole changes direction usually at about 200 to 250 yd (180–230 m) although some have a double dogleg. Dogleg holes invariably require the player to decide whether to hug the corner of the dogleg or play more conservatively.

The dogleg can be formed by trees, water hazards, boundary fences, ditches, mounds or slopes.

Dormie A matchplay term denoting the number of holes up as there are to play. Thus, a player is dormie 3 when he is 3 up with 3 to play. By the definition, players can never be 'dormie down' and the term cannot be applied (but is) to matches which have to be played to a finish, ie matches in championships where extra holes are employed to determine a result.

It originates from the French *dormir*, to sleep. Being dormie is being able to sleep in the knowledge that you cannot be beaten.

Draw A stroke executed by swinging the club from in to out, causing the ball to start to the right and curve back into the line required.

Also the draw for play giving opponents, partners, starting times, etc.

Drive The opening stroke from the tee where good distance is required. Most commonly played with the driver, the most powerful club in the bag although technical deficiencies, the conditions prevailing or special tactics cause players to drive with other clubs, frequently irons.

At short holes where length is often no criterion, the opening stroke is known as the tee shot.

Drop Under the Rules, players are commonly forced to drop or given the option of a drop. There is a set procedure but it is most likely done to replace a ball that is lost or put out of play, one that becomes unplayable or comes to rest in a water hazard, an area of casual water or ground under repair.

Duff A duff is a shot that is foozled or badly mishit. A duffer is a golfer whose game consists mainly of duffs.

E

Eagle A hole performed in 2 strokes better than par, 1 stroke better than a birdie—hence the term which implies a rarer bird. First mentioned in 1922.

F

Face The part of the club designed for hitting the ball.

Fairway Closely cut portion of the course between tee and green. The part on to which you should drive.

Flagstick The flagstick denotes the position of the hole on the putting green; it rests in the cup. The positions of the holes are changed to avoid too much wear and tear on one part. In big competitions, this is usually done each day.

Field The contestants in a competition.

Flat Used in describing a swing in which the plane is closer to the horizontal than the vertical. The opposite of steep or upright.

Flight The line which the ball takes through the air.

Fluff Akin to a duff, a foozled shot.

Follow through The part of the swing after the ball has been hit. It cannot alter the shot in any way, but it does indicate how the club has been swung. It is commonly regarded as a point of style.

Fore The golfer's cry of warning either that the ball has been hit and could endanger fellow players, spectators or bystanders; or, that a player is ready to hit and wishes to draw the attention of others to the fact.

It probably derives from 'beware before', a military command used in the 16th century to warn troops to drop to the ground in order that guns could be fired over their heads.

Fourball A match in which four players take part, each hitting his own ball.

Foursome A match in which four players take part, but only hit two balls. They take alternate shots. One of the very oldest forms of golf although a form very little played outside Britain. It is a form known in America as Scotch foursomes.

Freeze A condition in which players seize up over a shot and are incapable of movement.

G

Gimmie Shortened version of 'give me'; applied to a putt which is conceded, given, ie too short to miss. Originated in America.

Grip The part of the shaft which is held in the hands and covered to prevent slipping, etc.

Also used to denote the actual position of the hands on the club. There are many ways of holding the club.

Green The whole course over which the game is played. An ancient term which gave rise to such expressions as 'through the green' or 'rub of the green'; and more recently Green committee, meaning those responsible for the direction of the Green or entire course. It is a singular noun.

Green (used as a plural noun) also refers to the specially built, prepared and cut part of the course on which putting takes place. The areas where the holes are placed and marked by a flag.

Groove In the groove; an expression applied when a player's swing is repeating over and over again, and little goes wrong. Hence talk of a 'grooved swing'.

Ground the club The act of putting the club on the ground behind the ball before a stroke is played.

Ground under repair A temporary area, which should be clearly marked, from which a player is entitled to drop without penalty.

H

Half, Halve A match or a hole which finishes level. Another term for a halved match is All Square. Sometimes All Flat is used.

Half shot A controlled shot which is played with less than full power.

Handicapping The system whereby two players of differing ability can arrange a match which, theoretically, gives them an equal chance of winning.

Hazard The Rules of Golf define a hazard as any bunker or water hazard. Bare patches, scrapes, roads, tracks and paths are not hazards.

Head The part of the club designed to hit the ball.

Head-up The act of looking up too soon in the course of hitting the ball.

Heel The part of the clubhead nearest the shaft.

Hickory The wood from which the shafts of old golf clubs were made. The hickory is indigenous to North America.

Hole Two meanings: (1) The units into which a course is divided. Nearly every course consists of 9 or 18 holes. (2) The actual hole in the ground into which the ball is putted. It must be 4¼ in (107·9 mm) in diameter and at least 4 in (101·6 mm) deep.

Home One of the terms for denoting the second 9 holes of a course; the inward half. Hence the term 'home in 36'.

Honour The privilege of playing first from the tee either in strokeplay or matchplay. The honour is determined by whichever player or partnership won the previous hole or, if it was halved, the last hole to be won.

Thought to be derived from old courtly terminology, 'Pray, Sir, do me the honour of going first.'

Hook A stroke which starts to the right of the

target and finishes to the left. The opposite of slice although not so common among golfers.

I

Impact The moment when the clubhead meets the ball.

In The holes of the second 9 on a course. The inward half.

In play A ball is 'in play' as soon as the player has teed off. It remains in play until holed out, out of bounds, lost or lifted, or another ball is substituted under the Rules.

Irons Clubs made with metal blades for heads.

J

Jigger An obsolete iron club with a narrow blade. It roughly corresponds to a modern 3 iron.

L

Lie How the ball comes to rest, eg good lie, bad lie, cuppy lie, sandy lie or bare lie.

Also refers to the angle between the horizontal and centre of a club's shaft.

Line The direction in which the player intends the ball to travel.

Links Often thought to refer to courses with natural seaside qualities, sand-dunes, etc. In his *History of Golf*, however, Robert Browning took issue, stating that the area of ground over which the Royal Eastbourne course was laid out, was known as 'the Links' long before anyone thought of playing golf there; and it had downland character. Similarly some land at Cambridge was called 'the Links' although nobody considered playing golf there.

Some use the term 'links' as they might 'course'.

In modern parlance, it tends to be understood as meaning the country close to the sea which has little use except for golf. That part which lies between the sea and the more fertile parts, ie the link between the two.

Lip The edge of the hole.

M

Marker The small disc used to mark the position of the ball if lifted.

Also, somebody appointed to keep the score.

Mashie An old iron club, now obsolete, akin to a modern 5 iron. Possibly derived from the French word *massue*, a club.

Medal play A tournament or competition decided by counting the strokes taken; the opposite of matchplay.

The medallist is the person with the lowest score for the qualifying section of a matchplay tournament or championship. A predominantly American expression.

Method The manner of a player's striking and swinging.

N

Nap The grain of the grass on greens; less common than it was with the coarse-bladed grasses.

Nassau Three matches in one; a match for the first 9, one for the second 9 and one for the overall 18.

Net score A player's score when his handicap has been deducted.

Niblick Old-fashioned, lofted iron club. Used to be the most lofted club in the bag.

Nineteenth The club bar; or the first extra hole in a match undecided after 18 holes.

O

Out The first 9 holes. The holes on the way out to the turn. Opposite of the inward half.

P

Pacing Modern habit of pacing the ground in order that the player knows distances exactly.

Par Par is the exact score that an expert golfer would be expected to make for a given hole. Par means errorless play without flukes and under normal weather conditions; it also allows 2 strokes on each putting green.

In day-to-day language, one talks of being on a par (level); or below par (feeling unwell). The golfing term derives from this expression.

Penalty stroke A stroke added to a player's score under the penalty clauses in the Rules of Golf, eg accidentally moving the ball at address.

Pitch A shot in which the ball is played through the air into the target, usually the flag. Not always a full shot.

Pitch and run A shot played so that the ball will run along the ground after pitching. Common on hard ground.

Pitch mark The mark left in the ground when the ball pitches.

Play club An ancient driver.

Play-off The means of deciding the winner after two or more players have finished equal after the prescribed distance of a competition has been completed. Sometimes, it is over a set distance or, just as frequently, the play-off is sudden death.

Preferred lies A local rule allowing players to tee their ball up on the fairway in order to counter poor ground conditions. Usually used in winter play.

Pull A shot to the left of target although not as extreme as a hook.

Push The opposite of pull, a shot to the right of target although not as extreme as a slice.

Bobby Locke—one of the greatest putters lining up a putt (Action Photos)

Putting The part of golf which takes place on or just off the putting green. The ball is made to roll, not fly, into the hole.

The word 'putting' may be derived from the Dutch *putten*, meaning 'to place in the hole'.

Putting green The part of the course in which the hole is cut. It is specially prepared for putting, the grass being cut lower than on the fairway or approach. Usually just called the green.

Q

Quitting Quitting on a shot means not going through with it.

R

Rookie First year player.

Rough The part of the course which is neither, tee, fairway, green nor hazard. Usually long grass bordering the fairway.

Rub of the green Any chance happening while the ball is in play, something over which a player has no influence or control. Rather a case of taking the rough with the smooth.

An expression that has crept into non-golfing language.

Run The path of the ball along the ground after it has pitched. A lot of run is common on hard ground.

Run-up A stroke played usually with a straight-faced club where the ball travels close to the ground.

S

Sand iron The club which largely replaced the old niblick, a lofted club which revolutionised bunker play. Akin to a blaster.

Sclaff Old Scottish expression for hitting the ground behind the ball; not making a good contact.

Scratch golfer One who receives no handicap.

Semi-rough The lighter, graded rough nearest to the fairway.

Shaft The part of the club which is not the head. The grip surrounds the shaft.

Shank One of the most dreaded afflictions of golfers, where the ball is hit by the part of the club nearest the hosel, the socket on iron clubs into which the shaft is fitted. Explains why a shank is also known as a socket.

Billiard stroke—ingenious but illegal! (John Frost, Historical Newspaper Service)

Short game The part of the game played around the green, the shots relying on finesse and accuracy rather than power and distance. Consists of pitching, bunker play and putting.

Single A match between two players.

Sole The part of the club which rests on the ground.

Stableford A system of scoring, particularly popular in Britain, based on a points system devised by the late Dr Frank B Stableford of the Wallasey Club in Cheshire.

Stance The position of a player's feet when he addresses the ball.

Stroke The forward movement of the club made with the intention of hitting the ball. A stroke does not necessarily move the ball.

Strokeplay The opposite of matchplay, a competition where the players' total number of strokes for the round(s) are registered and counted.

Stymie An obsolete golfing term, but one which has been accepted in everyday language. It is akin to a snooker.

It meant a situation on the putting green in which the opponent's ball blocked the line to the hole, causing him to play round or over it. The opponent was said to have laid a stymie and the victim to be stymied. A stymie, however, did not apply if the balls were less than 6 in (152·4 mm) apart. The stymie was abolished in 1951.

Thought to have derived from the old Scots word 'styme' which appeared as early as 1300 in the phrase 'not to see a styme', ie not to be able to see at all. The golf term refers to the blinding of one ball by the other.

Sucker A ball embedded usually in soft ground or bunker faces.

Sway A lateral movement of head, shoulders or body in the backswing.

Swing The sweep of the club used in hitting the ball.

Also used to denote the borrow on a putt.

T

Takeaway The act of taking the club away from the ball. The first movement of the swing.

Texas wedge An American expression for using a putter from off the green. Most commonly adopted on hard ground—presumably such as is, or used to be, found in Texas.

Thin A shot hit off the bottom of the club. It flies low.

Through the green Whole area of the course except for the greens, tees and hazards.

Toe Part of the club furthest from the shaft. Opposite of heel.

Top A shot in which the ball fails to take off; usually it is hit a descending blow with the wrong part of the club.

Trap American term for a bunker; something which traps the ball.

Twitch An uncontrollable, nervous affliction, most commonly of putting. A convulsive movement of the hands.

U

Up A matchplay term used when a player has won more holes than his opponent; used to denote a current score, ie 1 up, 4 up.

Upright An upright swing is one which is nearer to the vertical than the horizontal plane. Opposite of flat.

W

Waggle The initial movement of the club at address. Used to lessen tension.

Woods The wooden-headed clubs, although term also refers nowadays to clubs of similar shape made from other substances.

STOP PRESS 1980

US Open

A championship in which records galore were broken, beginning on the first day with Tom Weiskopf and Jack Nicklaus equalling Johnny Miller's record of 63 for the lowest individual round in the Open. Nicklaus, in fact, missed from about a yard on the 18th green for a 62.

A second round of 71 lowered the aggregate for 36 holes and a further 70 lowered the 54-hole record, but it was a record shared by Isao Aoki of Japan who began with three 68s and chased Nicklaus hard in the last round.

A final 68 by Nicklaus gave him victory by 2 strokes and enabled him to break the record aggregate which he held jointly with Lee Trevino. He also joined Willie Anderson, Bobby Jones and Ben Hogan as the only four-time winners.

Aoki's second place was the best ever by an Asian golfer in the Open. Hubert Green's third round of 65 equalled the lowest third round and contained a record eight 3s in a row from the 9th.

Nicklaus's victory came 18 years after his first, a record span. It was the first time Nicklaus finished in the first six since 1973.

RESULTS

1980 Baltusrol GC, New Jersey

Jack Nicklaus	63	71	70	68	272
Isao Aoki	68	68	68	70	274
Lon Hinkle	66	70	69	71	276
Tom Watson	71	68	67	70	276
Keith Fergus	66	70	70	70	276

British Open

The British Open, the first officially scheduled to end on a Sunday, followed the US Open in providing a feast of record breaking. Isao Aoki had a third round of 63 to equal Mark Haye's record for an individual round in 1977; and, in the same round, played in unusually easy conditions, Tom Watson and Hubert Green returned 64s. The day before, Horacio Carbonetti, an unknown Argentinian, set a new course record with 64.

Watson's 64 allowed him to break his own record score for 54 holes but, more importantly, it enabled him to make up 2 strokes on the overnight leader, Lee Trevino, and then establish a 4-stroke lead. On the last day, he was never likely to be caught and he duly won his third victory, all in Scotland, by 4 strokes. He was only 3 strokes outside his own 72-hole aggregate of 268, and his 64 was the lowest round ever by a champion. In that third round, he came home in 30.

RESULTS

1980 Muirfield

Tom Watson, USA	68	70	64	69	271
Lee Trevino, USA	68	67	71	69	275
Ben Crenshaw, USA	70	70	68	69	277
Jack Nicklaus, USA	73	67	71	69	280
Carl Mason, USA, unattached	72	69	70	69	280

US Women's Open

Amy Alcott completely dominated the championship played at Richland CC, Tennessee. Having tied for the lead on the first day, she went away to win by 9 strokes with a total of 280. This broke the record set the previous year by Jerilyn Britz. Hollis Stacy finished as runner-up.

STERLING–US DOLLAR EXCHANGE RATES

This list represents the major dollar fluctuations, and will help the reader in converting the dollar rates given in this book.

$4·50–$5·00	Post War of Independence	1776
$12·00	All-time Peak (Civil War)	1864
$4·86 21/32	Fixed parity	1880–1914
$4·76 7/16	Pegged rate World War I	December 1916
$3·40	Low point after £ floated, 19 May 1919	February 1920
$4·86 21/32	Britain's return to gold standard	28 April 1925
$3·14½	Low point after Britain forced off Gold Standard (20 September 1931 [$3.43])	November 1932
$5·20	High point during floating period	March 1934
$4·03	Fixed rate World War II	4 September 1939
$2·80	First post-war devaluation	18 September 1949
$2·40	Second post-war devaluation	20 November 1967
$2·42	Convertibility of US dollar into gold was suspended on	15 August 1971
$2·58	£ Refloated	22 June 1972
$1·99	£ broke $2 barrier	5 March 1976
$1·56	£ At new all-time low	28 October 1976
$1·76	Bank of England buying pounds	10 October 1977
$2·00	£ breaks back to $2 level (1978 av. $1·91)	15 August 1978
$2·26	Dollar weakens	June 1979
$2·19	Iranian crisis unresolved	8 December 1979
$2·35	Dollar weakens	27 May 1980

Index

Page numbers in italics refer to illustrations

Index compiled by Anna Pavord